EARTH'S LAST
EMPIRE

EARTH'S LAST EMPIRE

THE FINAL GAME OF THRONES

JOHN HAGEE

WORTHY®
PUBLISHING

Worthy
Hachette Book Group
1290 Avenue of the Americas, New York, NY 10104
worthypublishing.com
twitter.com/worthypub

Originally published in hardcover in September 2018
Revised trade paperback edition: October 2020

Worthy is a division of Hachette Book Group, Inc. The Worthy name and logo are trademarks of Hachette Book Group, Inc.

The publisher is not responsible for websites (or their content) that are not owned by the publisher.

Unless otherwise noted, Scripture quotations are taken from the New King James Version®. © 1982 by Thomas Nelson. Used by permission. All rights reserved. | Scripture quotations marked NIV are taken from the Holy Bible, New International Version®, NIV®. Copyright © 1973, 1978, 1984, 2011 by Biblica, Inc.™ Used by permission of Zondervan. All rights reserved worldwide. www.zondervan.com. The "NIV" and "New International Version" are trademarks registered in the United States Patent and Trademark Office by Biblica, Inc.™ | Scripture quotations marked NASB are taken from New American Standard Bible (NASB) Copyright © 1960, 1962, 1963, 1968, 1971, 1972, 1973, 1975, 1977, 1995 by The Lockman Foundation.

Scripture quotations marked KJV are taken from the King James Version of the Bible. Public domain. Any emphases are the author's, and some poetry has been formatted as prose.

Published in association with Ted Squires Agency, Nashville, Tennessee

Library of Congress Cataloging-in-Publication Data

Names: Hagee, John, author.
Title: Earth's last empire : the final game of thrones / John Hagee. Description: Franklin, TN : Worthy Publishing, 2018. | Includes bibliographical references and index.
Identifiers: LCCN 2018033915 | ISBN 9781683972761 (hardcover : alk. paper) Subjects: LCSH: End of the world--Biblical teaching. | Eschatology--Biblical teaching. | Bible--Prophecies. | Bible--Prophecies--End of the world. |
Bible--Prophecies--International organization. | Bible--Prophecies--Armageddon.
Classification: LCC BS649.E63 H324 2018 | DDC 236/.9--dc23 LC record available at https://lccn.loc.gov/2018033915

ISBNs: 978-1-5460-1473-7 (revised trade paperback), 978-1-68397-206-8 (ebook)

Printed in the United States of America

LSC-C

Printing 4, 2020

He who gives a book
gives more than cloth, paper, and ink.
He gives more than leather, parchment, and words.
He reveals a foreword of his thoughts,
a dedication of his friendship,
a page of his presence,
a chapter of himself,
and an index of his love.
Author Unknown

It is my great privilege to dedicate this book
to one of the most beloved friends of my life,
Rabbi Aryeh Scheinberg.

With gratitude to my wife, Diana, and my executive assistant, Jo-Ann Coffey, whose love and passion for Israel and the Jewish people are reflected in this work.

Special Acknowledgment

Special thanks to Dr. David Crockett for his invaluable contribution to chapters 6 and 7 of this book. Dr. Crockett has dedicated his life to engraving young minds with the foundational truths concerning our nation's politics, with a focus on the American presidency—providing hope for America and the world.

CONTENTS

SECTION ONE

ALL ROADS LEAD TO JERUSALEM

MY JERUSALEM

Jerusalem is the only place on earth that is called the city of God. Benjamin Disraeli, prime minister to the United Kingdom under Queen Victoria, once said, "The view of Jerusalem is the history of the world—it is more, it is the history of earth and of heaven."

My personal encounter with Jerusalem began as an affair of the heart—for the City of the Great King connected heaven and earth within my soul. Once I stepped foot on its sacred soil, it became my Jerusalem.

> *Jerusalem, the center of the universe.*
> *Jerusalem, the City of Gold.*
> *Jerusalem, the undivided capital*
> *of the Covenant nation of Israel.*
> *Jerusalem, the place that the God of Abraham,*
> *Isaac, and Jacob calls home.*
> *Jerusalem, the experience that forever changed my life.*

From the moment I first walked the ancient cobblestone streets of that Holy City, I sensed a Divine Presence there—a type of supernatural peace known nowhere else. I have traveled the world, but only Jerusalem has felt like home.

Jerusalem is where Abraham, the father of all who believe, placed his beloved son, Isaac, on the altar of sacrifice at Mount Moriah, reflecting his absolute faith in God Almighty.

Jerusalem is the city King David conquered over three thousand years ago, making it the eternal capital of Israel.

Jerusalem is where Jeremiah and Isaiah penned the principles of righteousness that became the moral foundations of civilization.

Jerusalem is where a rabbi named Jesus of Nazareth established the covenants of my faith that are chiseled in the depths of my soul.

Jerusalem is where Messiah will rule the earth for one thousand years of perfect peace in the world to come.

Jerusalem is where God Almighty, the King of the universe, will establish His Eternal Throne.

Jerusalem is the city that holds my heart.

When I first prayed at the Western Wall, I stood next to a rabbi who bowed his head at every mention of God's Holy Name. I knew the Lord was listening to his prayer and to mine. At that very moment, I heard the Lord speak to my heart to bring Christians and Jews together in an atmosphere of unconditional love and mutual respect. It was a seemingly impossible task were it not for the help of the Almighty.

I entered Jerusalem a pilgrim…and walked out of its gates a Zionist. I believe all that the Holy Scriptures say of Jerusalem and have dedicated my life to sharing these truths with the world.

All of Zion rejoiced as Jerusalem celebrated its Jubilee, and we pray that God's continued favor will be its cherished hope for tomorrow. Yes, this holy place has forever changed my life.

Jerusalem is everlasting, for it is the "port city on the shore of eternity."[1]

CHAPTER 1

ISRAEL—
SEVENTY-TWO YEARS
OF MIRACLES

Great is the LORD, and most worthy of praise, in the city of our God, his holy mountain. Beautiful in its loftiness, the joy of the whole earth…Mount Zion, the city of the Great King (Psalm 48:1–2 NIV).

Ancient charts show Jerusalem as the center of the world, and for the Jewish, Christian, and Islamic faiths, this mapping certainly holds true. Historian Simon Montefiore exquisitely describes this unique city: "Jerusalem is the house of the one God, the capital of two peoples, the temple of three religions and she is the only city to exist twice—in heaven and on earth: the peerless grace of the terrestrial is as nothing to the glories of the celestial."[1]

The Midrash,[2] an ancient commentary on Hebrew Scriptures, states:

The Land of Israel is the center of the world—Jerusalem is the center of the Land—the Holy Temple is the center of Jerusalem—the Holy of Holies is the center of the Holy Temple—the Holy Ark is the center of the Holy of Holies and the Foundation Stone from which the world was established is before the Holy Ark.[3]

Jerusalem, first referenced as Salem in the Bible, is one of the oldest cities in the world and is introduced in Genesis 14:18–20 as the place where Abram paid tithe to Melchizedek after his glorious victory over the Canaanite Kings. Melchizedek was described as both a king (of Salem) and a priest, "...*king of Salem meaning 'king of peace,' without father, without mother, without genealogy, without beginning of days nor end of life, but made like the Son of God, remains a priest continually*" (Hebrews 7:1–3). Many biblical scholars believe that Melchizedek was in fact the first appearance of Jesus Christ in Scripture.

Jerusalem is not only an ancient city; *it is a consecrated city*—it is the city of God (Psalm 48:1–2). Jerusalem has been the spiritual epicenter of the Jewish people since 1010 BCE, when King David danced into the city before the Ark of the Covenant. It was here that he established Jerusalem as the capital of the Jewish nation (2 Samuel 6:14–15).

Teddy Kollek, former mayor of Jerusalem, beautifully described this city's connection to the Jewish people:

For three thousand years, Jerusalem has been the center of Jewish hope and longing. No other city has played such a dominant role in the history, culture, religion and consciousness of a people as has Jerusalem in the life of Jewry and Judaism. Throughout centuries of exile, Jerusalem remained alive in the hearts of Jews everywhere as the focal point of Jewish history, the symbol of ancient glory, spiritual fulfillment and modern renewal. This heart and soul of the Jewish people engenders the thought that if you want one simple word to symbolize all Jewish history, that word would be "Jerusalem."[4]

The sacred Scriptures not only laid the foundation of God's hallowed city—they also foretold its future (Psalm 132:14). Jerusalem is where the Final Throne will be established, for God declares,

This is my resting place for ever and ever; here I will sit enthroned, for I have desired it (Psalm 132:14 NIV).

During its long history, Jerusalem has been destroyed twice, besieged twenty-three times, attacked fifty-two times, and captured and recaptured forty-four times.[5] But no matter its struggling history, God has plans for Jerusalem to become the capital city of Earth's Last Empire in the future.

Again the word of the LORD of hosts came, saying, "Thus says the LORD of hosts: 'I am zealous for Zion with great zeal; with great fervor I am zealous for her.' Thus says the LORD: 'I will return to Zion, and dwell in the midst of Jerusalem. Jerusalem shall be called the City of Truth, the Mountain of the LORD of hosts, The Holy Mountain' (Zechariah 8:1–3).

For more than three thousand years, Israel has been a target for conquest and Jerusalem the reward; and its future is no different. However, another more important reality holds true—there is a God in heaven who declares, *"I am jealous for Jerusalem and for Zion"* (Zechariah 1:14).

Jerusalem is the Holy City of the past, present, and future. I have written books concerning Jerusalem through the years, motivated by biblical prophecy and the city's prominence in world news, and today is no different—Jerusalem is still at the forefront of global events.

The kingdoms of this earth want Israel and its capital city as their prize—the king of the North (Daniel 11:15–31) covets its warm-water ports for its global navy, the kings of the East (Revelation 16:12) are bent on world domination, the king of the South (Daniel 11:5) seeks to control all of God's Covenant Land, and the king of the West (Daniel 8:5–11) aspires to establish his apocalyptic throne there.

However, there is a King in heaven who protects Jerusalem day and night. *"Behold, He that keepeth Israel shall neither slumber nor sleep"* (Psalm 121:4 KJV). And there is room for only one throne—the Eternal Throne of the Living God—the One True God of Abraham, Isaac, and Jacob, and He will share the glory of Jerusalem with no one!

Abrahamic covenant…land grant…Israel…Jerusalem…blessing… prophecy…Gog and Magog…Armageddon. Most of us are familiar with the words, but how do they connect, and why are they import-ant to America, to the nations of the world, and to us personally?

My prayer is that the pages of this book will help the reader understand the importance of Israel, Jerusalem, and the Jewish peo-ple in the economy of God. There is no doubt that all roads in the future of the world lead to Jerusalem.

The covenant God made with Abraham, Isaac, and Jacob cen-turies ago exploded on the front pages of every newspaper in the mid-twentieth century on May 14, 1948, as Prime Minister Ben-Gurion announced the State of Israel's rebirth.

Israel lives—now and forever more!

THE PEOPLE OF ISRAEL LIVE

The year 2020 (5780 on the Jewish calendar) marked the seventy-second birthday of Israel's rebirth. The revival of modern Israel is by far the greatest miracle of the last century. In fact, the survival of the Jewish people as a culture, still anchored to the same Holy Scriptures, the same language, the same traditions, and the same land for more than three thousand years, is the greatest miracle since the resurrection of Jesus Christ.[6]

Despite all the tragedies and abuses the Jewish people have suffered, the descendants of Abraham are living and prospering in the land that God promised them in the book of Genesis. Israel's history over the last seventy-two years has been a continuous demonstration of the Lord's protection and blessing.

The miracle of Israel is perfectly summed up in the Hebrew phrase *Am Yisrael Chai*, which means "the people of Israel live." Israel and the Jewish people have experienced the adversity of defamation, persecution, dispersal, systematic annihilation, and crushing wars—and they have not only supernaturally survived—they have thrived!

When Israel was reborn in 1948, they had no one's help but God's. Today, this tiny nation is one of the most successful on earth. Israel's people have built cities out of swamps and transformed the desert into farmland. They have become global leaders in the technological and medical fields and one of the most advanced military forces in the world. Israel today is healthy, joyful, prosperous, and a true light unto the nations.

God Almighty gave Abraham the promise of a nation within the covenant of Genesis 12 and He has used this nation to bless the world. My hope is that Israel's amazing account will inspire and motivate you to take a bold and courageous stand on her behalf, for the story of Israel is the greatest drama ever to unfold on the stage of human history.

COVENANT, EXILE, AND RESTORATION

Israel is the only nation in the history of the world that was created by a sovereign act of God. But that didn't happen in 1948, it took place over four thousand years before (2100 BCE), when God made an everlasting covenant with Abraham and his descendants.

God Almighty clearly included both the Jewish people and the land of Israel in His covenant.

> *I will make you very fruitful; I will make nations of you, and kings will come from you. I will establish my covenant as **an everlasting covenant between me and you and your descendants** after you for the generations to come, to be your God and the God of your descendants after you. The **whole land of Canaan**, where you now reside as a foreigner, **I will give as an everlasting possession** to you and your descendants after you; and I will be their God* (Genesis 17:6–8 NIV).

When the Lord used the word *everlasting* to describe His covenant with Israel, He meant it—it stands *forever!* God's land covenant with Abraham and his descendants is mentioned throughout the Bible, and this foundational truth is absolutely essential for all peoples and nations to understand.

The God we serve does not break covenant. The Bible says, *"The LORD your God, He is God, the faithful God who keeps covenant and mercy for a thousand generations"* (Deuteronomy 7:9). That's one hundred thousand years when you consider that a generation, according to Genesis 15:16, is technically one hundred years. The meaning of this phrase is, "I am the Lord that keeps covenant longer than forever."

O seed of Abraham His servant, you children of Jacob, His cho-
sen ones! He is the LORD our God; His judgments are in all the
earth. He remembers His covenant forever, the word which He
commanded, ***for a thousand generations****, the covenant which*
He made with Abraham, and His oath to Isaac, and confirmed
it to Jacob for a statute, to Israel as an ***everlasting covenant****,*
saying, "To you I will give the land of Canaan as the allotment
of your inheritance" (Psalms 105:6–11).

God gave Abraham, and his descendants, through Isaac, the title deed to the land of Israel, and this ownership has never been revoked. But in the centuries that followed the creation of this binding contract, the Jews were driven from their land and scattered among the nations of the world. The dispersion of the Jewish people from their original homeland is called the *diaspora*.

Yet, despite the fact that many of the Jews were forced into exile by the Assyrians in 722 BCE, the Babylonians in 587 BCE, and the Romans in the year 70 CE, they always maintained a presence in their Covenant Land. Even though the Jewish people were not always in political control of the land and were not always the majority of the land's population, they have lived in Israel continuously from the time of Joshua's conquest at Gilgal (1500 BCE) until the present day.[7]

During the thousands of years of exile and unspeakable suffering, the chosen people never lost their hope of returning home. They clung to the many promises given through the Hebrew prophets that one day they would be restored to Zion, reclaiming their God-given inheritance.

The Jewish people base their right to the land of Israel on the following biblical and historical facts:

- First and foremost, God promised the land to the patriarch Abraham through an irrevocable covenant recorded in Genesis 12:1–3; 15:18; 17:8; 35:12.
- Second, the Jewish people settled and developed the land, as described by the prophet Jeremiah (Jeremiah 24:6; 42:10).
- Third, the international community granted political sovereignty to the Jewish people through the Balfour Declaration in 1917; the United Nations partition resolution of 1947; and Israel's recognition as a sovereign nation on May 14, 1948, fulfilling the prophecy recorded in Isaiah 66:8, 22.

THE INGATHERING

The appointed time for the rebirth of Israel had come at last. As promised throughout Scripture, God's mighty hand began to gather the exiles back to their Promised Land:

*Remember, I pray, the word that You commanded Your servant Moses, saying, "If you are unfaithful, I will scatter you among the nations; but if you return to Me, and keep My commandments and do them, though some of you were cast out to the farthest part of the heavens, yet **I will gather them from there, and bring them to the place which I have chosen as a dwelling for My name"** (Nehemiah 1:8–9).*

The LORD builds up Jerusalem; He gathers together the outcasts of Israel. *He heals the brokenhearted and binds up their wounds (Psalms 147:2–3).*

"Therefore behold, the days are coming," says the LORD, "that it shall no more be said, 'The LORD lives who brought the children of Israel from the land of Egypt,' but, 'The LORD lives

who brought up the children of Israel from the land from the north and from all the lands where He had driven them.' **For I will bring them back into their land which I gave to their fathers**" (Jeremiah 16:14–15).

Thus says the LORD GOD: "**When I have gathered the house of Israel from the peoples among whom they are scattered**, *and am hallowed in them in the sight of the Gentiles,* **then they will dwell in their own land which I gave to My servant Jacob.** *And they will dwell safely there, build houses, and plant vineyards; yes, they will dwell securely, when I execute judgments on all those around them who despise them. Then they shall know that I am the* LORD *their God*" (Ezekiel 28:25–26).

God was calling His people home.

REBIRTH OF ISRAEL: MAY 14, 1948

After thirty years of assurances from the British government and other world leaders, on November 29, 1947, the Jewish people finally received formal approval from the United Nations General Assembly for the recreation of an independent Jewish state located in the Promised Land. According to the partition plan, UN Resolution 181, the Jews would receive a tiny fraction of the land originally set aside for them by previous agreements.

Hesitant yet desperate, Jewish leaders accepted the offer of these disjointed scraps of land, and as the news spread, overjoyed Jewish families danced in the streets. However, irate Arab leaders rejected the partition plan and instigated months of attacks against their Jewish neighbors while preparations for statehood went forward.

On May 14, 1948, David Ben-Gurion proclaimed Israel's official independence. Eleven minutes later, President Harry Truman of the United States was the first world leader to officially recognize the rebirth of Israel. In that historic moment, God miraculously restored the land of Israel to His people and the ancient prophecy of Isaiah 66:8 was fulfilled:

> *"Who has ever heard of such things? Who has ever seen things like this? Can a country be born in a day or a nation be brought forth in a moment? Yet no sooner is Zion in labor than she gives birth to her children."*

However, the celebration was short-lived. The next day, Lebanon and Syria attacked from the north, Iraq and Jordan from the east, Egypt and Sudan from the south, and the Palestinians from within. Lacking in manpower, resources, and with almost no international assistance, Israel inexplicably survived and even gained ground. But the War of Independence came at a great cost. Israel lost 6,373 people in the war, nearly 1 percent of its entire population.[8]

After more than a year of fighting, the Arab nations finally made armistice agreements with Israel. For the first time in nearly two thousand years, since the 70 CE diaspora, the Jewish people would have sovereignty over their God-given national homeland.

REBUILDING A NATION (1949–1967)

Israel grew quickly as Jewish immigrants flooded back to their homeland from around the world. Jews who were interned in post–World War II refugee camps were finally allowed to leave Europe and go to Israel. The survivors of the war brought a wealth of skills, knowledge, and a passionate will to live in the Jewish state, but very little else.

At the same time, the surrounding Arab nations were so enraged by Israel's existence that they began harshly persecuting and evicting their Jewish citizens. More than 850,000 Jewish refugees from the Middle East and North Africa were forced to flee the communities where they had lived for nearly 2,600 years. These families, known as Mizrahi Jews, lost their homes, their possessions, their ancestral heritage, and their religious artifacts of worship—everything had to be left behind.[9]

Some of the Mizrahi Jews went to North America or Europe, but it was Israel that widely opened its doors to welcome them home. Those who immigrated to the newly reborn state were bound together by their divine destiny and desire to pioneer the land of covenant. They were also unified by the resurrection of the ancient Hebrew language that had been modernized by Eliezer Ben-Yehuda during the late nineteenth century, fulfilling the prophecy of Zephaniah 3:9:

> *For then I will restore to the peoples a pure language, That they all may call on the name of the Lord, To serve Him with one accord.*

Immediately, the Jewish people formed collaborative farming communities known as *kibbutzim*, where they worked together to transform the arid land into green fields. An Israeli pioneer invented the world's first drip irrigation system, which revolutionized not only Israel's agricultural industry but also transformed how farmers all over the world irrigated their crops.

Much of the country was dry and barren desert, and Israel faced a severe shortage of water needed for drinking, agriculture, and industry. For these reasons, finding a way to get a reliable source of water to all its cities and farms was critical to survival. By 1964, a massive project to transport water from the Sea of Galilee in the north to the center of the country and the southern communities in the Negev was completed and as a result the land began to bloom.

Through the Lord's blessings, and a tremendous amount of hard work, determination, and ingenuity, Israel flourished and grew stronger. Once again, the Jewish people participated in the fulfillment of biblical prophecy: *"The wilderness and the wasteland shall be glad for them, and the desert shall rejoice and blossom as the rose"* (Isaiah 35:1).

However, peace remained elusive, as Israel's Arab neighbors continued to brazenly threaten Israel with annihilation.

THE SIX-DAY WAR (1967)

For years, increasing terrorist attacks along Israel's borders plagued its citizens. Arab leaders spoke openly of their desire to wipe Israel off the map and massacre every Jewish man, woman, and child.

In April of 1967, Syria threatened Israel's water supply from the Jordan River, leading to a military confrontation. The Syrians called on their ally Egypt to attack Israel and, in May, Egyptian troops expelled UN forces stationed in the Sinai Desert and closed off Israel's access to shipping routes. The United States and Israel's allies in Europe refused to intervene and warned the Jewish state not to start a war, even though they faced an invasion of nearly half a million Arab troops positioned along all of their borders.

Lebanon, Jordan, and Iraq joined Syria and Egypt to fight against Israel. By June 1, it was clear that if Israel did nothing, these five Arab armies would wipe them out. Many Jews fled Israel, fearing extermination, while others dug graves anticipating the massive loss of Jewish lives. One celebrated Jewish rabbi sent a message of encouragement to the people of Israel reminding them that, *"He that keepth Israel neither slumbers nor sleeps."* Israel was forsaken by everyone—except God Almighty.

In the early morning of June 5, Israel's air force, under the leadership of Commander Mordechai Hod, launched Operation Focus, a surprise pre-emptive attack on Egypt's airfields destroying nearly all of the MIG-21 jets parked on the ground. Israel continued to fight and win astonishing victories over its enemies for five more days. But it was the battle for Jerusalem that became the pivotal moment that defined modern Israeli history.

Israel had lost the eastern half of Jerusalem during the 1948 War for Independence. The Old City, where Jews had lived continuously for centuries, even under foreign rule, was captured by Jordan. All Jews were forced out of their homes, and none were allowed to visit the Temple Mount or the Western Wall. The holiest site in the world for the Jewish people had been taken from them, and they mourned its profound loss.

Initially, Israel had no intention of fighting against Jordan to recapture eastern Jerusalem. But when King Hussein ignored Israel's pleas to stay out of the war, Israeli paratroopers stormed into the Old City on June 7. Within four hours, Israel had retaken control of the Temple Mount, and the world witnessed young Israel Defense Force (IDF) soldiers weep as they touched the Western Wall for the first time in almost two millennia.

Brigadier General Shlomo Goren, who later became the Chief Rabbi of Israel, sounded the *shofar* and led his troops in prayer after the battle for Jerusalem was over. There at the Western Wall, Israel's soldiers jubilantly rededicated Jerusalem to the Lord and mournfully remembered the lives they had lost to liberate the Holy City. IDF Commander Motta Gur issued these words to his troops:

> For some two thousand years the Temple Mount was forbidden to the Jews. Until you came—you, the paratroopers— and returned it to the bosom of the nation. The Western

Wall, for which every heart beats, is ours once again. Many Jews have taken their lives into their hands throughout our long history, in order to reach Jerusalem and live here. Endless words of longing have expressed the deep yearning for Jerusalem that beats within the Jewish heart. You have been given the great privilege of completing the circle, of returning to the nation its capital and its holy center. Jerusalem is yours forever.[10]

By the end of the Six-Day War, Israel had gained enough land to triple its size, yet most of it they would willingly exchange in future peace agreements. Even though the city of Jerusalem was considered too precious to give up or divide, then defense minister Moshe Dayan conceded Israel's sovereignty over the Temple Mount, only minutes after it was taken.

This concession has since been widely debated; Dayan gave up control of Judaism's holiest site to avoid further bloodshed, but as a result, the Jewish people have not been allowed to pray there ever since. However, after years of separation the Jewish people finally gained access to most of their holy places and, under Israeli control, Jerusalem was made safe for people of all faiths to live in and freely worship according to their own traditions.

The land Israel secured during the Six-Day War included the Sinai Peninsula, the Golan Heights, the Gaza Strip, and the ancient biblical heartland of Judea and Samaria. This miraculous military operation transformed the way the world saw Israel, and the way Israelis saw themselves. No longer was the Jewish state seen as weak and defenseless. However, Israel's enemies were not only defeated and humiliated—they were even more enraged.

This stunning victory came at a terrible price: In just six days, 777 IDF soldiers lost their lives, and 2,586 more were wounded in battle. The number may seem small, but proportionate to Israel's total population, this loss of human life is on par with the number of casualties the United States suffered during the eight devasting years of the Vietnam War.[11]

THREE NO'S

Although Israel had decisively won the Six-Day War, soon after, the Israeli government offered to give up the vast majority of its newly acquired territory in exchange for peace. On June 19, 1967, Israel offered to return the Sinai Peninsula to Egypt and the Golan Heights to Syria.

Despite the immense economic benefits and strategic military value of controlling these territories, Israel was willing to sacrifice this prized land if the Arabs would agree to accept their right to exist. However, the Arab leaders were in no mood to negotiate. Stung by their humiliating defeat and outraged by the reality that Jews had a right to live *anywhere* in the land, they immediately rejected Israel's offer of a permanent peace treaty.

Consequently, at the Arab League's Khartoum Conference in Sudan, Egypt, Syria, Jordan, Lebanon, Iraq, Algeria, Kuwait, and Sudan adopted an official position against Israel that included the infamous Three No's:

NO Peace
NO Recognition
NO Negotiation

For twelve years, the Three No's prevented all peace efforts, and to this day, they are still major obstacles to establishing peace between Israel and many of its neighbors.[12]

LAND FOR PEACE

The outcome of the Six-Day War not only angered the Arabs, the United Nations also viewed Israel's control of its new territories with disapproval. Since the beginning of time, nations have recognized the right of the victors in war to retain control of territory justly won in battle. Nevertheless, the UN decided that, in regard to Israel, this right was invalid, and on November 22, 1967, the Security Council passed Resolution 242.

This resolution became the foundation for all future efforts to influence peace between Israel and the Arabs. It called on Israel to trade land it had won in the 1967 war for peace agreements, and it called on the Arab states to recognize Israel's right to exist.

Israel has consistently shown its willingness to trade land for peace; in stark contrast, the Arab-Palestinian rejection of peace has invariably undermined all efforts to end the conflict. Moreover, the Palestinian leadership has yet to accept Israel's right to exist as a nation.

Radical Palestinians continuously seek ways to abolish Israel, even during so-called negotiations. For example, Palestinians claim that Arabs who left the fledgling State of Israel in 1948—and all of their descendants—have a "right" to return to the land of Israel (which they refer to as Palestine), even if they have never lived there. Such a policy would dissolve the Jewish state.

Until the Palestinians accept that Israel has a right to exist, the right to secure borders, and the right to defend itself by itself as an independent Jewish state, no international pronouncement or policy will serve to advance an end to this centuries-old conflict that first began with Ishmael and Isaac.

YOM KIPPUR WAR (1973)

It was Saturday, October 6, 1973, in Israel. The country was quiet and focused on observing the Day of Atonement, the holiest day in Judaism. Suddenly the solemn and sacred atmosphere was shattered.

While IDF soldiers observed Yom Kippur, Egypt and Syria launched a surprise attack simultaneously on two separate fronts. Fewer than 500 Israeli soldiers faced an overwhelming force of 600,000 Egyptians in the south, while in the north, 180 Israeli tanks defended the country against 1,400 Syrian tanks. US president Richard Nixon, motivated by fears of a Soviet-backed Arab victory, authorized a massive emergency airlift of weapons to Israel on October 12.

Though vastly outnumbered, Israel shocked the world by not only surviving the initial attacks, they also pushed the invaders back across their borders. Eighteen days after Egypt and Syria first attacked Israel, the Arab leaders agreed to a cease-fire rather than suffer further losses. Israel won the Yom Kippur War, but 2,688 Israeli soldiers sacrificed their lives to protect the Jewish homeland. It was another agonizing price to pay for peace; a price that the Jewish people have been paying for centuries.

Angered and stunned by yet one more miraculous Israeli victory, the Arab world realized that conventional warfare against Israel was not working. They changed their strategy and sought to isolate Israel from sympathetic foreign governments by declaring an oil embargo against the West. This oil ban created an energy crisis that lasted from October 1973 until March 1974.

The embargo worked as nations began altering their policies toward Israel. This model of economic and diplomatic warfare became the foundation for the anti-Israel Boycott, Divestment, and Sanctions (BDS) movement around the world.

Foreign attitudes grew increasingly hostile and irrational toward Israel after the Yom Kippur War. Then, in November of 1975, the United Nations General Assembly took it one step too far and declared that Zionism was a form of racism. It labeled the Israeli government as the "racist occupier and oppressor" of the Palestinian people.[13]

Israel was accused of being akin to the apartheid regime in South Africa, and this smear campaign did lasting damage to Israel's international reputation. The UN finally revoked this hateful and undeserved resolution (UNGA 3379) in 1991; nevertheless, Israel is still repeatedly singled out and condemned by the United Nations more than any other country in the world.

PEACE WITH EGYPT (1979)

Israel's first peace treaty with an Arab state began with Egyptian president Anwar Sadat's visit to Jerusalem in 1977. Sadat shocked and enraged the Arab world by standing in the Knesset and declaring that he sought peace between Egypt and Israel. Israel's prime minister, Menachem Begin, received this pronouncement in good faith and began making difficult and unpopular decisions to achieve peace.

The Camp David Accords took place as a series of meetings during the Carter presidency in the fall of 1978. The administration sought worldwide support for the negotiations and even asked religious leaders to pray for success. Finally, a peace treaty between Egypt and Israel was signed on March 26, 1979.[14]

The concessions Israel made for peace were painful. Menachem Begin agreed to return 91 percent of the territory it had won in the Six-Day War to Egypt, and willingly gave up the strategic and economic benefits of the Sinai Peninsula. Previously, in the 1956 Sinai Campaign, Israel had captured the peninsula in an attempt to deter terrorists and remove the Egyptian blockade of Eilat, a critical Israeli port.

The Sinai campaign not only increased the IDF's confidence, it also proved its ability to successfully engage in large-scale military operations, allowing Israel to gain respect in the eyes of the Western powers. Nonetheless, giving up land in both the 1956 Sinai Campaign and the later 1967 War was deemed a worthy sacrifice for peace, which Israel felt was necessary to achieving the security it had sought for decades.

Menachem Begin and Anwar Sadat were awarded the Nobel Peace Prize in 1978 for their courage in participating in the Camp David Accords. Unfortunately, the Arab League rejected Sadat's actions, and just two years after making peace with Israel, members of the Egyptian Islamic Jihad publicly assassinated Sadat.[15]

A *fatwa,* which is a religious ruling authorized by an Islamic ruler, sanctioned Sadat's murder. This fatwa was directed by Omar Abdel-Rahman, known in the United States as the "Blind Sheikh." Rahman was sentenced in 1995 to life in prison by a US court for being part of "an organization whose aim was to wage a *jihad* [Arabic for holy war or holy struggle] of terror against the United States."[16]

OPERATION BABYLON (1981)

For many years, Israel monitored Saddam Hussein's attempts to acquire nuclear weapons with alarm while the world looked the other way. France helped Iraq build research facilities, and resisted Israel's urgent warnings that Saddam Hussein intended to execute a nuclear holocaust against Israel.

America's defense secretary, Caspar Weinberger, and secretary of state, Alexander Haig, agreed with the Israeli assessment of the Iraqi nuclear program's goal of destroying Israel, but the United States refused to act.[17] Despite estimates that Iraq was only five to ten years away from acquiring nuclear weapons, and some reports predicting that Saddam Hussein could have the bomb within a year, world leaders also refused to take the threat seriously. Israel's pleas for help fell on deaf ears.

Israel did not have the luxury of hoping for the best. Past experience had proven that when an Arab dictator declared he intended to wipe Israel off the map, it was not an empty threat. History had also confirmed that Israel could not rely on any of its allies, even the United States, to intervene on its behalf when it came time for war.

After Israeli intelligence confirmed Iraq would complete the bomb within a year, Prime Minister Begin ordered a covert strike on the Osirak nuclear reactor. On June 7, 1981, fourteen F-15s and F-16s flew at low altitude over enemy airspace and launched a surprise attack on the nuclear facility. It was over in less than two minutes.[18] Immediately, a firestorm of criticism erupted around the globe. The United States was furious and voted for a United Nations Security Council resolution condemning Israel for the attack.

A NIGHT TO HONOR ISRAEL

While watching the news coverage, I grew extremely frustrated with America's outrage over Israel's strike on the Iraqi nuclear plant. I was so irritated that I decided to do something revolutionary by planning the first Night to Honor Israel. To my surprise, the local Jewish community was skeptical of my offer of support, believing I had a hidden agenda.

A gesture of unconditional love and support had never been extended before, but thanks to a courageous orthodox rabbi, the Jewish community agreed to the event. Despite death threats and harsh opposition from anti-Semites, I went forward and hosted the

Night to Honor Israel with the backing of my family, our church, one brave local pastor, and my newfound friend, Rabbi Aryeh Scheinberg.

On the appointed night of September 10, 1981, the standing-room-only crowd of Christians and Jews that gathered at the Lila Cockrell Theater in downtown San Antonio experienced a divine sense of brotherhood. To demonstrate our support, the Christians in the room raised $10,000 and presented the gift to Israel's Hadassah Hospital. As Rabbi Scheinberg gave the final benediction, the director of security quietly informed me that a bomb threat had been received.

No bomb went off that night in San Antonio—instead, a new movement exploded within our hearts. Since that historic night, Rabbi Scheinberg and I, along with the help of thousands of Christians and Jews in cities around the country and the world, have hosted hundreds of Night to Honor Israel events for nearly forty years. And because of this God-given desire to bless Israel and the Jewish people, another movement of solidarity was born—Christians United for Israel.

In February of 2006 I called four hundred of America's foremost Evangelical leaders together to form a national grassroots organization called Christians United for Israel. I asked for a vote of those who would support this revolutionary concept by a show of hands, and four hundred were instantly lifted. It was indeed a miracle from God.

It is my great privilege to report that through our united efforts, as of this date, Christians United for Israel (CUFI) is over 10 million members strong and now hosting more than fifty pro-Israel events every month throughout our great nation in churches, on college campuses, and within local communities. CUFI has been the tip of the spear in passing major legislation in Washington, DC, in our unwavering war against anti-Semitism.*

FIRST LEBANON WAR (1982)

Lebanon has long been a safe harbor for terrorist groups such as the Palestine Liberation Organization (PLO) and Hezbollah (Arabic for "the party of god"). The PLO was created in 1964 during the Arab League Summit in Cairo, Egypt, with the alleged purpose of the "liberation of Palestine." In reality, its main objective was the destruction of the nation of Israel through acts of terror.

In 1978, PLO terrorists penetrated the northern border of Israel and murdered thirty-nine innocent victims, including thirteen children. After this vicious attack and others like them, Israeli forces crossed into southern Lebanon, pushing the terrorists back from the border, but to no avail—the terror war continued.

Even after the United States helped broker a cease-fire agreement in 1981, the PLO repeatedly violated the truce and continued to build their forces and increase their arsenal while killing Israelis along the way. During the eleven-month "cease-fire" period, Israel endured 270 PLO terror attacks that killed twenty-nine Israelis and injured more than three hundred.[19]

---

* Additional legislation sponsored by Christians United for Israel:
- Never Again Education Act—2020
- Eastern Mediterranean Security and Energy Partnership Act—2019
- Adoption of IHRA definition of anti-Semitism for purposes of Title VI by White House executive order—2019
- Turkey removed from F-35 Joint Strike Fighter program—2019
- President Trump's designation of Iran's Islamic Revolutionary Guards Corps as a Foreign Terrorist Organization—2019
- President Trump's recognition of Israeli sovereignty over the Golan Heights—2019
- With CUFI's support, Kenneth Marcus is confirmed as the Department of Education's Assistant Secretary for Civil Rights—2018
- President Trump cuts off all US funding to UNRWA—2018
- Anti-Terrorism Clarification Act—2018
- Stop Using Human Shields Act—2018

In June 1982, the IDF once again moved into Lebanon to drive out the Palestinian terrorists through "Operation Peace for Galilee." Secretary of State and National Security Advisor under Presidents Nixon and Ford Henry Kissinger defended the Israeli operation: "No sovereign state can tolerate indefinitely the buildup along its borders of a military force dedicated to its destruction and implementing its objectives by periodic shelling and raids."[20]

The war in Lebanon was fought on two fronts—on the ground and in the media. Despite a series of attempted cease-fires by the Israelis, the PLO orchestrated assaults that generated required responses from the IDF. Unfortunately, the world press chose to accept the PLO's spin on the retaliation and blamed Israel—rather than the provocateurs—for the violence.

For the first time since Israel's rebirth, there was a civil debate on the war, and as a result of the extreme internal dispute, Israel pulled most of its troops out of Lebanon in 1985. Despite Israel's voluntary withdrawal, its civilians continued to suffer terror attacks along the Lebanese border.[21]

During the clashes between Israel and the PLO in the early '80s, Hezbollah gained strength and took root in southern Lebanon with the financial and military backing of Iran. Hezbollah later published an "open letter" identifying the United States as one of Islam's principal enemies and also called for the "obliteration" of Israel.

OPERATION MOSES (1984)

Israel's Knesset passed an extraordinary law in 1950 that essentially defined the nation's fundamental purpose: "Every Jew has the right to immigrate to this country . . ." This *Law of Return* established that all Jews everywhere are entitled to Israeli citizenship. After the rebirth of the nation of Israel, the two thousand years of wandering was officially over.

In 1975, Israel's Chief Rabbinate recognized the Ethiopian Jewish community (the descendants of Solomon and the Queen of Sheba) as Jews, which entitled them to the Law of Return, giving them the right to immigrate to Israel. For three thousand years, these displaced Jews had been faithful to the Torah and Jewish customs handed down to them by their ancestors. After Israel became a state, they desperately wanted to join their Jewish brothers and sisters in the Holy Land.

There was a problem, however. Ethiopia forbade the Jews to leave. Unwilling to accept their government's decision, thousands of Ethiopian Jews secretly traveled to the Sudanese border and waited for their miraculous transport to Israel. The journey was dangerous, and many died along the way. Reports reached Israel that thousands of Ethiopian Jews were perishing, and Israel decided to mount a rescue mission.

On November 21, 1984, the Mossad, Israel's national intelligence agency, collaborated with the CIA and the Sudanese National Intelligence and Security Service to covertly smuggle nearly eight thousand Ethiopian Jews out of Sudan. Over seven weeks, cargo planes made more than thirty secret flights to pick up the refugees while Israel clandestinely paid Sudanese officials to look the other way.[22]

Operation Moses gave thousands of Ethiopian Jews the hope of a new life in Israel and fulfilled three thousand years of longing to be reunited with their spiritual homeland. Today, after two more rescue operations in 1991 and again in 2010, there are over 150,000 Ethiopian Jews living and thriving in Israel, fulfilling the words of the Lord through the prophet Zechariah:

Thus says the LORD of hosts: "Behold, I will save My people from the land of the east and from the land of the west; I will bring

them back, and they shall dwell in the midst of Jerusalem. They
shall be My people and I will be their God, in truth and righ-
teousness" (Zechariah 8:7–8).

FIRST PALESTINIAN INTIFADA (1987)

A four-year period of violence and terrorism broke out in December 1987 after deliberate misinformation was spread in Gaza that Israel had killed four Palestinians in retaliation for the stabbing death of an Israeli. Massive riots soon broke out among the Palestinians, and each additional death added fuel to the fire. In the eyes of the international community, as in times past, Israel was seen as the guilty party and was harshly condemned for using necessary force in an attempt to quell the terrorism.

Enemy propaganda continued to circulate that Israel was murdering Palestinians. The UN investigated and determined the stories were false, but the damage had been done. The *intifada* (Arabic for violent uprising) continued to grow, and the IDF reported hundreds of attacks, to include bombings and shootings. What was reported in the world press as spontaneous mob violence was soon revealed to have been orchestrated and encouraged by Yasser Arafat, the PLO's leader.

To make matters worse, at the height of the intifada, King Hussein of Jordan decided to sever "administrative and legal" ties with Judea and Samaria (West Bank). This created an instant refugee problem with over one million Palestinian Arabs losing their Jordanian citizenship overnight. King Hussein explained his decision as one of deference to Yasser Arafat and his desire for national autonomy.[23] Arafat did not care about the welfare of his own people—he did not care how many suffered in the death camps that he helped create—he only cared about making the world believe the uprising was Israel's fault.

Meanwhile, the intifada became its own worst enemy. Many of the victims were themselves Palestinian, targeted by their own people who accused them of collaborating with Israel. The murder rate grew, and the Palestinian leadership could not put out the fire they had started. Arafat was losing control, and as a result, more extreme terrorist organizations emerged.

One such militant group to surface was Hamas. It was backed by the Egyptian Muslim Brotherhood and was not interested in a secular nationalist movement. Hamas's intent was to create an Islamist society of religious extremists engaged in a jihad against the Jews.

OSLO ACCORDS (1993, 1995)

Israel's success in trading land for peace with Egypt led them to believe they could accomplish the same with the Palestinians. Israel began secret negotiations with the PLO when Yasser Arafat announced a plan for a two-state solution in 1993.

Israel and the Palestinian leaders worked on a proposal to divide the West Bank, an area known to Jews and Christians by its biblical name of Judea and Samaria. In the years since 1967, Jewish pioneers had built towns in Judea and Samaria, and Israel's leaders wanted the majority to become part of the nation in any final peace accord. Under this plan, the undivided city of Jerusalem would also remain in Israel. After eight months of peace talks, Israel and the Palestinian leadership reached an agreement.

Israeli prime minister Yitzhak Rabin and PLO chairman Yasser Arafat signed the Oslo Accord in September 1993 at a public ceremony hosted by President Bill Clinton in Washington, DC. Arafat promised to recognize Israel's right to exist and renounce terrorism, and Rabin agreed to give up land and recognize the PLO as the leader of the Palestinian government. Under these terms, they pledged to seek a solution for the ongoing conflict.

The success of the accords encouraged Jordan to negotiate its own separate peace treaty with Israel. As a result, a final peace treaty was signed and a cooperative relationship was formed between Jordan and Israel in October 1994.

A second round of talks between Israel and the Palestinians, known as Oslo II, took place in 1995. The two parties agreed to a temporary system of government for the Palestinian Authority (PA) that still gave Israel security control over strategic areas. The agreement was supposed to expire in 1999, but the peace process stalled and the temporary arrangement has hung in limbo for more than twenty years.

Although Arafat told Israel and the United States that he had renounced violence and recognized Israel's right to peacefully exist, he told Arab audiences that his negotiations were merely a mechanism to buy time and gain a better position from which to launch future attacks. During the period after the Oslo Accords between September 1993 and September 2000, terrorists killed nearly three hundred Israelis.[24] Trust between Israel and the Palestinians broke down, and peace remained out of reach once again.

CAMP DAVID SUMMIT (2000)

Having brokered the Oslo Accords, US president Bill Clinton was eager to try again for an Israeli-Palestinian peace agreement before the end of his term in office. Israeli prime minister Ehud Barak and PLO chairman Yasser Arafat accepted Clinton's invitation to a summit at Camp David in July 2000.

Barak offered Arafat 91 percent of Judea and Samaria and 100 percent of the Gaza Strip for a Palestinian state. He even offered the Palestinians sovereignty over the Arab neighborhoods in Jerusalem, a plan that would divide the very heart of Israel and cause great emotional pain to the Jewish people. Arafat refused the offer and gave no acceptable terms of his own. The two-week summit ended without a deal.

SECOND PALESTINIAN INTIFADA (2000)

After the 1967 war, Israel immediately granted control of the Temple Mount to the Arab Muslim religious authorities in Jordan, restricting their own access to the area. This action prohibited the Jewish people from praying at the Temple Mount, which is Judaism's holiest site since King Solomon built the Temple in 957 BCE.

This heart-wrenching gesture by the Israeli government was extended to avoid a religious war over access to two Islamic sites on the Temple Mount: the Al-Aqsa Mosque and the Dome of the Rock, which were established in the seventh century CE. I cannot overemphasize all the sacrifices Israel has made in exchange for the mere possibility of living in peace with its Arab-Muslim neighbors.

The sacredness of the Temple Mount in Judaism is recorded in scripture. This mountain is where Abraham prepared to offer his son Isaac to God in 2054 BCE (Genesis 22:2). King David later purchased this biblical threshing floor for fifty shekels in 1000 BCE (2 Samuel 24:18–25), and it is the location of Solomon's Temple, 967 BCE[25] (2 Chronicles 3:1). One day it will be the home of the final Temple during the Millennium.

In September 2000, Prime Minister-elect Ariel Sharon visited the Temple Mount in Jerusalem after receiving permission and assurance from the head of the Palestinian Preventive Security Organization, who said, "If Mr. Sharon refrains from entering the mosques on Temple Mount, there will not be any problem."

Nevertheless, even with official Palestinian consent, Sharon's visit was used as a pretext by the PA to spark violent riots among the Palestinians. Yasser Arafat not only instigated the riots, but he had planned the intifada in advance of Sharon's visit to the Temple Mount. In November, the US sent a committee to Israel to investigate the root of the uprising, and by April 2001, the Mitchell Report concluded that the intifada had *not* been caused by Sharon's visit to the Temple Mount.[26]

This intifada was more deadly than the first due to the radical increase of suicide bombings. No one was safe. Over one thousand Israelis were murdered within the next six years through various acts of terror. This lethal violence compelled Israel to build a security barrier in 2002. The twelve-foot concrete fence was erected through parts of Jerusalem, Judea, and Samaria, to protect innocent civilians from sniper fire and suicide bombers.

In spite of the security barrier's obvious necessity and complete success, pro-Palestinian propagandists managed to convince many in the media and the international community that the fence was a burden to ordinary Palestinians. Anti-Israel activists oversimplified the issue and labeled the life-saving security fence an "apartheid wall."[27]

The United States tried to broker a peace agreement that would stop the unrelenting terror. In December 2000, Prime Minister Ehud Barak accepted a proposal from President Clinton that was even more generous to the Palestinians than what had been offered at Camp David five months earlier. Once again, Arafat said "No!"

After Arafat's refusal to make peace, the United States, the European Union, Russia, and the United Nations formed a mediating body called the "Quartet." In 2002, without including or consulting Israel, the Quartet created the "Road Map to Peace" and laid out a plan based on yet another "land for peace" scheme.[28] The Road Map to Peace failed, but Israel's security fence succeeded. In 2002, there were forty-seven suicide bombings; by 2006, after the building of the protective barrier, this number dropped dramatically to three.

WITHDRAWAL FROM GAZA (2005)

From its rebirth, Israel has held true to the fundamental goal to live in harmony with its Arab neighbors. Establishing peace is not only part of the foundation of Jewish tradition; it is also a "declared policy of the State of Israel," and it has come at a great price.[29]

In an attempt to ease tensions with the Palestinians, Prime Minister Ariel Sharon initiated a Disengagement Plan in 2005, which called for Israel's unilateral withdrawal from the Gaza Strip and northern Samaria. The plan's dual purpose was to increase Israel's security and create yet another opportunity for peace with the Palestinians. Sharon believed that in order for this peace initiative to work, it required the great sacrifice of the over nine thousand people who lived in the twenty-five settlements located in Gaza. It was yet another attempt to employ the failed policy of land for peace.

These brave families, who had worked hard for generations to establish a good life, abandoned their homes and livelihoods at the mandate of the Israeli government. The Israeli ambassador to the United States, Daniel Ayalon, called the Disengagement Plan a "test for the Palestinian leadership."[30]

Hamas met Israel's sacrificial gesture of faith and goodwill in the peace process with the immediate takeover of Gaza. Hamas had no interest in a peace agreement and used its new political power and strategic position on Israel's southwest border to begin launching daily rocket attacks into Israeli cities. This takeover hardened many Israelis on the idea of any future exchange of land for peace.

Hamas's unrestrained domination of the Gaza Strip has haunted Israelis and Gazans ever since. Their unrelenting pursuit of evil has led to tremendous suffering on both sides of the border. Israelis endure rocket fire, and Hamas terrorists divert humanitarian resources away from the Gazan people to buy weapons, build bunkers, and dig tunnels for their continued and escalated war against Israel.

Needless to say, the Palestinians failed the "test case for peace" and ultimately proved that radical Muslims want peace with Israel—one "piece of land" at a time.

SECOND LEBANON WAR (2006)

On July 12, 2006, Hezbollah crossed the Lebanese-Israeli border and ambushed an IDF patrol, killing eight soldiers and kidnapping two others. In the ensuing conflict, Israel bombed known Hezbollah strongholds while the terrorists launched rockets at Israel's northern population centers. For nearly five weeks, Hezbollah launched more than one hundred rockets per day into Israel as anxious Israeli families slept in their bomb shelters.

To make this onslaught of terror even more difficult to engage, the IDF faced a cowardly enemy who purposely hid among the civilian population in Lebanon. Hezbollah stored their weapons in private homes and fired their rockets from neighborhoods filled with women and children. Knowing that Israel values all human life, the terrorists used the Arab people as human shields. This barbaric tactic soon became Hezbollah's signature.[31]

Israel was under intense international pressure and criticism for unavoidable civilian deaths. By divine appointment, Christians United for Israel had formed in February of that year. Over 3,600 CUFI members descended on Washington, DC, for our first summit at the exact time the war broke out. We were able to meet with members of Congress and urge them to support Israel against the tidal wave of international condemnation. It was a time when Israel desperately needed friends, and by the grace of God, CUFI was prepared to speak out on their behalf during Israel's hour of need.

The war ended with a cease-fire on August 11, 2006. Israel withdrew without destroying Hezbollah; nonetheless, the IDF was able to severely cripple their operations in Lebanon. Sadly, the Second Lebanon War took the lives of 164 Israelis.

Two years later, Hezbollah released the bodies of the two kidnapped IDF soldiers captured at the start of the war in a prisoner exchange for five known terrorists. One of the terrorists was Samir Kuntar, who was convicted of viciously murdering four Israelis, including a father and his four-year-old daughter.[32]

After his release, Kuntar received Syria's highest medal and was honored by Iranian president Mahmoud Ahmadinejad while Israel grieved the loss of their fallen soldiers.[33] Kuntar later played an operational role, with the assistance of Iran and Syria, in "building up Hezbollah's terrorist infrastructure in the Golan Heights."[34]

OPERATION CAST LEAD (2008)

After three years of sustained rocket fire from Gaza, Israel's citizens had had enough. The IDF entered Gaza on December 27, 2008.

Hindered by Gaza's dense population and the fact that Hamas terrorists, like Hezbollah, hid among the civilians, the IDF was faced with a huge challenge. Hamas launched many of its rockets from schools, hospitals, and buildings owned by the United Nations. When Israel retaliated, the biased international media focused on stories about Israel bombing schools instead of blaming the terrorists for using human shields—once again, the propaganda war focused on vilifying the Jews.

To save as many innocent lives as possible, Israel voluntarily gave up the strategic advantage of surprise. The IDF sent voicemail messages and fliers in Arabic to thousands of Gazan residents before sending in an air strike. This gave civilians time to evacuate, but also warned the terrorists to escape. During the operation, Israel lost nine IDF soldiers.[35]

Still, a new day had dawned for the pro-Israel movement—during the three weeks of fighting, CUFI staff and lay-leadership organized multiple events around the country to draw attention to Israel's extraordinary efforts to save innocent lives. While Israel was being hammered in the media, Christians United for Israel was able to rally support in American communities and on college campuses with the truth.

OPERATION PROTECTIVE EDGE AND THE TERROR TUNNELS (2014)

"Terrorism is the best political weapon for nothing drives people harder than a fear of sudden death." —Adolf Hitler

For eight long years, Israelis living along the Gaza border had endured increasing daily rocket fire; but then in the summer of 2014, in just one twenty-four-hour period, Hamas fired more than one hundred rockets into Jewish neighborhoods. The situation became intolerable—Israel had to act.

In response, on July 8, the IDF launched Operation Protective Edge, with a ground incursion of Gaza. To minimize the risk of civilian casualties, the IDF was sent to fight in the cramped streets and booby-trapped buildings of Gaza.

What the IDF discovered as they entered Gaza was an even more chilling threat. Hamas had been secretly building a massive network of underground tunnels beneath their border with Israel. Since late 2009, the terrorist network had diverted hundreds of millions of dollars and supplies, intended as foreign aid for the war-torn Gazan population, toward the building of their terror tunnels.[36]

Israel has helped facilitate the transfer of goods provided by the United Nations and others into the Gaza Strip. I have personally witnessed eighteen-wheeler after eighteen-wheeler trucks stacked with humanitarian aid cross from Israel into Gaza. These trucks are filled with electrical appliances, iPhones, computers, cement, steel rebar, mattresses, washer/dryers, and even toys, supposedly intended to rebuild day cares and schools and improve the lives of everyday Gazans. In the first year alone, over 26,298 truckloads of humanitarian aid crossed the Gazan border, comprising nearly 600,000 tons of goods, and these massive deliveries continue to this day.[37]

Instead of using these materials to provide much-needed assistance to the people of Gaza, what Hamas didn't sell on the black market was used to build the tunnels and supply their military installations.[38] Hamas intended to use these tunnels to infiltrate Israeli towns with the goal of kidnapping and killing Jewish civilians. Terrorist groups were sent into Israel through these secret passages, sometimes disguised in IDF uniforms. Thankfully, none of their planned massacres succeeded, but the discovery of this new threat alarmed Israel. The tunnels had to be destroyed.

Meanwhile, anti-Semitism surged worldwide with huge anti-Israel rallies occurring in several Western countries. The pressure on Israel to withdraw from Gaza before their mission was complete grew intense. Israel desperately needed a friend, and Christians United for Israel became one of the leading voices speaking up for Israel's right to protect itself.

CUFI placed multiple full-page ads in national newspapers exposing Hamas's stated vow to destroy the Jewish state. Later that summer, CUFI organized an emergency pastors' solidarity mission to Israel with the express purpose of demonstrating unconditional Christian support for Israel's morally justified acts of self-defense.

Finally, Hamas accepted a cease-fire agreement. Israel had successfully destroyed the tunnels beneath the border and dealt a crippling blow to the terrorist infrastructure in Gaza. Yet Israel paid a painful price with the deaths of sixty-four soldiers and three civilians during the operation.[39]

Israel's humanitarian actions during the war were finally recognized. An independent assessment given by NATO military leaders exonerated and praised Israel, stating in their 2015 report that the IDF had conducted itself by the highest possible moral standards.[*]

STABBING INTIFADA (2015)

On Rosh Hashanah, in September 2015, a wave of violence emanating from Jerusalem began to spread across the country. This hostility was fueled by the hateful and deceitful rhetoric of the Palestinian Authority. Palestinian men, women, and even children began terrorizing Israelis, believing the lies spread by their media that Israel was threatening the Muslim holy sites on the Temple Mount. These assaults, which lasted for more than two and half years, became known as the "Stabbing Intifada." Along with the stabbings, many victims were shot, rammed with vehicles, firebombed, or beaten with large stones.

In the first several months, hundreds were injured in the riots and terror outbreaks. Jewish civilians were attacked in their cars, at bus stops, near holy sites, and even in their own homes. Twenty-seven Israelis were murdered before the end of 2015. Over the next few years, that number grew to include over sixty victims brutally killed and over nine hundred more wounded.

TAYLOR FORCE ACT (2018)

One of the victims of the Intifada was Taylor Force, a young American citizen on a study-abroad trip in Israel. Taylor, who had served his country in Iraq and Afghanistan after graduating

---

[*]   https://www.timesofisrael.com/israel-did-not-commit-war-crimes-in-gaza-says
       -multi-national-military-group/.

from West Point, was stabbed and killed by a Palestinian terrorist near Tel Aviv on March 8, 2016. The twenty-eight-year-old's
tragic murder led to the creation of the Taylor Force Act in the
United States. This legislation was designed to cut off the flow of
American tax dollars to the PA until they stopped all payments to
terrorists.

For many years, the Palestinian Authority rewarded terrorists
or their families with a lifelong pension worth more than most
Palestinians could hope to earn in their lifetime. This financial
incentive to commit terror was funded by international foreign aid,
to the tune of $350 million a year. When Americans discovered their
tax dollars were being used to reward terrorism, they were outraged.

Christians United for Israel members sent more than one million emails to Congress, insisting that they pass the Taylor Force
Act and end the PA's "pay-to-slay" policy. Thankfully, the law was
passed and signed by President Trump as part of an omnibus bill in
the spring of 2018.

IRAN, HAMAS, AND
THE MARCH OF RETURN (2018)

Iran has been firmly entrenched on Israel's northern border since
2011, when the Islamic Republic's military began operating in Syria
in support of President Bashar al-Assad's regime during its Syrian
Civil War. But Iran went beyond the Syrian border on the morning
of February 10, 2018, when they invaded Israeli airspace by sending
an unmanned drone equipped with explosives into Israel.

Within minutes, the IDF intercepted the drone with a Patriot
missile. In response to the blatant infringement, Israel's air force
attacked three military positions in Syria and made it clear that
they would not tolerate attacks on its sovereignty or its right to self-
defense. Only five months after Iran's attack, Syria infiltrated Israeli

air space with an unmanned aerial vehicle, which traveled 6.2 miles over the Sea of Galilee.[40]

Sadly, it will not be long before Iran, its terrorist army Hezbollah, and their Syrian allies defy Israel's sovereignty once again.

In the spring of 2018, another serious threat emerged along Israel's western border with Gaza. Hamas announced that it would sponsor a massive "March of Return" toward the security fence in protest of Israel's seventieth anniversary. A long-standing goal of Palestinian leaders has been to force Israel to accept the "return" of millions of Arab descendants from those who fled the 1948 war. As stated earlier, this "return" would mean the end of Israel as a Jewish state.[41]

It is important to reiterate that Israel withdrew totally from the Gaza Strip in 2006, and Hamas has had complete control since 2007. In reality, the March of Return was not a protest against Israeli "occupation" nor was it a protest against a disputed border, because the current border between Gaza and Israel follows the same line that has existed since 1949. Bottom line, these riots were not a protest at all—collectively, they were a deliberate and sustained act of choreographed mass terrorism.

Remaining true to their threat, beginning on the morning of Passover, March 30, 2018, tens of thousands of Palestinians began rioting along the Gaza-Israel security fence in an attempt to provoke a violent response from the IDF soldiers standing opposite them. This premeditated hostility was methodically organized and scheduled to increase daily over six weeks up to May 14, Israel's Independence Day. The Palestinians referred to this event as the *Nakba* (Arabic for catastrophe); it was also the day the US had scheduled their embassy dedication ceremony in Jerusalem. What was publicized as a "spontaneous show of peaceful protest" was not. I was there—the riots were orchestrated and deliberate.

Hamas furthermore emboldened the Palestinians to be as confrontational and violent as possible by offering a reward of $3,000 to the family of any Palestinian killed during the riots, and $500 for anyone seriously wounded by the IDF.[42] These "peaceful protesters" burned thousands of tires along the border to obscure the IDF's vision as they continued to try to sabotage and penetrate Israel's security fence and invade the Jewish state.

The Palestinian Authority, Hamas, and the Islamic Jihad acknowledged that many of the casualties resulting from the "March of Return" riots were in fact members of their radical terror groups. Moreover, in early June of 2018, the Palestinian ambassador to France disclosed that the Hamas demonstrations were "fully financed" by Tehran.[43]

Israel cannot and will not allow its border to be breached by even a single terrorist, much less thousands of hostile combatants. It might seem that the "March of Return" was a futile act, but in fact, it was designed to be a clever propaganda weapon to inflict massive political damage on Israel. Shamefully, the liberal anti-Israel media and the biased United Nations supported this orchestrated farce by publicizing the Palestinian Authority's staged photos and video footage, as well as disseminating the PA's exaggerated casualty reports.

Israel is currently surrounded by violence and threats of a much larger regional war. Behind the scenes, Iran's invisible hand is pulling the strings of its puppets Hamas and Hezbollah, the Syrian government, and smaller terrorist groups like the Palestinian Islamic Jihad, to squeeze Israel in a vice.

Eventually, Israel will be forced to defend itself in a major confrontation with Iran and its proxies. We can expect the United Nations and the international media to condemn Israel for any defensive action, as they continue to ignore the acts of aggression that force Israel to respond. What matters most is that Israel is morally and legally justified in defending its sovereignty, the security of its borders, and the safety of its people.

Despite the decades of war and terrorism, Israel has flourished, paving its future through creativity, innovation, and collaboration.

POWERHOUSE OF INNOVATION AND TECHNOLOGY

As a tiny nation dependent on making the most out of every resource, Israel has developed into a world-leading powerhouse of innovation.

Israel's government changed its economic policies in the 1980s to provide funding and incentives for startup companies. Government investment in the private sector led to a boom in high-tech innovation. By providing the venture capital for inventors and allowing private individuals the freedom to manage their work unhindered, Israel unleashed a powerful growth engine.

For example, a group of three young computer programmers created the world's first commercial firewall software in 1993. Their virus protection technology soon grew into one of the world's leading cybersecurity companies. Flash drive technology was invented in Israel, and after its release in 2000, this new data storage system was quickly adopted by every nation in the world.

One of the most popular navigation smartphone apps, Waze, was developed in Israel in 2008. Millions of people in major cities all around the world now use this app to track the flow of traffic and find the best route to their destination. Google, which has operated a research and development (R & D) center in Israel since the mid-2000s, purchased Waze for $1.1 billion and helped spur global interest in Israeli startup companies.

Google's partnership with Israel has been profitable. Its six-hundred-employee research center in Tel Aviv created Google's "autocomplete" search engine feature. Another tech giant, Microsoft, operates R & D centers in Haifa and Herzliya, where computer scientists developed motion-sensing cameras and facial-recognition software.

Because Israel was compelled to develop its own infrastructure so quickly, it was and is uniquely equipped to aid developing countries with innovations in agriculture, water management, education, and medicine, to name a few.

BLESSING THE NATIONS

The medical and technological advancements that have emerged from Israel are remarkable. The Jewish people continue to be at the forefront of major health breakthroughs such as the PillCam, which revolutionized the way doctors diagnose patients. Considered common today, this ingestible camera gives doctors a video recording of the intestinal tract.

In medical research facilities throughout Israel, scientists have discovered a compound that disables cancer cells, developed the world's first bone implant, created an artificial cornea, manufactured a flexible stent used to treat cardiac patients, and so much more. Israel is literally inventing ways for paraplegics to walk, giving sight to the blind, creating water out of thin air, and curing the worst diseases known to mankind.

Since 1995, Israeli doctors, through Save a Child's Heart, have provided free, lifesaving heart operations to more than 5,100 children from around the world. Ironically, half of these patients are from the Palestinian Authority, Iraq, Jordan, and other Arab nations.

Israel also shows compassion beyond its borders by playing a vital role in humanitarian aid during natural disasters throughout the world. They have provided medical supplies, support, and sustenance to victims of floods in Central America (1998); earthquakes in Turkey (1999) and Mexico (2017); hurricanes in the United

States (Katrina 2005), the Bahamas (Dorian 2019), and typhoon victims in the Philippines (2013). Most recently, in August 2020, a mammoth explosion at the port of Beirut caused massive damage, leaving hundreds dead and thousands wounded. Israel rose above the conflict between the two countries and immediately offered humanitarian and medical aid to Lebanon, extending a helping hand to its people.

During the novel coronavirus outbreak in 2020, Israel confronted the worldwide crisis head-on with ingenuity and generosity. For example, Israel Aerospace Industries engineers are developing a machine that uses ultraviolet light to kill bacteria and viruses on various surfaces.[*]

A unit in Israel's military is adapting bilevel positive airway pressure machines such as those used at home to treat sleep apnea, to properly ventilate coronavirus patients worldwide. Established companies and start-ups are producing items needed to fight the virus to include the ViriMASK, which offers front line full facial protection from the virus; and Soapy, a handwashing station that helps people effectively wash their hands, even in places without plumbing.[†]

Israeli authorities delivered coronavirus testing kits to the Palestinian Authority in Judea and Samaria and to the Hamas-ruled Gaza Strip, despite the thousands of rockets and bomb-carrying incendiary balloons that Hamas has launched toward Israel. In addition, Israel is continuing to work with Palestinian professional teams to prevent the spread of the virus.[‡]

From the outset of the outbreak, the country banded together

---

[*] Shoshanna Solomon, "From swords to plows: IAI seeks to battle coronavirus with UV-light tech" (March 30, 2020), *Times of Israel*, https://www.timesofisrael.com/from -swords-to-plows-iai-seeks-to-battle-coronavirus-with-uv-light-tech/, accessed April 2, 2020.

[†] https://www.israel21c.org/.what-the-us-can-learn-from-israels-handling-of -coronavirus-crisis/.

[‡] https://www.gatestoneinstitute.org/15739/israel-palestinians-coronavirus.

as in all other times of battle. The government enlisted the assistance of private business, medical researchers, the IDF, and even the Mossad.*

Israeli researchers have worked around the clock in finding a vaccine to combat the deadly virus and have made significant progress. Tel Aviv University recently announced that Professor Johnathan Gershoni was awarded a US patent for a vaccine that targets the "Achilles' heel of the corona viruses—that is their Receptor Binding Motif (RBM), a critical structure that enables the virus to bind to and infect a target cell."†

The promise of Genesis 12:3 stands; Israel is one of the world's first responder in times of crisis, and as such, has been a blessing to the nations of the world.

JERUSALEM JUBILEE (2017)

In 2017, Israel celebrated Jerusalem's Jubilee, the fiftieth anniversary of the reunification and restoration of Jerusalem as Israel's undivided capital. Remember this truth: God does everything at an appointed time, especially when it comes to Israel.

The importance of the Jubilee Year comes from Leviticus 25:10–11:

Consecrate the fiftieth year and proclaim liberty throughout the land to all its inhabitants. It shall be a jubilee for you; each of you is to return to your family property and to your own clan. The fiftieth year shall be a jubilee for you; do not sow and do not reap what grows of itself or harvest the untended vines. (NIV)

---

* https://www.nytimes.com/2020/04/12/world/middleeast/coronavirus-israel-mossad .html.

† https://nocamels.com/2020/04/israeli-scientist-nabs-us-patent-for-coronavirus -vaccine-design/.

From this passage, we know God measures time in modules of fifty years, and at the end of each module, He declares a Year of Jubilee. Furthermore, God's prophetic clock only runs when the Jewish people are in the Promised Land of Israel. This prophetic clock last stopped when the Roman army under General Titus conquered Jerusalem in 70 CE, destroying the Second Temple. According to the historian Josephus, over one million Jews were starved to death or slaughtered in the siege and hundreds of thousands more were taken as slaves to Rome or dispersed among the nations.

The clock began ticking again in 1917, with the creation of the Balfour Declaration. This British pronouncement stated that the Jewish people could return and rebuild their national home on a small piece of land representing only a fraction of the total real estate given to them by God in the book of Genesis.

When you add 50 to 1917, you reach the year 1967 when, in just six days, Israel miraculously defeated five Arab armies who were armed to the teeth by Russia. The astonishing victory of the Six-Day War more than doubled the size of Israel's land mass. But more importantly, Jerusalem was reunited with the nation of Israel for the first time since it was besieged by Rome. The Six-Day War was a war of miracles—and it happened in a Year of Jubilee.

Finally, add fifty years to 1967and you come to 2017. I believed with all my heart that this Jubilee Year would also be monumental for Israel and the Jewish people.

In the spring of 2017, I had the honor of meeting with President Trump and Vice President Pence in the White House, and of course, Jerusalem was on the agenda. We discussed the importance of moving the US embassy to Jerusalem, something every president since 1948 had failed to do, despite the law Congress had passed mandating the move over twenty years ago. God's prophetic clock hovered on the edge of striking fifty as the appointed time drew near.

On December 6, 2017, President Donald Trump stunned the world and all the foreign policy experts by publicly announcing that the United States recognized Jerusalem as the official capital of Israel. Just weeks later, President Trump announced that his state department would immediately begin preparations to move the US embassy from Tel Aviv to Jerusalem. I was privileged to personally participate in this historic and prophetic event by giving the benediction. Jerusalem's Jubilee Year ended with another miraculous event for the Jewish people.

PRESIDENT TRUMP'S VISION FOR PEACE

We are not here to lecture—we are not here to tell other people how to live, what to do, who to be, or how to worship. Instead, we are here to offer partnership—based on shared interests and values—to pursue a better future for us all.

—*President Donald J. Trump*

President Trump has proven to be the most pro-Israel president in America since President Harry Truman recognized Israel as an independent state in 1948. At the time of this writing, since President Trump's three years in office, he has kept his promises regarding Israel and the Jewish people.

In 2017, not only did President Trump recognize Jerusalem as the rightful capital to the State of Israel, he cut off all US funding to the United Nations Relief and Works Agency for Palestinian refugees (UNRWA), ending that organization's anti-Israel influence in the Middle East. In 2018, he signed into law the Taylor Force Act, which cut US aid to the Palestinian Authority until they stop paying terrorists and their families for murder.

After the US Embassy was moved to Jerusalem in May 2018, President Trump formally recognized Israeli sovereignty over the strategic Golan Heights in 2019. That same year he issued an executive order mandating the International Holocaust Remembrance Association's definition of anti-Semitism as US policy, protecting Jewish students on college campuses.

Most recently, in January 2020, President Trump unveiled a Middle East peace proposal that is sincere in its approach to bringing peace to the region. Israel's security is prioritized, Jerusalem remains undivided, and Biblical holy sites remain open to all faiths under Israel's sovereignty. In addition, the Trump Vision provides a clear path toward a prosperous tomorrow for the Palestinian people.

President Trump recognized that it was time to offer a new approach to achieving "peace, security, and dignity" for Israel and the Palestinians. This bold vision offers realistic and comprehensive benefits and conditions for both parties, providing hope for a productive future.

Prime Minister Netanyahu and the Israeli government, to include 75 percent of the Knesset, have endorsed President Trump's Vision for Peace. Though the Trump peace proposal is the most realistic approach ever advanced by an American administration, it has been attacked by those with maximalist demands, chief among them the Palestinian Authority. As of this writing, the extension of Israeli sovereignty to certain communities in Judea and Samaria under the peace plan has been temporarily suspended as Israel is in the process of establishing full diplomatic relations with additional Arab neighbors. In the past, Israel's Arab neighbors have repeatedly rejected peace with the Jewish state:

1. 1937—The Peel Commission: British Government
2. 1947—United Nations Partition Plan: UN General Assembly
3. 2000—Camp David Summit: President Bill Clinton, Prime Minister Ehud Barak, Yasser Arafat

4. 2005—Disengagement from Gaza: Prime Minister Ariel Sharon
5. 2008—Olmert Peace Offer: Prime Minister Ehud Olmert
6. 2020—Vision for Peace: President Donald Trump

Thus, the latest efforts to normalize ties between Israel and the Arab world are most welcome and serve as a reminder that the true impediment to peace in the Middle East is Palestinian rejectionism.

The Palestinian Authority effectively cut ties with the Trump administration after he moved the American Embassy to Jerusalem. Consequently, the Palestinians chose to reject the peace plan before it was even announced. President Trump considers "mere opposition to the peace proposal a declaration of support for the hopeless status quo that is the product of stale thinking."

The Palestinian leadership could learn from those of their Arab brethren who've chosen to pursue prosperity rather than conflict by normalizing ties with Israel. Sadly, as of today, they continue to refuse to do so.

AM YISRAEL CHAI

After nearly two thousand years of exile and longing, Israel was reborn as a modern independent nation, and the last seven-plus decades have been nothing less than miraculous. Despite all the wars, all the terrorism and all the sacrifice, the people of Israel are alive and well. Israel has thrived and the desert has bloomed like a rose.

Israel's awe-inspiring story throughout the last 3,500 years has indeed been supernatural. After God's eternal covenant with Abraham, Israel has overcome a relentless barrage of attacks, constant struggles and sacrifices, and heartrending tragedies. This is not a revelation to those of us who believe what the Word of God says, for He keeps His covenants for a thousand generations. The world may be mystified at Israel's perseverance and triumph, but we certainly are not.

The miracle of Israel's rebirth is that such a tiny nation surrounded by a massive sea of enemies has become in the last seventy-two-plus years one of the brightest torches of freedom, courage, and blessing in the world. While the rest of the Middle East has been a dark place of torment for thousands of Christians and other religious minorities, the Jewish state has been a place of refuge, safety, and prosperity. In Israel, all peoples are free to pursue their dreams, worship as they choose, and participate in every level of society.

This Covenant nation, restored by destitute refugees and Holocaust survivors, bequeathed a legacy of resilience, optimism, and faith to its more than 8.6 million modern descendants. With this legacy, the Jewish people have embraced peace instead of war, love instead of hate, and life instead of death.

Through the foundation of their faith, the Jews have found the divine grace to show compassion to all of humanity. Not only do the people of Israel live—they are an example to the rest of the world of how we can *all* live under the blessings and hope of God.

The God of Abraham, Isaac, and Jacob is unfolding Israel's prophetic destiny before our eyes. Christians everywhere should steadfastly stand with His chosen people as He fulfills His master plan, declaring with one voice, *"Am Yisrael Chai—the people of Israel live!"*

Shout it from the rooftops…*Israel lives!*

Shout it before the anti-Semitic members of the United Nations…*Israel lives.*

Shout it down the marble halls of those who chant "death to Israel" in Iran…*Israel lives.*

Shout it until all the anti-Semites of planet earth gnash their teeth in rage…*Israel lives, Israel lives…Israel lives!*

It is imperative that today's Christians understand how pivotal a role Israel and the Jewish people play in God's holy plan for mankind. Therefore, it is my continued mission in life to educate the world with the truth of God's Word and warn believers not to allow history to repeat itself.

We must not permit the war against the Jews to continue.

CHAPTER 2

THE WAR AGAINST
THE JEWS

Now there arose a new king over Egypt, who did not know Joseph. And he said to his people, "Look, the people of the children of Israel are more and mightier than we; come, let us deal shrewdly with them, lest they multiply, and it happen, in the event of war, that they also join our enemies and fight against us, and so go up out of the land" (Exodus 1:8–10).

There is no denial—the world has been at war with the Jewish people since the Pharaoh *"that knew not Joseph"* ordered all Jewish male babies drowned. This was the first recorded effort to exterminate the Jewish people.

With the extermination of the Jewish males, the Hebrew nation would have assimilated into oblivion in one generation. Remember this truth: Without the Jewish people there would never be the written Word of God, the patriarchs Abraham, Isaac, and Jacob, the Old Testament prophets, and King David, who became the forefather of Jesus Christ, the Redeemer of all mankind.

Most Christians do not understand our Hebraic roots, and even more are unaware of the atrocities that were committed against the Jewish people in the name of Christ during the eight crusades of the Middle Ages, the Spanish Inquisition, and the Holocaust. King Solomon declared, *"The mind of the prudent acquires knowledge, and the ear of the wise seeks knowledge"* (Proverbs 18:15 NASB). With this in mind, allow me to take you on a short journey of the endless war against the Jews.

Both biblical accounts and secular history give multiple examples of failed attempts to eradicate the Hebrew nation. This all-consuming hatred toward God's people has not been a consequence of their enemy's aims of achieving a political ideal, or the necessity to acquire vast resources, or even the objective to confiscate territory. The unrivaled animosity exists simply because they are Jews. This one-of-a-kind bigotry has been branded anti-Judaism or anti-Semitism.

ANTI-SEMITISM

Father Edward H. Flannery wrote in his book *The Anguish of the Jews*, "The sin of antisemitism contains many sins, but in the end it is a denial of Christian faith, a failure of Christian hope, and a malady of Christian love."[1] Bottom line: no one has to hate Jews in order to love Jesus.[2]

Anti-Semitism is an ancient and sustained crisis of civilization. It is one of the most malicious forms of racism in human history— it is a despicable fear, hatred, and contempt of the Jewish people without cause. This loathing for God's Chosen has remained so widespread since ancient times that recently the International Holocaust Remembrance Alliance—an intergovernmental group composed of thirty-four nations—adopted the definition of anti-Semitism as "'a certain perception of Jews, which may be expressed as hatred toward Jews that can also target the State of Israel."[3]

Early anti-Semitism was first termed *anti-Judaism* and was defined as the opposition to the Jewish faith and those who practiced it. At the core, anti-Semitism and anti-Judaism are one in the same.

When Jacob and his sons first entered Egypt to reunite with Joseph, they were honored guests, but this hospitality was short-lived. The book of Exodus records various examples of Jewish phobia and scorn toward God's people. One such example was Thutmos III, the pharaoh of the Exodus. He persecuted the Jewish people for fear they would overtake his reigning government, a myth that would live through the centuries. God chose Moses to deliver the Jews out of their oppression and foreboding demise.

After the Exodus from Egypt (1446 BCE), and forty years in the wilderness, Joshua walked the Israelites into the Promised Land and led them to victory in battles throughout Canaan. Following Joshua's death, Israel was ruled by a series of judges until the prophet Samuel appointed Saul and later David as kings of Israel. David conquered the Jebusites and made Jerusalem the capital of Israel (1010 BCE). After King David's death, his son Solomon built and dedicated the First Temple in the Holy City (960–953 BCE).

Solomon appointed no successor, and following his reign there was a breaking away of the Northern Kingdom of Israel (ten tribes) from the Southern Kingdom of Judah (two tribes). Eventually the Northern Kingdom of Israel was destroyed by the Assyrians, bringing about the deportation of ten of the twelve tribes throughout the Assyrian Empire (722 BCE).

A little over 130 years later, King Nebuchadnezzar conquered the Kingdom of Judah, resulting in the destruction of the First Temple and the exile of the Jews to Babylon (586 BCE). I will expand on this dispersion, or scattering of the Jews (diaspora), in a later chapter dealing with the capture and displacement of the prophet Daniel.

HAMAN'S FINAL SOLUTION

Throughout their time in exile, the Jewish people experienced indoctrination, torture, and death, but they remained faithful to the Torah. In time, the Babylonians were defeated by King Cyrus the Great of Persia in the fourth century BCE.

Eventually King Xerxes the Great, son of Darius, became the leader of the Persian Empire, which encompassed over 127 nations, to include the vast majority of displaced Jews. While a certain number of Jews were allowed to return to Jerusalem after the Edict of Cyrus to rebuild the temple, most remained in their displaced lands.

Esther and her cousin Mordecai lived in Shushan, a robust cultural, political, and religious center within the Persian Empire. The book of Esther records a deliberate incident of anti-Judaism, which began when King Xerxes appointed Haman, the Agagite, as his prime minister (475 BCE).

Haman was a descendant of Agag, king of the Amalekites, who were the first enemies Israel encountered after crossing the Red Sea en route to the Promised Land (Exodus 17:8–16). Haman demanded that the whole of the kingdom pay him homage. However, there was one who would not—Mordecai, the leader of the Jewish people. Mordecai refused to bow before Haman lest he offend the Lord.

Haman was incensed with Mordecai's defiance but was not satisfied with punishing one man; he instead devised a plan to eradicate the entire Hebrew population from the Persian Empire. Professor Rabbi Martin Lockshin proposes that "on the political level, Haman may have been the first to articulate the 'dual loyalty' argument, claiming that the Jews' allegiance to their own laws [the Torah] causes them to be disloyal to the laws of the state."[4]

Haman approached King Xerxes with his lethally deceptive and enticing offer:

There is a certain people [the Jews] scattered and dispersed among the people in all the provinces of your kingdom; their laws [Torah laws] are different from all other people's, and they do not keep the king's laws [dual loyalty]. Therefore it is not fitting for the king to let them remain. If it pleases the king, let a decree be written that they be destroyed, and I will pay ten thousand talents of silver into the hands of those who do the work, to bring it [the wealth of the Jews] into the king's treasuries (Esther 3:8–9).

Mordecai's nemesis proposed to increase the king's coffers by nearly two-thirds with the spoils he expected to seize from the Jews through his deceitful plot. Haman was one of the many "persecutor of the Jews" because of his attempt to exterminate the seed of Abraham. But the Lord remained faithful to His promise as recorded in Genesis 12 and totally destroyed Haman and his family instead.

THE GREEKS AND THE ROMANS

The Persian Empire, which included Judea, was conquered by Alexander the Great in 331 BCE. After Alexander's premature death at the age of thirty-three, the Greek Empire was divided among his four generals. One of the kings descending from this dispersion of power was Antiochus IV Epiphanes. This ruler was notorious for his cruelty toward the Jews of Judea and Samaria.

The Greeks wasted no time in introducing repulsive pagan rituals into the established customs and religious practices of the Jewish people. They attempted to "de-Judaize" observant Jews by forcing them to worship other gods; however, the majority of the Jews refused to denounce their faith. As a result, Antiochus ordered the plunder of Jewish property and the slaughter of the dissenters.

But ultimately, it was the desecration of the Holy Temple that drove the Jews to revolt against this Seleucid empire with its homegrown Hellenism.[5]

When the practice of the Mosaic law was outlawed, the Jewish citizenry became outraged and joined forces with a priestly family known as the Maccabees. The successful rebellion against Antiochus IV brought an end to Jewish oppression and allowed for the re-consecration of the defiled temple of Jerusalem (167–160 BCE).

The supernatural victory of the Maccabean Revolt brought with it a resurgence of national pride. This sense of liberation produced a wave of Jewish writings declaring the "glories of Israel and envi-sioned her ultimate triumph over all nations under the scepter of her Messiah."[6]

However, this newfound independence ended when the Roman general Pompey captured the city of Jerusalem from the Greeks in 63 BCE. Rome embraced the Greek disdain for the Jewish people, and as a result of Pompey's conquest, twelve thousand Jews were slaughtered and many more were exiled.

The Romans were proud of their gods and were absolutely intol-erant of any religion that would rival their own. On the other hand, the Jewish people knew that the God of Abraham, Isaac, and Jacob was a jealous God who forbade any form of idol worship. Once again, the Jewish people stayed true to their faith.

The Greeks and the Romans, like other societies before them, incessantly targeted the Jewish people because they would not adapt to their cultures or polytheistic religions. The Jews of the diaspora considered Jerusalem to be their Holy City and Jehovah God to be their *only* God. The refusal to embrace their Gentile ruler's demands prompted great resentment for the Jews and was viewed as a direct rebellion against the established government—Haman's lie of "dual loyalty" lived on.

What the Gentile nations failed to understand was that the Jewish people were set apart *to* God—*by* God. From the time Moses led the Israelites out of Egypt through the moment Joshua led them into the Promised Land, they were cast into a "religious and social solidarity." Edward Flannery describes this cohesion perfectly:

> From the heights of Sinai, the voice of Yahweh had thundered forth the tenet of unity: "I, the Lord, am your God... you shall have no other gods besides me" (Exodus 20:2–3); and Israel's election was made no less plain: "I, the Lord, am sacred, I, who have set you apart from the other nations to be my own" (Leviticus. 20:26).[7]

THE PHARISEES, THE SADDUCEES, THE ESSENES, AND THE ZEALOTS

A short history of the four sects of Judaism will help to understand both the religious and political integration of Jewish life during the Roman rule of first-century Jerusalem.

The Pharisees were known as the "spiritual fathers" of modern Judaism. They believed in the Torah or Written Law. They also believed in the Oral Law that God gave Moses at Sinai. This oral tradition was written down approximately three centuries later within the Talmud, which are rabbinical commentaries. The Pharisees considered the Torah and Talmud to be codependent, yet held that nothing superseded the authority of the written Word. They also believed that God gave Moses the interpretation and application of His laws.

The Pharisees supported the concept of the resurrection of the dead, the existence of an afterlife, God's punishment of the wicked and His reward of the righteous in the world to come. They also believed in a Messiah who would usher in an age of world peace.

The Pharisees continued to observe the principles of Judaism even after the destruction of the temple, including individual prayer and corporate gatherings in synagogues.

On the other end of the spectrum we have the "elitist" Sadducees, who wanted to uphold the priestly class. This sect of Judaism was freely tolerant of the integration of Hellenism into their everyday lives.

Hellenism was a "body of humanistic and classical ideals associated with ancient Greece." These Greek principles included the study of reason and the arts, the pursuit of secular knowledge and civic obligation, the development of the mind and body, and polytheism (the worship of many gods). In their purest forms, Hellenism and Judaism were opposing forces—the first believed in the *holiness of beauty* while the other believed in the *beauty of holiness.*

The Sadducees believed in the sacrificial rites of Judaism but rejected the idea of the Oral Law, insisting on a literal interpretation of the Written Law. Consequently, the Sadducees did not believe in an afterlife and primarily focused on partaking in rituals associated with the temple. Shortly after the destruction of the Second Temple, the Sadducees and their writings disappeared.

While the Sadducees led the good life and sought power in high places, the Pharisees believed that it was God's will for them to remain loyal to His Oral and Written Law. Enter the Essenes, who removed themselves from the struggle between the two opposing groups by retreating to their desert community. They believed in a stricter interpretation of the law and abstained from temple worship in Jerusalem. The Essenes were known for voluntarily living in poverty and devoted much of their time to studying the Torah.

At the beginning of the Christian era (Common Era), a fourth

Jewish faction rose among the Jewish people called the Zealots. Where the Essenes avoided confrontation, the Zealots welcomed it. These anti-Roman revolutionaries held the basic conviction that political and religious liberty from Rome was essential and should be achieved by any means possible.

Jerusalem had long been Hellenized by the Greeks, and now the Romanization of some within the Jewish community eventually brought with it a corruption that had previously flared under Antiochus IV Epiphanes. The Pharisees, led by Rabbi Yochanan ben Zakkai, were deeply opposed to the contamination of the Jewish religion, but they also opposed the Zealots' insurgence. Inadvertently, Rome created a "class divide" within the Jewish religion, and a Zealot uprising would later set off what history calls the Great Revolt (66–70 CE).

Josephus records the devastating defeat of the Jewish Revolt of Jerusalem by the Roman General Titus:

> The destruction of Jewish lives was relentless. Titus's ruthless and bloody assault ended with the destruction of the Second Temple and the slaughter of over one million Jews.[8]

The Jewish people were sent into exile as captives, slaves, and refugees, with nearly one hundred thousand taken to Rome to build the Colosseum. As foreigners and outcasts in the nations of their scattering, they were exposed to discriminatory laws, exorbitant taxes, humiliation, and active persecution, even more so after the rise of Christianity.

However, even through the centuries of exile, the hope for redemption of the land of Israel remained a central point of the Jewish faith and the people's beloved national identity.[9]

THE CHURCH FATHERS AND JUDAISM

By now, the majority of the Jews of Jerusalem were dispersed through-out the ancient world, and their unwavering devotion to their faith became an offense to the nations to which they were deported. For the most part, the Jews were tolerated; however, the expansion of the state church within the Roman Empire caused anti-Semitism to expand its ugly borders.

Initially, believers in Christ as Redeemer were recognized as just another Jewish sect, since Jesus and the disciples were Jewish and preached a form of Judaism. For a time, both groups main-tained some semblance of harmony. However, because of the man-date given in the Great Commission, the apostles evangelized all people with the Gospel through their travels in Europe and the Middle East. Soon, the followers of Christ exponentially multiplied to include non-Jews.

With the conversion of the emperors, beginning with the pagan Constantine, an idolatrous form of Christianity based on the princi-ples of Babylonism eventually became the recognized religion of the Roman Empire and the official successor to Judaism. Constantine's acceptance of Christ was motivated by political purposes and was, at best, a blend of paganism and a Hellenistic type of Christianity.

In an attempt to solve various doctrinal controversies facing the newly formed Roman Church, Constantine called for the Council of Nicaea (325 CE). This ecumenical gathering was the first empire-wide council of church leaders, which resulted in the creation and adoption of the Nicene Creed. By its end, the council successfully accomplished its goal to separate Christianity from Judaism.[10]

Several new doctrines were recognized by the Council of Nicaea that contributed to the church's formal disconnect with the Jewish roots of the newly established Christian doctrine and practices. In

Constantine's own words, the objective was simple: "ᴸ
nothing in common with the detestable Jewish crowd."[11]

From this point forward, Christians were prohibited from fo-
lowing the Torah and observing the Sabbath and the Jewish feasts.
With a stroke of the pen, the Council formally substituted the
observance of the God-ordained Passover Feast with the celebration
of Easter, adapted from the pagan feast of Ishtar, which will be further explained in a later chapter:

> We also send you the good news of the settlement concern-
> ing the holy pasch [Passover], namely that in answer to your
> prayers this question also has been resolved. All the brethren
> in the East who have hitherto followed the Jewish practice
> will henceforth observe the custom of the Romans and of
> yourselves and of all of us who from ancient times have kept
> Easter [Ishtar] together with you.[12]

However, observant Jews continued to adhere to the Torah,
which was the Word of God. They refused to participate in pagan
ritual practices and continued to faithfully observe the feasts of the
Lord. In addition, the Jewish people declined to accept Jesus as Lord
in obedience to the mandate of God to Moses declaring, *"Hear, O
Israel: The LORD our God, the LORD is one!"* (Deuteronomy 6:4).

These actions were collectively viewed as a deliberate defiance
against Rome's rulers and their newly adopted "Christian" faith,
which at this time embraced idols, remnants of pagan ritual worship, and in many cases, sustained polytheism.

Many early church fathers were trained in the principles of
logic and rational thought through the teachings of Greek philosophers such as Socrates, Plato, and Aristotle. However, even though

Judaism and Christianity were both rooted in the Old Testament, church leaders, like Ignatius, Origen, Martyr, Marcion, and others, thought it reasonable to affirm the newly found Christian doctrine by claiming it *superseded* Judaism.

For example, Ignatius, bishop of Antioch (98–117 CE), stated in his Epistle to the Magnesians, "For if we are still practicing Judaism, we admit that we have not received God's favor....It is wrong to talk about Jesus Christ and live like Jews. For Christianity did not believe in Judaism, but Judaism in Christianity."[13]

This doctrine of Supersessionism is very much alive in the modern church today. It argues that the Jews are no longer deemed to be God's chosen people and are "replaced" by the Church as a result of their rejection of Christ. This type of incessant denunciation of the Jewish people within the church's leadership contributed to the sustained animosity demonstrated against them.

Hatred for the Jews within the Christian movement grew exponentially as more church leaders like Justin Martyr ruthlessly vilified them. In his document *Dialogue with Trypho*, dated approximately 160 CE, Martyr stated:

The custom of circumcising the flesh, handed down from Abraham, was given to you as a distinguishing mark, to set you off from other nations and from us Christians. The purpose of this was that you and only you might suffer the afflictions that are now justly yours; that only your land be desolate, and your cities ruined by fire; that the fruits of your land be eaten by strangers before your very eyes; that not one of you be permitted to enter your city of Jerusalem. Your circumcision of the flesh is the only mark by which you can certainly be distinguished from other men....As I stated before, it was by reason of your sins and the sins of your

fathers that, among other precepts, God imposed upon you
the observance of the Sabbath as a mark.[14]

John Chrysostom (349–407 CE), referred to in history as the
"Golden Mouth," at times praised the Jews for being God's Chosen,
but he more often cursed and maligned them, calling them "wretched
and miserable," "good-for-nothing," and much worse after they
refused to convert to Christianity. An example of his anti-Jewish
vileness is as follows:

The Jews are the most worthless of men. They are lecherous,
rapacious, greedy. They are perfidious murderers of Christ.
They worship the Devil. Their religion is a sickness. The Jews
are the odious assassins of Christ and for killing God there is
no expiation possible, no indulgence or pardon. Christians
may never cease vengeance and the Jew must live in servi-
tude forever. God always hated the Jews. It is essential that
all Christians hate them.[15]

Chrysostom's warped theology was a continued form of
anti-Jewish Supersessionism, which was the precursor to modern
Replacement Theology.[16] His spiteful rhetoric was intended to dis-
courage Christians from observing the Jewish feasts and customs and
to prevent them from becoming "sick with a Judaizing disease."[17]
Sadly, Chrysostom's anti-Semitic rants, and those of other church
leaders before him, were later used to validate sustained hatred and
violence against the Jews.

Throughout the fourth and fifth centuries, discrimination
against the Jewish people continued to significantly increase, due in
part to the persistent denunciation by church fathers such as Saint
Augustine (354–430 CE), a contemporary of Chrysostom.

In his autobiographical work titled *Confessions*, Augustine wrote,

How hateful to me are the enemies of your Scripture! How I wish that you would slay them [the Jews] with your two-edged sword, so that there should be none to oppose your word! Gladly would I have them die to themselves and live to you![18]

Jews were officially ostracized from the societies they had lived in for generations. They were forbidden to marry Christians or even eat together with them. The Jews in Italy were confronted with forced conversion and in Carthage (modern-day Tunisia), they were expelled. Complete Jewish communities in Europe were destroyed. At the same time, Jews were banned from Jerusalem, and the Roman emperor Honorius called for the confiscation of all the gold and silver from the synagogues in the Holy City.

The next four hundred years (the fifth through the eighth centuries) were marked by more malicious milestones in the sustained war against the Jews. There was the creation and ratification of the Theodosian Code, which was a compilation of laws of the Roman Empire. In it, the Jewish people were prohibited from holding important financial positions as well as judicial and executive offices.

Muslim caliphs and medieval bishops mandated the use of an identifying badge to mark the Jews. The Jewish people were humiliated by having to wear "distinguishing garments" such as an emblem (yellow star), an insignia (Juden), or some other form of atypical clothing that set them apart from Christians.

Additionally, the ban against building new synagogues was reestablished. The Jewish people were forbidden from reciting the psalms while burying their dead, and in Spain, Jews were hanged or burned at the stake by the thousands for refusing to convert to Christianity.[19]

As the centuries passed, Jews were not allowed to join trade guilds. Jewish craftsmen such as goldsmiths, silversmiths, diamond cutters, and glass blowers began to fade away. Jewish people were excluded from owning land, holding office, and banned from becoming doctors or lawyers. In Canon 26 of the Third Lateran Council of 1179, Jews were forbidden to be plaintiffs or witnesses against Christians in court and were also prohibited from withholding an inheritance from their descendants who had converted to Christianity.

Within this time period, Pope Urban II of Rome decreed for the Christians of Europe to take up the cross and sword and liberate the Holy Land from the Muslims.[20] This call to action began the first of eight Crusades (1095–1291 CE). These violent campaigns against Muslims and Jews increased the ranking of European Christians within the region, giving them a major standing in the contest for land in the Middle East.

As a consequence of Rome's vicious campaign, sanctioned mobs of murderous vigilantes marched under the sign of the cross, looting, raping, and massacring tens of thousands of Jews on the road to Jerusalem.[21] Fundamentally, the seed of Abraham, the Chosen, the cherished, the Covenant people of God were slaughtered beneath the cross of Christ.

Evil lies about the Jews continued to surface, such as the fictitous tales of "blood libel." On Passover 1144, a Christian boy disappeared in Norwich, England. Immediately, the local citizens alleged that the Jews had murdered the young man in order to use his blood for ritual practices such as the making of matzo at Passover.[22]

It may be hard to believe, but radical Muslim communities teach this same treacherous lie to their children even to this day. They maintain that the Jewish people are the enemy of Allah and that Islam must continue to engage in a religious war against the Jews. Ultimately, this radical Islamic rhetoric teaches that killing Jews is a holy obligation.[23]

After my first trip to Israel in 1978, I began a two-year study of the historical relationship between Jews and Christians. I became deeply disturbed to learn that one of the great perpetrators of Jewish hatred was Martin Luther, the founder of Protestantism. After the Catholic Reformation of the sixteenth century, Luther became despondent that the Jews would not convert to his liberating form of Christianity. As a consequence of Luther's unrestrained anger, he authored a vile pamphlet entitled "On the Jews and Their Lies."[24]

In his book, Luther asserted that Jews were the Christ killers and demanded their torture and death. He stated that the Jews should have their tongues cut out through the back of their heads, their synagogues should be burned to the ground, and their children sold into slavery.

> Set fire to their synagogues or schools and to bury and cover with dirt whatever will not burn, so that no man will ever again see a stone or cinder of them. This is to be done in honor of our Lord and of Christendom, so that God might see that we are Christians.

These facts were never taught in any doctrinal seminars I attended.

The Nazis would reprint Luther's inflammatory pamphlet in 1935, which later helped spawn the evils of Hitler's Final Solution. Some historians believe that the slanderous attacks from church leaders such as Chrysostom and Luther marked the critical transition of "anti-Judaism" (the Christian hatred toward the Jewish religion) and "anti-Semitism" (the world's abhorrence toward the Jews as a racial group).[25]

John Calvin (1509–1564), a contemporary of Martin Luther, was a French theologian and spiritual statesman. Calvin is recognized as the most influential ecclesiastical leader within the second generation of the Protestant Reformation. But like others before him, his twisted views of the Jewish people continued to fuel the flame of hatred:

I have had much conversation with many Jews: I have never seen either a drop of piety or a grain of truth or ingenuousness—nay, I have never found common sense in any Jew.[26]

Their [the Jews] rotten and unbending stiffneckedness deserves that they be oppressed unendingly and without measure or end and that they die in their misery without the pity of anyone.[27]

There was no end in sight of the virulent spread of anti-Semitism from within and from outside of the church.

THE CRUSADES, THE POGROMS, AND THE GHETTOS

The crusaders were allegedly created to "liberate" Jerusalem from the infidels. However, during the First Crusade in 1095, Jewish communities were attacked on the road to Jerusalem using warped logic with the premise "Why fight Christ's enemies abroad when they are living among us?"

Consequently, nearly 5,000 Jews were murdered in cities throughout Germany alone during the first of these vicious campaigns. Later, in 1124, the entire Jewish quarter of Kiev, Russia, was destroyed, and in Morocco 100,000 Jews were massacred in Fez, along with another 120,000 in Marrakesh by angry anti-Jewish mobs.

The continued carnage of the Jewish people during the Crusades induced the birth of the *pogrom*. The word *pogrom* means "to destroy, to wreak havoc, or to demolish violently," and specifically refers to the outbreaks of anti-Jewish violence by non-Jews.

The first recorded pogrom arose against the Jews in 1241 in Frankfurt, Germany, after a debate over interfaith marriages between Jews and Christians. This assault, where 180 Jews were killed and 24 were forced to be baptized, is known as the *Judenschlacht,* or "Slaughter of the Jews." On Easter Sunday in 1389, the Jewish quarter in Prague, Poland, was burned and nearly 1,500 Jews were massacred.[28]

Increasingly, Jews were subjected to political, economic, and social discrimination. By the thirteenth century, Jewish people were systematically removed from their homes and required to live in designated communities, which eventually became known as the "Jewish Ghetto." The term *ghetto* originated in 1516 from the name of the Jewish quarter in Venice, Italy, where Jews were forced to live.[29] By the sixteenth and seventeenth centuries, Jewish ghettos were created in Frankfurt, Rome, Prague, and other cities throughout Europe.

The Jews were blamed for everything. Even the bubonic plague of the Dark Ages, which killed an estimated one-third of Europe's population, fueled further anti-Jewish hatred. The Jews were accused of poisoning wells, leading to the spread of the "Black Death," as this devastating disease was called. For this and other false allegations related to the plague, nearly one hundred thousand Jews were burned alive in Germany and Austria alone.[30]

By the 1800s, pogroms became commonplace as waves of anti-Jewish riots moved through Russia. During this time, more than two hundred anti-Jewish events occurred in Kiev and Odessa, Russia, as well as in Warsaw, Poland. The *New York Times* described the first Kishinev pogrom of Easter of 1903 with these words:

The anti-Jewish riots in Kishinev, Bessarabia [modern-day Moldavia] are worse than the censor will permit to publish. There was a well laid-out plan for the general massacre of Jews on the day following the Russian Easter. The mob was led by priests, and the general cry, "Kill the Jews," was taken up all over the city. The Jews were taken wholly unaware and were slaughtered like sheep. The dead number 120 and the injured about 500. The scenes of horror attending this massacre are beyond description. Babes were literally torn to pieces by the frenzied and bloodthirsty mob. The local police made no attempt to check the reign of terror. At sunset the streets were piled with corpses and wounded. Those who could make their escape fled in terror, and the city is now practically deserted of Jews.[31]

Pogroms became so prevalent and strongly associated with the persecution of Jewish people that in subsequent years historian John Klier stated, "By the twentieth century, the word 'pogrom' had become a generic term in English for all forms of collective violence directed against Jews."[32]

The church's violation of the Jewish faith and people is among the ever-present arguments over its contribution to the eventual attempted *extermination* of the whole Jewish race during the Holocaust.

Anti-Semitism

The term *anti-Semitism* was first conceived by Wilhelm Marr in his 1879 work *Victory of Judaism over Germanism.*[33] Known as the father of modern anti-Semitism, Marr believed the Jews should be barred from citizenship because of their conspiracy to rule the state—the spirit of Haman lives.

In the same vein, *The Protocols of the Elders of Zion* was published in 1905 by Russian writer and mystic Sergei Nilus. I want to emphasize that this document was completely fictitious and promoted, without substantiated proof, the perpetual myth that the Jews had devised a "secret plan to rule the world by manipulating the economy, controlling the media, and sponsoring various religious conflicts."[34]

These writings are seen as the "most notorious and widely distributed anti-Semitic publication of modern times."[35] *The Protocols* greatly contributed to the exponential rise in anti-Semitism and Jewish hatred. This anathema for God's people was additionally fueled by the development of Social Darwinism and other so-called scientific philosophies based on the bogus concepts of racial inferiority and superiority.

POST–WORLD WAR I GERMANY

Germany was humiliated by its defeat in World War I, and more so after the Treaty of Versailles. This accord obligated the German people to give up territory and pay reparations for the destruction they caused during the war.

Enter Adolf Hitler.

Hitler was a charismatic leader, and it was inevitable for the German people to fall in hypnotic obedience to his demagogic authority. He reminded the German masses of the "blood libel" lies and the fabricated Jewish root cause of the bubonic plague. He accused the Jews of conspiring to rule the world and perpetrated the "stab in the back" myth that blamed the Jewish people for benefiting from Germany's defeat in World War I. In addition, Hitler quoted the works of Chrysostom and Luther to promote fear within the people that the Jews and Judaism would in due course contaminate their "superior Aryan race."

The German people were desperate for any political and social revolution that would promise a return to their former glory days of European dominance while restoring Germany's lost dignity. This outcry for supremacy permitted Nazism to explode as a political movement that endorsed radically anti-Semitic philosophies as articulated by Adolf Hitler in his book *Mein Kampf* (translated *My Struggle*).

The demand for the resurgence of German national pride, coupled with Jewish hatred, culminated in Hitler's meteoric rise to power in 1933. His National Socialist regime promoted the methodical exclusion of Jews from society from its inception. The Jewish people were relentlessly demonized and accused of being the driving force behind international Marxism and what Joseph Goebbels called "immoral Capitalism."

Like Chancellor Bismarck before him, Hitler unified Germany by targeting a common enemy. He predicted that if left unchallenged, the Jews would eventually drag their beloved Deutschland into another world war. Goebbels and his Nazi propagandists convinced the German citizenry that the Jews were the root cause of every social, religious, and economic problem they faced; they *were* the perfect enemy.

Hitler was quoted as saying, "If the Jews didn't exist, we would have to invent them."[36]

Widespread anti-Semitic indoctrination saturated German society, resulting in the mass hatred of the Jewish people. Laws were ratified excluding Jews from state and civil service. The Bavarian Ministry of the Interior denied Jewish students entrance to schools and universities. Jewish doctors were forbidden from treating non-Jewish patients, and were denied reimbursement of services from public or state-supported health insurance funds, leaving them virtually bankrupt.

By 1934, Jewish lawyers and notaries were prohibited from participating in legal matters. Licensing credentials were revoked from Jewish tax advisors, Jewish actors were no longer allowed to perform on stage or screen, and Jewish butchers "could no longer slaughter animals according to ritual purity requirements, effectively preventing them [observant Jews] from obeying Jewish dietary laws."[37]

The question now arose—who was considered a Jew? Hitler believed he was the sole authority on racial policy and he had the final say about what the law stated. Therefore, on September 15, 1935, the Nuremberg Laws were swiftly ratified.

These anti-Semitic statutes marked a major step in clarifying Hitler's "ethnic purity" mandate and consequently removed all Jewish influences from Aryan society. The stated purpose of the Nuremberg Laws was to protect "German blood and honor" by regulating the "the problems of marriage between 'Aryans' and 'non-Aryans.'"[38]

Additional Nazi decrees were issued after the Nuremberg Laws that incrementally repealed a Jewish citizen's political, legal, religious, and civil rights. Ultimately, these decrees divested the Jewish people of their rights as human beings. They were deliberately designed to provide the legitimate path for the systematic discrimination, persecution, and subsequent extermination of the Jewish people in Germany and throughout their occupied territories.

The Reichstag, Germany's parliament, supported the philosophy of "racial hygiene" as a tool to build an Aryan "master race." In order to accomplish their diabolical plan, it was essential to establish "racial cleansing," which demanded the forced sterilization of the Jewish people and others deemed undesirable by the State. The integration of bogus medical science, unethical doctors, and inhuman medical practices would further the purpose of the Führer's National Socialism aim of racial integrity—a fundamental model within the Nazi doctrine.

By 1938, Jews could not legally change their personal names or the names of their businesses. The Order for the Disclosure of Jewish Assets required Jews to report all property in excess of five thousand Reichsmarks, while the Decree on the Confiscation of Jewish Property directed the transfer of assets from Jews to non-Jewish Germans.

Finally, the Reich Ministry of the Interior canceled all German passports held by Jews, with the stipulation that the passport could only be revalidated after the letter J was stamped on it. Violation of any of these decrees resulted in strict fines, incarceration, or deportation to labor camps.[39]

THE NIGHT OF BROKEN GLASS

On November 7, 1938, a young Jewish man learned that German police had confiscated his family's life possessions and had forcibly deported them to Poland. Living with an uncle in Paris, the seventeen-year-old became hopelessly distraught over his family's plight, and in blind retaliation he attempted to assassinate the German ambassador to France. However, his plan failed, and instead he fatally wounded an embassy undersecretary.

Joseph Goebbels, Hitler's chief of propaganda, immediately labeled the attack a conspiracy by "international Jewry." He announced to the German people that the deliberate act was a direct assault on the Führer. This ill-fated incident was all Goebbels needed to instigate retaliation against the Jewish people throughout Germany, Austria, and other newly acquired Nazi territories.

The sanctioned revenge against the Jewish people produced the infamous *Kristallnacht* or the "Night of the Broken Glass" of November 9 and 10, 1938. Within forty-eight hours, the Nazis burned down 200 synagogues, destroyed hundreds of Jewish homes, vandalized Jewish day schools, sacked and looted 7,500 Jewish shops, and murdered nearly 100 Jews throughout Germany and Austria. In the wake of this deadly violence, some thirty thousand Jewish men were arrested and sent to Dachau, Buchenwald, and Sachsenhausen—all established Nazi concentration camps.

Prior to Kristallnacht, the oppressive Nazi policies of anti-Jewish boycotts, staged book burnings, and sanctioned anti-Jewish legislation had been painfully hostile; however, after this two-day onslaught, conditions for German and Austrian Jews instantly grew far worse.

Within days of Kristallnacht, the Nazis issued a decree forcing all Jews to transfer their businesses to Aryan hands. Jewish students were expelled from all German schools, and the government levied a collective one billion Reichsmarks ($400 million) "penalty" against German Jews for the destruction of property during the reprehensible Night of the Broken Glass.[40]

A few months later, Hitler delivered his infamous speech to the Reichstag in celebration of the sixth anniversary of his ascent to power. Now holding the titles of both Führer and Reich Chancellor, Hitler made a self-proclaimed prophecy regarding the future of the Jewish people.

Today I will once more be a prophet: If the international Jewish financiers in and outside Europe should succeed in plunging the nations once more into a world war, then the result will not be the Bolshevization of the earth, and thus the victory of Jewry, but the annihilation of the Jewish race in Europe![41]

Germany was brainwashed into believing they had a widespread "Jewish problem." Prior to his Reichstag speech, Hitler's Third Reich took part in ongoing negotiations with the Intergovernmental Committee on Refugees regarding the complete deportation of Jews from Germany.

There was a glitch, however; the potential recipient nations did not want the Jews without their wealth, and the Reich was not willing to allow them to leave with any of their possessions, which they believed rightfully belonged to Germany.[42] There was no solution in sight; the gates of escape for the Jewish people were quickly closing.

PERSONA NON GRATA

After Hitler's prophecy, the Jewish people were personae non grata (unacceptable) throughout Europe. A classic example of their rejection among the nations is the voyage of the *St. Louis*. Following Kristallnacht, those Jews who could sought asylum in other countries, especially America. Some had by this time willingly emigrated from Europe, but others now considered relocating to the West as the only path to personal survival.

On May 13, 1939, 937 Jewish passengers boarded a German transatlantic liner named the *St. Louis* in Hamburg en route to Havana, Cuba. For most of the passengers, this voyage was the last hope to escape the horrors of Nazism. They took great pains to meet the strict immigration laws, which now involved increased levies, overpriced visas, and often mandatory sponsorship. The passengers of the *St. Louis* had secured travel vouchers and required visas; however, their visas were invalid by the time they arrived at the shores of Cuba.

The Cuban people were not happy with increased migration to their country. They believed that immigrants were the direct cause for a lack of jobs, which further negatively affected their failing economy. In response to their protests, Cuban president Federico Laredo Brú refused to allow the *St. Louis* to dock in Havana's port.

This denial was a perfect opportunity for the Nazis to justify their anti-Jewish goals and policies of forced emigration. Once again, propaganda mastermind Joseph Goebbel went into action and decided to use the *St. Louis* as part of a bigger plan. Goebbels sent his SS agents to Havana to provoke hatred against Jews using the same lies and distortions that had been so successful throughout Europe. He painted the passengers of this doomed voyage as "undesirables" too dangerous for the Cuban good.

The plight of the *St. Louis* gained international attention, and even though some countries sent the Cuban government telegrams of protest, no nation was willing to offer the Jews asylum. On June 2, the ship was forced to leave Cuban waters after only allowing 29 of the 937 passengers admittance to their country (28 had valid visas, and one passenger who had tried to commit suicide was evacuated to a hospital).

In desperation, international Jewish groups looked for a country willing to accept the refugees, yet no government granted safe harbor to the *St. Louis*.

While negotiations with other nations continued, the *St. Louis* sailed around Cuba, eventually reaching the coastline of Miami in anticipation that the United States would receive the refugees. However, the US Coast Guard prevented them from coming closer. In response to this travesty, a Virginia resident wrote,

[The] press reported that the ship came close enough to Miami for the refugees to see the lights of the city.... The U.S. Coast Guard, under instructions from Washington, followed the ship...to prevent any people landing on our shores.... When this horrible tragedy was being enacted right at our doors, our government...made no effort to relieve the desperate situation of these people, but on the contrary gave orders that they be kept out of the country.

...The failure to take any steps whatsoever to assist these distressed, persecuted Jews in their hour of extremity was one of the most disgraceful things which has happened in American history and leaves a stain and brand of shame upon the record of our nation.[43]

The captain had no choice but to return the *St. Louis* and its "banned cargo" to Europe. However, because of God's intervention and extraordinary negotiations, the American Jewish Joint Distribution Committee (JDC) was able to find several countries in Europe that would accept the refugees.

Thirty-six emotionally charged days after departing Germany, the ship was allowed to dock at Antwerp, Belgium, on June 17 with 907 passengers (one had died en route); 181 went to Holland, 224 to France, 288 to Great Britain, and 214 to Belgium.[44]

America accepted none.

Of the original 937 passengers who boarded the *St. Louis*, approximately 594 survived the Holocaust and 343 did not.[45] The damage was done. Goebbels had successfully spun the plight of the *St. Louis* into a worldwide propaganda bonanza, claiming it validated that Jews were universally detested, distrusted, and unwanted.

WORLD WAR II

The years between the first and second world wars were a time of international volatility. After World War I, President Woodrow Wilson founded the League of Nations in 1920, a global organization intended to regulate future conflicts between nations and preserve world peace. However, the League soon proved to be ineffective. Before long, international turmoil developed between world powers once again.

The financial devastation of America's Great Depression in 1929 plunged the world into a deep recession. When Hitler skyrocketed to power in 1933, he used this worldwide economic decline and the German people's deep resentment of the Treaty of Versailles to declare that his country needed to expand its "living space." As a result, in 1936 Hitler remilitarized the Rhineland, which was a direct violation of the Versailles Treaty.[46]

During this same period, Italy's prime minister, Benito Mussolini, elected to follow Hitler's example by conquering territory he thought rightfully belonged to Italy. The Italians had already colonized portions of Africa, believing this annexation would provide more job opportunities for unemployed Italians as well as let Italy acquire more mineral resources to drive back the effects of the world economic depression.[47]

These and other flagrant violations by Hitler and Mussolini confirmed the incompetence of the League of Nations, which did nothing to stop their aggression. Nazi Germany's goal of expansion through its methodical conquering and colonization of Europe and Mussolini's desire to re-create the Roman Empire by overtaking parts of the Mediterranean and Africa brought both nations into alliance—there was nothing to stop these dictators and their rabid agendas.

To add to this volatile coalition we insert Japan. The Japanese deeply resented America's refusal to recognize its racial equality clause in the covenants of the League of Nations. This rejection, along with the League's failure to flex its authority over Germany and Italy's aggression, led to Japan's alienation from the West.

As a means to resolve growing economic problems, Japan declared war on China in 1937. America demonstrated its opposition to Japan's onslaught by imposing trade embargoes and economic sanctions. Japan imported over 90 percent of its fuel, and the US oil embargo was the last straw. The world became ripe for war.

In late August of 1939, Hitler reached an agreement of non-intervention with Joseph Stalin of the Soviet Union known as the Hitler-Stalin Pact.[48] One week later, on September 1, Hitler invaded Poland, and in response, France and Great Britain declared war on Germany two days later. By the summer of 1940, Italy had allied with Germany.

The Nazis continued to advance through Europe and the Mediterranean and, as was Hitler's intent all along, targeted the Soviet Union. The Soviet Union kept Germany out of Moscow with a major offensive and as a result became a key player within the Allied powers (countries opposed to Germany).

America had avoided participation in Europe's war, but when Japanese bombers attacked Pearl Harbor on December 7, 1941, the United States declared war on Japan the next day. By December 11, Germany and Italy declared war on America. Once the lines were drawn, the combatants were defined as the Axis and Allied powers.

The Axis nations included Nazi Germany, fascist Italy, and imperial Japan. The Allied nations were composed of the constitutional monarchy of Great Britain, the communist states of the Soviet Union, and the democratic United States of America.

By its conclusion, World War II had engaged nearly every major nation on earth. For 2,190 consecutive days, more than 32,400 people were killed every twenty-four hours, making it the most destructive wartime conflict in human history.

However, few were aware that Hitler was also conducting his *secret war against the Jews* within the confines of his conquered territory. By the end of the war, the Nazis would be directly responsible for murdering two-thirds of the Jewish population of Europe.[49]

THE HOLOCAUST—
HITLER'S FINAL SOLUTION

From 1938 to 1942, the Jewish people of Europe suffered great humiliation, persecution, torture, displacement, and the loss of all their possessions, including their rights as German citizens and, in due course, as human beings. They underwent forced relocations into cramped disease-infested ghettos, eventually compulsory deportations to concentration camps, and finally, the death camps.

Throughout Hitler's reign, there were several contributing factors that ultimately influenced the evolution of Nazi racial anti-Semitism into Jewish genocide. Among the major influences were:

1. Hitler's never-ending lies depicting the Jews as an inferior race.
2. The incessant portrayal of the Jewish people as "communist subversives, as war profiteers and hoarders."
3. The false Nazi propaganda of the Jewish goal to gain world dominance at the expense of German Aryans.
4. Violent pogroms such as Kristallnacht.
5. The Nuremberg Laws.
6. The massive complications arising from the overcrowded, disease-infested Jewish ghettos and concentration camps.
7. Hitler's demand for a solution to the Jewish problem.[50]

In January of 1942, Reinhard Heydrich was delegated by Hitler to conceive a comprehensive plan for the Final Solution to the "Jewish problem." Heydrich, who was second in command of the SS, or *Schutzstaffel* (German for "Protective Echelon"), convened the Wannsee Conference in Berlin. He gathered fifteen top Nazi bureaucrats to coordinate a systematic plan to exterminate the entire Jewish population of Europe, which was projected to be approximately eleven million people.[51]

Every Jewish man, woman, and child in Europe and North Africa was tagged for annihilation, and eventually six million (including more than one million children) were murdered by the Nazis between 1942 and 1945. This supreme act of genocide is called the *Holocaust*.

The origin of the word *Holocaust* is from the Greek *holos* (entire) and *kostos* (burnt). Together, "entirely burnt" refers to the sacrifice, which was utterly consumed by fire on an altar. In Hebrew, the term *shoah* (sho-ah), which is found in the Bible several times (Psalms, Isaiah, Jeremiah, Lamentation, Ezekiel, Daniel, Micah, and Zephaniah), signifies complete and utter destruction.

To implement their grisly plan, the Nazis transported Jews to "purpose-built extermination camps" in occupied Poland. Once there, the Jewish captives were systematically murdered in gas chambers. By the time the war was over, a total of six killing centers and thousands of concentration camps existed in Germany and Nazi-controlled territory.[52]

It is impossible to sufficiently present the horrors of the Holocaust within this book; however, countless volumes have been written on the atrocities committed against the Jewish people, including first-hand accounts.

Christians must know the truth about what happened to God's chosen people. It is important to understand the cautious response of our Jewish friends when we extend our hand of friendship—a gesture they haven't seen in the past. I highly recommend you read as many reliable resources as possible to further educate yourself of the atrocities that were committed against the Jewish people in the name of Jesus Christ.[53]

We ask, how could this happen? How could civilized human beings murder over six million people in cold blood and the world stand idly by? How could the world's Christians ignore this atrocity? How is it that those who shared God's Torah with us, who brought forth the patriarchs, who gave us the apostles and, most importantly, our Redeemer, could be so despised? Why were we silent?

The church as a whole was silent in defense of the Jewish people, but it was not silent in condemning them. Holocaust historian Raul Hilberg described how anti-Semitism within the church presented the perfect atmosphere for Hitler's Final Solution of the Jewish problem:

> The missionaries of Christianity had said in effect: You have no right to live among us as Jews. The secular rulers who followed had proclaimed: You have no right to live among us. The German Nazis at last decreed: You have no right to live.[54]

Many have asked, "Why didn't America do more to intervene with the evil of the Holocaust?" The Allied nations ranked victory over their enemies above anything else. The humanitarian concern of saving the Jews from Hitler's Final Solution was not a top priority. In combination with anti-Semitic sentiments and domestic concerns, including unemployment and national security, there was little to no attention paid to the plight of European Jews.

Even though history records the actions of Jewish organizations and some righteous Gentiles throughout the world who bravely confronted the evils of anti-Semitism, most were apathetic and silent. At best, America was guilty of indifference.

Elie Wiesel, survivor of the Final Solution and my friend, provided an answer to the question *why*:

> The opposite of love is not hate, it's indifference. The opposite of beauty is not ugliness, it's indifference. The opposite of faith is not heresy, it's indifference. And the opposite of life is not death, but indifference between life and death.[55]

Elie also shared a painful truth: "What hurts the victim most is not the cruelty of the oppressor but the silence of the bystander."[56]

And it was our sin of silence that God Almighty heard the loudest.

CHAPTER 3

THE SIN OF SILENCE

Silence in the face of evil is itself evil: God will not hold us guiltless. Not to speak is to speak. Not to act is to act.
—*Dietrich Bonhoeffer*

Anti-Semitism is not only alive, it is ever-increasing. The mechanism by which this evil hatred displays its ugly talons is modernized, but the overall message is the same: dehumanize and demonize the Jewish people at every opportunity through all means possible.

One of the most prominent anti-Semitic propaganda movements to advance in the last twenty-plus years in North America and Western Europe has been the organized efforts to deny the existence or diminish the consequences of the Holocaust—the mass slaughter of six million Jews. Kenneth Marcus, in a blog post titled, "The Horror of Holocaust Denial," defined this deliberately orchestrated repudiation perfectly: "Holocaust denial is not just an ordinary form of ignorance but rather a modern cloak for the return of old-fashioned anti-Semitism."[1]

The primary premise of this evil distortion of truth is that if *no one* but the Jews actually experienced the Holocaust, then it didn't happen. Those who advocate this deceit claim that the Jews were, and continue to be, conniving perpetrators of lies and exaggerations to gain sympathy with the world for their personal benefit.

The Holocaust deniers attack four basic realities surrounding this heinous event. I will challenge their false assertions by presenting the truth about:

1. The existence of the extermination camps
2. The capacity of the gas chambers
3. The actual number of Jewish victims
4. The massive extent of the Nazis' crimes against humanity[2]

THE TRUTH ABOUT THE DEATH CAMPS

The Holocaust was the "systematic, bureaucratic, state-sponsored persecution and murder of six million Jews by the Nazi regime and its collaborators."[3] Hitler and many of his key Nazi leaders established in their speeches and writings the ultimate goal of the Final Solution: *"the annihilation of the Jewish race in Europe!"*[4]

Hitler stayed true to his word, and on December 12, 1941, one day after Germany declared war on America, the Führer called a meeting of the Reich Chancellery. It was here that he reaffirmed the imminent annihilation of the Jewish race to the top-ranking officers of the Nazi Party.

Hans Frank, governor general of occupied Poland, and Joseph Goebbels, the Reich's minister of propaganda, documented the details of the clandestine gathering. An excerpt of Goebbels's notes reads as follows:

[Regarding the Jewish question, the Führer] warned the Jews that if they were to cause another world war, it would lead to their own destruction [referring to the Reichstag speech of 1939]. Those were not empty words. Now the world war has come. The destruction of the Jews must be its necessary consequence. This question is to be regarded without sentimentalism. We are not here to have sympathy with the Jews, but rather with our German people. If the German people have sacrificed 160,000 dead in the eastern campaign, so the authors of this bloody conflict will have to pay for it with their lives.[5]

The chancellery meeting was a defining moment of the Nazi government's intent for the Jewish people. The decisions made here played a major part in the comprehensive transition from propaganda, terrorization, and assaults to the premeditated and calculated genocide of millions of European Jews. One month later, the Wannsee Conference of January 1942 introduced the "Final Solution to the Jewish problem," which included plans for the killing camps.

Julius Streicher, anti-Semitic propagandist and father of the German Socialist Party, wrote in his Nazi newspaper,

It is really the truth that the Jews, so to speak, have disappeared from Europe and that the Jewish reservoir of the East, from which the Jewish plague has for centuries beset the peoples of Europe, has ceased to exist. However, the Fuehrer of the German people at the beginning of the war prophesied what has now come to pass.[6]

And to accomplish their Führer's disturbing prophecy, the Nazis established death camps. Most refer to only a few of the twenty-three camps that existed throughout Nazi-occupied territory. However, what few people know is that within the twenty-three larger camps, including familiar names such as Auschwitz, Buchenwald, Dachau, and Treblinka, were various sub-camps connected to them.[7]

Current research has determined that the Nazis actually established about 42,500 camps and ghettos between 1933 and 1945. These sites included 30,000 slave labor camps, 1,150 Jewish ghettos, 980 concentration camps, 1,000 POW camps, 500 brothels filled with sex slaves, and thousands of other camps used for euthanizing the mentally disabled, sick, and elderly, as well as the infamous death camps that slaughtered the masses.[8]

Even though hundreds of thousands of Jews died in the rat-infested ghettos, through pogroms, on death marches, and in concentration camps, nearly one half of the six million who died in the Holocaust were exterminated within the six designated killing camps located in Nazi-occupied Poland. These camps were named Auschwitz-Birkenau, Treblinka, Belzec, Sobibór, Chełmno, and Majdanek.

THE TRUTH ABOUT THE GAS CHAMBERS

The Nazis were masters of efficiency and resourcefulness. They meticulously recorded everything, including the number of deported Jews, the names and tattoo numbers of concentration camp prisoners, and the location to which they were transported, and so on. The ovens were in operation twenty-four hours a day, seven days a week—so much so that witnesses said the oven doors melted off their hinges.

The Nazis instructed their Jewish workers, or *Sonderkommandos*, to "burn the corpses, stoke the fires, drain body fat, and to periodically turn over the 'mountain of burning corpses' for even combustion and a peak fire-temperature." These unwilling slaves did as they were told, even though they "were well aware that they, too, would meet exactly the same fate."[9]

With classic Nazi proficiency, all the physical remains of the dead were "recycled." Human hair was used for stuffing pillows and mattresses, and the human ash from the crematoriums was applied as fertilizer. The Nazis were "cost-conscious" as well; they made surviving Jewish families pay for as many items and services as possible.

When a Jewish person was murdered and cremated in the camps, his or her relatives would receive a postcard informing them that their loved one had died of a heart attack or some other natural cause. In addition, the card notified the family members that if they would "kindly send 3½ [German] Marks," the Nazi government would in turn send them the ashes of their loved one.[10]

The Nazis also developed various extermination methods to be as practical as possible in attaining the "Final Solution." Adolf Eichmann, who led the Gestapo Department for Jewish Affairs, was charged with implementing Nazi policies and procedures in all the sixteen German-occupied countries. As he rose through the ranks, Eichmann became one of the key logistical officials in charge of deporting and transporting the Jews throughout Europe to the death camps. It was said he kept the "trains rolling."[11]

On one occasion, Eichmann observed the Nazis lead Jewish men, women, and children at gunpoint to the outskirts of Minsk. Once reaching a selected area, they were taken en masse to the edge of a freshly dug ditch and forced to disrobe. They were then ordered to kneel, at which point German soldiers shot the defenseless prisoners. The victims fell into the mammoth grave, and Sonderkommandos immediately covered the bodies with mounds of dirt.

Eichmann coldly described the horrifying scene after the war at the Trial of the Major War Criminals before the International Military Tribunal in Nuremberg:

> The execution ditch had been covered over with dirt, but blood was gushing out of the ground 'like a geyser' due to pressure from the bodily gasses of the deceased.[12]

When Heinrich Himmler, one of the main architects of the Final Solution and Eichmann's superior, witnessed a similar bloody massacre and its gruesome aftermath to the one described, he almost fainted. Himmler decided to spare his men the trauma of this revolting sight. He consequently ordered Eichmann to develop and implement a more "humane method" to accomplish their grisly task. Please note that Himmler was not concerned for the Jewish victims but for the emotional protection of the perpetrators who carried out their execution. As a result of perfecting the killing procedure, the Nazis focused their efforts on gassing and cremating the Jews en masse.

To some degree, death by carbon monoxide gas was already in use within the Nazi "Euthanasia Program." Mobile gas vans were first used to streamline the existing operations for killing the elderly, the physically deformed, and the mentally impaired. Now it was time to expand their eradication program to include the building of gas chambers and crematoriums as a better way to rid the world of Europe's "sub-human vermin."

Rudolf Höss, the barbarous commandant of Auschwitz, was the poster child for both evil and proficiency. He, like so many other Nazi leaders, was a classic study in contradiction. Höss was described as a "mild-mannered, happily married Catholic who enjoyed normal family life with his five children," yet he represented humanity's utmost decline into the abyss of evil. Höss was the designer and administrator of the gas chambers and as the "architect of Auschwitz"—the largest of the killing centers—he became known as "history's greatest mass murderer."[13]

This well-ordered overseer analyzed the extermination procedures at other killing camps and "perfected" the process so he could more efficiently gas as many as two thousand Jewish victims at one time. He believed that the most effective way to kill the unsuspecting captives was by using a cyanide gas called Zyklon B instead of the carbon monoxide gas, which was previously used. Höss provided his personal account of the process:

> The gassing was carried out in the detention cells of Block 11. Protected by a gas mask, I watched the killing myself. In the crowded cells, death came instantaneously the moment the Zyklon B was thrown in. A short, almost smothered cry and it was all over....I must even admit that this gassing set my mind at rest, for the mass extermination of the Jews was to start soon, and at that time neither Eichmann nor I was certain as to how these mass killings were to be carried out. It would be by gas, but we did not know which gas and how it was to be used. Now we had the gas, and we had established a procedure.[14]

At full capacity, Auschwitz gassed and cremated an average of six thousand Jews per day. These numbers only reflect murders by gassing; death also came by disease, torture, starvation, shooting, and severe bludgeoning. Auschwitz was a place of suffering, torment, and slaughter—it was a living hell.

At Höss's trial, survivors testified that they remembered him "counting corpses with the cool dedication of a trained bookkeeper."[15] This cold-blooded murderer confessed before his execution how he repeatedly felt "weak-kneed at having to push hundreds of screaming, pleading children into the gas chambers":

> I did, however, always feel ashamed of this weakness of mine after I talked to Adolf Eichmann. He explained to me that it was especially the children who have to be killed first, because where was the logic in killing a generation of older people and leaving alive a generation of young people who can be possible avengers of their parents and can constitute a new biological cell for the reemerging of this people.[16]

Rudolf Höss was found guilty of the murder of 2.5 million Jews and was hanged next to the main crematorium at Auschwitz that he designed.

Another high-ranking Nazi party official was Hans Frank who, among his many other duties, was Hitler's personal legal advisor. As acting Bavarian minister of justice, Frank played a major role in revolutionizing the "New Order" of the Nazi state legal system. During his time in office, Frank kept a meticulous diary, which later was used to convict him and other Nazi criminals during the Nuremberg trials.

Frank's journal was composed of thirty-eight volumes in which he provided detailed descriptions of the daily, minute-by-minute brutalities that took place within the death camps. I have included one such despicable entry in Frank's diary not to *offend* but to *educate* with the *truth* of what happened within the death camps. The following is one of Frank's daily entries that depict the calculated mass herding, dehumanizing, and massacre of Jews in the gas chambers of Auschwitz:

The mass extermination of the Jews in Auschwitz occurred as follows. The Jews selected to be killed were led, men and women separately, as calmly as possible to the crematoria. In the undressing room, Sonderkommando prisoners [Jewish *slave* labor used to assist the Nazis] spoke to the Jews in their native tongue, telling them that they were only going to be bathed and deloused, that they should keep their clothes items together, and above all to remember where they left them, so that they could find them quickly after the delousing....After undressing, the Jews entered the gas chamber, furnished with showerheads and water pipes to give the impression of a bathhouse.

The women and children entered first, then the men, of whom there were always fewer....[The Jews] were calmed by the Sonderkommando prisoners...as well as one of the SS guards [who] always remained in the gas chamber until the last moment. Next the door was quickly closed and bolted, and the awaiting disinfectors immediately threw in the gas [pellets] through an opening in the ceiling down special pipes to the floor. This instantly caused the gas to dissipate.

Through a viewer in the door you could see that those nearest to the inlet pipes fell dead immediately. The remainder started to stagger, shout and gasp for air. The shouting, however, soon turned into wheezing, and, after a few minutes, everyone was down. After 20 minutes at most, no one was moving.

Loss of consciousness occurred just after a few minutes, depending on the distance from the inlet shafts. Those shouting, the elderly, the weak and the children died faster than the healthy and young. Within half an hour after the gas was thrown in, the door was opened and the ventilators were turned on. The extraction of the bodies commenced immediately. They showed no signs of physical change, contraction or discoloration. Only after they had been lying for several hours did post-mortem lividity appear. Bodies being soiled with feces was also rare. No physical injuries were ever identified....

The Sonderkommando pulled gold teeth out of the corpses, and the women had their hair cut off. Next the bodies were transported up in lifts to the already burning furnaces. Depending on the size of the bodies, up to three corpses could be fitted into one furnace chamber. Likewise, the cremation time depended on the type of corpse, but on average it lasted 20 minutes. As I mentioned earlier, crematoria I and II together were able to burn around 2,000 corpses within 24 hours. The burning of larger numbers of corpses was not possible without causing damage.

Crematoria III and IV were supposed to be able to burn 1,500 corpses within 24 hours, but I do not know whether that figure was ever reached. During the burning, the cinders and ashes constantly fell through the grids. They were also constantly taken away or first pulverized. The ashes and crushed cinders were transported in trucks to the Vistula, and there they were thrown into the water with spades to immediately flow away and disperse.[17]

Just another day…just another entry.

However, amidst the monstrous atrocities of the Holocaust, there was another Hand keeping even more painstaking records in the chronicles of heaven. It was a Jewish hand. Every tear was counted, every lash of the whip recorded, and every death mourned.

Sometime soon there will come the Judgment Day, when God

Almighty will settle the accounts of every act of anti-Semitism in the history of the world. The gates of hell will be fully opened, and there all who have not repented of their sin of hatred toward the Jewish people will be incarcerated for eternity (Deuteronomy 30:7; 1 John 3:15; 4:20; Romans 2:5–11).

THE TRUTH ABOUT THE NUMBERS

As noted, the Jews of Europe were the primary target and victims of the Nazis. In 1933, 9.5 million Jews lived in the countries that would eventually be occupied by Germany. By 1945, two out of every three European Jews had been murdered.[18]

I could present validated number after validated number in this chapter, but I ask, what's in a number?

The statistical figures mentioned in history of those that died in the Holocaust were more than numbers—they were people.

Can you determine the value of a person—of their soul—with a number? Can you tell what they looked like or what they studied in college? Can you know whom they married or how many children they had? Can you assume what they did for a living or what their gifts and talents were? Can you invision their dreams, their aspirations and what their future could have been? Can a number in a German log or on a Jewish arm reveal the significance of a human being?

Absolutely not!

Each one of the statistical figures mentioned in history books was God's creation. Each person who perished in the Holocaust was filled with a hope and a future. Each one was like you and me—someone with a life story, living every day to the fullest, anticipating the hug of a loved one after arriving home from a long day's work—*except they were Jewish.*

They were productive members of their communities where their ancestors had lived for generations—*except they were Jewish*. They were mothers, fathers, shopkeepers, doctors, rabbis, lawyers, students, craftsmen, bakers, poets, musicians, and professors; they were everyday people—*except they were Jewish.*

More than one million of them were young children, innocent about the evils of this world. They were like our children and grandchildren—full of goodness, living life with spontaneous laughter and joy—and some were yet unborn. Every one of them was known to God; He called them by name, *and yes, they were Jewish.*

No matter how alike or diverse the victims were. No matter the horrors of torture, starvation, pestilence, and disease they endured. No matter the name of the camp or the length of their imprisonment—the observant Jewish people remained faithful to the Lord by obeying His commandments.

If there was a Sabbath to welcome—they welcomed it; if there was a Passover to observe—they observed it; if there was a Hanukkah candle to light—they lit it; if there was a psalm to sing—they sang it; if there was a prayer to recite—they recited it. By whatever means they had—the faithful remained true to the God of Abraham, Isaac, and Jacob.

> *My son, keep my words,*
> *And treasure my commands within you.*
> *Keep my commands and live,*
> *And my law as the apple of your eye.*
> *Bind them on your fingers;*
> *Write them on the tablet of your heart.*
> (Proverbs 7:1–3)

Even though the Nazis kept fastidious records of deportations, internments, and gassings, no master list of those who perished in the Holocaust exists.

As the end of the war neared, the Nazis kept fewer tallies and destroyed many of their existing records in order to have more time to achieve as much of the Final Solution as possible and still hide the evidence that this diabolical plan had ever happened. Most who espouse Holocaust denial advocate that the death of nearly two-thirds of all the Jews of Europe was merely a result of collateral damage owed to the ravages of war—not so!

In spite of the whitewash of some German journal accounts, several trustworthy estimates of the total number of Jewish deaths have been given through the years. These recognized calculations were drawn using the existing Nazi records as well as criteria gathered in the comparison of before and after World War II population surveys. For example, during Operation Reinhard (March 1942–October 1943), over 1.7 million Jews from German-occupied Poland were exterminated. In an intense,100-day surge within this operation more than 25% of the Jews that perished in all six years of World War II were murdered by the Nazis within three death camps, Belzec, Sobibor and Treblinka.*

Trained historian Dr. Wilhelm Höttl initially cited the total number of Jewish people who died at the hand of the Nazis. Höttl served in the SS and testified at the Nuremberg trials of a conversation he had with Adolf Eichmann on the subject of numbers:

> Eichmann confided to [Höttl] in August 1944 that some four million Jews had been killed in the "various extermination camps," and another two million had been killed in other ways, mostly in shootings by Einsatzgruppen forces [death squads] in the course of the military campaign in Russia.[19]

---

* Lewi Stone, "Quantifying the Holocaust: Hyperintense kill rates during the Nazi genocide," *Science Advances* January 2, 2019: Vol. 5, no. 1, eaau7292 DOI: 10.1126/sciadv.aau7292.

Since then, there have been other notable scientific calculations to include those by Raul Hilberg, who determined there were a total of 5.1 million Jews killed in the Holocaust.[20] And those of Lucy Dawidowicz, who used prewar birth and death records to come up with the more detailed figure of 5,933,900 deaths.[21] And also German scholar Wolfgang Benz, who calculated a range of 5.3 to 6.2 million total Jewish victims.[22]

After Germany's surrender in May of 1945, Adolf Eichmann was arrested but later escaped and achieved asylum in Argentina under the assumed name of Ricardo Klement. In 1960, the Israeli Mossad captured Eichmann and took him to Jerusalem, where he was put on trial as a Nazi war offender and charged with crimes against humanity, specifically the Jewish people.

Over one hundred witnesses testified against him during the trial. When Eichmann spoke in his defense, he did not deny the existence of the Final Solution, dispute its horrors, or debate the vastness of its numbers—he merely said he was obeying orders.

Two of the most appalling statements Eichmann made throughout the trials were: *"I regret nothing"*[23] and *"I will leap into my grave laughing because the feeling that I have five million human beings on my conscience [is] for me a source of extraordinary satisfaction."*[24] Eichmann was found guilty on all counts by the Jewish court, sentenced to death, and hanged;[25] and I can assure you that he is not laughing now as he spends eternity in the bowels of hell.

In 2015, former SS officer Oskar Gröning, known as the "Accountant of Auschwitz," came forward after seventy years of silence and admitted to his role at the death camp. He was sentenced to four years after being tried and convicted of being complicit in the murder of three hundred thousand Auschwitz inmates. In his testimony, Gröning felt it was important to speak out in light of the mounting propaganda surrounding the Holocaust

denial movement; his message to the deniers was clear and
direct:

> I want to tell those deniers I have seen the gas chambers; I
> have seen the crematoria; I have seen the burning pits—and
> I want you to believe me that these atrocities happened. I
> was there.[26]

Ironically, his lawyers appealed the sentence, arguing that
Gröning's "fundamental right to life and physical safety was being
violated." However, the German court denied the appeal, ruling
in December of 2017 that Gröning "was part of the 'machinery
of death,' helping the camp function and collecting money stolen
from the victims to help the Nazi cause, and thus could be convicted of accessory to the murders committed there."[27] The ninety-
six-year-old Gröning died in March of 2018 before serving his
sentence.

Noted author and documentary film director of *Auschwitz: The
Nazis and the "Final Solution"* Laurence Rees said the following
about Gröning's trial and conviction: "It was too little too late."
In June of 2017, seventy-two years after World War II ended, the
German media reported that twenty-eight prosecutions against
alleged war criminals and concentration camp guards were in progress. However, the defendants were all over ninety years old; they
had led full lives—*it was too little too late*.

A calculation you might find troubling: there were nearly ten
thousand Nazis who worked at Auschwitz,[28] and unlike their victims, seven thousand of them survived the war. Of the seven thousand, fewer than eight hundred were put on trial. Of those tried,
fewer than eighty were prosecuted.[29]

THE TRUTH ABOUT THE CARNAGE

As the war was ending in the early fall of 1945, Allied troops swept throughout Europe with a chain of successful military incursions against the Nazis. It was then that they discovered the horrible truth of Hitler's Final Solution. The Allies found camp after camp packed with thousands of concentration camp prisoners—most of whom were the walking dead. What the Allies didn't see were the millions who had mercilessly died before the liberation of the death camps.

Most of the survivors had experienced years of untold cruelty and suffering, including the loss of all their family members. The prisoners were nothing more than human skeletons infested with fleas, lice, and rodent bites. All were suffering from the ravages of disease, infection, and extreme starvation. Even though the Allies were eyewitnesses, no one could wholly grasp the full extent of the Nazi horrors against the Jewish people.

One of the first Nazi camps to be liberated by American troops was Ohrdruf, a sub-camp of Buchenwald known as one of the largest forced-labor concentration camps within the old borders of Germany.

On April 12, Generals George Patton, Omar Bradley, and Dwight Eisenhower entered the gates of the camp and found, among many other atrocities, 3,200 naked, emaciated corpses in shallow graves, sheds holding stacks of dead bodies ready for cremation, and more victims partly incinerated on Nazi-constructed pyres.[30]

General Patton became physically ill and was so enraged by what he saw that he demanded that local German citizens of a nearby town take an immediate tour of the camp and witness what they had allowed to happen. Patton ordered more than two thousand residents of Weimar to view the carnage firsthand.

Weimar was famous for its classic poets Goethe and Schiller and its beloved composers Johann Sebastian Bach, Richard Strauss, and Franz Liszt. Now its citizens were touring a death camp where tens of thousands of Jewish people had been massacred. Weimer's inhabitants were visibly shaken yet claimed they were "unaware" of what was taking place, even though they lived barely four miles away.

General Bradley later commented, as they walked through the camp, that "the smell of death overwhelmed us." It was reported that General Dwight D. Eisenhower, the Supreme Commander of the Allied Forces in Europe, "turned white at the scene inside the gates, but insisted on seeing the entire camp." Eisenhower commented, "We are told that the American soldier does not know what he was fighting for; now, at least he will know what he is fighting *against*."[31]

Eisenhower gave the order that all American units in the area were to tour the camp. He felt it was imperative to have as many witnesses as possible to the insidious carnage the Jewish internees had suffered. Eisenhower immediately sent a message to his leadership in Washington, DC, referencing the Nazi camp:

> The things I saw beggar description....The visual evidence and the verbal testimony of starvation, cruelty and bestiality were so overpowering....I made the visit deliberately, in order to be in a position to give first-hand evidence of these things if ever, in the future, there develops a tendency to charge these allegations merely to "propaganda."[32]

Apparently General Eisenhower sensed, even then, that the inhumane brutalities against the Jewish people might one day be challenged or denied.

In order to get the truth to the world about what the Nazis had done, Eisenhower called on President Truman to send a congressional delegation along with members of the American press to personally witness the carnage. You must remember that there was a time in America when the media represented and reported the straightforward facts about history and current events versus today's mass liberal media, who merely broadcast their personal sociopolitical version and opinion of what they perceive to be true.

Truman granted Eisenhower's request, and within a short time, a congressional delegation accompanied by top journalists and skilled photographers arrived at the concentration camps. Once there, no one could believe what they saw.

Leading journalist Edward R. Murrow, who had become a legend on American radio during World War II, was among them. Murrow prided himself in taking the news to the world as it happened. It was said that when Murrow reported on the bombing of London it was as if he "burned the city of London in our houses and we felt the flames that burned it."[33]

In his legendary broadcast of April 15, 1945, Edward R. Murrow gave the American radio audience a heart-wrenching yet precise description of Buchenwald.

The main camp had 174 sub-camps, where prisoners were forced laborers, victims of horrific medical experiments, poisoned, starved to death, shot, or hung. The dead were either buried in mass graves or burned in crematoriums. Survivors and liberators alike testified that prisoners' skins were used to cover books, make lampshades, or simply taken as souvenirs.[34]

As many as 238,980 prisoners walked through Buchenwald's gates between 1937 and 1945, and of those at least 43,045 were murdered in one way or another; the balance were transported to the official killing camps.[35]

The following are excerpts of what Murrow described to America that day:

Permit me to tell you what you would have seen and heard had you been with me....There surged around me an evil-smelling stink. Men and boys reached out to touch me. They were in rags and the remnants of uniforms. Death had already marked many of them, but they were smiling with their eyes....

When I entered [the barracks], men crowded around, tried to lift me to their shoulders. They were too weak. Many of them could not get out of bed. I was told that this building had once stabled 80 horses. There were 1,200 men in it, five to a bunk. The stink was beyond all description.

When I reached the center of the barracks, a man came up and said, "You remember me, I am Petr Zenkl, one time mayor of Prague." I remembered him, but did not recognize him....

As I walked down to the end of the barracks, there was applause from the men too weak to get out of bed. It sounded like the hand-clapping of babies, they were so weak....As we walked out into the courtyard—a man fell dead. Two others...were crawling toward the latrine. I saw it, but will not describe it.

In another part of the camp they showed me the children, hundreds of them. Some were only six. One rolled up his sleeve, showed me his number. It was tattooed on his arm B-6030, it was. The others showed me their numbers. They will carry them till they die....I could see their ribs through their thin shirts....The children clung to my hands and stared.

We crossed to the courtyard. Men kept coming up to me to speak to me and touch me, professors from Poland, doctors from Vienna, men from all of Europe. Men from the countries that made America.

We went to the hospital; it was full. The doctor told me that two hundred had died the day before. I asked the cause of death. He shrugged and said: "Tuberculosis, starvation, fatigue, and there are many who have no desire to live. It is very difficult."...

We proceeded to the small courtyard....There were two rows of bodies stacked up like cordwood. They were thin and very white. Some of the bodies were terribly bruised, though there seemed to be little flesh to bruise. Some had been shot through the head, but they bled but little.

All except two were naked. I tried to count them as best I could, and arrived at the conclusion that all that was mortal of more than five hundred men and boys lay there in two neat piles. . . .

Murder had been done at Buchenwald. God alone knows how many men and boys have died there....I was told that there were more than twenty thousand in the camp. There had been as many as sixty thousand. Where are they now?

As I left the camp, a Frenchman who used to work for Havas [news agency] in Paris came up to me and said, "You will write something about this, perhaps?" And he added, "To write about this, you must have been here at least two years, and after that—you don't want to write anymore."

I pray you to believe what I have said about Buchenwald. I have reported what I saw and heard, but only part of it. For most of it, I have no words. Dead men are plentiful in war, but the living dead, more than twenty thousand of them in one camp...If I have offended you by this rather mild account of Buchenwald, I'm not in the least sorry.[36]

rts such as Murrow's, along with eyewitness testi-
ominent delegations, in addition to thousands of
expert and amateur photographers, as well as actual
the atrocities shown in theaters around the globe
contributed to a stark awakening. Finally, an otherwise clueless (or
indifferent) world acknowledged the horrible reality of what had been
done in an effort to eradicate all of the 11 million Jews of Europe.

THE RIGHTEOUS GENTILES

Most of us are familiar with Edmund Burke's statement, "The only
thing necessary for the triumph of evil is for good men to do nothing."
This profound truth resonated within the horrors of the Holocaust.

It has been said that had more people taken a stand for righteousness, many of the atrocities committed against the Jewish
people and other innocent victims could have been avoided, and
millions would have been saved. Jesus Christ will judge the nations
of the world for the sin of silence, as referred in Matthew:

*Then He will also say to those on the left hand, "Depart from
me…for I was hungry and you gave Me no food; I was thirsty
and you gave Me no drink; I was a stranger and you did not take
Me in, naked and you did not clothe Me, sick and in prison and
you did not visit Me." Then they also will answer Him, saying,
"Lord, when did we see You hungry or thirsty or a stranger or
naked or sick or in prison, and did not minister to You?" Then
He will answer them, saying, "Assuredly, I say to you, inasmuch
as you did not do it to one of the least of these my brethren [**the
Jewish people**], you did not do it to Me." And these will go
away into everlasting punishment, but the righteous into eternal
life (25:42–46).*

Erwin Lutzer recounts the gripping story from ar
Germany during the Holocaust. The congregants of
attempted to drown out the cries of God's people iı
trouble, instead of taking action in their defense:

> I lived in Germany during the Nazi Holocaust. I considered
> myself a Christian. We heard stories of what was happening
> to Jews, but we tried to distance ourselves from it because
> what could we do to stop it. A railroad track ran behind our
> small church and each Sunday morning we could hear the
> whistle in the distance, and then the wheels coming over
> the tracks. We became disturbed when we heard the cries
> coming from the train as it passed by. We realized that it
> was carrying Jews like cattle in the cars. Week after week
> the whistle would blow. We dreaded to hear the sound of
> those wheels because we knew that we would hear the cries
> of the Jews in route to a death camp. Their screams tormented
> us. We knew the time the train was coming, and when we
> heard the whistle blow, we began singing hymns. By the time
> the train came past our church, we were singing at the top
> of our voices. If we heard the screams, we sang more loudly
> and soon we heard them no more....Although years have
> passed, I still hear the train whistle in my sleep. God forgive
> me, forgive all of us who called ourselves Christians and yet
> did nothing to intervene.[37]

But there were others who did what they could to save the Jewish
people.

Those of us who saw the movie *Schindler's List* remember the riv-
eting closing scene where Oskar Schindler tearfully cries out, "Maybe

ould have saved one more—just one more!" All of humanity must ask the question of themselves, "If my Jewish friends and neighbors were threatened, would I risk my life and the lives of my loved ones in order to come to their rescue?" This is the question exceptional men and women answered during the Holocaust—and for those precious handful, their answer was *yes*!

"Righteous Gentiles" is a name given to non-Jews who took great risks to help rescue Jewish lives from the devastation of the Final Solution. The survivors identified hundreds of these honorable men and women, but hundreds more go unrecognized except by the Righteous Judge of Heaven. Allow me to share a few compelling stories of these brave rescuers.

Adelaide Hautval

A devout Protestant, Dr. Adelaide Hautval lived in southern France during World War II. Hautval was captured by German police in the spring of 1942 and transported to prison when she attempted to cross into occupied Paris after the Nazis denied her permission to attend her mother's funeral.

By that summer, Jewish captives wearing the yellow Star of David began to arrive at the prison. It became evident shortly after their arrival that the Jewish prisoners were being treated much more severely than the other inmates. Dr. Hautval courageously objected to their inhumane treatment, and the guards punished her by sentencing her to the same fate as the Jewish women. This did not influence the doctor's convictions—in response to her captors' pronouncement, Adelaide "pinned a piece of yellow paper to her clothing that read, 'Friend of the Jews.'"[38]

By early 1943, Dr. Hautval had been relocated to the Birkenau death camp, where she shared a barracks with five hundred Jewish women. This compassionate healer was soon nicknamed "the saint" because of her kindness toward her fellow Jewish inmates. With no medical resources at her disposal, she secretly treated and isolated those who were infected with contagious diseases. Dr. Hautval not only protected the healthier prisoners from illness, she also did not report the sick as she was instructed to—sparing hundreds of Jews from an instant death sentence.

Dr. Hautval was later transferred to Auschwitz I camp, where medical experiments were performed by the likes of Drs. Eduard Wirths, Wladislaw Dering, and of course, Josef Mengele. While at Auschwitz, she refused to participate in any medical experiments and boldly declared, "No person was entitled to claim the life or determine the fate of another."[39] Miraculously, Dr. Hautval was not killed for insubordination and was sent back to Birkenau and later to Ravensbrück, where she survived until freed by the liberators.

The Jewish survivors Dr. Hautval came in contact with remembered her compassion, encouragement, and determined dignity. Many quoted her as saying, "Here [Auschwitz] we are all under a sentence of death. Let us behave like human beings as long as we are alive." Hautval later provided eyewitness testimony against the doctors at Auschwitz at a hearing held in London and was described as "one of the most impressive and courageous women ever to testify before a court in Great Britain—a woman of strong character and an extraordinary personality."[40] Dr. Hautval proved to be a true friend to the Jews.

Roddie Edmonds

American master sergeant Roddie Edmonds of Knoxville, Tennessee, was credited with saving the lives of two hundred Jewish soldiers at a German prisoner of war camp. The righteous actions that Edmonds took personified the united stand the American people took against the Nazis once they were confronted with the carnage of the Holocaust.

Edmonds was taken prisoner and sent to Stalag IX-A by the Germans during the Battle of the Bulge. In January 1945, the German commandant of the camp announced that all Jewish prisoners of war were to report in front of their barracks the following morning. Edmonds deduced that the Jewish soldiers were going to be transported to a Nazi extermination camp.

As the highest-ranking soldier in the camp, Edmonds instead ordered all Jews and non-Jews to report to formation. Shocked by the over 1,270 inmates before him, the German camp commander shouted at Edmonds, "They cannot all be Jews!"

Edmonds firmly responded, "We are all Jews here."[41]

When threatened at gunpoint by the camp commander, Edmonds gave his name, rank, and serial number and declared to the commandant and all present, "If you shoot me, you will have to shoot all of us, and after the war you will be tried for war crimes."[42] Shockingly, after Edmonds's bold statement, the commandant walked away.

When testifying of the incident, a Jewish prisoner stated, "Although 70 years have passed, I can still hear the words he [Edmonds] said to the German camp commander." Another Jewish soldier who was imprisoned with Edmonds recalled, "There was no question in my mind, or that of Master Sgt. Edmonds, that the Germans were removing the Jewish prisoners from the general prisoner population at great risk to their survival. Master Sgt. Edmonds, at the risk of his immediate death, defied the Germans with the unexpected consequences that the Jewish prisoners were saved."[43]

There are only five Americans who are recognized as the Righteous Gentiles Among the Nations at Yad Vashem, Israel's

Holocaust memorial, and Master Sergeant Roddie Edmonds is one of them.

The Sleizen Family

Leah Berzak and her eldest daughter, twelve-year-old Renia, escaped the disease-infested Jewish ghetto of Baranovichi after the Nazis slaughtered Leah's husband, their three young children, and her mother. Seeking refuge, Leah and Renia hid in the frozen fields surrounding the city and begged the local farmers for help, but they were turned away time after time.

In desperation, Leah and her daughter managed to evade the Nazi guards and slip unnoticed into the outskirts of town to the farm of their Christian friends, the Sleizen family. Although they knew the severe penalty for hiding Jews was immediate deportation and execution, the Sleizens decided to do what was right in the sight of God.

Initially, Leah and Renia were hidden in the family barn. Eventually, the Sleizens dug a rectangular ditch under the floor of their home. The family set a rug and sofa over the grave-like pit to conceal its opening. The hiding place was just long enough to accommodate Leah's height and wide enough to cradle both mother and daughter as they lay side by side. This dark, cold, and damp sepulcher became their place of refuge.

Every morning at 3:00 a.m., Mrs. Sleizen would free Leah and Renia from their blackened tomb, feed them, and provide a brief opportunity to stretch their cramped bodies and relieve themselves. Day after day, the mother and daughter lay there motionless. When Renia cried in claustrophobic agony, Leah would lovingly touch her frightened daughter and say, "Soon the war will be over. We will be free and everything is going to be fine. Hashem will see to it my darling, Renia.... He will see to it!"

To bring her daughter peace, Leah would recite the *Sh'ma*. The Sh'ma is the most sacred prayer in Judaism, derived from Deuteronomy 6:4–9; 11:13–21; and Numbers 15:37–41: "Hear, Oh Israel, the Lord our God, the Lord is One. Praised be His Name. His glorious Kingdom is forever and forever."[44] It is said many Jewish people recited this prayer on their way to their deaths during the Holocaust.

The Sleizen farm was often subject to searches by SS soldiers. When the troopers approached the farmhouse hunting for Jews, the Sleizens would quickly signal Leah and Renia by having their young children sit on the sofa that covered their hiding place and sing special songs of warning until their stalkers left—it was only then that all could breathe a sigh of relief.

Finally, after 840 days—twenty-eight long months—mother and daughter were freed from their place of refuge and given Christian birth certificates and passports that the Sleizen family secretly obtained for them. Because of the help of their brave friends, Leah and Renia managed to walk from Poland through the Italian Alps and eventually arrived at a place called Palestine.

How do I know the details of Leah and Renia's story? Renia became the mother of one of our dearest friends, and my wife, Diana, and I had the honor of hearing her tell the personal account of her survival of the Holocaust.

Hitler did not extinguish this noble Jewish line; he could not, for it was redeemed by the Hand of God through the actions of Righteous Gentiles.

The Danes

How did nearly all of the Jews of Denmark survive the Holocaust? The answer is simple: Denmark was the only occupied country in Europe that stood for righteousness in defiance of the Nazis. Even though most Europeans did not actively participate in the Final Solution, they did little or nothing to prevent it. Professor of history and expert on the Holocaust Peter Longerich concluded that the success on the Holocaust was "dependent to a considerable extent, on the practical cooperation and support of an occupied country or territory."[45]

But not Denmark.

After the Nazi occupation, the Danes were covertly informed of the SS plans to deport the Jews of Denmark to the death camps. Instead of yielding to the horrific Nazi policies, the Danish government took action to protect their Jewish citizens. The Danes took a bold stand and believed that an attack on the Jews of Denmark was an attack on the whole nation. The extermination of a people—of an entire race—requires cooperation. Denmark refused to collaborate with the Nazis; therefore, the implementation of the Final Solution within their country became unachievable.

When the Nazis invaded, the Jews immediately sought refuge in non-Jewish farmhouses, homes, and churches—where they were all received. Next, the Danish government formulated a national effort to secretly transport all Jews to safety into the neutral country of Sweden. Because of the cooperation of the entire Danish citizenry, over 90 percent of the nation's Jews were able to clandestinely gather on the coast. Within a few days, fishermen succeeded in ferrying seven thousand Danish Jews across the Baltic Sea to their safe haven.[46]

Government officials did not shy away from their position, declaring,

The Danish Jews are an integral part of the people, and therefore all the people are deeply affected by the measures taken, which are seen as a violation of the Danish sense of justice.[47]

These and other honorable rescuers add to the list of witnesses against the lie that the Holocaust never occurred. The actions of these Righteous Gentiles attest that inherent goodness, moral conviction, self-sacrifice, and bold action can prevail even under unspeakable situations.

LEST WE FORGET

Diana and I have visited the Dachau concentration camp twice. The first time we walked the grounds alone, and the second time we had over two hundred of our ministry partners with us.

The camp is located in the city of Dachau, which is a short drive outside of Munich in the beautiful upper Bavarian countryside. It was the first Nazi concentration camp that opened shortly after Hitler became chancellor in 1933. In its early stages, Dachau initially held political prisoners, and later evolved into a death camp.

In the spring of 1984, I preached in West Berlin at the US military chapel and later, behind the Iron Curtain, to the people of East Berlin. After my engagement, Diana and I traveled to Munich because I felt I had a responsibility to see at least one of the death camps before returning home.

Diana and I stood at the entrance of Dachau and felt like we had been transported in time. We walked through Dachau's gate under the talons of the bronze Nazi eagle. The gate opened to a large courtyard where thousands of prisoners stood for hours several times a day while the captors methodically counted their captives—lest they attempt to escape their place of torture. I tried to absorb all that once happened there, but it was overwhelming, to say the least.

As we stood in the square, I had a sudden flashback of a story told to me by one of our many friends who had survived Dachau. Sandor "Shoney" Alex Braun had been incarcerated along with his father and brother at Auschwitz, then in one of the sub-camps, and finally Dachau. While in the sub-camp, the father observed a birthday. His sons could think of no better way to honor their beloved father than to give him their day's bread rations—the only thing of value they possessed.

Reluctantly, their father took the bread and slowly ate it with tears streaming down his face at the sacrificial gesture of his precious sons. Shoney's father, who had eaten more food that day (three small pieces of stale bread) than he had in months, fell fast asleep on the hard wooden bunk and missed morning roll call. Shoney then recounted what occurred at dawn that fateful day:

> One prisoner was missing. After several recounts…one prisoner was still missing. So the Kapos [prisoners assigned to supervise prisoners] went to the barrack to look for him. And they found the missing man sleeping in a corner. My father. They dragged him from his collar to the SS guard….And the SS guard turned to the assembly, to us, [and] said, "As I understand, the Jewish dog has here two sons. I want them to step out and come near him. Witness his punishment."
>
> So we had to step out…and we were standing near him [their father]. Then he [the SS guard] turned to the rest of them. He said, "This dirty Jewish dog kept Germany from victory ten minutes, because that's how long it took to find him." Then he gave a swift kick to my father, which signaled the Kapos to start the punishment.
>
> They rushed toward him…kicking and beating him from all directions…whipping him. We fell on our knees. And we turned to the SS and said, "Please, stop. Beat us. Please don't do that." The beating was even more severe.
>
> They were beating him until he collapsed; my father was

silent, except for his lips were moving…he tried to say something. I came closer, and I noticed that he was reciting the declaration of faith of the Jewish people, Sh'ma. The Sh'ma: "Sh'ma Yisrael, Adonai Elohenu, Adonai Echad—Hear, O Israel, the Lord our God, the Lord is One." Then he was very silent.

Diana and I continued our gloomy journey. We entered the cramped barracks where more than one thousand prisoners had been shoved into filthy bunks for a few hours' sleep each night before enduring eighteen hours or more of slave labor the next day.

We walked through the museums that displayed the instruments of torture as well as those used in brutal medical procedures by Josef Mengele, the mastermind behind the grotesque medical experiments on twins. It was Mengele, the "Angel of Death," who harvested "specimens" from every train delivery at Auschwitz.

As the human freight was unloaded from the trains, they were told to disrobe and await their fate. The Jewish captives stood before Mengele who, by the flick of his hand, determined who would go directly to the gas chambers, the slave labor camps, or the medical quarters. It was said that those who went directly to the gas chambers had a better fate compared to those who met their torturous death by Mengele's so-called medical research.

These death-inducing experiments were a wicked distortion of the medical profession, but more so, they were an insult to God and His creation. The sickening procedures were performed on the Jewish people because the Nazis believed them to be sub-human and therefore disposable. Mengele was not the only physician to take part in these malicious trials, but sadly, like Mengele, many of the participating doctors escaped criminal prosecution.

Diana and I walked beyond the barracks and came to the door

of the gas chamber where thousands had stood before us. The scores who were selected to go to the gas chambers had been told that they were to receive a much-needed shower, but instead, within minutes of the door shutting behind them, they gasped their last torturous breaths. We could still smell the stench of death and see their claw marks on the walls—it was heart-wrenching.

After the gas chamber, Diana and I walked into the crematoriums. By this point, we could hardly draw breath for the anguish that gripped our throats. There we saw leather cots leading into the ovens. I will always remember that the stretchers had the impressions of human bodies left on them from the thousands they had fed into the blazing inferno. Tall smokestacks jutted out of the building. In the days before the liberation of Dachau, these chimneys spewed the ashes of the dead twenty-four hours a day—seven days a week.

Diana and I continued to walk in silence as we viewed the balance of the museum displays. I remember thinking, *Oh my God, will we ever know the number of Your beloved who were sacrificed on the altar of hate?* There was no stopping the tears. By the end of our journey, I held Diana in an effort to console—I will forever remember that day.

I knew then that I had to bring others to see what we saw. My first objective was to show reverence to the thousands who had died at Dachau pledging that there would be more witnesses to the existence of this hideous place. Second, I wanted to somehow bring a degree of comfort and consolation to the relatives of the deceased who were sent to their deaths anywhere within the chain of concentration camps.

My thoughts went to the words of the prophet Ezekiel, who wrote, *"Then I came to the captives…and I sat where they sat, and remained there astonished among them seven days"* (Ezekiel 3:15).

I expressed to Diana my desire to return to Dachau for a "Lest We Forget" memorial service to remember the Jewish people who died in the Holocaust. A few months later, we brought over two hundred witnesses who could testify to their children and grandchildren that Dachau was a real place that housed, tortured, and killed thousands of Jewish prisoners.

Our group toured the repulsive camp where God's Covenant people had suffered and died. We did what Ezekiel did and stood where they stood. We lined up in formation on the camp's courtyard as thousands had stood before us. Each one of us wore a black armband with a yellow Star of David to symbolize the fact that those imprisoned at Dachau and at other camps within Nazi-occupied territories had committed no crime or broken no law—they were there simply because they were Jewish.

Rabbi Israel Ba'al Shem Tov taught that "forgetfulness leads to exile, but in remembrance lies the key to redemption."[48] We were there to remember—*lest we forget* what happened to our Jewish brethren at the hand of pure hatred. Our time in Germany was short—we were there less than thirty-six hours—but our mission was complete. We walked out of Dachau and left for our final destination: the State of Israel.

Soon after arriving in Israel, we gathered at the Night to Honor Israel Forest that Hagee Ministries established years before. While there, we planted two hundred trees in honor of the millions who died in the camps, wrapping the black armbands we had worn at Dachau around each trunk.

It was our way of symbolizing that the memory of those who had succumbed to the evil of the Holocaust would now forever be attached to the land of Israel. No longer would they be identified with a place of death; their sacred memory lives on—for *Am Yisrael Chai*—the people of Israel live!

FOUR KINDS OF PEOPLE

Despite the twisted reasoning used by Holocaust deniers to veil their attacks upon the memories of the survivors, *or* their blatant disregard of the liberators' eyewitness accounts, *or* their flagrant refusal to acknowledge the confessions of the agents of death who committed the crimes, Holocaust denial is still deeply rooted in anti-Semitism, and it has remained the universal language of hate.

It All Started with Words

My dear friend and Holocaust survivor Irving Roth often says of the Holocaust, "It all started with words." Matthew 12:34 reminds us that words reflect the condition of our soul, for the Word of God declares that "…out of the abundance of the heart the mouth speaks."

> *Watch your thoughts, they become your words;*
> *watch your words, they become your actions;*
> *watch your actions, they become your habits;*
> *watch your habits, they become your character;*
> *watch your character, it becomes your destiny.*

One of the most horrifying genocides the world has ever witnessed, the attempted systematic annihilation of the Jewish people, began with words. Anti-Semitism, the world's oldest hatred, eventually manifests in words, even though it is often sanitized, or draped in some social, political, or religious garb disguising the evil thoughts of men. These words will eventually transform a society leading to an irreversible hatred that condones segregation, persecution, and murder. It has happened in the past, and we must ensure that it never happens again.

---

* Lao Tzu.

For several years, anti-Semitism has been insidiously growing worldwide, and America is no exception—the question is, will we allow this evil to dictate our destiny?

Soon there will be no one left to tell the personal stories of their tormenting encounters with the evils of the Holocaust. Elie Wiesel said it well: "For the dead and for the living—we must bear witness."

In order not to repeat the mistakes of the past, it is crucial to remember that this catastrophic event involved four kinds of individuals: the mobs of torturous perpetrators, the millions of innocent victims, the few who righteously intervened, and far too many apathetic bystanders.

These diverse groups of people are still present in the world today; the question we must ask ourselves is: *Which are we?*

Even after the attempted annihilation of God's chosen people during World War II, a miracle was about to take place...the rebirth of the Jewish nation.

CHAPTER 4

BATTLE FOR JERUSALEM

Jerusalem is Israel's capital, will never be divided, and will remain the capital of the State of Israel, the capital of the Jewish people, forever and ever. —Prime Minister Benjamin Netanyahu

Many of the greatest civilizations have sought to rule over Jerusalem, yet only one people—the Jews—have been given the divine right to claim the Holy City as their eternal inheritance. And because God's Chosen have refused to relinquish this claim, they have paid a terrible price in blood and suffering.

Christian anti-Judaism and European anti-Semitism have historically produced massive horrors such as the Crusades, the Great Inquisition, the Russian pogroms, and Hitler's Final Solution.

Moreover, the continued struggle for control of the Holy Land, especially for the city of Jerusalem, has been stained with Jewish blood since King David conquered the city in 1000 BCE.

Yet, even after the Romans destroyed Jerusalem in 70 CE, where they massacred more than one million Jews and sent hundreds of thousands more into exile, there has always been a remnant of Jewish people who never left their biblical homeland since Joshua led them in at Gilgal. Israel's prime minister Benjamin Netanyahu explained this phenomenon well:

> In my office in Jerusalem, there's an ancient seal. It's a signet ring of a Jewish official from the time of the Bible. The seal was found right next to the Western Wall, and it dates back 2,700 years, to the time of King Hezekiah. Now, there's a name of the Jewish official inscribed on the ring in Hebrew. His name was Netanyahu. My first name, Benjamin, dates back a thousand years earlier to Benjamin—Binyamin—the son of Jacob, who was also known as Israel. Jacob and his 12 sons roamed these same hills of Judea and Samaria 4,000 years ago, and there's been a continuous Jewish presence in the land ever since.[*]

The Jewish people, who were dispersed to the nations of the world, were for centuries confronted with bigotry and hatred and considered outcasts in their host countries. Then, at His appointed time, the God of Abraham, Isaac, and Jacob began calling His people home. As a result of the Spirit's beckoning, many Jews began to grasp the notion that the only way to escape anti-Semitism and its deadly consequences was to regain their national independence.

HERZL'S JEWISH STATE

After nearly two millennia in exile, in the late nineteenth and early twentieth centuries, a new movement for Jewish sovereignty began

---

[*] https://mfa.gov.il/MFA/PressRoom/2011/Pages/Remarks_PM_Netanyahu_UN_General%20_Assembly_23-Sep-2011.aspx.

to gain worldwide traction. In 1896, Theodor Herzl's Zionist pamphlet, *The Jewish State*, laid out a vision that would eventually culminate in the rebirth of the State of Israel. Herzl believed he had the answer to the Jewish Question, which related to the civil, legal, national, and political status of Jews within world societies:

> We are a people—one people....We want to lay the foundation stone, for the house which will become the refuge of the Jewish nation. Zionism is the return to Judaism even before the return to the land of Israel.[1]

The ideal of Zionism, the belief that the Jewish people had a right to national independence and sovereignty as natives of their ancestral homeland, began to grow. Jewish immigrants flooded into what was then Palestine and began to purchase land from wealthy Arab landholders at exorbitant prices. The land had been mostly barren and sparsely populated for centuries, and to most, it seemed worthless. But to the Jews, who dreamed of coming home to their Promised Land, it was a fulfillment of prophecy.

Slowly, Palestine began to prosper as Jewish exiles cultivated the land, eliminated disease-infested swamps, and brought more economic opportunity to the area, creating a higher standard of living for all its residents.[2] The Arab population grew and flourished alongside their Jewish neighbors, and for a time the two groups peacefully coexisted.

Years of Zionist efforts resulted in the creation of the Balfour Declaration of 1917, which stated that the British government "views with favor the establishment in Palestine of a national home for the Jewish people and would use their best endeavors to facilitate the achievement of this object."[*] The British promised Palestine

---

*   Ibid.

to the Jewish people and assumed responsibility for guarding it through the process of Jewish statehood. This temporary steward-ship, called the Mandate for Palestine, was entrusted to Britain by the League of Nations.[3]

In 1919, an agreement between Zionist leader Chaim Weizmann and the Arab leader, Emir Faisal, was accepted.[4] The terms allowed for the notion of a Jewish state which also protected the rights of local Arabs in the land. However, by 1920, just as the mandate period began, a power struggle between two prominent Palestinian families caused a breakdown in the hope for peace between Arabs and Jews. Sadly, but not surprisingly, this disastrous feud evolved into an eruption of anti-Jewish violence.

A CENTURY OF TERROR BEGINS

In 1921, the British appointed Haj Amin al-Husseini the first *Mufti* (a Muslim legal expert who rules on religious matters) of Jerusalem. Much like Haman before him, the Mufti became paranoid that the growing Jewish population would impair Arab prominence in the land. His answer to the Jewish problem was to engineer bloody riots against Jewish settlements and recruit suicide squads to attack resident Jews in protest of the Balfour Declaration.[5]

Terrorism soon became the preferred political tool of extreme Palestinian Arab nationalists and set in motion another era of violence and hatred toward the Jewish people.

By this time, the British had divided the land set aside by the Mandate into two prospective states: 77 percent of the land for a proposed Arab state called Transjordan and the remaining 23 percent for a national Jewish homeland. However, the Arab riots of the 1920s and 1930s prompted Britain in 1937 to further partition the land, with 80 percent going to an Arab state and 20 percent to a Jewish state.[6]

Palestinian Arab leaders once again refused to accept this larger partition, and neither plan materialized.[7] Please note that any and all land offered to the Jewish people throughout history has been vigorously protested by their Arab neighbors.

Zionism was not very popular with many of the British officers assigned to administer the mandate power in Palestine. The bloody Arab uprisings further convinced the British that any promise of land made to the Jews was not worth the trouble.[8] In defiance of their *own* government's obligation to protect Jewish inhabitants, some British officers went so far as to encourage the Palestinian Arabs to use terrorism against the Jews in hopes the continued violence would cause Britain to entirely abandon the idea of a Jewish state.[9]

Jews were not allowed to own weapons or defend themselves against Arab extremist aggression, and those who did were arrested and sent to prison. Tragically, terrorists murdered hundreds of Jews during the British Mandate period.

Empowered and aided by British overseers, Haj Amin al-Husseini was given authority over the Muslim holy places and therefore wielded tremendous political and religious influence. From his position of control, al-Husseini continued to incite resentment and violence against the Jewish people.

Fearing that Zionism was gaining international financial backing, al-Husseini started a rumor of a Jewish plot to seize control of the Muslim holy sites, which successfully instigated even more riots.[10] The Mufti's propaganda tactic worked. British authorities uprooted Jewish families from their ancestral homes in Hebron and Gaza. The British also severely restricted Jewish immigration to Palestine and once again drastically reduced the size of the land intended for a Jewish state. Still, none of these extreme actions satisfied Arab leaders.

ARABS REJECT
ISRAEL'S RIGHT TO EXIST

Motivated by Hitler's hatred for the Jews and intrigued by his plans to annihilate them, al-Husseini traveled to Germany during World War II to meet with the Führer.[11] Following their meeting, the Mufti collaborated with the Nazi regime to recruit tens of thousands of Muslims for the *Schutzstaffel*—better known as the SS.

In the aftermath of World War II, al-Husseini was forced to flee prosecution for war crimes and lived abroad for the rest of his life. However, his legacy of terrorism and propaganda were used as a highly effective political tool against the Jewish state and became the prototype for future anti-Israel despots such as Yasser Arafat (PLO), Mohammed Badie (Muslim Brotherhood), Hassan Nasrallah (Hezbollah), Osama bin Laden (al-Qaeda), Abu Bakr al-Baghdadi (ISIS), and Ismail Haniyeh (Hamas).

Weary of the problem posed by Arab rejectionism and trying to work within the shadow of the horrors committed against the Jews during the Holocaust, Britain handed over responsibility of Palestine's future to the newly formed United Nations. On November 29, 1947, the United Nations voted in favor of Resolution 181 and adopted a partition plan for Palestine that divided the land west of the Jordan River into two states roughly equal in size but distinctly unequal in value.

The disjointed pieces of land reserved for the Jewish people consisted of mostly arid desert without defensible borders and excluded Jerusalem, which was designated an international city. Jewish leaders, desperate to build a national home and provide a refuge for the displaced survivors of the Holocaust, accepted the biased plan.

Arab leaders had previously established that they would not accept *any* proposal that included a Jewish state, and almost immediately made good on their threat to launch large-scale attacks on

Jewish communities. Consequently, hundreds of Jews were killed in riots and other terror attacks between November 29, 1947, and Israel's independence on May 14, 1948.[12]

Israel's existence as a Jewish state in the middle of what had once been an Islamic empire was entirely unacceptable to Arab leaders. They successfully conjured up rabid anti-Semitic fervor among their people as they called for a jihad. The day after the declaration of the partition plan, the British departed and the Palestinian Arabs were joined by five Middle East armies—Egypt, Syria, Transjordan, Lebanon, and Iraq—to launch a war of annihilation against the newly reborn State.

The international community stood back and silently watched without giving much hope for the fledgling state's survival of their war of independence.[13] But to the world's astonishment, Israel miraculously prevailed against their attackers. To avoid further disgrace and loss of territory, the Arab states signed an armistice agreement with Israel in March of 1949; however, their insatiable goal of destroying Israel remained. The next seventy-plus years would be marked by continued threats and attempts to wipe Israel off the map.

THE EVOLUTION OF ANTI-SEMITIC TERRORISM

The Arab extremists, bent on destroying Israel, learned of the power of radicalism during the British Mandate period. Terrorism was not only an effective political tool against the Jewish state, which weakened it internally; it also produced external pressure from the international community.

The generational goal to eradicate Israel fueled the rise of several Islamic extremist factions. Fundamental to each of these terrorist groups was an anti-Semitic interpretation of Islamic theology that left no room for acceptance of the State of Israel, the Jewish people, and, consequently, the possibility of peace between radical Islam and Judaism.

Muslim Brotherhood

One of the first extremist groups to form was the Muslim Brotherhood. It was initially founded in 1928 as a sociopolitical effort to bring back Islamic *Sharia law* (Islamic religious law) and reinstitute an Islamic Sunni *caliphate* (Islamic state) in the Middle East.

However, the Brotherhood soon embraced violent anti-Semitism as part of its ideology. During 1938 and 1939, the Brotherhood repeatedly attacked and threatened Egyptian Jews. Its leaders admired Hitler's plan to eliminate the Jews and passed out Arabic translations of Hitler's *Mein Kampf* and the Russian *Protocols of the Elders of Zion*.[14]

During the 1950s and 1960s, the radical Islamic scholar Sayyid Qutb officially branded the Jews as "nefarious agents of Satan" who planned to destroy Islam and corrupt their society's morals. He relied on the false doctrines of the *Protocols of the Elders of Zion* to "prove" his accusations, leaving no room for the possibility of the existence of "a good Jew." Qutb's solution for the Jewish "threat" was the same as all other anti-Semites since Haman: total extermination.[15]

The Muslim Brotherhood laid the ideological foundations for the rise of both Sunni and Shia Islamist extremist groups. The Brotherhood declared that it is incumbent on all Muslims to wage jihad over the entire world to "liberate" non-Muslim lands from the infidels.[16] The radical extremist theology and fanatical political goals of these groups rapidly evolved from the desire to win back lands that had once been under Islamic rule, to conquering and dominating the entire world under Sharia law. This remains their objective to this day.

By the 1960s, the Muslim Brotherhood had exported its anti-Semitic ideology and obsessive devotion to jihad across the globe. All radical Muslims were encouraged to become "martyrs" for the cause, which soon gave way to the phenomenon of suicide attacks.

Nearly every major radical Islamist terrorist group of the last fifty years can trace its warped ideological origins back to the Muslim Brotherhood and the teachings of Sayyid Qutb. In the West, the Brotherhood founded "nonviolent" Islamic institutions that preach the same hateful radical ideology while funneling money from their so-called charities to fund terrorist organizations around the globe.[17]

Palestinian Terrorism

Today, anti-Zionists assert that any terrorist actions against Israel and her citizens stem from the aftermath of the 1967 Six-Day War, which resulted in Israel gaining control of the Gaza Strip, Judea, and Samaria. Israel's detractors unjustifiably call this event "the occupation" of the Palestinian land and people by the Israeli army.

This deceitful label cannot be further from the truth. You cannot occupy land for which you possess the title deed. The Palestine Liberation Organization (PLO) was founded in 1964. At the time, Gaza was under the control of Egypt and Jordan, who also controlled Judea and Sam*aria. So, when the PLO began attacking Israelis in 1964, what "occupation" were* they fighting?

Obviously, the answer is that the Palestinian leadership has considered the entire State of Israel illegitimate, even though a Jewish remnant has remained in the land for more than three thousand years.[18]

The Palestine Liberation Organization

Created by the Arab League, the PLO was led by Yasser Arafat and his Palestinian nationalist party, Fatah. Arafat was an out-and-out terrorist, a cold-blooded killer who had more Jewish blood on his hands than any man in the twentieth century other than Adolf Hitler.

The PLO's national charter declared its intent to overthrow the State of Israel, calling Zionism an "illegal" and "colonialist" movement.[19] The charter further stated that the entire region designated as the British Mandate for Palestine in 1920, which includes all of modern Israel and Jordan, belongs entirely to the Palestinian Arabs. It asserted that only Jews who were living in the land prior to 1917 had a right to remain and finally, the PLO's charter proclaimed that violence was the only way to liberate Palestine from the Zionist presence.[20]

During the 1960s and '70s, the PLO and its affiliated groups conducted terrorist operations from Jordan, Lebanon, and throughout Europe. In May of 1972, Black September, a PLO splinter group, hijacked a Belgian airliner in Vienna bound for Tel Aviv. Four terrorists held ninety passengers hostage and forced the pilot to land in Israel while they demanded the release of 315 Palestinian terrorists from Israel's prisons. After disabling the plane, IDF commandos, disguised as maintenance workers, boarded the airliner and subdued the terrorists, but not before one of the passengers was fatally wounded.[21]

Later that year, Black September operatives broke into the apartments of Israeli athletes at the Munich Olympics, killed two in the initial scuffle, and took nine more hostages. German authorities attempted to rescue the hostages but failed, and all nine Israeli hostages were murdered.[22]

Another infamous Palestinian terror attack took place in 1976. Two members of the PLO faction named the Popular Front for the Liberation of Palestine and two German terrorist sympathizers hijacked a flight from Paris, forcing the plane to land at Entebbe Airport in Uganda.

After landing, the terrorists released the non-Jewish passengers and held 105 Jews hostage. For one week, Israel's government negotiated with the terrorists while the IDF planned a daring rescue mission. Seven days later, the IDF landed at Entebbe, and within an hour, the hostages were rescued. Israel lost three people that day—two hostages and the leader of the mission, Yoni Netanyahu.[23] Yoni's brother Benjamin would go on to become the prime minister of Israel and serve in that leadership role longer than anyone in Israel's history.

In 1978, members of the PLO operating in Lebanon hijacked an Israeli bus full of civilians and killed thirty-eight hostages. In response, the IDF crossed the Lebanese border to push the terrorists farther north. The ensuing conflict dragged on for four years while PLO terrorists hiding in Lebanon conducted hundreds of attacks on Israelis. Israel could no longer tolerate the buildup of a massive PLO army in Lebanon, and on June 6, 1982, launched a full-scale war known as Operation Peace for Galilee to root out Yasser Arafat and his terrorists thugs from southern Lebanon.[24]

A NEW ERA OF HOLY WAR

In 1979, the radical Shia Muslim leader Ayatollah Khomeini overthrew the shah of Iran and his secular government, instituting an Islamic revolution. Inspired by the writings of Sayyid Qutb and the ideology of the Muslim Brotherhood, Khomeini reinterpreted Shia theology and transformed the historically peaceful religious minority sect into one committed to violent jihad.[25]

What Qutb did to create extremist Sunni Muslims, Khomeini did for the Shiite Muslims, and thereby furthered the war against the Jews.[26] Iran's radicalized government during the 1980s and 1990s made jihad its primary focus against Israel, Jews, and their allies worldwide.

IRAN: THE HEAD OF THE SNAKE

In 2008, King Abdullah of Saudi Arabia repeatedly urged the United States to "cut off the head of the snake" by launching military strikes to destroy Iran's nuclear program.[*]

Despite the warning, the Obama administration chose to take another route by spearheading the Iran Deal, formally known as the Joint Comprehensive Plan of Action (JCPOA). The deal was a tragic miscarriage of foreign policy and has gone down as one of the worst diplomatic blunders in modern American history.

President Obama and the leaders of China, France, Germany, Russia, the United Kingdom, and other members of the European Union reached an agreement with Iran in 2015.[27] This fatally flawed pact released more than 100 billion dollars in cash to Iran—the world's leading terrorist state. Iran, in turn, used the cash to support its terrorist proxies and continue its maniacal dream of producing a nuclear bomb to annihilate Israel, America, and the entire western hemisphere.

As bad as this was, the situation got worse.

In the fall of 2016, President Obama authorized the government to shell out an additional $1.7 billion to Iran's coffers. Supposedly, America was paying back a deposit of $400 million plus $1.3 billion in interest which we "owed" as a result of a failed arms deal made between the Carter Administration and the shah of Iran in 1979. To add insult to injury, this "payback" was not wired bank-to-bank but was sent to Iran in various world currencies via US military cargo planes.[28]

One can only assume that the intended purpose of this clandestine transport of cash was for nefarious global transactions, to include Iran's funding of a massive buildup of missiles inside

---

[*]   https://www.reuters.com/article/us-wikileaks-iran-saudis/cut-off-head-of-snake-saudis
      -told-u-s-on-iran-idUSTRE6AS02B20101129.

Lebanon under Hezbollah's control. This calculated "reimburse-ment" was a deliberate act of betrayal against Israel—America's only friend in the Middle East.

On May 8, 2018, President Trump announced he would not renew the Iran sanction waivers established by the Iran Deal, effectively withdrawing the United States from the disastrous nuclear agreement with Tehran. It is hardly surprising that our president, an ardent supporter of Israel, chose not to continue this agreement, of which he said, "The Iran Deal was one of the worst and most one-sided transactions the United States has ever entered into."[*]

Prime Minister Benjamin Netanyahu later exposed, through Project Amad, the fact that Iran had lied to the International Atomic Energy Agency (IAEA) about shutting down their nuclear program. Netanyahu revealed on global television that the Mossad had discovered Iran's Atomic Archive and the existence of a secret nuclear facility, further confirming what we long believed: Iran's unrelenting pursuit of nuclear weapons continues to threaten the security of the entire world.

In addition to pursuing its nuclear capablities, the "head of the snake" used some of the funds to support terrorist armies such as Hezbollah in Lebanon and Hamas in Gaza. By late 2018, the Jewish Institute for National Security of America (JINSA), led by several retired senior U.S. military officials, reported, "Today, Hezbollah possesses more firepower than 95 percent of the world's conventional militaries, and more rockets and missiles than all European NATO members combined."[†]

Aside from the billions in cash, the Iran Deal contained within it a weak inspection and verification system, an automatic sunset

---

[*] https://www.whitehouse.gov/briefings-statements/president-donald-j-trump-ending-united-states-participation-unacceptable-iran-deal/.

[†] https://www.jns.org/hezbollah-has-more-firepower-than-95-percent-of-worlds-conventional-militaries-report-warns/.

provision, and no restrictions on Iran's ballistic missile program.[29] Most are not familiar with the critically short timeline of the sunset provision, which dictated the automatic expiration of the already feeble constraints included in the Iran nuclear deal.

In 2020, the UN ban on Iranian arms exports and imports would have lifted, allowing Iran to further support its terrorists proxies; by 2023 the UN ban on assistance to Iran's ballistic missile program and their ability to manufacture centrifuges would end; in 2025, most economic sanctions on Iran would cease; by 2026 nearly all nuclear restrictions would terminate; and by 2031 all restrictions would end, giving Iran multiple paths to a nuclear weapon in a very short period of time—a journey they have never strayed from.*

Since withdrawing from the Iran deal, the Trump administration has engaged in an ever-increasing campaign of maximum pressure against the Islamic Republic. This pressure campaign includes intensifying sanctions against specific industries, entities, and individuals associated with Iran's support for terrorism and its nuclear ambitions. The United States has made it clear that we will not sit idly by as Iran prepares to attack us and our allies.

Undoubtedly, the campaign is achieving its goals. For instance, Iran's oil exports decreased from 2.3 million barrels per day (bpd) in early 2018, prior to US sanctions, to just one tenth of that number, an estimated 248,000 bpd at the beginning of 2020.[†]

President Trump increased pressure on Iran in mid-2019, by imposing further sanctions on Iran's supreme leader and other high-ranking government officials, locking down billions of dollars

---

* https://www.aipac.org/-/media/publications/policy-and-politics/fact-sheets/other/the-iran-nuclear-deal-expiration-dates-and-consequences.pdf.

† Dalga Khatinoglu, "Iran Crude Oil Exports Drop to Less Than 250,000 Bpd in February" (March 2, 2020), *Radio Farda*, https://en.radiofarda.com/a/iran-crude-oil-exports-drop-to-less-than-250-000-bpd-in-february/30464729.html, accessed April 2, 2020.

in assets. As a result of combined sanctions, the Iranian economy has fallen into a deep depression, the value of their currency has taken a dive, leading to shortages of imported goods and products. Additionally, the International Monetary Fund projected that inflation would soon soar to over 35 percent.*

Hezbollah

When Israel withdrew from Lebanon, Hezbollah remained and grew stronger until it became a dominant political and military force in the country, effectively placing the Lebanese government under the thumb of Iran.[30] In collaboration with Iran, Hezbollah has become one of the deadliest terror organizations in the world. Motivated by the twisted theology that blames every social and political problem on the Jews, Hezbollah has spread its anti-Semitic terror throughout the world.

During the 1990s, Hezbollah sent its operatives to Argentina, where they bombed the Israeli Embassy in Buenos Aires. Two years later, they bombed a Jewish community center in the same city. In 2012, Hezbollah bombed an Israeli tour bus in Bulgaria.[31] Hezbollah's leader, Hassan Nasrallah, has made it clear he considers all Jews anywhere in the world to be targets for extermination.

Nasrallah was quoted in Lebanon's *Daily Star* as saying, "If they [Jews] all gather in Israel, it will save us the trouble of going after them worldwide."[32] Iran's leaders and its proxy, Hezbollah, have made no secret of their desire to complete Hitler's work of eradicating the Jewish people from the face of the earth. The State Department's 2018 Country Report on Terrorism confirmed Iran's expansive reach:

---

* Six charts that show how hard US sanctions have hit Iran https://www.bbc.com/news/world-middle-east-48119109.

Iran continued its terrorist-related activity in 2018, including support for Hizballah, Palestinian terrorist groups in Gaza, and various groups in Syria, Iraq and throughout the Middle East. Iran used the Islamic Revolutionary Guard Corps–Quds Force (IRGC-QF) to provide support to terrorist organizations, provide cover for associated covert operations, and create instability in the region. Iran has acknowledged the involvement of the IRGC-QF in the Iraq and Syria conflicts, and the IRGD-QF is Iran's primary mechanism for cultivating and supporting terrorists abroad. Iran also uses regional surrogate forces to provide sufficient deniability to try to shield it from the consequences of its aggressive policies.

In an interview with Iran's supreme leader, Ayatollah Ali Khamenei, Nasrallah stated the following:

It should be noted that all data, investigations and information show that such an event [the elimination of Israel] will occur, but the realization of this matter is not unconditional, and it would happen under certain conditions. Therefore, if we resist and continue on the path we have taken, factual and field conditions indicate that Israel will not be able to remain in the region in the next 25 years.[*]

IDF sources estimate that Hezbollah currently has an arsenal of 130,000 to 150,000 short-, medium-, and long-range missiles and rockets. During the entire Second Lebanon War, Hezbollah fired approximately 4,000 rockets into Israel. However, it is projected that during the next war, they will fire as many as 1,500 to 2,000 missiles into Israel *every day.* In addition, Hezbollah has amassed a trained

---

[*] Taken from the full text of Kamenei's interview with Sayyid Hassan Nasrallah October 1, 2019.

fighting force of approximately fifty thousand soldiers, with another ten thousand fighters in southern Syria ready to join the fight.[33]

Sadly, the lethal goal of wiping Israel off the map is not letting up. In June of 2018, the Ayatollah Ali Khamenei once again threatened to annihilate Israel on social media, anti-Semitism's latest propaganda tool.

> "Our stance against Israel is the same stance we have always taken. #Israel is a malignant cancerous tumor…that has to be removed and eradicated: it is possible and it will happen."[34]

The significance of the Ayatollah's statements was not lost on Israel's prime minister, Benjamin Netanyahu, who responded to the threat by declaring,

> Ayatollah Khamenei, the ruler of Iran, declared his intention to destroy the State of Israel. Yesterday he explained how he would do this—with the unrestricted enrichment of uranium in order to produce an arsenal of nuclear bombs. We are not surprised. We will not allow Iran to obtain nuclear weapons.[35]

In early July 2020, a massive explosion at Iran's highly sensitive Natanz uranium-enrichment nuclear complex was believed to have been an act of sabotage. The Natanz facility, known as the Iran Centrifuge Assembly Center, was permitted to operate under the terms of the 2015 Iran nuclear agreement. Experts agree that with additional processing, the uranium could potentially be converted into weapons-grade fuel for nuclear bombs. Iranian officials stated that the blast caused "significant" damage and implied that

US or Israeli operatives were responsible, however, neither country has acknowledged any involvement in the incident.* The significant damage caused by the explosion has set back Iran's uranium enrichment program for now.

To intensify this volatile situation, Iran's support of Hamas and the Palestinian Islamic Jihad in Gaza, its military entrenchment in Syria, and its support for Hezbollah in Lebanon makes it the largest state sponsor of terror in the world and positions itself on three of Israel's borders.

Time is running out.

Al-Qaeda

The era of the Islamic fundamentalist revival which produced Iran's Islamic Revolution and generated Hezbollah, also birthed al-Qaeda in the 1980s. Osama bin Laden, perpetrator of the 9/11 attacks on the United States, was likewise motivated by the anti-Semitic writings of Sayyid Qutb and embraced his theology of jihad as a major tenet of faith.[36]

Surprisingly, or perhaps not, both al-Qaeda and Osama bin Laden's successors found a sympathetic partner and safe haven in the Republic of Iran, despite their different interpretations of Islamic theology. Predictably, their common bond is their hatred of the Jewish people and America, Israel's strongest ally.

ISIS

Out of al-Qaeda was born a radical and barbaric splinter group now known as the Islamic State in Iraq and Syria (ISIS).[37] In 2014, President Obama infamously dismissed ISIS as the "JV team." However, the world soon learned how naïve his assumption was and

---

* https://www.washingtonpost.com/national-security/signs-increasingly-point-to-sabotage -in-fiery-explosion-at-iranian-nuclear-complex/2020/07/06/d10.

witnessed a surge in mass-casualty terrorism at the hands of ISIS fanatics as they beheaded their victims, including Jews, Christians, and Muslims alike.

ISIS's goal of creating an Islamic caliphate in the Middle East appears to have been weakened by recent losses in Syria and Iraq, helped in part by President Trump's military mission to eradicate them in Syria. Nevertheless, ISIS has been extraordinarily successful at exporting its anti-Semitic and anti-Western theology over the internet to a new generation of homegrown terrorists across the globe.

With their dreams of a caliphate slipping away, ISIS has turned its attention to Israel. Israel's intelligence experts are carefully watching the growth of ISIS in the Sinai Desert along Israel's western border with Egypt and the attempt by ISIS operatives to challenge Hamas for supremacy in Gaza.

In October 2019, the US conducted a raid to capture Abu Bakr al-Baghdadi, the leader of ISIS. To evade capture, al-Baghdadi detonated a suicide belt, killing himself and three children in the blast.[*] With its leaders gone, the terrorists are attempting to regroup.

General Joseph Votel, former commander of US Central Command, testified to the House Armed Services Committee that ISIS is lying in wait for a resurgence. "ISIS made a 'calculated decision' to preserve their capabilities by taking their chances in camps for internally displace persons [refugee camps] and going to ground-in remote areas [caves and tunnels], waiting for the right time to resurge."[†]

Remember this truth—Even though ISIS's leader is dead, ISIS is not.

---

[*] https://www.bbc.com/news/world-us-canada-50200339.
[†] https://www.wilsoncenter.org/article/timeline-the-rise-spread-and-fall-the-islamic-state.

Hamas

Hamas, an Arabic acronym for the Islamic Resistance Movement, was created by the Muslim Brotherhood in the 1980s. It supposedly originated as a "social welfare" organization for the benefit of Palestinians in Gaza.[38] However, this radical group quickly mutated into a terrorist organization dedicated to attacking Israel and brutally enforcing strict Islamic law on the Palestinians under its influence.

Hamas gained power due to the frustration of some Palestinian extremists with Yasser Arafat's political doublespeak. Arafat often engaged in "diplomatic" talks with Israel in which he promised to restrain the PLO and the Fatah party's support for terrorism. But in reality, Arafat was only posturing for sympathy from the United Nations and never renounced terrorism. But his mere pretense of compromise with Israel enraged Islamist radicals. Thus, Hamas recruited an even more extreme brand of terrorist than the PLO and dedicated itself to the complete destruction of Israel with no room for negotiation.[39]

In an attempt to garner goodwill from the Palestinians, while also relieving the IDF's burden of overseeing the Gaza Strip, Israel unilaterally withdrew from Gaza in 2006. In addition, nine thousand Jewish families left their homes and livelihoods to give peace yet another chance. Hamas, however, took advantage of the power vacuum created by Israel's absence and easily won the 2007 elections. Instead of providing a foundation for future reconciliation, Gaza has become a launching pad for continuous rocket fire into Israel to this day.

After their defeat, the Fatah-led Palestinian Authority government was forced out of Gaza. The results were immediately disastrous. Hamas murdered Palestinians suspected of sympathizing or collaborating with Israel or its political rivals. While creating horror on the streets of Gaza, the newly elected Hamas-controlled government also maintained a constant barrage of missiles into Israel.[40]

Hamas's charter, like that of Hezbollah, specifically dedicates itself to the total annihilation of the Jewish state. Moreover, like Hezbollah, Hamas intentionally targets Israeli civilians and uses its own civilian population as human shields. One of the worst crimes against humanity perpetrated by these two terrorist organizations is their practice of deliberately hiding their weapons in civilian areas. This attempt to force Israel to kill innocent men, women, and children in order to defend itself from the terrorists is a barbarously calculated maneuver.[41]

The purpose of such an evil strategy is obvious: Hamas wants to inflame worldwide hatred against Israel and thereby force the Jewish State to either commit national suicide by standing down or suffer extreme worldwide political and economic retaliation for acting in self-defense. This despicable plan has empowered Israel's enemies to falsely portray the Jewish nation as a "cold-hearted monster," when it is Hamas and Hezbollah who are guilty of war crimes under international law. This is a classic illustration where truth becomes a lie and lies have become truth.

Since the spring of 2018, terrorists in the Gaza Strip have launched hundreds of helium balloons and kites bearing flammable materials into Israeli territory, starting over 2,300 fires. The "terror kites," some of which are decorated with swastikas, are fitted with a long string to which a Molotov cocktail, a pouch of burning fuel, or an improvised explosive device is attached causing them to explode upon impact.

Nearly 8,700 acres, or 13.5 square miles, of agricultural fields, forest, and grasslands,* which is more than half of Israel's nature reserves, have been burned due to these destructive kites, causing

---

* *The Times of Israel*, July 10, 2019, Judah Ari Gross.

multiple millions of dollars' worth of damage.[42] As the IDF has declared, "It's not a game—it's a war."[43]

In the middle of July 2018, shortly after the start of the kite onslaught, Gaza terrorists fired over two hundred rockets at Israeli border towns. This massive rocket barrage is the most serious outbreak of fighting since Operation Protective Edge in 2014. In response, the IDF bombed dozens of Hamas posts in the Gaza Strip including two terror tunnels, a Hamas headquarters post, and a high-rise building that served as a Hamas urban warfare training facility.[44] Prime Minister Netanyahu said of the incursion, "Our policy is clear—if anyone attacks us, we will deal them a forceful counterattack. I hope that they [Hamas] got the message. If not, they will in the future."[45]

Israel cannot tolerate this devastation much longer. The Gaza Strip is a ticking time bomb that could explode into a full-fledged war against Israel at any moment.

Remember this truth: Hamas has no interest in a Palestinian state alongside Israel, regardless of whatever concessions Israelis are willing to make on borders or within the city of Jerusalem. Hamas wants it all, and it won't stop until it achieves its goal.

Additionally, Hamas's ceaseless fight for control of the Palestinians in Judea and Samaria (West Bank), and its growing popularity there, threaten to unseat Fatah as the ruling party of the Palestinian Authority. The sustained incitement to terrorism and the extreme anti-Semitic rhetoric coming from the PLO, Hamas, and ISIS, have inspired a new breed of terrorism. Whereas previous terror attacks were usually planned and carried out by organized terror cells, deadly "lone wolf" attacks have become commonplace since 2015.

Lone Wolf

Lone Wolf terrorists are often young Palestinian men and women who spontaneously attack Jews with whatever weapon is at their disposal. The PLO encourages these attacks by providing pensions and salaries to the murderers and their families.

In early 2018, the United States passed a law, the Taylor Force Act, restricting American foreign aid to the Palestinian Authority until it ends their "pay to slay" reward system. However, in defiance, the Palestinian Authority announced that it was increasing the budget for this terrorist incentive from $347 million to $403 million.[46]

Clearly, this "unholy" war against the Jews over the last century, and the emphasis on violent jihad in the last forty years, are far from over. Although the various radical Islamic terror groups are in competition with each other, they are united in their intense hatred of Israel and the Jewish people. The spirit of Haman and Hitler lives within their theology, their political discourse, their youth brainwashing programs, and their culture of death worship.

Looming above it all is the shadow of Iran's ambition for a nuclear holocaust that threatens to spark a third world war with the goal of destabilizing the entire Middle East and rebuilding the Persian Empire.

Iran's subversive acts mark its obsession with anti-Semitism which leads people to value death more than life. This warped philosophy produces suffering for millions of innocent Arabs, Christians, and Muslims alike, who become collateral damage in the ongoing war against the Jews.

THE RESURGENCE OF JEWISH HATRED

Jewish hatred did not originate or end with Adolf Hitler. As I have discussed, God's Chosen have suffered harassment and persecution since ancient times, and this unrivaled animosity lives on worldwide.

Anti-Semitism has never truly disappeared from society; however, for a season, the terrors of the Holocaust significantly suppressed its public expression. Jewish bigotry in America never advanced to the lethal level of Nazi-led Germany, but it was nonetheless widespread.

As the years have elapsed, recollections have become dim, and many of the survivors have passed on, and as a result, the global condemnation of the Jewish State of Israel and its people has intensified. Anti-Semitism can hide in plain sight but is still very prevalent in social, religious, political, and educational circles, as well as within some so-called influential progressive movements.

Moreover, the advent of social media has caused anti-Semitic propaganda and threats against Jews to soar. Sadly, the internet provides the "facelessness" that cowardly anti-Jewish extremists thrive on, giving them the opportunity to influence millions with their false rhetoric.

In recent years, there has been a deeply concerning upsurge of anti-Semitism. Some of the settings may have changed, but the hateful discourse remains the same—accusing the Jewish people of long-standing claims ranging from dual loyalty to using their influence to control the world because they have a "disproportionate amount of political and economic power."

The manifestations of Jewish hatred are becoming increasingly blatant as we witness an increase of violent anti-Semitic incidents worldwide. We see it with the reemergence of Replacement Theology within the church, and the BDS movement.

Malcolm Hoenlein, a close friend who leads the Conference of Presidents of Major American Jewish Organizations, believes that for several years it was accepted for Americans to say that they were *anti-Israel*; however, "today it is accepted to say I am *anti-Jewish*." This, Hoenlein believes, is partly due to the anti-Israel BDS movement, which provides a "cover for anti-Semitism."[47]

College campus students and tenured professors have become more comfortable with not only criticizing Israel but also attacking

Jewish students for simply being Jewish, or because they support the ideals of the Jewish state. Increasingly, non-Jewish students are being maligned and spat upon for supporting their Jewish friends on campuses throughout America and the world.

Why have America's college campuses become a hotbed for anti-Semitism? Because the enemy knows the future belongs to the next generation. Here, hatred for Israel is disguised as a deserved consequence for the false accusation that the Jewish nation is an "aggressor" against the "oppressed" Palestinians. This deceptive portrayal of being an "apartheid regime"—one that discriminates on the grounds of race—has caused severe damage to the way the world views Israel.

No one can deny that anti-Semitism is raging in today's society. Sadly, in the last few months we have seen the horrifying consequences of this growing evil. The year 2018 recorded 1,879 anti-Semitic incidents in the US, including the deadliest attack on Jews in the history of our nation: the massacre of eleven Jewish worshippers at the Tree of Life Synagogue in Pittsburgh.[*]

While anti-Semitic attacks were flat from the previous year, the 2018 total is 48 percent higher than the number of incidents documented in 2016 and 99 percent higher than 2015. The 2019 totals, though not yet final, are pointing to a nearly 20 percent increase.

On the last day of Passover in 2019, a man walked into a Chabad synagogue near San Diego and opened fire, leaving one woman dead and three other people injured.[†] In mid-December, three civilians, one officer, and two suspects were killed after a targeted attack inside the JC Kosher Supermarket in Jersey City, New Jersey.[‡] On the

[*] https://www.adl.org/news/press-releases/anti-semitic-incidents-remained-at-near-historic-levels-in-2018-assaults.
[†] https://www.usatoday.com/story/news/nation/2019/04/27/passover-shooting-california-synagogue-poway-san-diego/3600900002/.
[‡] https://www.jns.org/shooting-near-kosher-supermarket-in-new-jersey-dead-and-wounded/.

seventh day of Hanukah, five members of an ultra-Orthodox Hasidic Jewish congregation were stabbed by a man wielding a machete-type knife who barged into the holiday celebration at a rabbi's home in a New York City suburb.[*]

The novel coronavirus outbreak did not deter anti-Semitism; instead it caused some to "retool" their prejudices against the Jewish people and Israel. Neo-Nazis spread new conspiracy theories that the Jews were responsible for creating the coronavirus pandemic, similar to the false claims regarding the Black Death of Europe in the fourteenth century. A professor at California State University tweeted in reference to Israel's shutdown during COVID-19 that, "Israel will—I am sure—have different medical procedures for Jews and non-Jews. Non-Jews will be put in mass prisons."[†]

How quickly we have forgotten that words and deeds matter.

It sickens my heart to think of what our Jewish friends are thinking and feeling as they are confronted with the vicious scourge of anti-Semitism once again. What do they tell their children and grandchildren? Who will stand beside them? Who will come to their defense?

While in recent decades, Christians have embraced the post-Holocaust slogan *Never Again*, the majority have remained heart-breakingly silent. However, Elie Wiesel poignantly defined this phrase,

"Never again" becomes more than a slogan: It's a prayer, a promise, a vow. There will never again be hatred...Never again jail and torture. Never again, the suffering of innocent people, or the shooting of starving, frightened, terrified

* https://www.nbcnews.com/news/us-news/four-shot-injured-southern-california -synagogue-n999191.

† https://www.washingtonexaminer.com/opinion/anti-semitism-rages-during -coronavirus.

children. And never again the glorification of base, ugly, dark violence. It's a prayer.

Remember this truth—Never Again is more than a slogan—it is also a verb. Never Again requires more than words—it requires action!

You may tag a sophisticated label on anti-Semitism, but it is still sin, and as sin, it damns the soul. This Jewish hatred is once again spreading like a contagious virus. It is a cancer growing on the soul of America and the world. Anti-Semitism is not just a Jewish problem—it's the world's problem. I fully agree with Malcolm Hoenlein that fighting anti-Semitism starts with the Jewish community, but he continues:

> ...it doesn't end with it. This is not our problem. It's society's problem. It's Christianity's problem. It's everybody's problem, when there's hatred against Jews. We're the victims; we're not the cause of it. It's not because we did something wrong. It's because of who we are and our values.[48]

THE BLESSING OF BLESSING ISRAEL

How does our Christian walk intersect with Israel? I have said that it is not possible for Christians to love Jesus Christ and hate the Jewish people living across the street. The thousands of years of Jewish hatred that is imbedded in our world culture has caused many Christians to have anti-Semitic leanings or, at best, to be indifferent toward the Jewish people.

I was guilty of indifference—I knew that the nation of Israel was important in Bible prophecy, but I did not connect my personal involvement with the Jewish people as being a vital part of God's plan for all believers until I visited Israel.

I made my first journey to the Holy Land over forty years ago, and as I mentioned earlier, I went there a tourist and returned home a Zionist.

I stood at the Sea of Galilee where Jesus miraculously fed the multitudes and healed the sick. I prayed at the Western Wall where the prophets Ezra and Nehemiah sought the face of God, and I walked the cobblestoned streets of the Old City where my Redeemer carried His cross to Calvary—I had found my spiritual home.

I left Israel with a longing to discover the history of the Promised Land, and during my years of study, I unearthed the Jewish roots of my Christian faith. Sadly, I also came face-to-face with the virulent bigotry that birthed the Crusades, the Spanish Inquisition, and the harvest of hatred that produced the Holocaust.

But most importantly, I realized God's boundless love for the Jewish people, for His Covenant Land, and for the city of Jerusalem. Jesus Christ was and always will be Jewish. When He spoke to the Samaritan woman, He identified Himself with the Jewish people, *"You worship what you do not know; we [Jesus and the Jewish people] know what we worship, for salvation is of the Jews"* (John 4:22).

God promises to bless those who bless Israel and His people. Paul wrote, *"For if the Gentiles have been partakers of their [the Jews'] spiritual things, their [the Gentiles'] duty is also to minister to them in material things"* (Romans 15:27). Repeatedly Scripture chronicles the principle of God blessing those who bless the Jewish people.

Jacob and Laban

This Bible principle is illustrated with the story of Jacob and Laban. Jacob, one of the patriarchs, worked for a Syrian by the name of Laban. Laban changed Jacob's wages ten times, each time to his loss. Jacob became disillusioned and informed Laban he was leaving.

Laban responded remorsefully, saying, *"Please stay, if I have found favor in your eyes, for I have learned by experience that the LORD has blessed me for your sake"* (Genesis 30:27).

Laban was one Gentile who recognized that the blessings of God followed the Jewish people.

Joseph and Pharaoh

The promise of blessing continues in the story of Joseph and Pharaoh. Joseph saved the Gentile world from starvation through his divine power to interpret dreams. Pharaoh blessed Joseph by making him the prime minister of the nation and by giving to his family the rich farmlands of Goshen, which were the best in Egypt. Pharaoh treated Joseph and the Jewish people as an extension of his own family.

In accordance with Joseph's interpretation of Pharaoh's dream, the seven years of abundance began, and Joseph erected large storehouses all over the country, gathering the surplus of grain that flooded the markets. The seven years of plenty passed and the years of famine began; now the entire country found itself dependent upon the provisions stored away under the wise administration of Joseph.

During the time of lack, the people sold their land and livestock to Pharaoh in exchange for food. Through the genius of Joseph, the stored food not only provided nourishment for the masses but also purchased vast amounts of real estate outside of Egypt, thereby enlarging Pharaoh's kingdom. The Gentile king blessed the Jewish people, and God saw to it that he was blessed beyond measure.

The Centurion's Servant

Why was Jesus Christ willing to go to the house of the centurion in Capernaum and heal his sick servant? The Roman centurion deserved God's blessing, for he demonstrated his love for the Jews by building a synagogue in Israel (Luke 7:5).

When you display practical acts of love to bless the Jewish people and the State of Israel, God will bless you.

Cornelius of Caesarea

Why did God the Father select the house of Cornelius in Caesarea to be the first Gentile house in Israel to receive the Gospel? The answer is given repeatedly in the book of Acts, which says: *"a devout man [Cornelius] and one who feared God with all his household, who gave alms generously to the people, and prayed to God always"* (Acts 10:2). What *people* did Cornelius give alms to? They were the Jewish people who lived around him.

Acts 10:4 states, *"Your prayers and your alms have come up for a memorial before God."* Acts 10:31 reads, *"Your alms are remembered in the sight of God."*

The point is made three times in the same chapter: a righteous Gentile who demonstrated his unconditional love for the Jewish people in a practical manner was divinely selected by heaven to be the first house to receive the Gospel of salvation and the first to receive the outpouring of the Holy Spirit.

These combined scriptures verify that prosperity (Genesis 12:3; Psalm 122:6), divine healing (Luke 7:1–5), and the outpouring of the Holy Spirit (Acts 10) came first to the Gentiles who blessed the Jewish people and the nation of Israel in a practical manner.

The Bible also teaches that love is not what you say—love is what you do (1 John 3:18). It has been said that "a bell is not a bell until you ring it…and love is not love until you give it away."[49]

It is imperative that we express our unconditional love and support for Israel and the Jewish people through practical acts of kindness and prayer.

Pray for Jerusalem

Remember this truth: When it comes to prophecy and the End of Days, it's all about Jerusalem. In Psalm 122:6, King David commands all people to *"pray for the peace of Jerusalem: 'May they prosper who love you.'"* Righteousness and peace are destined to spring forth from Jerusalem to all the nations of the earth; therefore, it benefits all people to pray for her good. It is the only city God mandates us to pray for in Scripture.

Daniel prayed three times each day toward the city of Jerusalem while he was in Babylon. Even though these prayers were outlawed by the government, he chose to remain in prayer at the cost of facing the lions' den. The Lord protected Daniel for his courage and obedience and intervened on his behalf so he could continue to pray for the City of God.

The scriptural principle of personal prosperity is tied to blessing Israel and praying for the city of Jerusalem. This prosperity is not purely associated with material blessings but also includes the Lord's spiritual blessings, supernatural protection , and abundant favor.

The principle of blessing the Jewish people is as applicable today as it was in biblical times, and it will be especially relevant in the days to come, especially as Jerusalem becomes the pawn for those who desire to bring destruction to the Jewish state.

The Watchmen

The future of Jerusalem is at the core of God's blueprint for eternity. Make no mistake: God will remove, reclaim, restore, reorder, renovate, redistribute, recommit, and redeem until the Holy City becomes the crowning gem of all the cities on earth.

Biblical watchmen were stationed on city walls (2 Samuel 18:25; 2 Kings 9:18; Psalms 127:1; Isaiah 62:6), on watch towers (2 Kings 9:17; 17:9; 18:8), or on hilltops (Jeremiah 31:6). It was their duty to alert the king of an imminent hostile action against the city (2 Samuel 18:24–27; 2 Kings 9:17–20).[50] The past atrocities committed against the Jewish people and the city of Jerusalem attest to the reality that the church, as a whole, has failed to accomplish the mandate God set before us as watchmen over Israel.

> *I have set watchmen on your walls, O Jerusalem; they shall never hold their peace day or night. You who make mention of the LORD, do not keep silent, and give Him no rest till He establishes and till He makes Jerusalem a praise in the earth* (Isaiah 62:6–7).

Martin Luther King Jr. said, "There comes a time when silence is betrayal." Watchmen should not remain silent or passive when Jerusalem is threatened—we must act in its defense. God has appointed Christians as guardians, and as such, we should never allow Jerusalem to be threatened—by suicide bombers, missile attacks, political propaganda, or as a "bargaining chip in achieving peace."[51]

The Jews are God's Covenant people, and Jerusalem is His everlasting city. Jehovah God never intended the heart of Israel to be divided. Israel, including Jerusalem, belongs to the Jewish people, and the Almighty declares that anyone who attempts to persuade, coerce, or terrorize His chosen people to end Jewish control of Israel, including Jerusalem, is in direct opposition to His known will (Joel 3).

The God of Abraham, Isaac, and Jacob intends for His people to shine forth as a bright light to the Gentiles. He loves and delights in the Jewish people and rejoices over them—they are the apple of His eye. The Lord will protect His Holy City at all costs. Rest assured that Jerusalem's future will not be dictated by "The Quartet"

(United Nations, United States, European Union, and R
Vatican, by Iran or any radical extremist terrorist groups—
is in the hands of God Himself.

Unlike during World War II, this time Christians must accept our role as watchmen on the walls of Jerusalem and sound the alarm with our united voices when Israel and the Jewish people are threatened—God Almighty has entrusted our generation with this crucial assignment, and we must not fail.

The world is still grappling with the age-old conflict between two half-brothers—one, the father of the Jewish nation, and the other, the father of the Arab states. The outcome of this struggle will affect every person on earth. Results from any future negotiation for peace or the lack of it will be noticed at the gas pump, the grocery store, and with banking institutions worldwide. If you think the battle for Jerusalem won't affect you—think again!

Please note that the battle for control over the Promised Land, and specifically Jerusalem, is not merely political or economic. This is foremost a spiritual struggle, and the repercussions of the strife between these ancient foes will continue to reverberate across the globe until Messiah comes.

I encourage you to understand God's plan for His Holy City, because with every passing sunset, we move one day closer to when Jerusalem will take center stage in world events. As the conflict rages and world leaders strive to find a peaceful solution to the problems in the Middle East, the significance of Jerusalem will only increase.

This Time

The nation of Israel was rebirthed out of its passion for survival. The Jewish people must never be without a country again. From out of the concentration camps and crematoriums of Europe echoes the cry, "Never again!" Let our united voices of unconditional love and steadfast support be heard in the courts of heaven until the End of Days when Jerusalem becomes the praise of all the earth.

Our generation is headed for a perfect storm, and in order not to repeat the mistakes of the past, we must learn from this simple mandate: "Thou shalt not be a victim, thou shalt not be a perpetrator but, above all, thou shalt not be a bystander."[52]

This time in world history Christians must not stand idly by.

This time righteous people must take a stand against evil.

This time we must circle the wagons and fight the battle against Jewish hatred.

This time Christians and Jews must unite and win the war against anti-Semitism.

SECTION TWO

THE EMPIRES

CHAPTER 5

THE BIRTH OF
THE EMPIRES

This agglomeration which was called and which still calls itself the Holy Roman Empire was neither holy, nor Roman, nor an empire. —Voltaire

---

An empire is a political concept in which one state dominates over another state, or a series of states. An emperor or monarch commonly rules over an empire. On the simplest level, the control of the "core state" over the "peripheral state or states" is accomplished through military occupation or other formal political intervention, but it can also include economic, cultural, religious, and ideological influence.[1]

Since the beginning of time, it has been man's desire to rule over others. Conquerors have taken lands by persuasion, by treaties, and often, by force. Those who lived in seized territories would either surrender their allegiance to the new leaders or face enslavement or execution. History is cluttered with kingdoms that rose and fell from power, which are now forgotten and consigned to obscure and dusty corners of abandoned libraries.

The desire to amass an empire, with all its inherent wealth and power, has never escaped man's imperious nature. However, as civilization has evolved, so too have the mechanisms of gaining and maintaining power. In today's world, at least in the familiar cultural confines of Western civilization, most who seek to build and control an empire attempt to do so through business agreements, mergers, or diplomatic negotiations rather than by bloody battles.

The notion of emperors and empires is outdated in most parts of the world where individual freedoms and democratic forms of government have replaced violent conquests and authoritarian rule. It is important to remember that democracies (governments ruled by the people) are a relatively new concept when viewed in the scope of human history. Yet what goes around comes around, and in some places of the world, the means of attaining power by force is once again gaining ground.

America is an oddity in world history. Since winning our independence, the idea of being conquered and subjugated by a demagogic ruler is foreign to us. As a nation, we have never known an emperor or a king. We were birthed out of a revolution against tyranny and have remained intact even after a devastating Civil War. Additionally, since the end of World War II, we have managed to quell any further full-scale worldwide conflicts. This is mainly due to backroom deal making, dubious diplomacy, political pandering, and threatening arms races. However, because we can play "the game" so well, we have been lulled into a false sense of security, but that bubble is about to burst. The Fourth Reich is coming.

THE COMING EVIL EMPIRE

When we hear the word *empire*, we automatically think of some of the largest, most powerful, and highly influential kingdoms that have crossed the stage of world history. The top five empires that come to mind are the Persian, Roman, Arab (Caliphate), Mongol, and British. However, few of us would consider Germany as one of the most dominant empires ever to exist.

The German word *reich* means "realm of an empire or kingdom" and describes three historical periods during which Germany aspired to dominate Europe and expand its power across the world. The First Reich (The Holy Roman Empire), existed from the tenth to the nineteenth centuries, spanning the territories originally conquered by Charlemagne. The Second Reich (The German Empire) lasted from 1871 to 1918, and included the united Germany under Otto von Bismarck, and ended with its defeat after World War I, and the birth of the short-lived Weimar Republic. The Third Reich (Nazi Germany) lasted from 1933 to 1945, and at its height it controlled most of Europe, regions in North Africa and Asia. The Nazi Empire ended with Hitler's defeat in World War II.

These Reichs were precursors to the future Fourth Reich, which will force the citizens of the world to live under the political, religious, and financial dictatorship of one man: the Antichrist.

The reign of the Antichrist will begin when he makes a seven-year peace treaty with Israel which he will break in three and a half years—it will end forty-two months later. The Antichrist will come as a man of peace and prosperity but will in fact become the most vicious monster the world has ever known.

As we have learned, this will not be the first time man has attempted to come against God's Chosen. The pages of history are filled with stories of emperors and empires who shared a common hatred for the Jews, but where are they now?

Pharaoh's horsemen and chariots chased the Jews through the Red Sea, and God turned them into fish food (Exodus 15:19).

Where is the Babylonian Empire? Gone.

Where is the Medo-Persian Empire? Gone. Where is the Greek Empire? Gone.

Where is the Roman Empire? Gone.

Where are the Third Reich and the goose-stepping barbarians who followed Adolf Hitler? Gone—buried in the boneyard of history awaiting their day of judgment before the throne of God Almighty.

I ask, where is Israel? Israel is alive and thriving.

The coming Fourth Reich of the Antichrist will be earth's last empire of evil until the glorious return of the Messiah. After His coming, the God of Abraham, Isaac, and Jacob will establish the Eternal Kingdom in the holy city of Jerusalem.

THE GERMAN EMPIRES

The following pages will briefly cover the times and events surrounding the First Reich (962–1806), the Second Reich (1871–1918), and the infamous Third Reich of Hitler (1933–1945).

This is not merely a history lesson. Many people are unaware of the deep-rooted anti-Semitic foundations upon which these empires were built. Since Genesis, Satan has sown seeds of hatred, prejudice, jealousy, murder, and lust for power that led ordinary people to commit grotesque acts of evil without even a prick of conscience as described in 1 Timothy 4:1–2,

Now the Spirit expressly says that in latter times some will depart from the faith, giving heed to deceiving spirits and doctrines of

*demons, speaking lies in hypocrisy, having their own conscience
seared with a hot iron.*

FROM THE ROMAN EMPIRE
TO THE HOLY ROMAN EMPIRE

The Roman Empire (27 BCE–476 CE), established by Octavius
Augustus, was a vast and powerful domain that ruled on three continents for over five hundred years. Believing that the empire was too
large for one emperor to govern, Diocletian (284–305 CE) divided
the kingdom in two portions.[2] Later, Constantine defeated both
the eastern and western parts and became the sole emperor of the
Roman Empire (306–337 CE).

The Roman empire was eventually ripped apart by internal
and external forces. As Roman power weakened in Europe, the
Germanic tribes asserted dominance over the region. In the year
410 CE, German Visigoth warriors sacked Rome, which by then
was the capital city of only the western half of the former glorious Roman Empire. This invasion sent shock waves throughout
Europe—a classic example of "you reap what you sow."

By 476 CE, the Western Roman Empire's ruler, Romulus
Augustulus, was forced to surrender to the German chieftain
Odoacer. Thus, the Roman Empire in the west died, while its stronger and wealthier eastern half, the Byzantine Empire, continued to
dominate the Middle East until it finally fell to the Ottoman Turks
during the fifteenth century.[3]

Between the fall of the Western Roman Empire and the establishment of the Holy Roman Empire (First Reich), central Europe
contained hundreds of small kingdoms ruled by tribal chieftains,
warlords, and minor kings. It was also within this period that the
Roman Catholic Church split into the Orthodox Church in the east
and the Roman Catholic Church in the west.

However, the Roman Church would remain a powerful religious and political institution due to the conquering Germanic tribes converting to Catholicism.[4] Eventually, it would be the Western Roman Catholic Church that provided the key to unifying the independent tribes and kingdoms into one empire.

THE FIRST REICH— THE HOLY ROMAN EMPIRE (962–1806)

The First Reich, or Holy Roman Empire, was centered in Germany and soon stretched across central Europe, including present-day Austria, the Czech Republic, Switzerland, the Netherlands, Belgium, Slovenia, parts of eastern France, western Poland, and northern Italy. The empire began with the crowning of Otto the Great in 962 CE and lasted for more than eight hundred years.[5]

There had been previous attempts to establish a new Roman Empire since Pope Leo III crowned the Frankish (German) conqueror Charlemagne in the year 800 CE. However, the new empire did not truly exist until Otto I succeeded in the unification and subjugation of all the warring regions in central Europe.[6]

Otto I was the strongest of the warring Germanic kings, crushing several rebellions, which helped to protect the Roman Catholic Church and its territories. These successful campaigns won the support of Pope John XII, who anointed Otto I as emperor of the new Roman Empire.

The link between Otto I's empire (the new Roman Empire) and the ancient Roman Empire was established through the medieval model of *translatio imperii,* meaning, "translation of rule or empires."[7] This concept is believed to have originated in Daniel 2:39–45 with the young prophet's interpretation of Nebuchadnezzar's dream.

Later, the Roman Catholic philosopher St. Augustine expanded the theological division of world history into six periods of time or ages.[8] This is commonly referred to as the Seven Ages of Dispensation, with the "seventh age" encompassing the Millennial Reign of Christ.

Dispensationalism

Dispensationalism is a series of defined periods, or ages, in history where God's purpose and assigned stewardship for mankind is found.

There are references to "ages" and "dispensations" in scripture and each of these words carries a different connotation. Whereas "age" has to do with a period of time, "dispensation" refers to an assigned stewardship occurring within a time or age; either with part of an age, a complete age, or even a sequence of ages.

The seven dispensations distinguishing God's work on earth are as follows:

- The first age is called the Dispensation of Innocence, which begins with the creation of Adam and Eve and ends with their fall and eviction from the Garden of Eden (Genesis 1:26; 2:16–17; 3:6; and 3:22–24).
- The second age is known as the Dispensation of Conscience, which began with the expulsion from the Garden and lasted through the Antediluvian Flood (Genesis 3:7,22; 6:5, 11–12; and 7:11–12, 23).
- The Dispensation of Human Government is the third age, and it began with Noah and his family after the flood and lasted through the Tower of Babel with the establishment of various world nations and cultures (Genesis 9:1–2 and 11:1–8).
- The fourth age is called the Dispensation of Promise. It began

with God's covenant call of Abraham and ended with Moses receiving God's Law at Mount Sinai (Genesis 12:1–3; 15:5; 26:3; 28:12–13; 13:14–17 and Exodus 1:13–14).

- The Dispensation of Law is the fifth age, and it began with the Exodus until the death of Jesus Christ in CE 30–33 (Exodus 19:1–8; Romans 3: 19–10 and 10:5; Acts 2:22–23 and 7:51–52; Galatians 3:10 and 2 Kings 25:1–11).

- The sixth age is called the Dispensation of Grace, or the Church Age, and it began on the Day of Pentecost (Acts 2:1–4) and ends with the Rapture of the church (I Thessalonians 4). It is the present age, and it occurs between the sixty-ninth and seventieth week of Daniel's vision (Daniel 9:24).

- The end of the Dispensation of Grace is unknown—it will be followed by the seventh and final age, called the Millennial Reign of Christ (Revelation 20:4). This age of perfect peace will last a thousand years and will end with the Great White Throne Judgment of the wicked (Revelation 20:1–15). The Almighty will then destroy the heavens and the earth by fire, creating a new heaven and new earth. Afterward, the God of Abraham, Isaac, and Jacob will establish His Final Throne in the city of Jerusalem (Revelation 21).[*]

During the fourth and fifth centuries, Catholic writers built on Augustine's theory and began viewing four of the ages as a succession of world empires: Babylon, Persia, Greece, and Rome— the four kingdoms of Daniel's vision. The next recognized transition of empires was that of Charlemagne, who became the first emperor to rule from western Europe since the fall of the Western Roman Empire three centuries earlier. Following this line of logic, Otto I, who was considered the natural successor to Charlemagne,

---

[*] https://www.compellingtruth.org/seven-dispensations.html.

represented the sixth world empire, which would supposedly exist until the second coming of Christ.

Although Otto I aspired to be the emperor of only Germany and Italy, with the blessing of the pope to give him added legitimacy, it was actually his son, Otto II (967–983 CE), who added "Roman" to his title of emperor. It was his way of competing with the Byzantine emperor Basil II, who had ambitions of reacquiring control of southern Italy.[9]

By the reign of Emperor Conrad II (1027–1039)—the name of the kingdom became commonly known as the Roman Empire (referring to Germany). In the first few centuries of the Golden Era (973–1056), the German emperor was the most powerful political and religious figure in Europe. He was regarded as the guardian of Christendom,* and his office had supreme authority over the church, with the power to appoint or unseat the pope in Rome as he desired.

The emperor's supremacy was eventually challenged when Pope Gregory VII (1073–1085) asserted his independence from Henry IV of Germany (1056–1105). This struggle between the political and religious authorities prompted megalomaniac Emperor Frederick I (1157), also known as "Red Beard," to rename his empire *The Holy Roman Empire* emphasizing his authority over church and state.[10] Red Beard's ambition for power was limitless, and he considered himself second only to God.

Because of this sustained contention, the Holy Roman Empire not only lost territory in Italy but also the guaranteed support of the Roman Catholic Church. By the thirteenth century, the German kingdom (aka Holy Roman Empire) had rivals in France and Italy for imperial power in Europe. In one of the great ironies of history, eighteenth-century French philosopher Voltaire declared that

---

* https://www.britannica.com/biography/Charlemagne/Emperor-of-the-Romans.

the Holy Roman Empire "was neither holy, nor Roman, nor an empire."[11]

Yet the name remained, and so did the idea that Germany should be the guardian of Christendom. This self-appointed commission would eventually become the foundation to its cultural and ethical convictions of superiority and natural right of rulership over Europe. Every empire in history believed in its own imperiousness, and Germany was no different.

By the early sixteenth century, competing forces were pulling the Holy Roman Empire apart both politically and religiously. Not only was the empire in crisis, but so was the Roman Catholic Church. The lines of succession had become blurred, and multiple contenders fought each other for the titles of emperor and pope. Like previous empires in history, the First Reich searched for a scapegoat to blame as the source for all the unrest—they chose the Jews.

The historical treatment of Jews in Europe had been growing worse over the centuries. The divergence of power between the emperors and the popes, and its subsequent effect on the supremacy of papal authority over every Christian kingdom in Europe, resulted in an expansion of religious law and a hardening of church doctrine.

This stringent policy gradually emphasized corporal punishment for sin and apostasy, and the Jews were the natural target.[12] Heresy, which any observant Jew was guilty of by the standards of medieval Christian theology, became a crime punishable by torture, imprisonment, or death.

A few earlier popes made some occasional statements against the forced conversion of Jews, while others asserted the Jews at least deserved protection from physical harm. However, the majority stood firmly against the Jewish people and their faith.

The short-lived tolerance disappeared as the church grew more powerful and the empire's grip on its territories grew more precarious.

In competition for supreme authority over Europe's citizens, the church and the empire both exploited the latent anti-Jewish feelings of medieval Christians to their own advantage.

European Jews were routinely accused of blood libel and their religious books burned as dangerous heretical teachings; they were forced out of many occupations and segregated into ghettos. The period of the Crusades yielded extreme feelings of hatred for religious outsiders, which included the Jews, and precipitated several shocking massacres, especially in Germany's Rhineland.[13]

I have well documented the persecution of the Jews by the Roman church during this time period. Please remember that the Roman Church doctrine of this era did not reflect the teachings of Christ. Furthermore, many of the policies inflicted on the Jews by the early church fathers were later adopted by the Third Reich. Church edicts such as requiring Jews to wear identifying clothing later inspired Hitler. This forced practice of selective ostracism also foreshadows the prophesy of the coming Fourth Reich, which will require those left behind after the Rapture to either take the mark of the Beast or be killed.

Even though by the thirteenth century, the Holy Roman Empire no longer enjoyed the status of being the pope's chosen kingdom in Europe, it still upheld church law to give legitimacy to its claim as the guardian of Christendom. Convinced by his advisors that the Jewish religion was a threat to not only Christianity but also the stability of his empire, Holy Roman emperor Maximilian I ordered all Jewish books other than the Hebrew Bible to be gathered and burned in 1509.[14] Increasingly, Jews were treated as dangerous intruders in Germany and a threat to both the church and the empire.

In 1517, the tensions between Pope Leo X and the Holy Roman Emperor Charles V were exacerbated by Martin Luther's rebellion against the Roman Catholic Church, which precipitated the

Protestant Reformation.[15] Luther's challenge to papal authority led to a crackdown on perceived heretics everywhere, especially the Jewish people.

The Holy Roman Empire, afraid of losing its authority because of Luther's teachings, decided to help eradicate the "heretic Jews" by forcibly expelling them from parts of their empire. This practice spread across Europe during the Middle Ages, resulting in the banishment of entire Jewish communities.

In 1670, Holy Roman emperor Leopold I issued an order that all Jews had to leave Austria by August 1. This was the second time Jewish citizens of Austria had been banished by the empire—the first expulsion took place in 1421 and lasted over two hundred years.[16]

As time passed, the Holy Roman Empire was gradually forced to concede much of its centralized authority to the princes and rulers of its local territories. During its final two hundred years, this Germanic empire existed more on paper and in the imaginations of its citizens than in reality.

Nonetheless, up until the very end of the Holy Roman Empire, Jewish communities were subjected to cruel and bigoted treatment. In 1802, just four years before the empire dissolved, a Jewish delegation pleaded with Emperor Francis II (1792–1806) to grant them the rights of German citizens and abolish their many restrictions, including the discriminatory poll tax that German Jews had to pay in order to enter any town or province. Their request was denied.[17]

Weakened by internal feuds and the political impact of the French Revolution, the Holy Roman Empire finally dissolved in 1806 when Francis II abdicated the throne in order to avoid being overthrown by Napoleon Bonaparte's triumphant march across Europe.[18]

BETWEEN THE REICHS

Just as the German emperors believed they had inherited the Holy Roman Empire through *translatio imperii,* Napoleon fancied himself to be the rightful successor to the conquered fragments of the Holy Roman Empire. At first, it seemed that Napoleon Bonaparte might be a different kind of emperor, one who was willing to give the Jews of Europe the rights of citizenship and who promised to allow the Jewish people to return to their homeland after his attempt to conquer Palestine, but those hopes were soon dashed.[19]

Napoleon's "Infamous Decree," published two years after he unseated the Holy Roman Empire, imposed economic restrictions on eastern European Jews and limited their freedom of movement across the continent. Napoleon's short-lived reign was the catalyst for major social upheaval in Europe that actually strengthened the perceived conflict between Jews who remained loyal to the Torah and their righteous traditions, versus those who assimilated to the new concept of modern nationalism.

Another important effect of Napoleon's conquest of Europe was the change in the balance of power between the Roman Catholic Church and the kingdoms of Europe.[20] Prior to Napoleon's conquest, the pope had enjoyed a symbiotic relationship with the kings and queens of Europe. Since the thirteenth century the heads of state acted as enforcers of church policy and in turn relied upon papal support to retain control.

However, after Napoleon rose to power, he oversaw a movement to secularize much of the national government and placed himself above the authority of the pope. Napoleon's example changed how future European rulers viewed the relationship between church and state.

After Napoleon's defeat at Waterloo by the British Alliance in

1815, Pope Pius VII (1800–1823) tried to reassert his authority, but the Roman Church never regained the same level of political power it had enjoyed during the days of the Holy Roman Empire. Napoleon Bonaparte may have successfully ended the First Reich, but it had already left an indelible mark on Germany's culture.

For sixty-five years, Germany's imperial ambitions would lie dormant, but would once again rise up within the Second Reich.

North German Confederation

During the six and a half decades after Napoleon's defeat, the disjointed German states attempted to regroup under new leadership but struggled to form a lasting alliance. Initially, thirty-nine German states struck a bargain for a mutual defense pact, but once again, the lust for ultimate power led to a war between rival German leaders, which resulted in a Prussian state victory.

In 1866, the ambitious Prussian prime minister Otto von Bismarck established the North German Confederation and succeeded in unifying twenty-two of the thirty-nine German states under his authority.[21] This laid the foundation for the rise of the Second Reich. The confederation united the twenty-two states under a single judicial and legal code, and placed economic authority in the hands of the federal government in which individual states would retain control of their religious and educational affairs.

France declared war against the North German Confederation in 1870 because it feared Prussia's ambition of German unification would shift the balance of power in Europe. However, France's declaration backfired and caused the remaining seventeen German states to affirm their loyalty to Prussian King William I.

It was during this Franco-Prussian War that the bitter seeds of World War I were sown by the rivalry of France and Austria against Germany. At the end of the war, Germany decided to humiliate their defeated enemies by imposing a debt of 5 billion francs. This was a foreshadowing of their own future humiliation via the Treaty of Versailles after Germany's defeat in World War I, which ultimately led to World War II.[22]

In 1812, Prussia had passed a law allowing its Jewish residents to claim all the rights, privileges, and responsibilities of Prussian citizens. When Prussia became the dominant member of the North German Confederation, citizenship was extended to all Jews within the confederation. After the German unification in 1871, all German Jews were declared legal citizens for the first time in Germany's history.

This law, however, did not remove the deep anti-Semitic root that had been planted centuries earlier. Even though the German government could see the advantage of securing the loyalty of the Jewish people by giving them citizenship, their fellow German countrymen deeply resented this change in their long existing social tradition.[23]

THE SECOND REICH (1871–1918)

The Second Reich was formed in January 1871 when Prussian king William I was declared emperor of the united German states. The new German empire, called the *Deutsches Kaiserreich*, retained most of the North German Confederation's constitutional provisions, and annexed the conquered French province of Alsace-Lorraine into their empire against the will of its French population.[24]

At this time, Chancellor Otto von Bismarck led the German Empire into a direct confrontation with the Roman Catholic Church, further ingraining the German culture's ideal of their government's inherent authority over church doctrine. The chancellor strongly objected to the 1870 ruling of the First Vatican Council that conferred infallibility upon the office of the pope. Consequently, he led the German Catholic people to split off and form their own Old Catholic Church.[25] However, this separation was more for political reasons than for any strong religious conviction.

The split from the Roman Church caused the erosion of traditional Christian practices throughout Germany. In the year after the Vatican Council adjourned, Bismarck launched the *Kulturkamph* (culture war), which gained strong support from German liberals who embraced secularism. This culture war yielded the Pulpit Law of 1871, making it a crime for any cleric to "discuss public issues in a way that displeased the government." The pulpit regulation led to a new mainstream mind-set making the Roman Church of Germany effectively impotent.

Within the cultural shift, Bismarck secularized marriage, removed Roman Catholic officials from government, and seized the church's control of education. In hindsight, these moves were the beginning of a trend to prepare German citizens for replacing the authority of the church with a combined religious and political loyalty to the state.

A key philosophical foundation of Bismarck's approach to complete government authority was his belief that he needed to provide the German people a "common enemy" in order to unify them and maintain control. This philosophy still remains the preferred way for dictators and despots to distract their people from internal problems and hold on to power.

Throughout his time as chancellor, Bismarck chose various "enemies" with which to unite the German people. First with foreign wars, then by fighting the Roman Catholic Church, and later by targeting the socialist politics of Karl Marx.[26]

In several ways, Otto von Bismarck paved the way for Adolf Hitler's ascension to power. Bismarck laid the groundwork for instituting the German state's national government. He gave the chancellorship supreme authority and effectively overturned centuries of local German political autonomy.

Like Bismarck, Hitler recognized that the best way to secure control of the German people was to elevate the power of the state over the church and present the "common enemy" philosophy.

German Nationalism

The growing nationalism of the German people demanded the expansion of the empire during the Second Reich. Bismarck had built his career by provoking conflict with neighboring states in order to keep the German people unified under his leadership. However, in the later years of his rule, he found himself having to play an increasingly complicated game of substituting one bogus enemy for another as he instigated minor conflicts along Germany's borders to appease factions within the empire.[27]

Chancellor Bismarck governed for nearly twenty years but failed to create a system of government that could survive once he no longer held the reins of power. After the death of the original kaiser, William I, and then the untimely demise of his heir apparent, the German Empire was left in the hands of his young grandson, Emperor William II, who had no loyalty to Bismarck. Asserting his constitutional authority, Emperor William II forced Bismarck to resign in 1890, beginning the demise of the Second Reich.[28]

The young emperor was unprepared to deal with the challenges Germany faced as it entered the twentieth century. Bismarck's previous two decades of cultivating war with France as a means to solidly unify the German people's nationalism resulted in a mutual animosity between the two countries. In addition, Germany found itself increasingly isolated from foreign allies who had been alienated by Bismarck's hostile policies.

Emperor William II made a catastrophic miscalculation by

disregarding the limits to Germany's power. While Bismarck had been shrewd enough to try to restrain the German people's appetite for imperial expansion, the new kaiser foolishly believed the conquest for new territory was his and Germany's supreme mandate.

By 1914, William II had gained popular support for a confrontation against France and Russia, setting in motion a military build-up that he was powerless to stop.[29] By June, World War I had begun, and it became a self-perpetuating calamity. Germany expected the war to be over in six months; instead, it lasted four years. World War I evolved into one of the deadliest conflicts in human history, with more than 16 million people losing their lives, including nearly 1.8 million Germans.

In order to end the war, Germany signed a peace agreement with the Allied powers of Great Britain, Russia, France, Italy, Romania, Japan, and United States. The armistice required Germany to transition its government to a constitutional monarchy. Faced with an internal revolt, Emperor William II stepped down from his throne.

After the emperor's abdication, the German party of the Socialist Democrats combined with the established military leadership to form a new democratic republic.[30] This effectively ended the Second Reich, and introduced the disastrous period between 1918 and 1933 known as the Weimar Republic.

THE WEIMAR REPUBLIC (1918–1933)

The aftermath of World War I created feelings of humiliation, shame, frustration, and resentment among the German people, and it was the Weimar Republic that took the blame for it. In reality, those most responsible for the war, and the accompanying economic disasters that followed, gladly handed their fiasco over to this newly formed democracy, a type of government that had not previously existed in Germany.

To make matters worse, the very essence of democracy found in the Weimar Bill of Rights, and free elections, which were available to all German citizens, including the Jewish people, had a devastating side effect. The repercussions of the war produced an aggressive increase in anti-Semitic sentiment among Germans who strongly resented their Jewish neighbors being given increased freedoms while they felt theirs had been stripped away.[31]

Even though German Jews had bravely fought alongside their Christian counterparts during World War I, anti-Semitic propaganda was spewing a different tale. The Jews were portrayed as slackers who avoided fighting on the front lines. During the post–World War I civil revolution of 1918–1919, angry mobs in Munich and Berlin viciously attacked Jewish citizens.

Many Germans believed that World War I was lost because they were "stabbed in the back" by traitors to the German cause. Consequently, the Weimar Republic, liberal socialists, war profiteers, and of course the Jews were blamed for undermining the war effort. To add to the discord, America's Great Depression of 1929 aided in plunging Germany into a disastrous economic freefall.

The political consequences were immediate: the coalition government collapsed, while the Nazis and Communists saw upsurges in their membership. Germany's twelve-year experiment with democracy ended, creating a vacuum that would soon be occupied by yet another Reich.*

Morever, the evil propaganda espoused by both the state and the church that had circulated in Germany for centuries had successfully persuaded average German citizens that all their problems could be rationally attributed to the Jews.

---

* https://encyclopedia.ushmm.org/content/en/article/the-weimar-republic.

THE RISE OF THE THIRD REICH (1933–1945)

The impact of the previous two Reichs had perfectly positioned the German people to accept and follow Adolf Hitler's satanic cult called Nazism:

- The Holy Roman Empire established a mythology of grandeur among the German people that enabled centuries of their leaders to exploit the inherent national German pride in their superiority and right to safeguard the "Christian" culture of Europe.
- The struggle between the emperors of the First and Second Reichs and the Roman Catholic Church had gradually established a tradition that placed the people's ultimate loyalty in the hands of the state over the church, even in matters deciding religious doctrine.
- The anti-Semitic policies pursued by the Holy Roman Empire, the Roman Catholic Church, and the Protestant Reformation, combined with the propaganda taught during the Middle Ages, were later resurrected, reminding German Christians that Jews were considered enemies of the state and a threat to the stability of the nation.

There was also a strong element of economic envy prevalent within German anti-Semitism. After World War I, the ascent of the National Socialist German Workers' Party (Nazis) reinvigorated the old beliefs that Jews were unfairly profiting off their Christian neighbors.

Adolf Hitler embodied the sentiment of the times. He understood the disillusionment of his fellow countrymen with the status quo. He identified with Germany's desire to regain world supremacy as it held during the First and Second Reichs. Hitler knew the

German people were looking for someone to blame for their dismal status—again the Jews were the ideal scapegoat.

It is important to note that Hitler became both chancellor and Führer of Germany in less than two years—creating a vast evil empire in which he had total control. The Third Reich occupied territories as far north as Barentsburg in Norway, as far east as Mozdok in the Soviet Union, as far south as the island of Gavdos in Greece, and as far west as the island of Ushant in France.

*

Hitler was determined to be Germany's leader—its savior—and in the end, its messiah. His meteoric rise to power sadly demonstrates how swiftly the geopolitical climate of the world can change.

A DICHOTOMY OF MORALITY

By the late nineteenth century, Germany was one of the most cultured and educated countries in Europe. It published the most

* https://www.jewishvirtuallibrary.org/german-occupied-europe.

books, had the highest literacy rate, and housed some of the most prestigious institutions of higher education in the civilized world. This is the era into which Adolf Hitler was born.

By 1933, nearly 99 percent of the German population considered themselves Christians (80 percent Protestant; 19 percent Roman Catholic).* However, it was becoming increasingly obvious that neither culture, education, nor religion guaranteed the making of a God-honoring society. The so-called gatekeepers of the faith had morphed into something incredibly evil.

As the Third Reich rose to supremacy, all religious belief that worshipped anyone or anything above Hitler was unacceptable. The Nazis had their own brand of "religion"; it was the highest form of self-adulation since Lucifer fell from the Third Heaven.

The Reich opposed traditional Christian values and replaced them with the ideals of a "reformed religion" that would fully incorporate Nazi principles. Instruction in conventional Christian doctrines in schools was first made optional, then altogether replaced with mandatory teachings encompassing Hitler's philosophies. Eventually, the crucifix was replaced with photos of Adolf Hitler, and in due course, the Nazi regime became the new state religion of the Third Reich.*

As Hitler ascended to power, he surrounded himself with elite thinkers. His top ten advisors were learned economists, lawyers, and philosophers. Others were recognized ambassadors and experts on world affairs. Another was a specialist in designing mass transportation and infrastructure.

Hitler's associates had strong family units, enjoyed the arts, attended church, and were passionate about their beliefs. One could

---

* https://encyclopedia.ushmm.org/content/en/article/the-german-churches-and-the
  -nazi-state.

easily conclude that the Führer's inner circle was, at the very least, the best Germany had to offer.

In reality, Hitler surrounded himself with an elite gang of fanatical yes-men. The Führer's neurotic leadership, coupled with his followers' obsessive commitment to his warped ideology, generated political, economic, and social institutions of legitimized terror.

Hitler's leaders, who had been entrusted with the management of the Third Reich, were the epitome of contradiction. On the surface, all seemed to be in excellent order.

Hitler's henchmen went to church and sang the hymns, worshipped baby Jesus, heard the homilies, and kissed the toe of the Virgin Mary. Then these monsters left their places of worship and with cold-blooded deliberation commanded Mary's descendants into the gas chambers and flung their lifeless bodies into the ovens.

They were brilliant, yet they had no conscience. Their psychotic behaviors produced indescribable atrocities, yet after receiving psychological exams during the Nuremberg trials, they were declared "normal."

Most of the perpetrators defended their conduct and claimed they were simply following orders—few regretted their actions. Remember, it is the evolution of leadership that ultimately determines the direction a nation will follow.

As Thomas Jefferson said, ". . . man cannot be trusted with the government of himself. Can he, then be trusted with the government of others?...Let history answer this question."*

---

* https://www.brainyquote.com/quotes/thomas_jefferson_109179.

CHAPTER 6

THE EVOLUTION
OF AMERICAN
LEADERSHIP

"I urge, then, first of all, that petitions, prayers, intercession and thanksgiving be made for all people—for kings and all those in authority, that we may live peaceful and quiet lives in all godliness and holiness." —*1 Timothy 2:1–2 NIV*

Many Americans are unaware of our country's deep roots regarding democracy and the fundamental way our government functions. We started as colonies under the watchful tyrannical eye of the British Empire. Our resources, livelihoods, and basic religious freedoms were under attack...so we rebelled against one of the largest military forces ever assembled.

There had never been a revolution such as ours—we were the first independent, foreign-recognized nation and the first European colonial entity to break from its mother country. However, were we destined to become our own empire or a true democracy by the people and for the people?

THE AMERICAN EMPIRE

While Americans do not typically think of the United States as an empire, the idea of an "empire of liberty" goes back to Thomas Jefferson. And while it was hardly a global power at its birth, the United States grew in influence to become the dominant world power after World War II, and the only truly global power after the Soviet Union broke apart in 1991. Thus, any analysis of empires past, present, and future must come to terms with the American story.

Leadership in the United States runs along two tracks: moral leadership that is based on the founding principles of the American republic, and political leadership that is situated in a constitutional system and alternately empowered or constrained by a cycle of partisan eras.

In this chapter we will explore these two types of leadership and then trace their development through American history up to the present day. That story will help clarify the nature of America's current struggles and leadership crisis—a crisis that cannot help but have an impact on global politics.

Moral Leadership: America's Genetic Code

Americans celebrate the birth of the United States every July 4, marking the unanimous adoption of the Declaration of Independence. This document contains several foundational principles that are part of the DNA of the American republic. The document, however, did not spring out of nothing. Underappreciated by Americans is the fact that the colonists wrestled with the principles and processes of liberty for over 150 years before John Hancock affixed his famous signature to the Declaration of Independence.

Americans were governed by such documents as the Mayflower Compact (1620) and the Massachusetts Body of Liberties (1641) long before 1776, and most of the ideas that lay at the foundation of democracy, self-government, and majority rule arose in church debates in the 1600s before they became political debates in the 1700s.

The Founders of the American republic established their system of government on what Michael Novak called the "two wings" of common sense and religious faith. The commonsense reasoning of such thinkers as Aristotle, Cicero, John Locke, and Baron de Montesquieu was baptized, in a sense, by a biblical worldview that was partly Protestant, but even more so Hebraic.[1]

Many Americans saw the United States as an "American Israel," with George Washington standing in the place of Moses. The dynamic collision of these different but complementary perspectives caused most of the Founders to understand and agree with a very simple set of precepts.

First, liberty is the goal or objective of the American republic. Second, liberty cannot exist without virtue. Liberty *needs* virtue to thrive and succeed. Third, virtue is impossible without religion. Therefore, because liberty requires religion, the American experiment can only succeed in a healthy religious environment.[2]

We can see evidence of this perspective in the Declaration of Independence itself. In that document, Thomas Jefferson famously referred to the "Laws of Nature and of Nature's God"— language that borrows explicitly from the natural law tradition of Cicero and Thomas Aquinas. Jefferson also declared the existence of several self-evident truths: "that all men are created equal, that they are endowed by their Creator with certain unalienable Rights, that among these are Life, Liberty, and the pursuit of Happiness."

To call a truth "self-evident" is to say that it is basic and fundamental. There are no truths more fundamental than these truths, and they are knowable by human beings with the unaided power of reason. There is in the very structure of the created order of the universe—given by God—a set of objective moral principles or universal truths by which we can evaluate and judge human laws, politics, and customs.

Human nature itself is fixed and unchanging, and the existence of a fixed human nature means there are fixed and permanent natural rights that come from a source higher than the state, putting constraints on the state. These fixed moral principles guide government power and provide for limited constitutional government, which in turn protects life, liberty, and property.

These objective moral principles inform us that all human beings are created equal. We are not, of course, equal in every area of life. We are obviously not equal when it comes to economic condition, talents and skills, intelligence, moral virtue, and character qualities. But we *are* all equally human. No one is more human than anyone else.

That means we are all equal under the law. And because of that innate equality of all human beings, we all have the same natural rights to life, liberty, and the pursuit of happiness. Positive rights are given by the government, and therefore the government can take them away. But natural rights—what Jefferson called unalienable rights—are given by God, and government cannot legitimately take them away.

Jefferson and the Constitution

Jefferson argued that securing these rights is the very reason we have government, an assertion that connects the Declaration of Independence to the Constitution. The central reason why the Framers of the Constitution separated the powers and functions of government into separate bodies of officials was to prevent any single individual or group of individuals from accumulating all powers into their hands, leading to tyranny.[3]

Thus, embedded into the very structure of the American constitutional order is a concern to protect the rights and liberties guaranteed by the Declaration of Independence. The Constitution itself replaced the Articles of Confederation, which proved inadequate to securing "the blessings of liberty to ourselves and our posterity."

Just in case anyone was in any doubt about these principles of liberty, the first task of the First Congress was to draft and ratify a Bill of Rights. This document, comprising the first ten amendments to the Constitution, further reinforces basic and fundamental principles of liberty. Most important, the First Amendment guarantees the free exercise of religion, a fact that provides more evidence of the central place of religion in the thinking of the Framers. We also enjoy freedom of speech, freedom of the press, the right to bear arms, and various rights of the accused—all designed to protect citizens from the unjust, coercive, and intrusive power of the state.

These are the fundamental principles embedded into the genetic code of what it means to be an American. It is a genetic code supported by both the philosophy and religious worldview of the architects of the American political system. The great French commentator Alexis de Tocqueville understood the important role religion played in supporting and sustaining liberty, arguing in the 1830s that the common Judeo-Christian morality taught by all religious sects in America helped regulate and constrain its politics.

He no doubt had in mind some of the more radical and d[?]tive schemes of his own nation's French Revolution. This is wny Tocqueville called religion "the first of their [America's] political institutions."[4]

America is strong when it understands and embraces these foundational principles—and its strength is endangered when it forgets them. America is now in a revival of paganism and secularism; the more secular we become, the more godless we become. It's time for a revolution of righteousness to sweep America.

The Place of the Presidency

In many nations, the focal point for moral leadership may be found in a monarch. Whether king, queen, kaiser, czar, or emperor, these individuals, even as mere figureheads, embody a nation's identity and values. They represent the nation on the world stage. Dictators, führers, ayatollahs, and "Dear Leaders" (Kim Jong-Un) do the same for tyrannies.

Although the United States is not a monarchy, that does not mean it has no need for political leadership. In fact, the Framers of the constitutional system understood the need for leadership, and carefully constructed the federal political institutions to provide for it. Leadership is not a quality often found in Congress, but that is hardly the fault of national legislators.

Congress is not designed to provide national leadership. It is a plural institution designed to implement policies that reflect the popular will of the people. It is structured to make deliberation about the merits of policy more likely through its large, two-chambered structure and frequent elections (every two years for the House of Representatives). Action and efficiency are not qualities Congress possesses.

Nor do we find national leadership in the federal court

system—an institution composed of a small group of highly educated experts who have job security so that they can protect individual rights and liberties by accurately interpreting and applying the law in cases and controversies.[5]

Instead, the focal point for national leadership is the presidency. Its function, in the words of Alexander Hamilton, is to concern itself with "the execution of the laws and the employment of the common strength."[6] In some ways the president is a type of clerk to Congress, for the Constitution charges him to "take care that the laws be faithfully executed." But the president is also a leader—an independent constitutional officer designed to clarify and set goals and respond to crises, whether they be of an economic, a national security, or a natural disaster variety.

The very fact that the presidency is composed of one individual makes the office "the bulwark of the national security," and enables the president to act swiftly and decisively, with "vigor and expedition."[7] The unitary nature of the office also allows citizens and voters to hold the individual accountable for his actions—to be able to give credit or lay blame for the president's conduct of his office.

However, it would be a mistake to assume that all presidents are created equal, with equal opportunities to accomplish their objectives. Presidential greatness surveys that rank presidents from one to forty-five feed this mistaken perspective. In fact, most presidents have only a marginal ability to control their own success or failure. Larger forces are already in place whenever a new president takes office, and the most important thing a president can do is have a strategic sense of what he can accomplish within his term.

What is the nature of these larger historical constraints? American political history can be divided into a series of political eras that tend to favor one party over the other. We can think of the advantaged party in an era as the "governing party" and the disadvantaged party as the "opposition party." For example, the Democratic Party during the Jacksonian era enjoyed a natural advantage over the Whig Party. That does not mean that the Whigs never won elections, only that the natural advantage lay with the Democrats.

Similarly, the Democratic Party during the New Deal era enjoyed a natural advantage over the Republican Party. The principal advantage enjoyed by the governing parties in these eras is that they retained the power to define what the political debate was about—which issues dominated and how we talk about them. The core ideology of the governing party becomes the dominant governing philosophy of the nation for that era.

We can see American history, then, as a cycle of partisan "regimes." One party takes control in a redefining election, becomes the major player for several decades, loses office a couple of times, but always comes back to power. Then the party becomes weak and vulnerable, and less able to adapt to changing issues and circumstances. It eventually loses power to the opposition party in some sort of crisis that delegitimizes its leadership, and the opposition party takes control in another redefining election…and the cycle begins all over again.[8]

The important question for any president, given this cyclical understanding of American history, is where in the cycle he takes office. The presidents with the greatest abilities to truly lead and reshape politics in America in a genuinely transformational way are those who come at the beginning of the cycle. These are the epoch-making regime founders who come to power opposed to the previous regime when that regime is weak and vulnerable and collapsing, usually due to some trigger event that causes a crisis of legitimacy.

Constitutionally, then, all presidents are leaders. Historically, all presidents must adjust their leadership goals to account for their placement in the partisan era of their time. In *all* cases, presidents, as the embodiment of America on the world stage, represent the basic foundational principles of the American republic—those self-evident truths Jefferson wrote about. To the extent that presidents and their parties faithfully adhere to those transcendent truths, the nation thrives. When the presidents and their parties stray from these principles, the nation is endangered. It is to that story that we turn next.

PRESIDENTIAL LEADERSHIP FROM THE FOUNDING TO THE CIVIL WAR

We can trace the two-party competition that marks American political history back to the founding era, where the first battle was fought over the ratification of the Constitution. Federalists supported ratification, while Anti-Federalists opposed it. Federalists won the initial dispute, but the argument splashed over into the administration of George Washington.

George Washington, America's first president, was perfectly fitted for the job. Washington had chaired the Constitutional Convention, and when the Framers were debating the structure and powers of the presidency, they had their eye on the man at the front of the room—the man everyone knew would first inhabit the office. Washington understood that everything he did as president would set a precedent for future presidents, from how to conduct foreign policy to how to employ the veto.

Washington was both a national founder (an architect of the American republic) and a regime founder (of the Federalist era). In the great debate between his secretary of the treasury, Alexander Hamilton, and his secretary of state, Thomas Jefferson, Washington sided with Hamilton. Hamilton and Jefferson became the leaders of America's first political parties, the Federalists and the Democratic-Republicans.

These parties separated in disputes over the power of the federal government, whether there should be a national bank, and whether the United States should favor France or Great Britain in foreign policy. Washington claimed for the presidency powerful administrative and foreign policy authority, and his economic policies helped put the young nation on a much firmer financial foundation.

Despite Washington's success, the two parties of the 1790s hated each other and saw each other as borderline treasonous. Jefferson's Democratic-Republicans saw the Federalists as undemocratic, commerce-loving monarchists who betrayed the accomplishment of the revolution, while John Adams's Federalists saw the Jeffersonians as godless, French-loving, agrarian radicals.

Neither party had any sense that the other group represented a legitimate presence in American politics. Jefferson's victory over Adams in 1800 sent the Federalists into a death spiral from which they never recovered, leaving Jefferson's party as the only significant force in American politics—a period known somewhat inaccurately as the "Era of Good Feelings."[9]

Thomas Jefferson was the chief architect of this new era, which saw three straight two-term presidencies, all from Virginia. Unquestionably, Jefferson's most significant accomplishment was the acquisition of the Louisiana Territory from France, an act that immediately doubled the size of the nation and extended its reach to the Pacific.

Jefferson's successors asserted themselves on the international stage by declaring the hemisphere off-limits to European meddling in the Monroe Doctrine and made the first significant attempt to manage the slavery issue with the Missouri Compromise. Jefferson's party was so dominant that when James Monroe ran for reelection in 1820, he faced no opposition, winning every electoral vote but one.

Political ambition and competition do not rest, however. Just as the Jeffersonian system reached its zenith, the presidential nomination process broke down. In a four-way split in 1824, Andrew Jackson won more electoral votes than anyone else. He failed to win a majority, however, and the House of Representatives selected John Quincy Adams to be president. Jackson spent the next four years castigating Adams as corrupt, and the Jeffersonian system collapsed as Jackson won the presidency in 1828.

Andrew Jackson's presidency witnessed a resurgence of party competition, with Jackson serving as the founder of the new Democratic Party, and the various factions opposed to Jackson coalescing under the banner of the Whig Party. Both parties evolved out of different factions of Jefferson's Democratic-Republicans. They stood for different policy choices and philosophies of governance, and both believed they were faithful defenders of the Constitution, as well as of the basic principles of American government articulated in the Declaration of Independence.[10]

Jackson's Democrats clearly dominated the era, however, which is named after him. The president launched a successful assault on the Second Bank of the United States, a symbol of elite power against the masses, by vetoing its 1832 attempt to be rechartered. Jackson also sought to secure western expansion, and part of that project included the removal of the Cherokee Nation from the state of Georgia in the "Trail of Tears," an event that violated the natural rights principles of the American republic.

Jackson enforced his policy by flagrantly ignoring a Supreme Court decision mandating a return of Cherokee lands, an act that undermined separation of powers.[11] Every policy decision by Jackson's followers, from the destruction of the Second Bank to the acquisition of Texas, prompted counterefforts by Whig leaders.

The Great American Original Sin

Had the political battle been limited to economic policy and western expansion, the party system could have regulated the typical conflict that marks such disputes. Instead, slavery—the great American original sin—took center stage. Slavery was part of American politics from the beginning, of course, but in the early years of the republic, it was seen by all sides as an unfortunate institution.

People like Washington, Jefferson, and Madison—all slave owners—knew the institution was unjust and corrupt, but they were unsure how to deal with it. In fact, a famous quote by Jefferson summed up their dilemma: "But, as it is, we have the wolf by the ear, and we can neither hold him, nor safely let him go. Justice is in one scale, and self-preservation in the other." The geographic phenomenon of slavery centered in Southern states created tensions with the acquisition of new states, leading to famous conciliations like the Missouri Compromise and the Compromise of 1850.

But the Indian Removal Act of 1830 placed the Democratic Party on treacherous ground where "unalienable rights" were concerned, and the annexation of Texas—begun by Whig-in-name-only John Tyler and completed by Jackson's protégé, James K. Polk—pushed the nation toward a crisis of "self-evident truths."

The self-evident truths Jefferson wrote about have their own power, and their inherent logic gave rise to the abolitionist movement. Unfortunately, the two political parties were not capable of regulating the discourse about slavery. Anti-slavery elements rightly argued that slavery was oppressive and despotic—a violation of the principles of the Declaration of Independence. No one likes being called immoral, so Southern Democrats began to make arguments that slavery was not just an unfortunate institution; it was actually a positive good, both for the slave master and for the slave.

People like John C. Calhoun made the argument that white Europeans and African slaves were not equal, physically, morally, or intellectually. In fact, Calhoun explicitly rejected Jefferson's argument that all men are created equal, saying, "There is not a word of truth in it."[12] Others called it "a self-evident lie."[13]

A party that was descended from Jefferson explicitly rejected his most important political insight, arguing, in effect, that all men are *not* created equal, and thus do *not* have natural rights to life, liberty, and the pursuit of happiness. This argument constituted a rejection of the objective moral principles and universal truths the nation was founded upon.

The Whig Party—also descended from Jefferson—proved not much better. Although not a pro-slavery party, the Whigs wanted the issue of slavery kept off the political scene just as much as Democrats did, because they knew how unsettling the issue was. But as events moved forward, with the Fugitive Slave Act (enforced by Whig president Millard Fillmore) and the Kansas-Nebraska Act (pushed by Democratic president Franklin Pierce), those who opposed slavery bolted from their respective parties. Democrats survived as a party because of their regional strength in the South, but the Whigs self-destructed and disappeared.

The new Republican Party arose to replace the Whigs as the second major party in American politics, founded as an anti-slavery party, pledging not to get rid of slavery in the South but to prevent it from spreading into new territories and states. It was a party founded on Jefferson's original argument that all men are created equal—this notion, again, that there are self-evident truths and objective and universal principles, right for all and known to all at all times, in all places and cultures.

These ideas, part of America's DNA, are also part of the genetic code of the Republican Party, which came into existence as an attempt to reclaim these ideas for the nation at a time when both political parties had forsaken them.

We can see this in the way Abraham Lincoln, one of the founders of the Republican Party, talked about this basic dispute. Lincoln explicitly invoked Jefferson's language from the Declaration, that all men are created equal. And although Lincoln was hardly a racial progressive the way we might think of the concept today, he understood that slavery is despotism. It was one man governing another without his consent—an explicit rejection of the principles of our founding documents.[14]

The first time the Republican Party ran a presidential candidate was 1856, and the party platform could not have been clearer. The platform resolved that "the maintenance of the principles promulgated in the Declaration of Independence, and embodied in the Federal Constitution is essential to the preservation of our Republican institutions, and that the Federal Constitution, the rights of the States, and the union of the States, must and shall be preserved." The platform repeated the self-evident truths that all men have unalienable rights to life, liberty, and the pursuit of happiness. The party opposed both slavery and polygamy as barbaric institutions.[15]

However, a Supreme Court stacked by Jacksonians declared in the 1857 *Dred Scott* case that slaves were "beings of an inferior order, and altogether unfit to associate with the white race."[16] Slaves had no rights, despite the clear understanding of the Declaration that some things are *never* right if they violate natural rights.

Alexander Stephens, who became the vice president of the Confederacy, rejected Jefferson's language as "fundamentally wrong." He said the cornerstone of the Confederacy was the "great truth, that the negro is not equal to the white man; that slavery...is his natural and normal condition."

In fact, according to Stephens, African slaves were unequal because the Creator made them that way, and the true natural law was the subjugation of one race by another.[17] This was the position defended by the final Jacksonian presidents: Franklin Pierce and James Buchanan, whose lack of moral leadership encouraged the secession crisis and consequently ended the era of Democratic Party dominance.

The pro-slavery argument worked like a cancer, metastasizing in a threat to national union. This disease infected the American constitutional order and attacked the most basic principles of the Declaration of Independence. The Republican Party was a party established to reclaim the political and moral fact that there are some universal principles that are right for everyone, because we are all equally human. The argument against slavery was also an argument for an entrepreneurial society where people were economically independent, socially mobile, and free from class conflict and the agitation of rich versus poor.

THE PROGRESSIVE THREAT TO AMERICA

The end of the Civil War allowed the Republican Party to achieve its core objectives in exceptionally swift fashion. The party retained its basic economic vision, as well as its focus on civil rights, natural rights, and transcendent moral truths. Lincoln's Republican successors often blur together in a collage of unknown bearded presidents: Ulysses Grant, Rutherford B. Hayes, James Garfield, Chester Arthur, and Benjamin Harrison.

Operating in Lincoln's shadow, these men sought for and achieved the first civil service reform. They fought for sound monetary and fiscal policy, working for balanced budgets and a strong economy. The party continued to fight to secure the rights of freed slaves against the terrorism of the Ku Klux Klan. It fought for voting rights for women, low taxes, and a strong commercial republic. Under William McKinley, the United States became an international power with its victory in the Spanish-American War. Theodore Roosevelt continued to expand America's global influence, inserting himself into international affairs and building the Panama Canal.

By the turn of the century, another threat arose to the basic principles of the American republic: the rise of the Progressive movement. Just as pro-slavery elites rejected the self-evident truths of the Declaration, and in turn endangered the integrity of the constitutional order, so the Progressives launched their own attack on these fundamental principles.

Progressives believed that the central defect of the American constitutional order was the "separation of powers" system, which gets in the way of an activist government that seeks to expand its scope of power and control in an effort to regulate ever larger portions of our lives. And because separation of powers is linked to the self-evident truths of the Declaration, Progressives also rejected the natural rights understanding of that document. Regrettably, they sought to put in place instead a "living" Constitution that could grow and adapt to allow political leaders to do anything they wanted to do.

This new virus infected both parties. Woodrow Wilson claimed the Progressive mantle for the Democratic Party, and it was fully embraced by the time of Franklin Roosevelt. But there were also progressive Republicans, most notably Theodore Roosevelt. He began his presidency operating as a more traditional Republican, albeit with his own unique style. But as he moved forward in his career, especially when he ran for a third term in 1912 by attacking the more traditional constitutionalist Republican president William Howard Taft, Roosevelt fully embraced the Progressive critique of the American founding.

Progressives believed that human nature was not fixed. There were no permanent "laws of nature and nature's God." They rejected the natural rights tradition, arguing instead that rights come from the state, and the state can revise those rights to account for modern problems. Roosevelt himself once said that the rights articulated in the Declaration were merely "sentimental attachments."

Individual rights, private property, and limited government were outmoded notions. In their place, Progressives sought to install centralized planning, regulation, and redistribution. All of these notions constituted a direct assault on the founding principles of our nation. The very notion of a fixed and unchanging human nature means there are natural rights that come from a source higher than the state, putting constraints on the state. If human nature is not fixed but is malleable, then neither are natural rights fixed—and there is nothing higher than the state constraining them.[18]

Woodrow Wilson was an opposition president—one of only two Democratic Party presidents elected to office in the long Republican era that stretched from Lincoln to Herbert Hoover. He was consequential, however, in establishing many Progressive policies and institutions that laid the foundation for the later New Deal. Wilson fully accepted the Progressive criticism of separation of powers, reinterpreting the role of the president to be a popular leader capable of moving Congress and public opinion in his desired direction as an agent of rapid change.

Wilson adhered to a Darwinian understanding of politics, with government (and the Constitution) as a living and adapting phenomenon. There should be no limits on this change, so Wilson advocated discarding or ignoring the first two paragraphs of the Declaration of Independence, rejecting the natural rights understanding of the American republic and empowering a growing administrative state to manage national life.[19] Wilson demonstrated what a national leader can do if he articulates a different under-standing of human nature and political philosophy.

Wilson's insertion of the United States into World War I contin-ued the expansion of American global influence begun by McKinley and Roosevelt. Wilson overreached, however, failing to recognize the reluctance of many Americans to embrace his League of Nations and the diminishing of national sovereignty that would come with entrance into that organization.

In fact, because of the excesses of Wilson's presidency, Progres-sives did not find an easy home in the Republican Party. Republicans Warren G. Harding and Calvin Coolidge represented a conservative rejection of progressivism, and a restoration of a more traditional understanding of the constitutional order. In fact, Calvin Coolidge understood the conservative-progressive debate better than we give him credit for. He understood that the basic principles of the Declaration are final and unchanging.

Coolidge stated, "If all men are created equal, that is final. If they are endowed with inalienable rights, that is final. If governments derive their just powers from the consent of the governed, that is final. No advance, no progress can be made beyond these proposi-tions."[20] This sense that some things are permanent and unchanging is the very antithesis of progressivism.

THE GREAT DEPRESSION

The Great Depression brought the long Republican era that began with Abraham Lincoln to an end. When one party dominates American economic policy for seven decades, it gets the blame for the nation's greatest economic crisis.

While Woodrow Wilson failed to make a reality out of the Progressive vision, Franklin Roosevelt used the Great Depression to fulfill Wilson's dream. The New Deal represented a transformation of the role of the federal government in American life.

Roosevelt was shrewd enough to realize that Americans would not tolerate an open rejection of the principles of the Declaration of Independence, so he simply amplified the concept of rights. In addition to freedom of speech and freedom of religion, Roosevelt added freedom from want and freedom from fear—two goals that cannot help but infuse greater power in the state.

We have a right to life, but now we also have a right to a comfortable living. We have rights to liberty and the pursuit of happiness, but now we also have rights to a job, a decent home, medical care, a good education, and the protection from the economic fears of old age, sickness, accident, and unemployment. We have, in short, the right to a risk-free life, secured by the power of an enlightened administration. And that enlightened administration would be concentrated in a newly expanded and empowered White House that centralized control in the Oval Office.[21]

Thus, Roosevelt inaugurated a new era of Democratic Party dominance: the New Deal era. He was not particularly successful in pulling the nation out of the economic catastrophe, but American involvement in World War II made the nation a true military and economic world power. In the greatest conflict in world history, Roosevelt stands on equal footing with some of the most significant world leaders of the century—men like Hitler, Stalin, Tojo, de Gaulle, and Churchill.

He holds the record for the longest presidency in American history, winning four straight elections, and the combination of his administration with that of Harry Truman gave the Democratic Party twenty years of control over the executive branch. Most of this period was marked by strong Democratic Party majorities in both houses of Congress, and Roosevelt and Truman together appointed all nine justices on the Supreme Court. The destruction of the Axis powers and the subsequent fall of the British Empire made the United States the most powerful country in the world, with a monopoly (briefly) on nuclear weapons.

For twenty years after World War II, American politics traveled along two tracks. In the area of domestic policy, the programmatic liberal New Deal paradigm reigned supreme. Conservative Republicans tried to figure out how to rescind the New Deal, but after two decades of Roosevelt and Truman, they were not a strong enough faction to determine the direction of national policy.

Even Republican president Dwight Eisenhower accepted the New Deal as a fact of life and sought not to get rid of it but to manage it more efficiently, making the New Deal a bipartisan endeavor. When John F. Kennedy and Lyndon Johnson restored Democrats to the White House, they pushed the New Deal agenda more aggressively. Johnson pledged to end poverty and racial injustice—with all the government programs that necessarily come with such a promise. As the role of government got bigger and bigger, the place for freedom and liberty got smaller and smaller.

In the area of foreign policy, the United States entered nearly forty-five years of a Cold War with the Soviet Union, in a duel of superpowers that flared hot in places like Korea and Vietnam, but avoided nuclear annihilation. Because Eisenhower embraced the basic precepts of American global leadership—containment of communism and the spread of freedom and democracy—there was a rough bipartisan consensus in many areas of foreign policy.

What separated Truman, Eisenhower, and Kennedy were questions of emphasis and tactics, not national strategy. Soviet leaders like Stalin, Khrushchev, and Brezhnev tested American leaders, but the rough foreign policy consensus held until Vietnam blew it apart.

The cultural war had begun!

CHAPTER 7

THE CONSERVATIVE RESURGENCE

When you open your heart to patriotism, there is no room for prejudice. The Bible tells us, "How good and pleasant it is when God's people live together in unity." —President Donald Trump[1]

The assassination of President John F. Kennedy brought Lyndon Baines Johnson to power in the early '60s and had a Pandora's box effect. Lyndon Johnson's excesses—the combination of the costly, ill-advised Vietnam War and his New Deal on steroids, aka the Great Society—nearly drove the Democrats off the national stage. Then Richard Nixon proved unwilling to pursue conservative leadership, opting instead to govern essentially as a moderate Democrat, until his own personal demons caught up with him in the Watergate scandal.

This collapse of moral leadership put the nearly defunct New Deal on life support during the 1970s, as Gerald Ford was forced to basically tread water. Jimmy Carter inherited an exhausted administration, and with his own foreign policy debacles, he helped set the stage for a genuine conservative resurgence.

THE CULTURAL WAR BEGINS

As early as 1964, Ronald Reagan warned of the growing power of the central government and cautioned that natural rights were now seen more as a privilege of the state—a perversion of the Framers' original design. Barry Goldwater's campaign for president that year articulated a staunch conservative political philosophy that marked a direct frontal assault on the New Deal system.

Goldwater lost badly to Lyndon Johnson, but in the process, he pushed the Republican Party to become a more consistently conservative force in American politics, centered on more traditional notions of liberty and limited constitutional government.[2]

The contemporary conservative political movement got its greatest push from the turmoil of the 1960s. The period between Johnson's landslide election in 1964 and his departure in 1969 witnessed what appeared to be a collapse of the social order. Urban riots sparked by racial tensions exploded each summer in American cities, capped by the assassination of Martin Luther King Jr.

Student unrest at "Johnson's War" in Vietnam led to campus violence, street protests, and the burning of draft cards and American flags. Liberation was a dominant theme, especially with the new hedonism and *Playboy* philosophy of the sexual revolution. Traditional social mores fell under attack as the political philosophy of the Progressive elites and academics from earlier decades became the popular philosophy of the masses.

CONSERVATIVES Believe . . .	PROGRESSIVES Believe . . .
that there is a transcendent moral order that sets moral standards, and by which we can evaluate and judge human institutions and politics. They believe nature is fixed and normative, which is why things like slavery, abortion, drug use, and sexual perversion are not wrong at one point in time and right in another—they are always wrong.	that nature is plastic, changing, and adaptable, which is why we cannot speak of natural rights that are right always and everywhere. Some things that were once considered perverted may become normalized.
that history can teach us something and that tradition contains the wisdom of the past.	that history is something we can escape from as we move into a more utopian future.
that people have different social roles and responsibilities, and that there are differences between men and women, and between parents and children.	that distinctions between men and women are arbitrary and oppressive and should be abolished, and that men and women are exactly alike.
that progress is dubious at best—not that we cannot do some things better, but that we cannot merge heaven and earth.	that we can engage in experiments in living to discover better ways of ordering society.
that equality in our human nature and natural rights allows us to pursue liberty.	that equality requires limitations on liberty as we seek to bring everyone to the same economic level.[3]

Where the Framers of the American republic envisioned a system of ordered liberty channeled by moral virtue, the architects of the protest movements of the 1960s understood true liberty to be freedom from any old-fashioned moral constraints.[4]

The list of hot-button issues is familiar to anyone who has paid attention in the past few decades. Abortion, drugs, school prayer, pornography, gay rights, racial and gender quotas, sexual experimentation, skyrocketing out-of-wedlock births, fatherless families, situational ethics, moral relativism—Conservatives could rightly believe that society was experiencing a disintegration of traditional values.

Some scholars see this period as the beginning of a "culture war" based on competing religious perspectives. Traditional Protestants, Catholics, and Jews became united in their commitment to a transcendent authority against progressive Protestants, Catholics, and Jews, as well as against secularists, who adapted their faith to modern sentiments. The result was a cultural realignment that set the stage for the rise of Ronald Reagan.[5]

This cultural realignment brought into the open the central conflict between Conservatives and Progressives.

Dred Scott Decision and Roe v. Wade— The Battles for Equality

There is, in fact, continuity between the contemporary culture war and the earlier crisis of self-evident truths of the 1850s in the linkage between slavery and abortion. The central question in the infamous *Dred Scott* Supreme Court decision in 1857 was whether the slave was primarily and essentially a human person, and thus entitled to the personal liberty guaranteed by the Constitution.

The central question in the *Roe v. Wade* decision in 1973 was whether the fetus is a person within the meaning of the Fourteenth

Amendment. The Supreme Court's position in *Dred Scott* was that the slave was not a person within the meaning of the Fifth Amendment, arguing that blacks, whether slave or free, were "beings of an inferior order…and so far inferior that they had no rights which the white man was bound to respect."

The Supreme Court's position in *Roe* was that the unborn are not persons within the meaning of the Fourteenth Amendment's due process clause, arguing that "we need not resolve the difficult question of when life begins," while at the same time apparently resolving that question by asserting that the unborn are merely "potential life" and "prenatal life"—two concepts that are mutually exclusive.

Dred Scott declared slavery legal and constitutional; *Roe* declared abortion legal and constitutional. The first said blacks may be human, but they were not persons in a constitutional sense; the second said the unborn may be human, but they are not persons in the constitutional sense. In both cases, blacks and the unborn do not merit legal protection.[6]

Broadening the scope beyond Supreme Court jurisprudence, proponents of slavery said slaves were the property of their owners; proponents of abortion rights say the unborn are the property of their owners. One said the right to property trumped the right to *liberty*; the other says the right to personal liberty trumps the right to *life*.

Alternatively, the right to personal liberty for one person (slave owner or pregnant woman) supersedes the right to personal liberty for another (slave or unborn). One defended slavery using the argument that abolitionists should not impose their morality on the rest of the nation; the other defends abortion using the argument that those who support the right to life of the unborn should not impose their morality on the rest of the nation.

Finally, one led to the perverse conclusion that slaves were partially persons in *some* circumstances (they could be held responsible for their actions under the law) but not in others (they were also regarded as property and as extensions of their masters' will); the other led to the perverse conclusion that the unborn ought to be protected in *some* circumstances (we have laws that punish the killing of the fetus in an unlawful way, such as assault or drunk driving), but not in others (it is permissible to destroy the fetus if you are the mother).

Put simply, one side in both debates is "pro-choice," and the other is "pro-life" and "pro-liberty." In both cases, the "pro-choice" side rejects the natural rights perspective of the Declaration of Independence, leading to a similar rejection of the limited government understanding of the American Constitution.

THE REAGAN REVOLUTION

Ronald Reagan's inauguration as president in January 1981 reinserted these themes into the national dialogue. The realignment of American politics that followed made the Republican Party a conservative party, because the party attempted to conserve the permanent truths about human nature, natural rights, and limited constitutional government.

Reagan pursued this agenda in three major areas. First, in the area of economic policy, Reagan sought to cut taxes in order to starve "big government" of the funding necessary to sustain it. This would reduce the footprint of the federal government in American life and expand the scope of personal liberty.

Though less successful in reversing the growth of government, Reagan did succeed in slashing income tax rates that had exceeded 90 percent at the height of the New Deal era to less than half that level. The basic argument has hovered around that lower level ever

206 | THE EMPIRES

since, for no serious Democratic Party presidential candidate advocates returning to income tax rates in excess of 90 percent.

Second, in the area of foreign policy, Reagan sought not a truce with expansionist communism but victory over it. The principal objective behind Reagan's military buildup and programs like the Strategic Defense Initiative was to end the Cold War on American terms. Reagan understood that the totalitarian impulse of the Soviet Union represented a clear assault on the central moral principles of the American constitutional system, against permanent and eternal truths.

Reagan had the moral vision to call the Soviet Union the "focus of evil in the modern world"[7] and to call for the tearing down of the Berlin Wall, the stark symbol of the Soviet threat. In this campaign Reagan was joined by British prime minister Margaret Thatcher and Catholic pope John Paul II. Less than a year after Reagan left office, the Berlin Wall fell. Two years later, the Soviet Union broke apart.

Finally, in the area of social policy, Reagan sought a return to traditional virtues that supported the family and fought against the erosion of the culture. Pro-life, pro-family, anti-pornography, "just say no" to drugs, resistance to the increasing dependency of American citizens on the state—these too were part of Reagan's agenda. This was his most difficult task, for presidents have much less power to move culture in their desired direction than they do to implement tax policy and foreign policy.

Some of these items required changes on the Supreme Court, and progressive forces fought successfully to kill the nomination of Robert Bork, a man who would have provided the necessary fifth vote to overturn *Roe v. Wade* in 1992. University academics had already succeeded even before Reagan came to office in corrupting the standard moral language. They favored and taught "subjective" truth and "values" as opposed to simple truth and virtues. This indoctrination of the young minds with terms such as *values clarification* and *lifestyle choices* created a wider chasm between Progressives and Conservatives.

With the rise of postmodernism, any attempt to make the case for Jefferson's "laws of nature" and "self-evident truths" would be branded as oppressive, patriarchal, and culturally insensitive—a perspective embraced by the elite news media and popular culture. Reagan's efforts injected a strong rhetorical opposition to the progressive Left, but the battle continues.[8]

THE DECLINE OF POWER— POST-REAGAN PRESIDENCIES

The Reagan era is not exempt from the normal pattern of political cycles. Reagan was clearly the founder of a conservative era that transformed the way Americans think about politics. His immediate successor, George H. W. Bush, inherited the burden of following in Reagan's footsteps, trying to serve as a type of third Reagan term the same way Madison, Van Buren, Grant, and Truman followed their founders.

Bush attempted to follow the path laid out for him by Reagan, to varying degrees of success. He demonstrated in the Persian Gulf War that the post–Cold War American military was unmatched by any other military in the world. But Bush also reversed his "no new taxes" campaign pledge, earning the wrath of conservative purists. The entrance of independent candidate Ross Perot in the 1992 presidential race split the Republican Party and gave the presidency to Bill Clinton.

Clinton was a classic opposition president. With the end of the Cold War, a draft-dodging child of the 1960s took advantage of the lack of a significant national security threat to win the presidency. He attempted to govern as a progressive president, with his signature domestic agenda centered on universal government-run health care.

Clinton did not recognize that he was president in an era in which Reagan conservatism and suspicion of government programs was still resilient. In 1994, Republicans took control of both houses of Congress for the first time in forty years, prompting Clinton to move toward the center, declaring that the era of big government was over and pledging to balance the budget.

He also signed welfare reform and the Defense of Marriage Act, which defined marriage as a relationship between a man and a woman. Clinton's own immoral sexual indulgences, however, cost him greatly in his second term, leading to only the second impeachment trial of a president in American history.

Clinton's own quibbling over the meaning of the word *is* exemplified the classic moral relativism and postmodern abuse of language that Conservatives fought against. The fact that Clinton retained very strong public approval ratings during this period testifies to the durability of the more lax code of ethics inherited from the 1960s.

George W. Bush restored the Reagan agenda after the close election of 2000. He succeeded in cutting income taxes twice, in a direct extension of the Reagan revolution. He also attempted to further a social conservative agenda with his Supreme Court appointments, staunch support of marriage, and resistance to federal funding of embryonic stem cell research. He welcomed religious groups into the White House and encouraged their unique activities in American public life.

Most consequentially, the terrorist attacks of September 11, 2001, transformed the Republican national security posture from an out-of-date Cold War setting to a global contender in the war on terror. Bush succeeded in toppling the Taliban regime in Afghanistan and Saddam Hussein in Iraq, but as the American body count rose, the two wars became increasingly unpopular. The double shot of war and financial crisis in 2008 gave the presidency to another opposition president, Barack Obama.

BARACK OBAMA—
THE SOCIALIST AGENDA PRESIDENT

Obama represented a distinct threat to the vitality of the aging Reagan era. He clearly wanted to be the founder of his own progressive regime. His agenda was staunchly liberal, with health-care reform representing the summit of leftist dreams for decades. He ran a campaign on "change we can believe in." He rescinded the "don't ask, don't tell" policy on homosexuals serving in the military and ceased to enforce the Defense of Marriage Act.

Obama was always supportive of abortion on demand, dismissing the question of the moral status of the unborn as "above my pay grade."[9] He launched a campaign against religious freedom through the mechanism of the Affordable Care Act and his eventual open support of gay marriage. In almost every way, Obama's social agenda represented an attempt to repudiate the Reagan stance and win the culture war.

He arguably accomplished this project, at least in part, in the campaign to redefine marriage, a pre-political institution that has been understood as a conjugal relationship between a man and a woman—part of the "laws of nature and of nature's God"—for millennia. Obama had the full weight of the cultural elite on his side, aided by a Supreme Court—though staffed with a majority of Republican appointees—that overturned the Defense of Marriage Act in 2013 and legalized gay marriage in 2015. Obama continued his campaign to transform the culture with his imposition of transgender rights late in his second term.

In the area of economic policy, Obama proved willing to increase spending to almost unthinkable levels, working vigorously to expand the scope of federal action in American life. But he proved incapable of truly reversing Reagan in the area of income taxes, promising tax cuts for almost all Americans—except for the top 1 percent. The focus on the top 1 percent marked a return to a class-based politics that placed inequality at the center of Democratic Party discourse, making it possible for a socialist candidate, Vermont senator Bernie Sanders, to mount a serious threat to the presidential nomination of the Democratic Party in 2016.

In the area of foreign policy, Obama retained a variety of Bush era security policies but chose to confront the war on terror through drone aircraft, drastically reducing our military presence in the campaign against Islamic extremism. During this time, the radical Islamic terrorist organization ISIS rose from the ashes in Iraq, seizing territory and surreptitiously using social media as a recruiting tool to gain foot soldiers.

While Obama referred to them as "a JV team,"[10] these terrorists were prepared to commit vile attacks throughout Europe and the United States. Their goal was not only to wipe Israel "off the map," but to remove all who opposed them.

Yet Obama worked to diminish American influence in the world, choosing to "lead from behind" and often focused on America's faults in his public rhetoric, unwilling to draw clear distinctions between good and evil, virtue and vice. Despite his efforts to destroy America and its values, the Republican Party, led by an energized Tea Party movement, captured control of the House of Representatives in 2010 and the Senate in 2014.

Lacking control of the legislature, Obama proceeded to enact as much of his anti-American agenda as he could through executive power. From selective enforcement or nonenforcement of federal

statutes, to the use of unilateral foreign policy power in forging a
nuclear deal with Iran, which never would have been allowed to see
the light of day if it had required a treaty ratification fight in the
Senate, Obama found a way. All of which brings us to our current
leadership crisis.

DONALD J. TRUMP—
MAKING AMERICA GREAT AGAIN

President Trump inherited an exceptionally dangerous leadership
challenge. He has to restore the Reagan revolution to renewed vigor
and dominance while adjusting it to changing times as he attempts to
turn back the resurgent progressive forces who believe that Obama's
agenda represented the future of the nation—or who believe that
Obama's agenda was not progressive enough for the nation.

Trump has to articulate the virtues of a conservative economic
agenda, including limited government and federalism, while trying
to tame a seemingly intractable national debt. Trump has to restore
America's global leadership at a time when the growing threats to
national security seem to multiply daily with a military force armed
with aging weapons systems and a population suspicious of foreign
engagements.

Trump has to make a compelling case for conservative views
on social issues. Most important of these is the issue of religious
freedom in the face of an aggressive "marriage equality" movement.
He must confront the spread of social radicalism on our college
campuses, which now requires universities to supply safe spaces for
"marginalized groups" or suffer economic ramifications under civil
discrimination suits.

Trump has to do all of this in a period that has witnessed increasing political polarization, as the Republican Party has become
increasingly and more uniformly conservative and the Democratic

Party increasingly and more uniformly liberal. Such polarization—the highest it has been since the Civil War—makes it difficult to push a legislative agenda through a narrowly divided Congress, as each side sees the other as a dangerous threat to the republic. Progressive forces are entrenched in the elite news media, higher education, and popular culture in opposition to the central principles of the Reagan era.[11]

Finally, Trump is attempting to accomplish these objectives in the midst of an unprecedented natural disaster: a global pandemic, the novel coronavirus COVID-19, which originated in China, and in the span of a few weeks disrupted every aspect of the world's economic life. The impact of the pandemic on the 2020 presidential election remains highly unpredictable.

Thus, Trump is presented with two leadership problems: how to be successful as a conservative political leader late in the Reagan era and how to be successful as a moral leader in an age that no longer recognizes the "laws of nature and nature's God."

Trump's Accomplishments

At the time of this writing, as Donald Trump's first term as president transitions into a reelection campaign, it would be useful to briefly survey the political landscape and see what Trump has been able to accomplish given his constrained circumstances.

In the area of economic policy, Trump followed in the footsteps of Reagan by signing into law a $1.5 trillion tax cut, lowering the income tax rates for individuals while also reducing the corporate tax rate from 35 percent to 21 percent.[12] This tax cut legislation also simplified the income tax process by reducing the standard 1040 tax form to the size of a postcard. It eliminated the individual mandate of the Affordable Care Act (Obamacare).

While the Republican-led Congress could not agree on a specific legislative package to replace Obamacare, the end of the individual mandate guts the law of its primary fiscal lifeline. With this one move, Trump succeeded both in restoring Reagan-era tax policy to prominence while also attacking and undermining the accomplishments of the president who most threatened the vitality of the Reagan era. And, although Obamacare has survived several court challenges to date, the Supreme Court will soon hear a new case that could undermine the law, brought forward by more than a dozen Republican states, led by Texas.

The Trump administration has also made significant progress in cutting regulations. Trump promised to eliminate two regulations for every new one created, a ratio he has frequently surpassed. He used the Congressional Review Act sixteen times by the summer of 2019 to end Obama-era regulations—a tactic used only once before in history, by George W. Bush. Federal agencies have shifted their focus from writing regulations to cutting them, resulting in billions of dollars in savings. This reduction of the footprint of the federal government in American life expands the scope of personal liberty following eight years of movement in the opposite direction under President Obama.

The result of these moves led to a healthy economy and continued growth. Many corporations publicly announced major bonuses for employees after passage of the tax cut. The stock market hit a historic high of 9569.58 points in February 2020*, job growth increased steadily month to month, wages rose, and the unemployment rate sank to 3.5 percent in September 2019, the lowest level in fifty years. Add to that a steady GDP, relatively low inflation, and historically low unemployment rates for youth, women, African Americans, and other minorities[13]—it would be difficult to find an

---

* https://tradingeconomics.com/united-states/stock-market#:~:text=Historically%2C %20the%20Dow%20Jones%20Industrial,updated%20on%20July%20of%202020.

earlier period with healthier economic numbers until the negative impact of the novel coronavirus hit.

In the area of social policy, clearly the most important development was Trump's nomination and appointments of Neil Gorsuch and Brett Kavanaugh to the United States Supreme Court. Trump received a major assist in this area from the Republican-controlled Senate.

The unexpected death of conservative icon Antonin Scalia early in 2016 gave President Obama the opportunity to shift the basic balance of power on the Supreme Court decisively in a liberal direction with his nomination of circuit court of appeals judge Merrick Garland. However, Senate majority leader Mitch McConnell refused to hold hearings on the nomination, effectively killing the nomination when Trump won the presidency. The consequences of this blocking tactic cannot be exaggerated. Garland represented a fifth and decisive liberal voice on the Court, potentially shifting the Court to the left for a generation. Instead, Gorsuch's appointment solidified the conservative bloc.

President Trump strengthened the conservative majority on the Court in 2018 when he nominated Judge Kavanaugh to replace retiring Justice Anthony Kennedy. Despite a fierce and brutal assault on Kavanaugh's character, the administration and Republican Senate held firm, and Kavanaugh took his place on the Court next to Gorsuch.

With two liberal justices over the age of eighty, the chances of Trump getting one or two more nominations in a second term are very high—a fact that highlights the importance of the 2020 presidential election. The impact of Trump's appointments on everything from abortion to free speech rights to religious liberty is beyond calculation. The Trump Supreme Court will control the legal destiny of America for the next forty years.

Trump's accomplishments in judicial nominations are not limited to the Supreme Court. Most judicial matters never get to that level; they are instead settled at lower levels of the federal judiciary. With the cooperation of Republicans in the Senate, Trump has nominated and appointed federal judges at a record pace—almost two hundred judges over the course of three years, comprising over a quarter of all federal appeals court positions. This includes a reshaping of the infamously liberal Ninth Circuit Court of Appeals, which now has ten Trump-appointed judges out of twenty-nine seats.* Trump's concentrated efforts in this area will shape the future trajectory of the judicial branch for years to come.

In addition to using executive power to reinstate pro-life policies, Trump followed the examples of Reagan and George W. Bush by speaking live via video feed to the 2018 March for Life. In 2020 he personally attended the march, a first for a sitting president. He has consistently supported the Second Amendment, speaking at the National Rifle Association's annual conference in 2017, 2018, and 2019. Federal agencies have begun reversing Obama-era policies and supporting religious liberty and conscience protections.[14] The administration has even slowed down and reversed efforts to advance the gender identity campaign.

In the area of foreign policy and national security, the president has much greater leeway to act at his own discretion. Trump has been more noticeably and openly critical of the United Nations since taking office. He has pushed NATO members to increase their defense spending. He also revoked the Iran nuclear deal.

Trump withdrew the United States from the Trans-Pacific Partnership on trade and renegotiated the North American Free Trade Agreement, culminating in the new United States–Mexico-Canada

---

* Ronn Blitzer, "Trump Heads into 2020 with 'Historic' Judicial Appointments" (December 22, 2019), https://www.foxnews.com/politics/trump-heads-into-2020 -with-historic-judicial-appointments.

Agreement (USMCA). He also renegotiated the United States–Korea Free Trade Agreement, and continues to work on other bilateral trade agreements, including one with post-Brexit Great Britain.

He imposed tariffs on steel and aluminum and began several trade actions targeting China. In 2018 Trump withdrew the US from the United Nations Human Rights Council over bias against Israel and its ineptness to prevent abuse by "the world's most inhumane regimes."[15]

Between 2006 and 2016, the United Nations Human Rights Council passed sixty-seven resolutions condemning human rights violations around the world, to include the massacre of half a million people in Syria, the genocide in Darfur, and the execution of lesbian, gay, and bisexual people in Iran.

In that same decade, the Human Rights Council passed sixty-eight resolutions condemning Israel for fighting for its life against murderous terror organizations. This flagrant injustice reflects the appalling discrimination of the UN when it comes to Israel.[16]

Trump also took an aggressive stance against ISIS, targeting its strongholds in Syria, Iraq, and Afghanistan. The terrorist group has lost most of the territory it once controlled. In 2019 American military forces tracked down and killed infamous ISIS leader Abu Bakr al-Baghdadi. Then, in early January 2020, Trump authorized an air strike that killed Iranian general and head of the Quds Force Qasem Soleimani.

Trump has demonstrated a much firmer hand against the use of chemical weapons in Syria and leveled sanctions against Russia for its use of chemical weapons against two citizens in Great Britain. He has made national security concerns a central feature of the administration's immigration policy, using his discretionary authority to divert federal funds to the construction of a wall on the border with Mexico.

Trump has taken a much more aggressive stance against N Korea, officially designating the rogue nation a state sponsor terrorism, while at the same time expressing a willingness to speak with North Korean leader Kim Jong-Un. This face-to-face meeting, something never before done in American foreign policy, occurred in June of 2018. Kim Jong-Un began making overtures of peace to South Korea, talking about formally ending the Korean War and eliminating all nuclear weapons from the Korean peninsula.

In June 2019 Trump became the first president to step across the border of South Korea into North Korea. A nuclear deal remains elusive, but Trump has demonstrated a consistent willingness to act against conventional wisdom in pursuit of larger goals.

Finally, Trump visited Israel in May 2017, the fiftieth anniversary of the Six-Day War and Israel's reunification with Jerusalem. In December of that year, he officially recognized Jerusalem as the capital of Israel and ordered the State Department to begin the process of moving the American embassy from Tel Aviv to Jerusalem.

On May 14, 2018, the United States embassy was officially opened in Jerusalem, despite a United Nations Security Council resolution condemning the move. I had the honor of participating in the opening ceremony of the US embassy in Jerusalem by offering the benediction prayer. It will be a day etched in my mind forever!

Trump's Challenges

In all of these areas, Trump has worked to advance the basic principles and commitments established at the dawn of the Reagan era, at the same time working vigorously to reverse and cancel the progressive gains of the Obama presidency. It has not been an easy road for the administration. In some cases, the pushback has been predictable. For example, presidents typically lose ground in Congress in midterm elections, and Trump was not immune to this constitutional feature.

Although Republicans gained two Senate seats in the 2018 midterm elections, defying the historical pattern, they lost forty House seats, as well as control of that chamber. When the new Congress convened in January 2019, Trump faced a divided government: a Senate narrowly controlled by his party, but a House now under the leadership of Democrat Nancy Pelosi.

In other cases, the pushback against Trump represented a fierce battle of Democrats to delegitimize and even end his presidency. Before Trump even took the inaugural oath a "resistance" movement formed to question his legitimacy and fight him every step of the way.

Maintaining control of the Senate was exceptionally important, given the success Senate majority leader Mitch McConnell has had in pushing through judicial nominations. All other policy arenas, however, became much more tenuous as House Democrats began a series of oversight investigations that eventually led to the impeachment of the president in December 2019. This was the first completely partisan impeachment of a president in American history, as all House Democrats voted to impeach Trump while all Republicans voted against the procedure.

The trial in the Senate was predictable. Sixty-seven votes were needed to convict President Trump; the eventual vote to acquit was almost as partisan. All Democrats voted to convict the president, while all but one Republican voted to acquit. The various phases of the impeachment effort dominated the political calendar for months, preventing action on other important issues.

At the same time, the lengthy 2020 presidential campaign season got underway, with more than two dozen Democrats vying for the nomination. The field spanned a wide spectrum of policy proposals and ideologies, from moderate or establishment candidates to far more leftwing options. Most notably, independent and self-described Democratic Socialist Vermont senator Bernie Sanders, who had harassed Hillary Clinton on her road to the nomination in 2016, came back to seek the nomination again.

Sanders (and to a lesser extent Massachusetts senator Elizabeth Warren) represented a concentrated attack on the very foundations of most features of the Reagan era. His rejection of capitalism and the free market represents a rejection of Reagan-era economic policy. Indeed, Sanders proposed to raise taxes to historic levels in a massive redistribution scheme designed to guarantee a variety of "benefits" to the population, including free health care, free public college, and the retirement of all student debt.

He regularly attacked "Wall Street" in a naked attempt to foster class warfare. He also rejected most elements of conservative social policy, especially in the area of sexual liberty and abortion. He was also a frequent critic of just about every form of American foreign policy, with a long career marked by embracing and praising a number of Communist dictators and criticizing Israel.

The fact that a self-described socialist could threaten to seize control of the Democratic Party nomination process and make a serious run at the nomination itself, despite the fact that he was not even a member of the party, demonstrates how far to the left he helped push the party in his losing effort in 2016. Policy proposals that seemed extreme in 2016 were mainstream in 2020.

More ominously, the percentage of Americans who view socialism positively has risen in recent years. A Gallup poll in November 2019—at the height of the Democratic Party pre-primary debates—found that Gen Xers and Baby Boomers have been fairly consistent in their views of socialism and capitalism.

Roughly two-thirds of them view capitalism positively, while only one-third view socialism positively. For Millennials and Gen Zers, however, ages eighteen to thirty-nine in 2019, about 50 percent have positive views of socialism, while the positive views of capitalism have declined from 66 percent in 2010 to 51 percent in 2019.[*]

While the youngest cohort of voters turns out to vote in the smallest numbers—much to the chagrin of Bernie Sanders—the fact that the youngest cohort has such positive views of an ideology that has never performed better than 6 percent in a presidential election (1912) suggests that what Bernie Sanders represents may become increasingly popular as this group ages and becomes more reliable in their voting habits.

The COVID-19 global pandemic could be one of those once-a-generation trigger events that changes the trajectory of American politics—along the lines of the Great Depression or the social disruption of the 1960s. For example, the repercussion from Hurricane Katrina in 2005 was the catalyst which promoted the popular approval rate for President George W. Bush to decline, and ultimately paved the way for the rise of Barack Obama. In like manner, the devastation of the novel coronavirus represents a clear threat to President Trump's accomplishments and political future.

The economic devastation has been stark. The unemployment rate tripled in April 2020 to 14.7 percent, the highest level since the Great Depression. By mid-May more than 20 million people were out of work, with projections that the unemployment rate could move as high as 25 percent.[†]

From a record high approaching 30,000 points in mid-February,

---

[*] Lydia Saad, "Socialism as Popular as Capitalism Among Young Adults in U.S." (November 25, 2019), https://news.gallup.com/poll/268766/socialism-popular -capitalism-among-young-adults.aspx.

[†] Brendan Morrow, "Goldman Sachs Economists Forecast Unemployment Rate Will Reach 25 Percent," *The Week* (May 14, 2020), https://www.msn.com/en-gb/news/politics /goldman-sachs-economists-forecast-unemployment-rate-will-reach-25-percent /ar-BB142GRy.

the Dow Jones Industrial Average suffered six quadruple-digit losses over the next five weeks, plunging over 30 percent, erasing trillions of dollars of wealth and ending an eleven-year bull market.[*] Early federal government efforts to address the crisis totaled more than two trillion dollars, swelling the federal budget deficit to a projected 3.7 trillion dollars for the year. The Federal Reserve responded by slashing interest rates to zero.[†]

Sports, from the professional level down to juvenile leagues, cancelled entire seasons; musical ensembles ended their seasons in mid-stride; movie theaters went dark for several months, schools at all levels closed down and resorted to remote, online education. The economic consequences of these developments cascaded down through all levels of government.

Shelter-in-place policies that led to these massive job losses resulted in minimal commercial activity, and the loss of sales tax revenue in turn means state and local governments are experiencing huge budget shortfalls that will adversely impact their ability to provide basic and necessary services to their communities. Oil prices crashed, putting additional stress on the energy sector of the economy, and there is no guarantee that once commercial activity resumes businesses will immediately rehire all the employees who were laid off.

In the meantime, in mid-May, House Democrats approved an additional multi-trillion-dollar, 1,800-page relief bill. This bill directly conflicted with the aims of the Republican-controlled Senate, with both chambers of Congress facing off against President Trump, who had his own ideas about further stimulus efforts.

---

[*] Kimberly Amadeo, "How Does the 2020 Stock Market Crash Compare with Others?" *The Balance* (April 27, 2020), https://www.thebalance.com/fundamentals-of-2020-market-crash-4799950.

[†] Jeanna Smialek, Jim Tankersley, and Emily Cochrane, "Fed Chair Touts More Help for Economy," *New York Times* (May 14, 2020).

dueling proposals reflected the competing political objec-
the two parties, a further manifestation of the polarization
of contemporary politics. Democratic House efforts, for example, include provisions to reduce immigration enforcement, provide checks to illegal immigrants, shore up the Postal Service, and
require that national elections be held by mail. Former Democratic
Party presidential candidates Bernie Sanders and Kamala Harris
proposed that Americans be given two thousand dollars a month for
the duration of the crisis.

Democratic Party efforts, then, represent an effort to make use
of the pandemic to further the party's own ideological agenda—
to take advantage of a crisis to gain what it could not in regular
elections. Joe Biden understands the need to gain the support of
Sanders's energetic progressive base. Even though Biden is not the
most progressive candidate in history, it is likely that Sanders's influence will cause the party platform to be the most progressive platform in history.

Biden is becoming increasingly tied to Sanders and Sanders's
most vocal ally in the House, New York congresswoman Alexandria
Ocasio-Cortez, named by Biden as a co-chair of his climate change
task force. Biden has already pledged to name a woman as his running mate, and the forces in the party most attuned to identity politics are pressuring him to name an African American woman to
the ticket.

Ironically, this decision came at the same time that Biden was
accused of sexual harassment by a former subordinate. The difference in reaction by the Democratic Party establishment and the
mainstream news media compared to the accusations against Brett
Kavanaugh exemplifies the hypocrisy of the Left, and the nature of

the conflict Trump faces. Not surprisingly, Biden won the Democratic Party Nomination for the 2020 presidential election.[*]

The uncertain trajectory of the pandemic makes it impossible to predict its influence on the November election. For the most part, Republicans allied themselves to the "open now" faction, while Democrats embraced the "keep things closed" faction. Political polarization provides little to no room for compromise on options, and the decreasing number of true swing voters will decide the election based on their perceptions of who has been most successful addressing the crisis.

History is often unkind to incumbent presidents who preside over bad economic times, as seen by the failure of Herbert Hoover, Jimmy Carter, and George H. W. Bush to win reelection. However, Americans have also been known to give incumbents a pass on economic bad times if they believe other forces are responsible, as seen by the electoral success of Franklin Roosevelt and Barack Obama. For President Trump and his work to restore the Reagan agenda, everything hinges on which group of presidents the American voters associate Trump with come November.

What Is Our Future?

Reagan succeeded in recalibrating the public debate over these timeless values, but he did not succeed in defeating the many forces conceived in the Progressive movement and birthed in the 1960s. For Trump to succeed, he will have to reset the political clock of the Reagan era for another generation and clearly articulate the historic

---

[*] As of this printing, Joe Biden and Kamala Harris have accepted the nomination of the Democratic Party for the offices of president and vice president, respectively. President Donald Trump and Vice President Mike Pence accepted the Republican Party nomination to pursue a second term as president and vice president.

understanding of the universal and absolute truths of the American Founding.

If President Trump fails, we will more than likely enter a new progressive era—a prospect that does not bode well for liberty, limited government, and self-evident truths. It will produce a liberal dictatorship that will attack religious freedom and traditional marriage and will advance the slaughter of the unborn and embrace social revolution where tyranny and anarchy in the streets of America overwhelm the police forces.

"Equal justice under the law" will be a mere slogan chiseled over the doors of the Supreme Court building, not a fact of life any longer in these United States.

Make way for the New World Order!

CHAPTER 8

THE NEW WORLD ORDER

Believe me, National Socialism would not be worth anything if it were to be confined to Germany and did not secure the rule of the superior race over the whole world for at least one or two thousand years... National Socialism will use its own revolution for establishing a new world order. —Adolf Hitler

A "New World Order" (NWO) is any period of history that demonstrates a dramatic change in world thought, causing a shift in the balance of power among the geopolitical actors on the global stage. Since the post–Cold War era, the universal meaning of the NWO was redefined as an alliance of sovereign nations working together for the world's common good.

The New World Order is not a novel phenomenon. Its origins can be traced to the book of Genesis with the building of a stronghold that symbolized man's arrogance, lust for power, and ultimately, their absolute rebellion against God.

NIMROD:
BABEL'S NEW WORLD ORDER

Shortly after creation, the Lord commanded mankind to populate and cultivate the whole earth:

> *Then God blessed them, and God said to them, "Be fruitful and multiply; fill the earth and subdue it; have dominion over the fish of the sea, over the birds of the air, and over every living thing that moves on the earth"* (Genesis 1:28).

Yet, the people at the time of Noah defied God and lived only for themselves. They used violence and force against their weaker neighbors for gain, having no regard for any system of laws. After generations of disobedience, wickedness and corruption, the Lord used a flood to destroy humanity, saving only Noah and his family:[1]

> *So the LORD said, "I will destroy man whom I have created from the face of the earth, both man and beast, creeping thing and birds of the air, for I am sorry that I have made them." But Noah found grace in the eyes of the LORD* (Genesis 6:7–8).

After the Flood, in obedience to God's mandate, Noah and his sons, Shem, Ham, and Japheth, began to repopulate the earth.

The Bible records a pivotal incident resulting in Noah pronouncing a curse on one of his sons and blessing the other two. Finding his father drunk in his tent, Ham exposed Noah's disgrace, while his brothers, Shem and Japheth, dutifully covered their father's shame (Genesis 9:18–24). Noah spoke a curse over Ham after learning of his disrespect, and in contrast, Noah rewarded Shem and Japheth's righteous actions with his spoken blessing (Genesis 9:25–27).

Why is this event significant? Abraham and the Jewish people are direct descendants of Shem—they are the righteous line (Genesis 15:6; 18:19). The Gentiles descended from Japheth's line—we are the branches that were grafted into the root according to the book of Romans (11:17, 19).

Ham's sons were Cush, Mizraim, Put, and Canaan. His descendants, which included the Jebusites and other Canaanite people, represented the ungodly and rebellious line, who were later conquered by Israel (Joshua 24:11). It is from this lineage that the concept of the New World Order originated.

The generation after the Flood was different than the generation before. The individual was now part of a united front that submitted themselves to the desires of the group. But the great strength which eventually grew out of their consolidation made them believe they were self-reliant, and that deceptive independence turned them against God.

The people rejected God's revelation concerning access to His presence. Moreover, they turned away from being governed by God or His chosen representatives. The Almighty divinely established the institutions of religion and human government as two distinct entities managed by two separate individuals. The government would be administered by a ruler from the tribe of Judah (Genesis 49:10), and the system of religion was to be led by a priest from the tribe of Levi (Joshua 13:33), with the exception of Melchizedek, as mentioned in the first chapter.[*]

Mankind's defiant will to remain together in one place was an affront to God and in direct conflict with the command He gave to Noah and his sons (Genesis 9:7). This was the generation into which Nimrod was born.

It has been said that *the purpose of life is life's purpose,* and in order

---

[*] J. Dwight Pentecost. "The Prophetic Word and Romanism." *The Prophetic Word in Crisis Days,* edited by G. Vernon McGee. CreateSpace, 2015.

to accomplish our divine destiny, our aspirations should always align with that of our Creator.

Cush, Ham's son, begat Nimrod, who scripture describes as *"a mighty hunter before the LORD"* (Genesis 10:9; 1 Chronicles 1:10; Micah 5:6). Nimrod's name in Hebrew means "revolt," and his purposes were outside of God's authority and divine plan for mankind. This Cushite became known as "a mighty man of sin, a murderer of innocent men and a rebel before the Lord."*

Nimrod was the first personal kingdom builder. He constructed four cities in Assyria: Nineveh, Rehoboth Ir, Callah, and Resen (Genesis 10:11–12); and on the plains of Shinar, he built Babel, Erech, Accad, and Calneh (Genesis 10:10). Nimrod's obsession with self-adulation and supreme power birthed a tyrannical type of government as well as an idolatrous religious system.

Babel, which means "confusion," is where Nimrod chose to erect a tower that would reach the heavens. Later known as Babylon, this city was intended to be the seat of Nimrod's new self-ruled government, and its stronghold, referred to as "the house of Nimrod,"† was to become the center of worship. Babel and its tower were symbols of man's sinful pride—the same pride that cast Lucifer out of the Third Heaven. (Genesis 10:8–12; 11:1–4; 1 Chronicles 1:10; Micah 5:6).

Josephus said the following of Nimrod and his diabolical objective:

He [Nimrod] also gradually changed the government into tyranny, seeing no other way of turning men from the fear of God, but to bring them into a constant dependence on his power. He also said he would be revenge on God, if He

---

* http://www.the-ten-commandments.org/origin_of_babylon_sun_worship.html.
† http://www.jewishencyclopedia.com/articles/11548-nimrod.

should have a mind to drown the world again; for that he [Nimrod] would build a tower too high for the waters to be able to reach and that he would avenge himself on God for destroying their forefathers![2]

In response to Nimrod's rebellion, God destroyed the tower of Babel, confused the language of the people and scattered them throughout the world (Genesis 11:5–9).

Nevertheless, Nimrod's compulsion for absolute control set the foundation for the first New World Order. It was Nimrod's intent to become the supreme leader of both a universal government and its counterfeit religion. To accomplish his perverse plan, Nimrod married his mother, Semiramis, declared himself the king of Babylon and his mother-bride as its first queen and high priestess of idolatry.*

The incestuous couple introduced Ba'al worship to the people and demanded they pay homage to this false god known as Prince, Lord of the Earth.† Remember this truth: Satan is the Great Imitator. His design was to use these rabid occultists to divert their followers from the God of Noah and enslave them to the king of darkness.

Joshua 2:11–13 refers to this abominable idol worship:

Then the sons of Israel did evil in the sight of the Lord and served the Baals, and they forsook the Lord, the God of their fathers, who had brought them out of the land of Egypt, and followed other gods from among the gods of the peoples who were around them, and bowed themselves down to them; thus they provoked the Lord to anger. So they forsook the Lord and served **Baal** *and the* **Ashtaroth [Semiramis]**.

---

* https://www.bibletools.org/index.cfm/fuseaction/Topical.show /RTD/cgg/ID /3048Mother-Child-Worship.htm.
† https://www.britannica.com/topic/Baal-ancient-deity.

Semiramis [Ashtaroth], who is said to have conquered much of Asia Minor, Libya, and Ethiopia and built the walls of Babylon, is recorded in history as the only woman to have ruled the Assyrian Empire.* She was influential enough to be referred to on ancient monuments in Iraq and Turkey, having her own obelisk placed in prominence in the city of Ashur with the following inscription:

> Stele of Sammuramat [Semiramis], queen of Shamshi-Adad, King of the Universe, King of Assyria, Mother of Adad Nirari, King of the Universe, King of Assyria, Daughter-in-Law of Shalmaneser, King of the Four Regions of the World.†

Semiramis is depicted in Babylonian mythology as both the mother and wife of Nimrod, who miraculously conceived and birthed a son.‡ As part of the first unholy trinity, Semiramis claimed she was the woman of the promise of which we read about in Genesis 3:15: "*I will put enmity between thee and the woman, and between thy seed and her seed: it shall bruise thy head, and thou shalt bruise his heel,*" and that her son, Tammuz, was the *"seed of the woman."*§

Nimrod, Semiramis, and Tammuz, the headship of this rogue cult order, were derailed when Nimrod met his demise at the hand of another great hunter named Esau—son of Isaac and grandson of Abraham, one of Nimrod's adversaries. After Nimrod's death, the followers of Ba'al worshipped in secret.[3]

---

* https://www.nationalgeographic.com/history/magazine/2017/09-10/searching-for-semiramis-assyrian-legend/.
† Joshua J. Markby Joshua J. Mark published on 18 August 2014 Ancient History Encyclopedia-Semiramus.
‡ The Prophetic Word in Crisis Days; Chapter 12 The Prophetic Word.
§ Ibid.

The One World Religion of the Mother-Child Cult

Historian and Bible scholar Alexander Hislop states

> The Tower of Babel was actually the worship of Satan in the form of fire, the sun and the serpent. However, Satan worship could not be done openly because of the many who still believed in the true God of Noah. So a mystery religion began at Babel where Satan could be worshipped in secret.[4]

Semiramis, however, would not settle for an underground form of worship. This egomaniacal queen consoled the people after Nimrod's death alleging to be the Queen of Heaven of the Babylonian religion, thereby securing direct access to God.

According to legend, her son Tammuz was killed while hunting a wild boar. At this time, Semiramis called her virgin followers to forty days of prayer and fasting. After their intercession, Semiramis declared that Tammuz had been resurrected from the dead as a result of her intervening powers. This counterfeit religion, known as the "Mother-Child Cult," was depicted by the iconic symbol of a mother holding an infant in her arms.

The forty-day fast became an annual observance of mourning and sacrifice throughout Babylon. At the end of the fast, the Feast of Ishtar was celebrated in honor of Semiramis and her son. Here colored eggs, the symbol of Tammuz's resurrection, were exchanged. In addition, during the winter solstice, evergreen trees were erected to mark Tammuz's birthday, symbolizing his eternal life.

The prophet Jeremiah describes this latter form of idol worship with a perfect word-picture:

> *Do not learn the way of the Gentiles;*
> *Do not be dismayed at the signs of heaven,*

For the Gentiles are dismayed at them.
For the customs of the peoples are futile;
For one cuts a tree from the forest,
The work of the hands of the workman, with the ax.
They decorate it with silver and gold;
They fasten it with nails and hammers
So that it will not topple (Jeremiah 10:1–4).

Great Abominations

In chapter 8 of the book of Ezekiel, the prophet writes of *"great abominations"* and even *"greater abominations"* that are being committed within the Holy Temple of Jerusalem. (verse 6). He sees unclean animals desecrating God's sanctuary and the elders of Israel, believing they were beyond God's sight, worshipping the graven images of idols (verses 10–12).

Ezekiel witnesses yet another repugnant pagan practice of *"women…weeping for Tammuz"* (verse 14). Lastly, God shows *"about twenty-five men with their backs toward the temple and their faces toward the east, and they were worshipping the sun [Ba'al] toward the east"* (verse 16). This is clearly a pagan sunrise service, where the men of Israel dishonored the God of Abraham, Isaac, and Jacob by turning their backs on Him, while paying homage to the sun god.

There are additional biblical and historical references to the Queen of Heaven and "Mother-Child" worship.* This false religious system may have had different names in Phoenicia, Egypt, Greece, and Rome, but the message was the same—"salvation is through the mother of the Mother-Child Cult."† Semiramis, known in various cultures as Ashtaroth, Ishtar, Aphrodite, Venus, and Isis, effectively

---

* Jeremiah 7:18; 44:17–19, 25; Judges 2:13; 10;6; I Samuel 7:3–4; 12:10; 1 Kings 11:5, 33; 2 Kings 23:13.
† J. Dwight Pentecost. "The Prophetic Word and Romanism." *The Prophetic Word in Crisis Days*, edited by G. Vernon McGee. CreateSpace, 2015.

established a global apostasy that continues to dominate the world to this very day.

With the Babylonian Empire ever expanding and it being the seat of pagan worship, the Mother-Child Cult and its practices soon spread to Phoenicia. First Kings 16:30–33 records the far-reaching corruptions of this forged religion even into the palace of the king of Israel:

> Ahab son of Omri did more evil in the eyes of the Lord than any of those before him…he also married Jezebel daughter of Ethbaal king of the Sidonians, and began to serve Baal and worship him. He set up an altar for Baal in the temple of Baal that he built in Samaria. Ahab also made an **Asherah pole** and did more to arouse the anger of the Lord, the God of Israel, than did all the kings of Israel before him.

After the Medes and the Persians conquered Babylon in 539 BCE, the majority of the pagan priests associated with Ba'al worship were forced to relocate to Pergamos. Christ referred to this city as the throne of Satan in His letter to its citizens:

> I know your works, and where you dwell, where **Satan's throne** is. And you hold fast to My name, and did not deny My faith even in the days in which Antipas was My faithful martyr, who was killed among you, where Satan dwells (Revelation 2:13).

From Pergamos, the pagan priests migrated to Rome and Alexandria, where they set up the sun worship under its emperors.[5] Socrates Scholasticus, the author of *Historia Ecclesiastica* (Church History), documents this shift of ancient Christianity during the years 305 to 439 CE:

For although almost all churches throughout the world celebrate the sacred mysteries [of the Lord's Supper] on the
Sabbath of every week, yet the Christians of Alexandria and
at Rome, on account of some ancient tradition, have ceased
to do this.[6]

Since 12 BCE, the Caesars were crowned with two crowns.
They were both emperor of the secular government and Pontifex
Maximus, the leader of the Roman church system.[*] In 313 CE, while
emperor of the Western Roman Empire, Constantine issued the
Edict of Milan, legalizing Christianity. This decree was an attempt
to form an alliance with the followers of Christ for the purpose of
social stability.[†]

After gaining complete control of Rome in 324 CE, Emperor
Constantine convened the First Council of Nicaea, resulting in the
creation of the official Roman Church doctrine, called the Nicene
Creed (325 CE).[‡] Sixty-eight years later, Theodosius I issued the
Edict of Thessalonica (380 CE), making "Christianity" the autho-
rized state religion of the Roman Empire.[§]

But what kind of Christianity were Rome's citizens professing?
They were certainly not following the righteous teachings of Jesus
Christ of Nazareth. Many of these newly dubbed "Christians" were
fervent disciples of the "Queen of Heaven" and the Mother-Child
god, Tammuz.

After the Edict of Thessalonica, practicing pagans went back
to the same temple, worshipped the same Mother-Child god and
observed the same rituals. They celebrated Lent with a forty-day
fast, Easter with colorful eggs, and the midwinter celebration by

---

[*]   https://www.sjsu.edu/faculty/watkins/caesaraugustus.htm.
[†]   https://en.wikipedia.org/wiki/Edict_of_Milan.
[‡]   https://en.wikipedia.org/wiki/First_Council_of_Nicaea.
[§]   https://en.wikipedia.org/wiki/Theodosius_I.

cutting down trees in adoration of Tammuz. The only difference was that by an official Imperial decree, they all became "Christians."

With these three rulings, Babylonian paganism was merged into the Roman Church, which became the reigning religious system of the Dark Ages. This was the same Roman Church whose Crusaders marched to liberate Jerusalem in the Middle Ages while slaughtering Jewish families along the way.

This was the same Roman Church that gave King Ferdinand and Queen Isabella their blessing for the Edict of Expulsion (1492), which demanded all Jews leave Spain or face death.

This was the same Roman Church that supported the Third Reich.

As the centuries passed and the seed of anti-Semitism took root, Satan laid the foundation for every future evil world empire. His ultimate goal is to foil God's plan of redemption by destroying the Jewish people from which comes our Messiah.

And it was from the Holy Roman Empire (Germany), that the Evil One chose to spawn another self-adulating megalomaniac by the name of Adolph Hitler.

HITLER AND THE NEW WORLD ORDER OF THE THIRD REICH

After the Paris Peace Conference, President Woodrow Wilson founded the League of Nations in 1920.[7] This intergovernmental organization was intended to oversee the nations of the world in an effort to avoid another catastrophe like World War I.

Sixty-three nations participated in the League, eventually including Germany. Ironically, even though the US established the group, we chose not to be a part. Our leaders wanted to avoid any further involvement in Europe's disputes in order to circumvent being ensnared in another global war.

Then, in 1933, the world dramatically changed when a demonized madman by the name of Adolf Hitler was appointed chancellor of Germany. In less than ten months after taking office, Germany withdrew from the League of Nations, due to the league's refusal to acquiesce to the newly appointed chancellor's demands for military parity with the Western powers.* Little did the League know that this one man would shatter their dreams of achieving world peace.

Adolf Hitler was born in Austria in 1889 and moved to Germany when he was twenty-four years old. After serving in World War I, he joined the German Workers Party in 1919 and became its leader by 1921. While imprisoned in 1923, after a failed coup against the government, Hitler wrote his infamous book *Mein Kampf*.

Following his release from prison in 1924, Hitler immediately gained widespread popularity by attacking the much-despised Treaty of Versailles, the "traitorous" Weimer Republic, and the rise of communism, all the while promoting Pan-Germanism (the union of all German people) and anti-Semitism. Hitler began to advance the idea of a Führer as an absolute ruler who would bring unity to the German people and lead the "Aryan race" to world supremacy—his well-synchronized tactics worked.

In January of 1933, in an effort to neutralize Hitler's increasing popularity, the ailing German president Paul von Hindenburg appointed this "bohemian corporal," as he referred to him, chancellor. But the chancellery was just the first phase of Hitler's calculated plan in his lust for power. By August 19, 1934—seventeen short days after Hindenburg's death—Hitler assumed the office of the president and merged it with the office of the chancellorship. Then, as a result of his mesmerizing influence and systematic fear tactics, Hitler received 90 percent of the majority vote from Germany's parliament: He was now both chancellor and Führer.

---

* https://www.wdl.org/en/item/11598/.

As the army took an oath of loyalty to its supreme commander-in-chief, the last fragments of the nation's democratic government were ripped apart, making way for Hitler's Third Reich. This unprecedented consolidation of power made Adolf Hitler Germany's dictator.

Hitler's strategy was to conquer Europe and become the savior of Germany and ultimately the ruler of the world. This failed artist and puffed-up corporal of the German army thought of himself as god, and his Third Reich, an empire that would last a thousand years.

Joseph Goebbels, the Reich Minister of Propaganda, said of Hitler's vision:

> The Führer gave expression to his unshakable conviction that the Reich will be the master of all Europe. We shall yet have to engage in many fights, but these will undoubtedly lead to most wonderful victories. From there on, the way to world domination is practically certain. Whoever dominates Europe will thereby assume the leadership of the world.[*]

Hitler swore to the citizens of Germany that he would bring a new world order producing peace, prosperity, and global power. He adopted the political directive of *Neuordnung* (New Order), which Nazi Germany would attempt to impose on all of their conquered territories.

Even though this New Order had begun shortly after Hitler assumed leadership in 1933, he declared, the "... *year 1941 will be, I am convinced, the historical year of a great European New Order.*"

This New Order was a springboard for Hitler's attempted global conquest and the establishment of a world government under

---

[*] Jonathan Adelman, *Hitler and His Allies in World War Two*, Routledge, 2020.

German control. The strategy for the revival of the Holy Roman Empire entailed the following:

- The creation and supremacy of a pure Aryan-Nordic master race structured according to Nazi ideology.
- Massive territorial expansion into Central and Eastern Europe.
- The physical annihilation of the Jews, Slavs (Poles and Russians), Roma (gypsies), and others considered "unworthy of life" and "racially inferior."[*]

The masses, including the *Hitlerjugend* (Hitler Youth), hypnotically followed the Führer, making their Nazi salute a symbol of praise to the new pagan god of Germany. Hitler strongly believed in ensuring the future of the Third Reich by captivating the minds of the next generation,

We have set before ourselves the task of inoculating our youth…at a very early age.…This new Reich will give its youth to no one, but will itself take youth and give to youth its own education and its own upbringing.…When an opponent declares, "I will not come over to your side," I calmly say, "Your child belongs to us already.…What are you? You will pass on. Your descendants, however, now stand in the new camp. In a short time, they will know nothing else but this new community."[†]

But not all of Germany was deceived by Hitler's vision. There were those who rightly discerned the nation's future path of destruction.

---

[*] https://www.warhistoryonline.com/instant-articles/hitlers-plans-for-a-new-world.html.

[†] *Nazi Conspiracy and Aggression*, Vol 5, by United States Office of Counsel for the Prosecution of Axis Criminality, U.S. Government Printing Office 1946, pp. 196–198.

During Hitler's dramatic rise to power, Lutheran pastor Dietrich Bonhoeffer stated, *"Germany cannot have two masters. Either we will serve the God of the Bible or we will serve Herr Hitler ... but we cannot serve both."*[8]

Bonhoeffer was arrested and died in prison for having the courage to speak the truth against the Führer's monstrous regime. His words, however, were seared into the hearts of believers for generations to come: *"To see evil and not call it evil is evil. Not to speak is to speak. Not to act is to act. God will not hold us guiltless."*[9]

Instead of ruling the world for a thousand years as predicted, Adolf Hitler's reign was destroyed after twelve years. And instead of peace, prosperity, and power, the Führer and his satanic SS led the German people into the bowels of a living hell.

Hitler's Third Reich would eventually evolve into an occultist, merciless, and godless empire that would catapult the nations of the globe into World War II. This false messiah transformed Europe into a battlefield turned red by rivers of human blood resulting in the death of more than 40 million people in the European theater alone.*

Hitler's New Order destroyed Europe's control over much of the world and its influence over the rest. After half-hearted and doomed attempts to resist Hitler's expansionism, many European nations willingly participated in the dismantling of what they had once thought of as their "birthright." Within fifteen years of the end of the war, Britain, France, Belgium, and the Netherlands relinquished their empires, after having lost the will, the energy, and the wealth to maintain their power.

Geopolitical analyst George Friedman further addressed Europe's loss of free thinking, which Hitler deemed suspect to the

---

* https://en.wikipedia.org/wiki/World_War_II_casualties.

goal of Nazism. By prostituting the classic German philosophers like Friedrich Nietzsche and Richard Wagner to accomplish his ends, Hitler stripped Europe of much of its intellectual heritage.[*]

Adolf Hitler also cost Europe its spiritual awareness. It is alarming, the extent to which Europe abandoned Christianity for secularism. The train wreck that Hitler's New Order made of Europe created a human secularism not only in relation to Christianity, but in all attempts to recreate the depth of European culture that once existed.[†] Hitler's New Order forever changed the world.

The Führer was as a self-proclaimed prophet who declared,

In a hundred years' time, perhaps, a great man will appear who may offer them [the Germans] a chance at salvation. He'll take me as a model, use my ideas, and follow the course I have charted.[‡]

Enter the Antichrist.

THE ANTICHRIST AND THE NEW WORLD ORDER OF THE FOURTH REICH

The leader of the Fourth Reich will be the Antichrist—the satanic counterfeit of Christ. This evil ruler who is "opposed to Christ" and all He represents will derive his power and authority from Satan. The Antichrist will be the final absolute ruler of man's earthly empire—the revived Roman Empire. This Fourth Reich will encompass the world and will be more wicked than all preceding empires.

The Antichrist will be to Satan what Christ is to God the Father and the false prophet will attempt to rival the supporting role of the

---

[*] https://www.forbes.com/sites/stratfor/2015/09/02/pondering-hitlers-legacy/#75a08fe84227.

[†] Ibid.

[‡] https://libquotes.com/adolf-hitler/quote/lbj0j9p.

Holy Spirit. Satan, the Antichrist, and the false prophet will comprise the unholy trinity of the Fourth Reich.

The Antichrist was introduced in Scripture by the prophet Daniel and is also referred to by Ezekiel, Matthew, Paul, and John the Revelator.

The Antichrist will among many things:

- Be a cunning political leader who will deceive many and control the world and its economy (Matthew 24:4-5; Revelation 13: 5–7; 16–17).
- Make and break a peace treaty with Israel (Daniel 9:27).
- Denies the Lordship of Christ, claiming to be God and demanding worship (1 John 2:22; 2 Thessalonians 2:3–4).
- Plan to destroy Israel and the Jewish people (Daniel 11:40–41).

I have often asked myself the question, How quickly will the Antichrist come to power after he is introduced onto the world stage? After learning how rapidly Adolf Hitler became the supreme dictator of Germany and then witnessing how swiftly the world came to its knees after COVID-19—the answer to my question is—*not long!*

I stated how the Treaty of Versailles and the Great Depression helped to catipulte Hitler's ascent to power in less than 550 days. Yet, in this twenty-first-century world of hypoconnectivity, the ripple effects of the coronavirus pandemic have influenced more than a region of the world—it has impacted the nations of the globe—and done so very quickly.

Most countries isolated themselves from the rest of world, attempting to curb the lethal effects of the virus while internally grappling with the nearly impossible decision of reopening their economies and possibly exposing their citizens to further infection.

As a result of the economic shutdown, the fierce escalation

of debt is of great global concern for individuals, corporations, and governments alike. The pandemic rate of infection in some of the oil-producing nations also caused many to run to the International Money Fund for emergency funding.[*] It is predicted that as soon as revolving credit lines run dry, many people will file bankruptcy or simply walk away from their overwhelming debt while businesses will go under or merge with other desperate corporations.

By looking back at history, the more we can envision how our global society can radically and rapidly be reshaped by the coronavirus pandemic. The Mongol Empire, which I previously referenced as one of the greatest territorial realms in history, was fractured by the Black Death epidemic of the fourteenth century. This form of bubonic plague directly contributed to the fall of the mighty Mongol Empire, which disappeared within twenty-two years of the plague's outbreak. The global effects of the coronavirus pandemic, even though it has not claimed as many lives, will emerge far more quickly.[†]

The questions now are—will we become a more resilient global system in the aftermath of this pandemic—or will we endeavor to be part of a New World Order that will provide the economic life-preserver we so desperately desire?

Could it be that the mechanisms are in place that will allow for a united world, with one world currency and one supreme leader?

THE UNITED NATIONS

Founded in the fall of 1945, the United Nations (UN) replaced the ineffective League of Nations created after World War I.

---

[*] https://www.imf.org/en/About/FAQ/imf-response-to-covid-19.

[†] Parag Khanna and Karan Khemka, "The coronavirus butterfly effect: Six predictions for a new world order." *Fast Company*, 4/14/20, accessed 7/17/20. https://www.fastcompany.com/90488665/the-coronavirus-butterfly-effect-six-predictions-for-a-new-world-order.

The stated goals of the United Nations are to maintain world peace by:

- Keeping worldwide security.
- Developing relations among nations.
- Fostering cooperation between nations in order to solve international economic, social, cultural, or humanitarian problems.[*]

After fierce negotiations, fifty nations agreed to a charter that begins with, "We the peoples of the United Nations...". *Why is this phrase important?*

Man, since the Tower of Babel, has had a fervent longing to unite the world under one banner. However, history has proven that the "banner" is usually controlled by a select few, and the United Nations is no exception. The UN seems to serve only the narrow national interests of some of its 193 member countries—specifically, the most powerful.

The opening session of the United Nations General Assembly becomes the global platform where heads of state present speeches that are often filibusters of their own country's ideals. The UN introduces hundreds of resolutions annually, and most fall into forgotten archives while others draw worldwide attention, like the 1975 resolution that equated Zionism with racism. After the speeches and resolutions, the General Assembly becomes the "arena where largely symbolic diplomatic jousts are won and lost."[†]

In theory, each country, no matter its size or economic strength, has equal clout through their one vote—however, the genuine power resides within the fifteen-member Security Council. The five victors

---

[*] https://www.un.org/en/sections/what-we-do/.

[†] https://www.nytimes.com/2017/09/17/world/americas/united-nations-un-explainer.html.

of World War II, the United States, Britain, China, France, and Russia, are the permanent members of the council; the remaining ten nations are chosen by secret ballot and hold a two-year term.[*]

Members of the "P5" have the power to veto any measure, which usually protects itself or its allies. Since 1990, the United States has vetoed sixteen council resolutions, most of which concern the Israeli-Palestinian relations.[†]

Another question arises, *Can the United Nations achieve its founding mandate of uniting the world to make it a more peaceful place?*

The ability for the Security Council to maintain international peace has been severely limited for decades, primarily because of hostile divisions between Russia and the West. The council has been ineffective in several major conflicts, such as the handling of the civil war in Syria, with Russia backing the government of President Bashar al-Assad, and the United States, Britain, and France supporting opposition groups.

In the 1990s there was the failed "Oil-for-Food" program through which Iraq's dictator, Saddam Hussein, profited 11 billion dollars. In early 2000, the UN sanctions against Afghanistan's Taliban did nothing to bend or reign in the activities of Al-Qaeda.[‡] In addition, the regime of North Korea, an ally of China, has repeatedly ignored the United Nations' ban on their nuclear tests, and on intensifying its arms buildup.

It seems that the same impotence of the League of Nations afflicts the UN.

What can unify the UN? The European Union has joined forces with the United Nations in building a more "cooperative world order." Federica Mogherini, the European Union's former High Representative for Foreign Affairs and Security Policy, stated, "The

---

[*] https://www.un.org/en/ga/62/plenary/election_sc/bkg.shtml.
[†] Ibid.
[‡] https://www.cfr.org/backgrounder/un-sanctions-mixed-record.

European way is the United Nations way....The European vision is the United Nations vision."[10]

Why is the European Union important in prophecy?

The European Union is fundamentally a federation, which is a political entity defined by an alliance of partially self-governing nations under the control of a central federal government.* John the Revelator refers to an apostate church, the Antichrist, and a forthcoming union of nations in Revelation 17:3:

So he carried me away in the Spirit into the wilderness. And I saw a woman [apostate church] sitting on a scarlet beast [Antichrist] which was full of names of blasphemy, having seven heads and ten horns [leaders of nations].

The Antichrist will have authority over the federated states of Europe; however, he will be controlled by a politico-religious system referred to as the Great Harlot in Revelation 17:5:

MYSTERY, BABYLON THE GREAT,
THE MOTHER OF HARLOTS
AND OF THE ABOMINATIONS OF THE EARTH.

We have established some of the players; now back to the question of unification. Past world dictators have united their citizens through a common enemy.

The efficiency of the truly national leader consists primarily in preventing the division of the attention of a people, and always in concentrating it on a single enemy.
—Adolf Hitler

* https://papers.ssrn.com/sol3/papers.cfm?abstract_id=2731552.

Could that common enemy be Israel and the Jewish people?

Prime Minister Benjamin Netanyahu said the following of the UN in 2009:

> …this is an unfortunate part of the UN institution. It's the theater of the absurd. It doesn't only cast Israel as the villain; it often casts real villains in leading roles: Gadhafi's Libya chaired the UN Commission on Human Rights; Saddam's Iraq headed the UN Committee on Disarmament. Hezbollah-controlled Lebanon is on the UN Security Council. This means, in effect, that a terror organization presides over the body entrusted with guaranteeing the world's security. You couldn't make this up…[*]

It does seem that opposing Israel is a unifying factor. In the seventy-fourth session of the UN General Assembly (2019–2020), the members of the European Union states voted for thirteen out of eighteen resolutions singling out Israel.[†] Moreover, based on Scripture, several of these member-nations of the UN Security Council will be part of the army that comes against God's covenant nation in the future.

Could a seven-year peace treaty with Israel bring the unity the UN seeks?

I believe that the eventual goal of the United Nations will be to create one world government with one constitution, one world bank with one currency and one world army with one supreme leader.

---

[*] *The Israel-Arab Reader: A Documentary History of the Middle East Conflict*, Edited by Walter Laqueur, Dan Schueftan, 8th Revised Edition, Penguin Books, NY, NY, 2016.

[†] https://unwatch.org/2019-un-general-assembly-resolutions-singling-out-israel-texts-votes-analysis/.

Whoever Owns the Gold Has the Power

The best way to attain a stable currency is to link it to gold. People used gold and silver as a financial method of exchange for nearly five thousand years. Because of the inconvenience of weighing and assaying the medals, coinage became the preferred method for financial transactions.[*]

Paper money first surfaced in eleventh-century China but was not used in Europe until after 1850. Now the world is planning to fade out paper currency altogether as more and more financial transactions occur without it.

America had operated under the gold standard (a monetary system in which currency is backed by gold), since 1879, other than a short embargo on gold exports during World War I. Then came the Great Depression of the 1930s, which caused some banks to fail and the public to frantically hoard gold.

On June 15, 1933, President Franklin D. Roosevelt froze US bank assets and ordered all gold coins and gold certificates in denominations of one hundred dollars or more to be turned in and exchanged for cash. The purpose of this directive was to give the Federal Reserve the opportunity to raise its money supply, thereby fighting off an economic downturn.[†]

In June 1934, exactly one year later, gold was re-established as the standard to back up the American dollar. However, the world was about to dramatically change after World War II, as a more robust and open global market would take center stage.

As nations became more competitive in global exports, in addition to weakening US balance of payments, increased military spending and foreign aid, there was a large supply of dollars circulating

---

[*] https://qz.com/1646318/why-trump-and-judy-shelton-want-the-us-back-on-the-gold-standard/.

[†] https://www.history.com/this-day-in-history/fdr-takes-united-states-off-gold-standard.

around the world. Soon, there were more foreign-held dollars than the United States had gold. The country was vulnerable to a run on gold, and there was a loss of confidence in the US government's ability to meet its obligations, thereby threatening the dollar's position as reserve currency.[*]

Several years later, President Richard Nixon confronted the international dilemma of a looming gold run and the domestic problem of inflation by taking the US off the gold standard in August of 1971. However, Nixon's attempted permanent fix to the financial crises yielded an unsuccessful outcome. In less than two years, the United States entered into a drawn-out recession. As a result of this economic downturn, the American public lost trust in their elected officials and the world lost significant confidence in the American dollar.

Currently, governments hold a monopoly on printing money and can issue new currency at almost no cost. Add to this equation that most governments are run by vote-seeking politicians who promise the moon to win re-election. Therefore, the only logical outcome is more promises, more money, more money, more inflation.

According to American economist Milton Friedman, preventing inflation requires fixing the money supply. To accomplish this task, we must limit the dollars the government can print to the weight of gold it holds in reserves, which would mean going back to the gold standard.[†] However, until if and when America reestablishes the gold standard, who currently holds the world's economic power?

It is interesting to note that although the US ranks number one, owning 8,133.5 tons of gold, it is *Germany* that ranks second in

---

[*] https://www.federalreservehistory.org/essays/gold_convertibility_ends.

[†] https://qz.com/1646318/why-trump-and-judy-shelton-want-the-us-back-on-the-gold
    -standard/.

the world, with 3,372 tons—the Holy Roman Empire keeps rolling. The third through fifth spots are all European: the International Monetary Fund (IMF), who headquarters in Belgium, has 2,814 tons; Italy owns 2,451 tons; and France rounds out the top five with 2,456 tons.[11]

According to the World Official Gold Holding chart, as of the fourth quarter of 2019, Russia has been busy expanding its reserves over the past two years, moving from seventh to sixth place, and now owns 1,890.8 tons. It is important to note that Russia "doesn't need to import [gold] to add to its stockpile…as it has a billion-dollar gold mining industry."[12] China, however, *is* the world's largest gold producer, ahead of Australia and Russia, and is currently ranked seventh, owning 1,842.6 tons.

Remember this truth—Whoever owns the gold holds the power. George Bernard Shaw expressed this reality in 1928:

> The most important thing about money is to maintain its stability…You have to choose between trusting the natural stability of gold and the honesty and intelligence of members of government. With due respect to these gentlemen, I advise you, for as long as the capitalist system lasts, to vote for gold.*

China and Russia are part of the world coalition calling for a one world currency. *Why?* Because they have become major players in the gold market. Many financial experts believe these major players are underreporting their holdings,[13] which can only mean they are preparing for a major upheaval in the world's economy.

To contribute to the looming upheaval, the coronavirus pandemic has negatively affected global economies, placing them in a

---

* Ibid.

tailspin. Who would have thought that the nations of the world would be limited or prevented from buying or selling goods and services?

Another point to consider in this imminent upheaval is the increasing demand by the Democratic Socialists of America to adopt an economic system that financially supports the majority of Americans and illegal immigrants without offering a way to sustain their entitlement philosophy.[*]

As I mentioned before, the gold standard limits government spending to only what it can raise in taxes or borrow against its gold reserve. It also prevents the government from simply printing money to pay its debts or provide entitlements. The Democratic Socialists, however, promise to radically raise taxes, and because we are off the gold standard, nothing prevents the printing of more and more money. How long can we fund entitlements before America financially implodes from within?

The apostle John put his pen to parchment on the Isle of Patmos and wrote that there is coming a day, at the end of time as we know it, when the world will have a one world economy limited only to those who have the mark of the Beast:

> He [Antichrist] causes all, both small and great, rich and poor, free and slave, to receive a mark on their right hand or on their foreheads, and that **no one may buy or sell** except one who has the mark or the name of the beast, or the number of his name. Here is wisdom. Let him who has understanding calculate the number of the beast, for it is the number of a man: His number is 666 (Revelation 13:16–18).

---

[*] https://www.theguardian.com/politics/2019/aug/06/democratic
-socialists-us-alexandria-ocasio-cortez-bernie-sanders.

While there is a debate about what this mark may be, perhaps even a vaccination microchip or whether the number of the Antichrist is a literal "666," what we can be sure of is that the New World Order, with its one world economy, will be eagerly embraced by the nations of the world.

ONE WORLD CURRENCY

The coronavirus crisis effectively paralyzed America and the world. Our economic engines were shut down. We lived in social isolation for months, people died alone without a loved one by their side; graduations, weddings, and funerals were postponed or cancelled, and we were prevented from gathering in our houses of worship.

Because of the Great Lockdown of 2020, financial experts are predicting the world will experience the worst recession since the Great Depression of 1929 and far greater than the global financial crisis of 2009. This mandatory global shutdown, deemed necessary to contain the virus and preserve life, has resulted in a collapse of economic activity "the magnitude and speed of unlike anything experienced in our lifetimes."[*]

The nations of the world are juggling with several disasters simultaneously, which relate to each other in complex ways. Whole countries are not only dealing with the lingering effects of a deadly health crisis, they are also faced with the aftermath of a financial devastation that resulted in a radical collapse of the price of goods and services (gross domestic product, or GDP). Governments provided unparalleled funding to individuals, businesses, and financial markets, creating insecurity about how the economic landscape will evolve when we finally emerge from the effects this lockdown.

Experts are saying that the collective loss to global GDP over

---

[*] https://blogs.imf.org/2020/04/14/the-great-lockdown-worst-economic -downturn-since-the-great-depression/.

2020 and 2021, owed to the pandemic crisis, could reach as high as 9 trillion dollars, which is greater than the economies of Japan and Germany combined.[*]

The coronavirus pandemic has also disrupted the supply chains across our nation as farmers were forced to destroy acres and acres of crops, dump hundreds of thousands of gallons of milk, and throw out tons of perishable goods that couldn't be stored. With the closing of restaurants and schools, the demand for food products led to the shutting down of meat plants, resulting in the loss of millions of animals like chickens, pigs, and cattle.[†]

Turning off our economic engines caused the stock market to experience a rapid series of record gains and breathtaking losses. And to add fuel to the fire, Saudi Arabia and Russia glutted the world oil market during the pandemic in an attempt to bring American independent oil producers to their knees, causing them to give up their market share and board up their oil wells. As a result, the price of oil plummeted to an all-time low due to the unprecedented excess, the huge gap between supply and demand, and the exorbitant cost of storing the physical crude.[‡]

As of June 2020, storage capacity was being tested as a worldwide glut of fuels and crude expanded due to the destruction of demand by the coronavirus. Still, there were some tentative signs of a fledgling recovery in demand.[§] Only time will tell if we ever regain our footing in the oil market.

Mark my words—we will return to 1979 when, during the

---

[*] Ibid.

[†] Ron Insana. "Op-ed: Recovering from this unprecedented oil crash could take years and may not benefit Saudi or Russian producers." CNBC, 4/21/20, accessed 7/17/20. https://www.cnbc.com/2020/05/02/coronavirus-devastates-agriculture-dumped-milk-euthanized-livestock.htmlhttps://www.vox.com/2020/5/4/21243636/meat-packing-plant-supply-chain-animals-killed.

[‡] Ibid.

[§] https://www.worldoil.com/news/2020/4/29/oil-prices-rise-as-production-cuts-begin-worldwide.

Carter administration, Americans lined up for blocks waiting to purchase a rationed amount of fuel. America will once again be at the mercy of Saudi Arabia and other foreign oil-producing nations for our petroleum needs.

Furthermore, cash is no longer king in a world suffering the overwhelming financial effects of the coronavirus pandemic. When the World Health Organization released a statement in early spring of 2020 recommending that people turn to cashless transactions to fight the spread of COVID-19, a number of governments and retailers across the world immediately acted on the warning. At the first hint that paper money was a potential carrier of the coronavirus, a growing number of businesses and individuals stopped using physical currency, fearing it could be a path for the spreading the deadly virus.[*]

Why was this ban on paper currency so readily accepted? Could it be that the public worldwide has been willingly schooled to deal in cashless transactions through the exclusive use of credit cards, debit cards, Apple Pay, Zelle, Venmo, and Google Pay as means to transfer digital financial information via a smartphone?

Will the pandemic make cash obsolete? More and more you hear the terms digital dollar, digital wallet, digital currency, or digital cash—all describing cashless transactions. The US was on the verge of issuing a digital dollar as part of the early draft for the COVID-19 stimulus package. Separate House and Senate bills proposed creating digital dollars as an effort to reduce the shock of the economic lockdown due to the spread of the novel coronavirus.[†]

Why is this important? Because a "cashless transaction" is the forerunner to a global currency.

It's important to note that China has already transitioned to

---

[*] https://www.legalexecutiveinstitute.com/will-covid-19-make-cash-obsolete/.
[†] Ibid.

an almost complete cashless society where its citizens generate 80 percent of all expenditures digitally. Nearly everyone in China uses quick read codes (QRC) to exchange virtual money in person or through digital wallets online.

The People's Bank of China will soon issue a digital currency electronic payment (DCEP) system using blockchain technology, which is a decentralized, distributed ledger that records the origin of *all* digital assets. China plans to rollout DCEP globally, especially in Asia and Africa. As this digital currency is used, the Red Communist state will have direct insight into the finances of everyone in the country and beyond.*

Thomson Reuters's financial technologist and futurist Joe Raczynski believes that "dramatic shifts are about to take place (globally) with our primary forms of money. With the advent of blockchain technology, there will be a fission between state-sponsored fiat money and privately-run currencies."†

What is fiat money? Fiat money is "government-issued currency that is not backed by a physical commodity, such as gold or silver, but by the government that issued it. The value of fiat money is derived from the relationship between supply and demand and the stability of the issuing government. Most modern paper currencies are fiat currencies, including the U.S. dollar, the Euro, and other major global currencies."‡

Is the use of one global currency far in the future? Facebook's Libra project is an attempt by a private company to issue a global currency. If Facebook succeeds, it could create a currency usable by half the world population *overnight*, which is extremely powerful, yet threatening to sovereign nations.§

---

* https://builtin.com/blockchain.
† https://www.legalexecutiveinstitute.com/will-covid-19-make-cash-obsolete/.
‡ https://www.investopedia.com/terms/f/fiatmoney.asp.
§ https://www.legalexecutiveinstitute.com/will-covid-19-make-cash-obsolete/.

China, India, and Russia have already called for one world currency. And in 2009, at the G8 meeting, Russia's president presented a gold coin with the number "1" stamped in the middle of it, which he recommended to be the currency for the global economy.[14]

More than thirty years ago, the cover of a 1988 Rothschild publication, the *Economist*, showed a phoenix rising from the flames of a pile of burning bank notes—dollars, pounds, and lira; all were ablaze, predicting the death of currency as we know it.[15]

"A REPUBLIC, IF YOU CAN KEEP IT."
—Benjamin Franklin

Another major event marking the advent of the New World Order is the destruction of patriotism. To be a patriot is to love your country, be willing to defend it, and give your life if necessary to preserve its freedom. Remember this truth: If we do not use our freedom to defend our freedom, we will lose our freedom.

America is in the midst of a major identity crisis; we do not seem to know who we are, what we believe in, or what we are willing to defend as a nation or as individuals. We witness millionaire athletes refuse to stand and honor the flag—whose own freedoms were purchased with the blood and sacrifices of our military heroes—and still debate whether this disrespect is acceptable.

We see anti-Jewish and Christian insolence sweeping America like a wildfire. Anti-Semitism has resulted in, among other things, the desecration of synagogues and cemeteries while Christians who stand with Israel and the Jewish people are ridiculed and spat upon. Furthermore, anarchist students protesting on elite college and university campuses are led on by leftist professors who have programmed these young, pliable minds to hate America.

Tomorrow's leaders are rebelling without knowing what they

truly stand for or against—and this my friends is dangerous. If we continue to tolerate these reproachful behaviors, our nation will self-destruct.

In the first quarter of 2020, President Trump declared himself a "wartime president," which was accurate. The president aggressively fought an unprecedented war on two fronts: domestic health and the economic crisis. While these battles raged, there was a third front that hid in the trenches—the rise of national democratic socialism.

Our millennial generation has been deceived by the false promises of a social system of government and it has become their "moral high ground." The very system of capitalism that affords our citizens the benefits they take for granted is now equated with corporate greed, immigration abuse, and global warming.

Socialism is communism with lipstick—they are two left-wing schools of economic thought and both oppose capitalism. The basic principles of socialism surround the political and economic theories that promote the concept that production, distribution, and exchange of goods and services should be owned and/or controlled by the community as a whole. Socialism emphasizes equality rather than achievement.

All factories, farms, and machinery and the labor used to produce and distribute goods and services are controlled by the government, which not only determines their output but also regulates their pricing. Under socialism, individuals rely on the state for everything. As fellow socialist Adolf Hitler said, "Why nationalize industry when you can nationalize the people?"[*]

And in order to create dependence on the state, you create more and more entitlements. The current leaders of this democratic socialist movement propose to "tax the hell out of the wealthy" (as defined by their criteria), in order to fund government entitlements

---

[*] *The Nazi War on Cancer*, Robert N. Proctor, Princeton University Press, NJ, 1999.

relating to housing, student loan debt, universal health care, and climate change.

Modern socialists like Bernie Sanders, Elizabeth Warren, and Alexandria Ocasio-Cortez walk in the footsteps of founding socialists before them such as Karl Marx, Friedrich Engels, and Vladimir Lenin. And like them, they use every opportunity to unify against a common enemy (capitalism) and propagandize, with the help of a liberal media, any and all self-perceived political and economic injustices.[*]

Emil W. Henry Jr., former U.S. assistant treasury secretary (2005–2007), warned that this third front is the true existential battle for the survival of our country. There is a Trojan horse temptation in our midst "of state-sponsored security at the expense of freedom, innovation and growth. Overflowing hospitals? Time for Medicare for all. Joblessness and bankruptcies? Time for Universal Basic Income."[†]

Our nation was founded on the principles of popular majority rule while at the same time preserving a stable government that protects the rights and liberties of all citizens. Upon leaving the Constitutional Convention, founding father Benjamin Franklin was asked what sort of government the delegates had created. His answer was simple yet profound, "A republic, if you can keep it."

Franklin was saying that "democratic republics are not merely founded upon the consent of the people; they are also absolutely dependent upon the active and informed involvement of the people for their continued good health."[‡]

Are we invested enough in preserving our nation and its

---

[*] "Will Corona Launch the Second Wave of Socialism?" Emil W. Henry, Jr., March 26, 2020.

[†] Ibid.

[‡] *Perspectives on the Constitution: A Republic, If You Can Keep It* by Richard R. Beeman, PhD.

constitution to *keep it?* I am afraid the answer to that question is *no.*
Hitler said it perfectly:

> How fortunate for governments that people do not think.
> There is no thinking except in giving and executing com-
> mands, if it were otherwise human society could not exist.[*]

The times are ripe for a radical transformation in our nation and
world as we know. Even the best-intentioned global leaders have lost
control.

Take heed—the stage is being set for the Antichrist. He will
come to power and rule the world as a ruthless dictator on the
wings of a financial crisis just as Hitler did. And just as the German
people were clamoring for a savior who would bring them back to
European prominence, prestige, and power, so will the modern-day
leaders seek a new Caesar. He will come as the prince of peace and
prosperity, but in reality, he will be ruthless—those he does not kill,
he will enslave.

Make no mistake: a New World Order will come to power. The
Antichrist will rule the world. What should be our attitude concerning the future? Not one of doom and gloom. Jesus said,

> *Now when these things begin to happen, look up and lift up your
> heads, because your redemption draws near"* (Luke 21:28).

A final throne will be established, and its ruler will be Jesus
Christ—the Son of God. He will rule the world for a thousand
years from the city of Jerusalem. Kings, queens, presidents, prime
ministers, statesmen, and the rich and powerful of the world will

---

[*] *Hitler's Tischgespraeche im Fuehrerhauptquartier* 1941–42 H. Picker, edited by P. E.
Schramm et al., Stuttgart, 1963, p. 159.

line up in the streets of the Holy City to climb the Temple Mount and bow before the Carpenter's Son.

> *...that at the name of Jesus every knee should bow, of those in heaven, and of those on earth, and of those under the earth, and that every tongue should confess that Jesus Christ is Lord, to the glory of God the Father* (Philippians 2:10–11).

The Word of God shall go forth from Jerusalem. The Son of King David is coming with power and great glory. He will return to rule and reign over the whole earth with a rod of iron. Christ and Christ alone is the King of all kings and the Lord of all lords. Lift up your heads people and rejoice.

SECTION THREE

FROM AMALEK
TO ARMAGEDDON

CHAPTER 9

FASCINATION WITH THE FUTURE

Never be afraid to trust an unknown future to a known God.
—*Corrie ten Boom*

Mankind has always been fascinated with the future. People have long been captivated with horoscopes, futuristic movies, and science fiction books that attempt to predict the unknown. This mysterious attraction has led to an equally unconventional preoccupation with the "end of the world."

Questions like, "When will the end come?" "How will it come?" and "Who will survive it?" have prevailed throughout human history.[1] Yet, even with the meteoric rise of knowledge experienced by the human race, and the high-tech explosion available at everyone's fingertips, man has not accurately been able to forecast the future outside of the prophetic Word of God.

World history records a myriad of human obsessions with the End of Days to include: The Assyrians prediction of the end of the world as recorded on a clay tablet discovered in Nineveh dating to 2800 BCE; The Mayans' cataclysmic 12/12/12 calendar; and the Y2K Myth.

No matter the source or purpose of various "end time" theories, the same questions still arise:

- Are we nearing the end of the world as we know it?
- Is the Apocalypse, with all of its horror and calamity, just before us?
- Will we know the season of its appearing?

The answer to these questions is *yes!* However, we must first study the Word of God, which reveals His truth concerning the End of Days.

CAN WE KNOW THE FUTURE?

The Bible is a book of profound mysteries and glorious unveilings. To the carnal mind, the Scriptures are no more than foolish contradictions, but to the believer, the Word of God is the embodiment of precise logic and the manifestation of eternal hope.

The Bible has been described as a house with many rooms; to the outsider looking in, it is unknown as to what makes up each room. However, for the one who holds the key to the house and has access to its interior, there is no secret to what each room contains.[2]

As believers in Christ, we are given the access key to the revelation of Scripture, for Jesus declared, *"Most assuredly, I say to you, unless one is born again, he cannot see the kingdom of God"* (John 3:3).

Christians are eager to learn about healing, prosperity, and supernatural favor, but some are often intimidated by the study of biblical prophecy, even though we hold the key to the "prophecy room" and can know what lies within. Jesus considered prophecy important, saying, *"Do not think that I came to destroy the Law or the Prophets. I did not come to destroy but to fulfill"* (Matthew 5:17).

The Rabbi from Nazareth often spoke about coming events, and He rebuked those who did not recognize the importance of the signs that were occurring around them. In fact, Christ scolded those who surveyed the stars to foretell the weather but were blind to the prophetic indicators of the times. In Luke 12:56, Jesus said, *"Hypocrites! You can discern the face of the sky and of the earth, but how is it you do not discern this time?"*

It was no small thing to Jesus that the people of His generation remained ignorant to God's prophetic Word. And as believers in this generation, we too are mandated to study all Scripture as a guide for righteous living in preparation for the Lord's return.

WHY STUDY BIBLICAL PROPHECY?

Approximately one-fourth of the Word of God was prophetic at the time it was written. The obvious conclusion is—if the Almighty devoted so much of His Word to prophecy, it certainly benefits every believer to study it. The knowledge of biblical prophecy produces the following important results.

The Bible's Authority

First and foremost, the study of the prophetic scriptures and their fulfillment attests to the *authority* of the Word of God. The detailed descriptions of coming events and their precise fulfillment validate that, "Scripture is of divine origin, trustworthy, and to be studied with confidence."[3] All that man knows of God is recorded in His Word; without this assured foundation, we are nothing.

For I am God, and there is no other; I am God,
and there is none like Me,

> *Declaring the end from the beginning,*
> *And from ancient times things that are not yet done,*
> *Saying, "My counsel shall stand,*
> *And I will do all My pleasure"* (Isaiah 46:9–10).

Remember this truth: The Holy Scriptures were authored by God; they are *His Spirit, His voice* and *His authority*—man was merely the scribe.

> *Knowing this first, that no prophecy of Scripture is of any private interpretation, for prophecy never came by the will of man, but holy men of God spoke as they were moved by the Holy Spirit* (2 Peter 1:20–21).

The Bible's Accuracy

Studying prophecy confirms the *accuracy* of God's Word. The Bible is not just an account of historical events—it is a living, accurate, and commanding message from God to His people. Christ acknowledged the Scriptures in His earthly ministry by referring to the Old Testament writings as those things "spoken to you by God."[4]

Saint Peter wrote,

> *We heard this voice which came from heaven when we were with Him on the holy mountain. And so we have the prophetic word confirmed, which you do well to heed as a light that shines in a dark place, until the day dawns and the morning star rises in your hearts* (2 Peter 1:18–19).

An eyewitness account is the highest standard of accuracy possible, but Peter declares that biblical prophecy is even more accurate than an eyewitness.

There are 353 prophetic scriptures in the Old Testament dealing with the birth, ministry, death, and resurrection of Jesus Christ. These accounts were recorded centuries before He came to earth, and every word has been fulfilled.[5] Man, with all of his knowledge and with the assistance of all the technology afforded him, cannot come close to this degree of accuracy—only God can.

The fulfillment of the following Old Testament prophecies concerning the life of Christ further testifies about the infallible precision of God's Word.

- His royal lineage: 2 Samuel 7:12–16; Psalms 89:3–4; 110:1; 132:11; Isaiah 9:6; Matthew 22:44; Mark 12:36; Luke 1:69–70; 20:42–44; John 7:42.
- His virgin birth: Isaiah 7:14; Matthew 1:23.
- His birth in Bethlehem: Micah 5:2; Matthew 2:6; John 7:42.
- His return from Egypt: Hosea 11:1; Matthew 2:15.
- His coming revealed by God's messenger: Isaiah 40:3–5; Malachi 3:1; 4:5; Matthew 3:3; 11:10–14; Mark 1:2–3; Luke 3:4–6; 7:27; John 1:23.
- His anointing by the Holy Spirit: Psalm 45:7; Luke 3:22, 4:1; John 1:33.
- His ministry in Galilee: Isaiah 9:1–2; Matthew 4:15.
- His use of parables: Psalm 78:1–2; Isaiah 6:9–10; Matthew 13:14–15.
- His healing of the sick: Isaiah 53:4; Matthew 8:17.
- His teachings and miracles rejected: Isaiah 53:3; John 12:37.
- His triumphal entry into Jerusalem: Psalm 118:26; Isaiah 62:11; Zechariah 9:9; Matthew 21:5; John 12:14–15.
- His betrayal by a friend: Psalm 41:9; John 18:2.
- His being forsaken by His disciples: Psalm 31:11; John 18:25.

- His being condemned with criminals: Isaiah 53:9, 12; Luke 22:37.
- His garments being divided by lot: Psalm 22:18; John 19:24.
- His being offered vinegar on the cross: Psalm 69:21; Matthew 27:34; John 19:29.
- His side being pierced without His bones being broken: Exodus 12:46; Numbers 9:12; Psalm 22:14, 16; 34:20; Zechariah 12:10; John 19:36–37.
- His dying words foretold: Psalm 31:5; Matthew 27:46; Mark 15:34; Luke 23:46.
- His resurrection: Job 19:23–27; Psalm 17:15; 1 Peter 1:3, 3:21; Acts 4:33.

God's Wisdom

Prophecy reveals the *wisdom* of God. Only the Almighty, in His infinite insight, could inspire the compiled writings of sixty-six books that were penned on three continents in three different languages—Hebrew, Aramaic, and Greek.

The Holy Scriptures were recorded by approximately forty people of diverse education and backgrounds, including kings, shepherds, scientists, attorneys, an army general, fishermen, priests, and a physician, most of whom never met.[6]

> *Oh, the depth of the riches both of the wisdom and knowledge of God! How unsearchable are His judgments and unfathomable His ways!* (Romans 11:33 NASB)

The greatest harmony ever heard is within the symphony of the Word of God. This sacred masterpiece was composed over a period of about 1,400 years, covering over 4,000 years of human history.

There are 1,239 prophecies found in the Old Testament and 578 prophecies in the New Testament, for a total of 1,817, which comprise 8,352 verses.[7]

God revealed Himself to and through men with these sacred writings, which began with the prophet Moses and ended with John the Revelator. Yet, as inconceivable as it may seem, every word of the Scripture is orchestrated to harmonize with all other scriptures.

God's Power

The study of prophecy testifies to the *power* of God.

> *The* LORD *said to Moses, "Is the* LORD's *power limited? Now you shall see whether My word will come true for you or not"* (Numbers 11:23 NASB).

What was happening at this moment in scripture? Moses and the children of Israel were in the wilderness, and the Lord was about to discipline them for their constant murmuring and unbelief. Moses, thinking in the natural, questioned God's ability to carry out His judgment (Numbers 11:21–22).

Moses' doubt challenged the power of the Divine (vv. 1–15). Had Moses forgotten that he had been not only a witness but also an instrument of the Almighty's work?

God's matchless power had not waned from the time He had inflicted the plagues on Egypt, parted the Red Sea, and rained manna from heaven. The Great I AM had not become weak or weary—He remained the same, and His power was undiminished.

The study of prophecy and its fulfillment reveals that God's powerful hand will stretch as far as needed to achieve His divine plan.

This is the same power that measures the depth of the seas and the heights of the heavens (Isaiah 40:12). Saint Paul desired that every believer would grasp the presence of God's power:

> *...the eyes of your understanding being enlightened; that you may know what is the hope of His calling, what are the riches of the glory of His inheritance in the saints, and what is the exceeding greatness of His power toward us who believe, according to the working of His mighty power which He worked in Christ when He raised Him from the dead and seated Him at His right hand in the heavenly places, far above all principality and power and might and dominion, and every name that is named, not only in this age but also in that which is to come* (Ephesians 1:18–21).

The greatest proof of God's power lies within His Word and its fulfillment, which includes our personal redemption from sin and conformity to Christ's resurrection. It is through this supernatural fulfillment that God responded to Moses's doubt.

Remember this truth: God *is* power. His Word *is* power; therefore, when God speaks—*His power enables His Word to come to pass*.

God's Promises

Studying prophecy reaffirms God's fulfilled *promises*. Consider the rebirth of the nation of Israel (Isaiah 66:8). Every major prophet in the Old Testament foretold that God would bring the Jewish people "out of their Gentile graves," which were the nations into which the Jewish people had been dispersed following various conquests.

Isaiah spoke of this phenomenon:

The Sovereign LORD declares—he who gathers the exiles of Israel: "I will gather still others to them besides those already gathered" (Isaiah 56:8 NIV).

The Lord, through the prophet Jeremiah, declared the following about leading His Covenant people home:

"I will be found by you," declares the LORD, "and will bring you back from captivity. I will gather you from all the nations and places where I have banished you," declares the LORD, "and will bring you back to the place from which I carried you into exile" (Jeremiah 29:14 NIV).

Ezekiel prophesied concerning the restoration of the Jewish people into the land of Israel:

I will bring you from the nations and gather you from the countries where you have been scattered (Ezekiel 20:34 NIV).

Amos foretold of the same ingathering:

And I will bring my people Israel back from exile. "They will rebuild the ruined cities and live in them. They will plant vineyards and drink their wine; they will make gardens and eat their fruit" (Amos 9:14 NIV).

Jewish immigrants began returning to their homeland from around the world in the 1880s. This migration was known as the first *aliyah* (immigration to Israel). Theodore Herzl, motivated by Zionist ideology and Jewish persecution, inspired the second *aliyah*, from 1904 to 1914. By the beginning of World War I, the number of Jews living in the Promised Land was somewhere between eighty to ninety thousand.[8]

By May 14, 1948, when the United Nations officially recognized the State of Israel, over 800,000 Jews had fulfilled the prophecies of the ingathering. Per the Central Bureau of Statics, there are 14.6 million Jewish people in the world, and more than 6.7 million have been regathered to Israel.[*]

Only God could have foreseen this miraculous ingathering and rebirth over 2,500 years before it began, and only God had the power to make it happen.

God's Purposes

Studying prophecy makes known the *purposes* of God. God Almighty demonstrates beyond any doubt that He knows the end from the beginning and is orchestrating the events on earth to fulfill His perfect plan. The study of prophecy provides a better understanding of the current economic and political events in the world that will bring the Antichrist to power.

Because of fulfilled and future fulfillment of prophecy, we can better comprehend a few of the signs reflecting the season of Christ's return to rule the earth from the Temple Mount in the city of Jerusalem (Matthew 24):

- The appearance of a great pandemic (Jeremiah 29:17–18; Luke 21:11; Matthew 24:7).
- The global rush for a one-world currency (Revelation 13:17).
- The creation of a one-world government (Revelation 13:2, 7).
- The birth of a one-world religion (Revelation 13:12–16).

---

[*] https://www.jpost.com/Israel-News/Number-of-Jews-in-Israel-and-worldwide-on-the-rise-reports-603033.

- The resurgence of Russia as a military superpower (Ezekiel 38:2, 5–7).

1.

God's Peace

Studying prophecy produces *peace* in the heart of every believer. As we watch the daily news reports of North Korea and Iran preparing for nuclear proficiency; of the spiraling growth of anti-Semitism; of Iran's backing of Hamas, Hezbollah, and the barbaric Syrian regime, producing continued turmoil and mayhem in the Middle East and the world. And finally, with Russia and China coming into the region as a major players, all the while being distracted and alarmed by the liberal media fearmongers covering the COVID-19 crisis—it is no wonder we question the future.

When Jesus spoke of His approaching death and resurrection with His disciples, they naturally became troubled. Similarly, many today are also anxious due to the disturbing world conditions. We ask the same questions the disciples most likely asked themselves: "What are we going to do? Who will watch over us? Who will defend us from our enemies?"

And just as Jesus spoke these words to the disciples, He reassures all believers, *"Let not your heart be troubled; you believe in God, believe also in Me"* (John 14:1). Jesus, knowing the disciples were concerned about their future, further calmed their fears with these prophetic words:

In My Father's house are many mansions; if it were not so, I would have told you. I go to prepare a place for you. And if I go and prepare a place for you, I will come again and receive you to Myself; that where I am, there you may be also (John 14:2–3).

Because they had witnessed the fulfillment of Scripture through the life and ministry of Jesus, the disciples trusted Him when He gave the prophetic promise of His return. Therefore, we too must trust, believe and be comforted by the Lord's fulfilled promises, which confirm that every event on earth occurs by divine design:[9]

- Noah believed and his family was saved from destruction (Hebrews 11:7).
- Abraham believed and he became the father of all who believe (Hebrews 11:8–12).
- Joseph believed and he became the ruler of Egypt (Genesis 41:37–39).
- Moses believed and he led God's people to freedom (Hebrews 11:29).
- David believed and he defeated the giant and became king (1 Samuel 17:45–51; 16:1, 13; 2 Samuel 2).
- The Virgin Mary believed and she gave birth to the Son of God (Luke 1:38).
- Saint Paul believed and he wrote thirteen books of the New Testament (Acts 9:1–20).
- John believed and he received the book of Revelation (1 John 1:1–4; Revelation 1:1).

Blessed are those who have not seen and yet have believed (John 20:29).

TIMELINE OF THE PROPHETS

In the next three chapters, we will explore some of the most notable men in biblical history who were shown the future by the Lord Almighty. Their revelations and the interpretation of those revelations were recorded in Scripture for coming generations.

- Abraham saw the Promised Land (Genesis 15).
- Daniel saw the dawn of eternity (Daniel 12).
- Ezekiel saw the judgment and redemption of God's people (Ezekiel 38–39).

To better understand God's message to His people, I have presented a timeline[10] of a few of the prophets and their prophecy, along with some of the major biblical events that occurred between the birth of Abraham and the birth of Jesus Christ.

YEAR (BCE)	EVENT
2001	Birth of Abraham (Genesis 11:26).
722	Assyrians conquer Tribe of Israel—Northern Kingdom (1 Chronicles 5:26; 2 Kings 15:29).
650	Birth of Jeremiah.
628	Birth of Daniel.
627	Jeremiah prophesies the Assyrian attack on Judah (Jeremiah 11:1–8; 17; 19–27).
622	Birth of Ezekiel.
612	The Babylonians destroy Nineveh and became the new world superpower (Nahum 1–3).
608	Josiah, king of Judah, is killed in battle with Egyptians (2 Chronicles 35:20–25). • Jehoahaz becomes king but is taken to Egypt (2 Kings 23:31–33). • Jehoiakim becomes king (2 Kings 23:36). • The prophet **Jeremiah** is declared a traitor and imprisoned (Jeremiah 37:12; 38:28).
606	Habakkuk delivers a prophetic message to Jerusalem (1:5–17).

YEAR (BCE)	EVENT
605	Jeremiah proclaims God's judgment on Judah as it's besieged by the Babylonians (Chapter 25).
605	King Nebuchadnezzar of Babylon captures Jerusalem; exiles the best and brightest descendants of the king to Babylon, which includes Daniel, Hananiah (*Shadrach*), Mishael (*Mishach*), and Azariah (*Abed-Nego*) (2 Kings 24–25; 2 Chronicles 36:6).
604	Daniel interprets Nebuchadnezzar's dream (Daniel 2).
598	Second Exile to Babylon (3,023 captives). • King Jehoiakim of Judah dies; Jehoiachin reigns (2 Kings 24:6).
597	Third Exile to Babylon (ten thousand captives) • King Jehoiachin and prophet **Ezekiel deported** (**2 Kings 24:12–14**). • The poorest are left in the land; Zedekiah begins his reign (verse 14).
593	Ezekiel receives visions of heaven (Ezekiel 1:3; 3:14, 22; 8:1; 33:22; 37:1 and 40:1).
586	Babylonians plunder and destroy Jerusalem and the temple (2 Kings 25:1–7; 2 Chronicles 36:12; Jeremiah 32:4–5; 34:2–3; 39:1–7; 52:4–11).
580	Jeremiah is freed from prison and is allowed to stay in Jerusalem (Jeremiah 39:11; 40:6).
570	Daniel interprets Nebuchadnezzar's vision of a tree (Daniel 4).
570	Jeremiah dies in Egypt.
565	Ezekiel completes his book and there is no other recording of his life.
550	Daniel receives vision of four beasts (Daniel 7).
548	Daniel receives vision of the ram and the goat (Daniel 8).

YEAR (BCE)	EVENT
539	**Daniel interprets handwriting on the wall. (Daniel 5).** • Belshazzar is murdered. • Cyrus the Great captures Babylon. • Persia becomes the new world superpower.
539	**Medo-Persian Empire is established (Daniel 2:36–43).**
536	**Daniel is given the interpretation of the seventy-week prophecy.** • King Cyrus enables the building of the Second temple (2 Chronicles 36:23).
537	**Daniel's Final Visions:** • Receives a vision of the Messiah (Daniel 10). • Is shown the future kings of Persia and Greece (Daniel 11:2–34) and the future leader of a world government **during the end times tribulation (Daniel 11:35–12:13).**
536	**The prophet Daniel dies in captivity.**
536	**Exiles return to Jerusalem.**
520	**The prophet Zechariah, whose name means "Yahweh Remembers," is brought to Jerusalem as a youth and begins his ministry.**
519	**Zechariah receives eight visions:** 1. The Man among the Myrtle Trees (1:7–17). 2. The Four Horns and the Four Craftsmen (1:18–21). 3. The Surveyor with a Measuring Line (2:1–12). 4. Cleansing and Crowning of Joshua, the High Priest (chapter 3). 5. The Gold Lampstand and the Two Olive Trees (chapter 4). 6. The Flying Scroll (5:1–4). 7. The Woman in a Basket (5:5–11). 8. Four Chariots (6:1–8).
485	**Xerxes I begins his reign as King of Persia (Esther 1:1).**
480	**Esther becomes Queen of Persia (Esther 2:17).**

YEAR (BCE)	EVENT
480–470	Zechariah receives vision of the redemption of Israel, the coming Messiah, and His Millennial reign (Zechariah 14).
445	Artaxerxes decrees rebuilding of Jerusalem (Nehemiah 2:1).
331	Alexander the Great Conquers Persia (Daniel 8:5–8; 21–22).
63	Roman general Pompey conquers Jerusalem (Daniel 2).
6 CE	Birth of Jesus Christ (Luke 1:1–20).

As Christ mandated, we must learn to discern the signs of the time. The end of the world as we know is casting a giant shadow in our world today. The ingathering of the Jewish people to the land of Promise, the rebirth of the nation of Israel, the rise of religious apostasy, the technological explosion of knowledge, the revival of the Roman Empire in Europe, the resurgence of Israel's ancient enemies, the rise of Russia as a military power, the expansion of China's world economy—all are preparing the way for the anti-Christ.

It is now time to go "back to the future" as God reveals His eternal plan for all humanity through the prophets Abraham, Daniel, and Ezekiel.

CHAPTER 10

ABRAHAM'S VISION— THE PROMISE

I will make you a great nation. —Genesis 12:2

Every serious student of eschatology has the privilege of drawing fresh water from the deep and refreshing wells of wisdom carved out by respected biblical scholars such as Clarence Larkin, Arthur Pink, Myer Pearlman, J. Dwight Pentecost, and Derek Prince—and I am no exception. My purpose in this section is to condense and, at times, complement the vital works of these giants of Bible prophecy so that the reader can effectively use this knowledge to better understand the foreshadowing of things to come.

THE PURPOSE

For the first two thousand years after creation, the earth was a spiritual wasteland; Jewish scholars refer to this season as "two thousand years of desolation." It was a time when God allowed the world to exist purely out of His goodness and mercy. This barrenness lasted until Abraham brought forth the seedlings of holiness that culminated in the giving of the Torah at Mount Sinai. The Word of God was "a spiritual sunrise after a night of almost endless blackness."[1]

God used the first eleven chapters of the Bible to introduce the whole human race. Then in chapter 12, He chose one family, specifically the family of Abraham, through which he continued to weave His scarlet thread of redemption. God Almighty made an everlasting covenant with Abraham, Isaac, and Jacob and their descendants that produced the Old Testament prophets, the kings of Israel, and in due course, led to Bethlehem's manger.

The Almighty reveals His purpose for mankind through personal visitation, His written Word, and by dreams and visions to the few He calls His messengers. Ultimately, the Architect of the universe desires that good triumph and that evil is conquered. This is a theme that consistently runs through biblical prophecy, yet *how* God chooses to fulfill His purpose is often complex and inconsistent to human reasoning.

For example, there are times when we see good rewarded and evil punished. There are other times, however, when evil seems to prevail, and goodness stands disgraced. No matter how hard this is to understand, we must trust that God's plan is not hindered. This one thing we know: we will not fully understand the ways of the Almighty until we are with Him in eternity. In the meantime, God, in His infinite wisdom, chooses what and when to conceal or reveal to His children.

God's vision is perfect—ours is not. Man's vision has been likened to what a fly sees when it lands on an artist's painting—the broad scope of the entire canvas is impaired because the fly can only see minute parts of the whole. Rabbi Hersh Goldwurm explains it this way: "Until we see the whole, we cannot understand the parts; when we see the whole—sometimes after generations, sometimes not until the End of Days—we will understand why each ingredient had to enter the picture when it did and as it did."[2]

THE COMMAND

At His chosen time, God Almighty allows His creation to look into the heavens and witness scenes that reveal future events. One such vision was given to Abram, as recorded in Genesis 15. Here, God made known to the *"father of all those who believe"* (Romans 4:11), the future of the Jewish people for thousands of years to come.

The prophetic use of dreams and visions is emphasized in Scripture from the book of Genesis through the book of Revelation. When Aaron and Miriam rebelled against Moses, the Lord defended Moses with these words: *"If there is a prophet among you, I, the LORD, make Myself known to him in a vision; I speak to him in a dream"* (Numbers 12:6).

Before we can fully appreciate what Abram saw, allow me to give you a short synopsis of who he was.

Abram was a Semite, a descendant of Shem, Noah's son. He lived in the city of Ur, where his father was an idol merchant. In order to fulfill His plan, God called Abram out from his pagan-worshiping land through the commands and promises of Genesis 12,

> Now the LORD had said to Abram: *"Get out of your country, from your family and from your father's house, to a land that I **will** show you. I **will** make you a great nation; I **will** bless you and make your name great; and you shall be a blessing. I **will** bless those who bless you, and I **will** curse him who curses you; and in you all the families of the earth shall be blessed"* (vv. 1–3).

Acts 7:2–3 refers to this appearance of *"the God of glory"* to Abram while he was still in Mesopotamia shortly after the destruction of the

Tower of Babel, which is recorded in Genesis 11 and discussed in chapter 8 of this book. God was about to intervene in the life of Abram in a manner that would forever change his future and the future of mankind. While Genesis 11 was about the rebellion of man against the authority of God, Genesis 12 is about the eternal plans of God for Abram, the Jewish people, and the nations of the world.

This glorious appearance of God to mankind was the first recorded since the expulsion of Adam and Eve from the Garden. After centuries of continued disobedience, the Lord chose a man among the world's idolaters (Deuteronomy 14:2) who would be faithful to respond to His revelation and teach His precepts to his descendants (Proverbs 22:6). From this point forward, Abram and his seed are the major focus of Scripture.

Arthur W. Pink states, "The Lord's commands are rarely accompanied with *reasons,* but they are always accompanied with *promises,* either expressed or understood."[3] Genesis 12 is no exception. God Almighty used the phrase "I will" five times within the sevenfold blessing to emphasize that He meant what He said, and as is His nature, the Lord has fulfilled every one of His declarations.

The first "I will" referred to the future State of Israel; the crown jewel among all nations. And in fulfillment of His promise, the Jewish people have blessed the nations of the world despite the efforts of many to eradicate them.

Through the centuries, God's chosen line has miraculously survived the wicked plans of dictators, despots, psychopathic Caesars, expulsions, pogroms, and mass executions. And no matter how vicious and horrific the campaigns, the Jewish people have miraculously survived and overwhelmingly blessed humanity by scripting the Word of God and by giving us the patriarchs—Abraham, Isaac, and Jacob, the Old Testament prophets, and the First Family of our faith—Mary, Joseph, and Jesus. Christianity certainly owes a debt of gratitude to the Jewish people. Remember this Truth: Judaism does not need Christianity to explain its existence; however, Christianity cannot explain its existence without Judaism.

BLESSINGS OR CURSINGS

The decline and demise of nations in both ancient and modern times, which plagued Israel and tormented the Jewish people, can be directly attributed to God's *"I will"* promise to *"curse him who curses you"* (Genesis 12:3). Here are just a few examples recorded in history.

The Assyrian Empire existed from 900 BCE to 600 BCE. They invaded Israel in 722 BCE, initiating the first Jewish diaspora, which forced the Jewish people to assimilate throughout the Assyrian province. Soon after, Assyria fell to its ardent enemies: the Babylonians (612 BCE). Today, ancient Assyria is composed of parts of Iraq, Turkey, Iran, and Syria—all of which are war-torn countries marching toward the mountains of Israel for the coming Gog and Magog Wars, where they will encounter the judgment of God.

The Babylonian Empire (626–539 BCE) ushered in an era of cultural renaissance in the Near East. The Babylonians, under Nebuchadnezzar, conquered Jerusalem (586 BCE), destroyed the First Temple, and exiled the Jewish people to Babylon. They soon fell to Cyrus the Great, king of Persia (539 BCE).

King Cyrus blessed the Jewish people, as foretold by the prophet Isaiah. He permitted the exiled Jews to leave Babylon and return to their Promised Land. In Jerusalem, they would live under a form of Jewish home rule and be allowed to rebuild the temple (Isaiah 44:28).

The effect of King Cyrus's blessing upon the Jewish people continued for over one hundred years, until 411 BCE, when a Persian by the name of Bagoas was made governor of Jerusalem. During his ruthless tenure, he tormented the Jews by levying burdensome taxes and desecrating their temple. Within the course of time, the evil Bagoas became the power behind the throne of Persia by governing through weak puppet-kings such as King Darius III.

Bagoas attempted to poison King Darius, as he had assassinated the previous kings, but instead was forced to drink the poison himself. Soon after Bagoas's death, Alexander the Great destroyed the Persian Empire (332 BCE) and conquered Judea.

The promise of God's curse on anti-Semitism continued. After the Greeks besieged the Jewish people and desecrated their holy altar, they were in time conquered by Rome (146 BCE).

Rome too viciously oppressed and tortured the Jewish people, and under the siege of Titus in 70 CE, destroyed the Second Temple. During this horrific siege, one million Jews died by either starvation or the sword. Titus commanded the Roman Tenth Legion to tear down the Second Temple until not one stone remained on top of another. Then seventy thousand Jewish men were taken prisoners, forced to march to Rome, and build the celebrated Roman Coliseum. The God of Israel witnessed Rome's cruel treatment of the Jewish people and upheld His promise of the curse.

By 285 CE, Rome's emperor was dealing with internal chaos, moral decadence and political corruption and chose to split the empire in two. This separation created an Eastern and Western Empire, which weakened Rome's overall dominance. Then in 476 CE, the Germanic king Odoacer overthrew what was left of the Western Roman Empire.

Modern nations have not circumvented the curse of Genesis 12, nor will they in the future. Prior to the Inquisition and the Edict for Expulsion of 1492, Spain was considered the first global superpower. But in less than two hundred years following this anti-Semitic edict, which forced the Jews to convert to Christianity or leave the country within a period of twelve days, Spain became fully bankrupt.[4] This marked the beginning of the end of Spanish imperialism.

Germany was in ruins after igniting the furnace of the vilest of Jewish propaganda, persecution, and pogroms, which culminated in the Final Solution where over six million Jews perished at the hands of so-called baptized Christians. The judgment of God was poured out on Hitler's mighty army as 5.3 million German soldiers perished during World War II.[*] This was followed by the brutality of the Russian invasion, during which thousands of women were raped and murdered, and hundreds of thousands more died from forced labor in the Soviet Union.[†] Finally, many Germans endured decades of living under the oppressive boot of communism behind the Iron Curtain. Still Germany has not paid its debt in full.

A Gatestone Institute article stated, "Mass migration from the Muslim world is fast-tracking the Islamization of Germany, as evidenced by the proliferation of 'no-go' zones, Sharia courts, polygamy and child marriages. Mass migration has also been responsible for a host of social disruptions, including jihadist attacks, a migrant rape epidemic, a public health crisis, rising crime and a rush by German citizens to purchase weapons for self-defense—and even to abandon Germany altogether."[5] The curse continues.

At its peak, the British Empire was the world's foremost global power. By 1922, it was the largest empire in history, governing over one-quarter of the earth's total land area. However, the United Kingdom no longer governs any major land mass in the world other than England, Scotland, Wales, and Northern Ireland.

---

* Rüdiger Overmans, *German Military Losses in World War II*. Oldenbourg, 2000, p. 228.
† "Challenge Population: on developments of modern thinking about the population before, in and after the Third Reich Ingo Haar, "population balance sheets and displacement losses." On the History of German Victims from Escape and Expulsion Publisher for Social Sciences 2007.

The British Empire lost its world dominance when it violated its trust with the Jewish people through actions such as expelling the Jews from England (1290), failing to vote for Israeli statehood (1947), and for its continued anti-Semitic stand with the Boycott, Divestment, and Sanctions campaign against Israeli products and businesses. Thankfully, Britain's current prime minister, Boris Johnson, is expected to unveil proposed legislation aimed at undermining the BDS campaign.

In a 2015 BBC interview, then-Mayor Johnson stated that he could "not think of anything more foolish than to say that you want to have any kind of divestment or sanctions or boycott against a country that, when all is said and done, is the only democracy in the region."* Prime Minister Johnson has also called out the UN's anti-Israel bias, and was the UK's first foreign secretary to vote against Item 7, a perpetual anti-Semitic agenda item of the UN Human Rights Council singling out Israel for criticism.

I want to clearly state that our nation is no exception to God's promise of Genesis 12:3. As long as we have stood by God's Chosen, we have experienced His blessings. This promise can be traced back as far as 1492, when we became a refuge for the Jewish people from the horrors of the Spanish Inquisition and was especially prevalent when we recognized Israel's statehood.

However, during Barack Obama's eight-year tenure as president, he deliberately put daylight between America and our only democratic ally in the Middle East by orchestrating the traitorous Iran Deal. President Obama seriously risked Israel's right to exist by obliging Iran. He pandered to radical Islamist theocrats who daily threaten to wipe the Jewish people off the map. Make no mistake, Iran's chants of "Death to America" and "Death to Israel" are expressions of intent, not just frenzied rhetoric.

---

* https://www.timesofisrael.com/boris-johnson-set-to-move-forward-with-anti-bds-law/.

Ultimately, America betrayed the trust of the Jewish state, and as a consequence of this and other fundamentally disloyal actions against Israel, America lost its status as a respected world leader largely because our allies couldn't trust us, and our enemies didn't fear us.

God in His infinite mercy has given America an opportunity to reverse the promise of the curse under the leadership of President Trump, who has pledged to stand by Israel and the Jewish people. During his first term, President Trump has proven his resolve to bless and defend Israel's right to exist.

The president has strengthened the cooperation between the US military and the IDF, bolstering the security of both our countries. His administration has sought to promote peace in the region to ensure Israel and the Jewish people will remain strong and protected. These examples of President Trump's steadfastness toward Israel, as well as all the accomplishments listed in previous chapters, gives us hope for the future. "He who blesses Israel will be blessed!"

I, along with millions of other believers, pray that our country continues to make every effort to strengthen our relationship with Israel. I have said it before, and it bears repeating—those nations that have come against the Jewish people are in the boneyard of human history while the State of Israel lives and prospers. God's promises never fail!

SET APART

We must remember that Almighty God will have nothing to do with an idolatrous people or nation. God demands that His people be set apart to Him. The Creator of heaven and earth has great plans for His Covenant Land and His people,

"And you shall be holy to Me, for I the LORD am holy, and

have separated you from the peoples, that you should be Mine" (Leviticus 20:26).

God has not changed, and His precepts remain the same. The promise of Genesis 12 continues in verse 7, when God gave the land to Abram. The Lord used a variety of ways to bring Abram into his sevenfold blessing, however, Abram first had to completely separate himself from his idolatrous past, his family, and his country.

In Genesis 13, an argument arose between Abram's herdsmen and those of his nephew Lot. In an effort to bring peace, Abram divided the grazing land and allowed Lot to choose the best real estate for himself. It is significant to note that Lot's name means "veil." In other words, no matter how close Abram and his nephew were, Lot was an *impediment* that prevented Abram from *seeing* his inheritance and from achieving God's destiny.

Abram was now in a place of divine separation where God could fully bless him. Bible history proves that what you are willing to walk away from will determine what God can bring you to. Abram walked away from Ur, his idolatry, his family, and all else God had commanded him to leave behind. Because of his obedience, Abram became one of the most prosperous and revered men in world history.

The Lord reaffirmed to Abram what He promised in Genesis 12—the giving of the land to him and his descendants forever.

MELCHIZEDEK

Lot was now living in Sodom, and during this time in history, King Chedorlaomer of Elam, who followed in the way of Nimrod, conquered the lands as far west as Canaan and exercised authority over its southeastern part.[6] The five local kings of these regions, after paying tribute to him for twelve years, rebelled, but within a short time, Chedorlaomer and his three collaborating kings crushed their uprising.

During the battle, Chedorlaomer's legions plundered the region of the Dead Sea and took Lot captive. Abram came to Lot's rescue in the first war ever mentioned in Scripture and, in doing so, delivered the kings of Sodom and Gomorrah and their allies (Genesis 14).

After the victory, Melchizedek, the king of Salem, who was also the priest of the Most High God (Hebrews 7:1), blessed Abram: *"Blessed be Abram of God Most High, Possessor of heaven and earth; and blessed be God Most High, who has delivered your enemies into your hand"* (Genesis 14:19–20). After the blessing, Abram presented *"a tithe of all"* (v. 20) to Melchizedek.

Melchizedek embodies the foreshadowing of the millennial glory of Christ as he meets Abram upon his return from the slaughter of the kings, and Lot symbolizes the Jewish remnant during the tribulation period. So will it be when our Lord returns to usher in the Millennium. He will overthrow the Beast and his forces in this same *"King's Valley"* (v. 17), deliver Israel out of their hands, and bless the descendants of Abraham.

And just as Abram acknowledged the authority of Melchizedek by paying him tithes, so will Israel acknowledge their divine Melchizedek and claim Him as their Priest and King.[7]

THE VISION

After these things the word of the LORD came to Abram in a vision, saying, "Do not be afraid, Abram. I am your shield, your exceedingly great reward." But Abram said, "Lord GOD, what will You give me, seeing I go childless, and the heir of my house is Eliezer of Damascus?" Then Abram said, "Look, You have given me no offspring; indeed one born in my house is my heir!" And behold, the word of the LORD came to him, saying, "This one shall not be your heir, but one who will come from your own body shall be your heir." Then He brought him outside and said, "Look now toward heaven, and count the stars if you are able to number them." And He said to him, "So shall your descendants be."

And he believed in the LORD, and He accounted it to him for righteousness. (vv. 1–6)

These verses introduce several first-used concepts in Scripture that transformed Abram's life and the lives of all who believe. A few of the more significant words are "vision," "afraid," "believed," "accounted," and "righteousness." To better understand their importance, let us consider their intent.

Why did the Lord speak to Abram through a vision? And why was he afraid?

Think of it—Abram led his small squadron of 318 armed servants—the first IDF commandos—in a surprise night attack, gaining a supernatural victory against four kings and their seasoned armies.

Chedorlaomer and the three kings were dead, Lot was liberated, and the riches that had been taken from Sodom and Gomorrah were recovered. Abram acknowledged that it was God who had gloriously intervened—*but what now?*

Abram feared that the successors of the four kings would gather even larger armies in retaliation for his victory, and he was anxious as to whether God would deliver him once more. In order to comfort Abram, God appeared to him in a vision, saying, *"Do not be afraid, Abram. I am your shield, your exceedingly great reward"* (Genesis 15:1).

However, Abram had an even more desperate concern: *"Lord GOD, what will You give me, seeing I go childless?"* (v. 2). In the times of Abram, going childless meant his legacy would fade away, for it was believed that "heirship is based upon sonship."[8]

At this time in Abram's life, he would have to leave all his possessions to his trusted servant, who would become his heir by adoption. However, God, in His sovereignty, knew that He would make a covenant with Abram, give him the "son of promise" and have a relationship with his descendants for eternity (see Galatians 4:22–23).

God's timing was crucial—He would wait until both Abram and Sarai were outside of their childbearing years (Hebrews 11:12). In doing so, God manifested His never-ending faithfulness and His miracle-working power once more. Just when Abram's dream seemed absolutely impossible—God showed up. Remember this truth: When you are down to nothing, God is up to something!

In answer to Abram's deeper-rooted fear, Jewish scholars teach that the Lord comforted Abram through two prophetic experiences—in a vision and with the spoken Word:

> *He brought him outside and said [spoken Word], "Look [physical vision] now toward heaven, and count the stars if you are able to number them." And He said [spoken Word] to him, "So shall your descendants be [prophetic vision]"* (Genesis 15:5).

The combination of these events (spoken Word, and the physical and prophetic visions) confirmed that God's promise of protection would not only comfort Abram but also his descendants whenever they were confronted with impending danger.[9] How did Abram respond? Abram *"believed in the LORD, and He accounted it to him for righteousness"* (v. 6).

Abram did not limit God's power with the doubts of his own

natural mind; rather, he had confidence in the spoken Word—God said it, and he believed it. Abram grew both in his faith *in* God and in his obedience *to* God. And the Almighty rewarded Abram's great trust with a binding and unbreakable covenant.

Derek Prince describes God's next step perfectly:

> The final commitment of God to do whatever He's promised is in a covenant. Once God has made a covenant, there is nothing more He can do to commit Himself.[10]

The interaction between God and Abram in the next few verses led to a remarkable binding ceremony that stood at the time it was made, still stands today, and will stand throughout eternity.

Remember this truth: God will always perform what He promises.

THE COVENANTS

In order to appreciate the magnitude of the irrevocable agreement God made with Abram, we must have a clear understanding of the types of covenants found in the Bible. First, God's covenants are *literal*, and any covenant pertaining to Israel is *eternal*, with the exception of one—the Mosaic covenant, which was to continue only until the coming of the "Promised Seed,"[11] our Lord and Savior Jesus Christ.

Scripture records two types of covenants—conditional and unconditional.

A conditional covenant is a two-sided agreement in which a proposal is made between two parties and is characterized by a qualifier—*if you will, then I will*. Man's compliance or failure to keep his part of the agreement may result in either his blessing or his curse. Two such conditional covenants are the covenant with

Adam in the Garden of Eden (Genesis 2:15–17) and the covenant made between God and the nation of Israel at Mount Sinai (Exodus 19–24).

An unconditional covenant is a one-sided promise and *solely depends upon the integrity of God for its fulfillment.* It is a sovereign act of God. In it, He completely commits Himself to bring to pass specific blessings and conditions for the people with whom He has made a covenant.

As mentioned in the beginning of this chapter regarding the promise of Genesis 12:1–3, this type of covenant is characterized by the principle of God's *"I will,"* which emphasizes His resolve to do as He said.

There may be terms God asks the participant to meet within the covenant, but they *do not* alter the unconditional character of it, nor are they the basis of God fulfilling His promises of blessings. An unconditional covenant is made possible by the unmerited grace of God.[12]

The following are four examples of unconditional covenants found in Scripture:

- Noahic (Genesis 9:1–17)
- Abrahamic (Genesis 12:1–2, 7; 13:14–17; 15:1–21; 17:1–21; 22:15–18)
- Davidic (2 Samuel 7:8–16)
- New (Hebrews 8:6–13)

COVENANTS WITH ISRAEL

The unique nature of the unconditional covenants with Israel, aside from their literal meaning, is that they either have been or will be fulfilled; therefore, an unconditional covenant is in no way restricted or altered by time.

Once sealed, the contents of the covenant may go into effect immediately while some may go into effect in the near future, or certain provisions may manifest in the distant prophetic future.

Another distinct nature of unconditional covenants is that they were exclusively entered with one people:

> ...*who are Israelites, to whom pertain the adoption, the glory, the covenants, the giving of the law, the service of God, and the promises; of whom are the fathers and from whom, according to the flesh, Christ came, who is over all, the eternally blessed God. Amen* (Romans 9:4–5).

Paul underscored this fact in Ephesians 2:11–12 by declaring that Gentiles were considered *"strangers from the covenants."* Our hope as Christians is found in the following verse, *"But now in Christ Jesus you who once were far off have been made near by the blood of Christ"* (v. 13).

It is also important to reemphasize that these unconditional covenants were not and will not be withdrawn or revoked because of Israel's disobedience. These covenants are solely dependent upon the faithfulness of God for fulfillment.

ABRAHAMIC COVENANT

The vision of Genesis 15 leads to the Abrahamic covenant. This covenant is an eternal covenant—a binding and unconditional contract between God and man (Genesis 17:7, 13, 19; 1 Chronicles 16:17; Psalm 105:10).

The word *covenant* in Hebrew, *b'rit*, means a formal agreement or pact. The Hebrew verb meaning to "seal a covenant" literally translates "to cut." To "cut a covenant" implies the shedding of blood as part of the confirmation of the agreement.

God chose to "cut covenant" with Abram in this manner, which conveys the magnitude of the pact they entered into. If the Abrahamic covenant is the foundation of the things to come, then the knowledge of its details is essential to understanding its message.

So He said to him, "Bring Me a three-year-old heifer, a three-year-old female goat, a three-year-old ram, a turtledove, and a young pigeon." Then he brought all these to Him and cut them in two, down the middle, and placed each piece opposite the other; but he did not cut the birds in two. And when the vultures came down on the carcasses, Abram drove them away.

Now when the sun was going down, a deep sleep fell upon Abram; and behold, horror and great darkness fell upon him. Then He said to Abram: "Know certainly that your descendants will be strangers in a land that is not theirs, and will serve them, and they will afflict them four hundred years. And also the nation whom they serve I will judge; afterward they shall come out with great possessions. Now as for you, you shall go to your fathers in peace; you shall be buried at a good old age. But in the fourth generation they shall return here, for the iniquity of the Amorites is not yet complete."

And it came to pass, when the sun went down and it was dark, that behold, there appeared a smoking oven and a burning torch that passed between those pieces. On the same day the LORD made a covenant with Abram, saying:

"To your descendants I have given this land, from the river of Egypt to the great river, the River Euphrates—the Kenites, the Kenezzites, the Kadmonites, the Hittites, the Perizzites, the Rephaim, the Amorites, the Canaanites, the Girgashites, and the Jebusites" (Genesis 15:9–21).

Let us study certain key words and phrases used within the covenant to paint a word picture of what transpired between God and Abram. Jewish scholars state that the covenant is a "permanent bond between two parties, symbolizing a friendship so close that they are like a single body and that each is as responsible for the other as for himself.... The two parties entering into the covenant are to be as one body, each ready to risk danger if necessary to help the other."[13]

- *"Bring Me"*: signifies that the sacrifice belonged exclusively to God and would have the status of an irrevocable oath.
- "*a three-year-old heifer, a three-year-old female goat, a three-year-old ram*":
    1. Both Christian and Jewish scholars agree that the three years of each animal's life reflect the perfection of the sacrifice at its peak of maturity and strength.
    2. The heifer is referenced several times in Scripture as a sacrificial offering for the purification from sin as mandated by God through the Mosaic law (Numbers 19:1–10; 1 Samuel 6:7–12; Job 21:10; Isaiah 7:21). The heifer would be sacrificed on the most sacred of all the Hebrew holidays, Yom Kippur—the Day of Atonement (Leviticus 16; Numbers 29:7–11).
    3. Similarly, the goat signified the sin offering presented by an individual on the Day of Atonement (Leviticus 4:28; 16:15).
    4. The ram is linked to the Levitical guilt offerings connected with consecration (Leviticus 8:1–10).[14]

- *"a turtledove, and a young pigeon"*: The turtledove is one of the smaller members of a species of birds also referred to as pigeons. Genesis 15:9 is the first time a turtledove is referred to in Scripture. Later, Levitical law would dictate that a pair of turtledoves or young pigeons was allowed as a sacrificial substitute for those who were too poor to provide a lamb.[15] A pair of these birds was offered by Mary as sacrifice at her purification (Luke 2:24).

Because of its habit of pairing for life and its fidelity to its mate, the turtledove was a symbol of purity and an appropriate offering for the Abrahamic Covenant. Biblical scholars compare these birds to Israel because, like doves, they would be preyed upon by their enemies and yet would remain faithful to the God of Abraham.

The regular migration of the turtledove in the winter and its return in the spring is mentioned by Jeremiah and King Solomon and is significant to prophecy:

Even the stork in the heavens knows her appointed times; and the turtledove, the swift, and the swallow observe the time of their coming. But My people do not know the judgment of the LORD (Jeremiah 8:7).

For lo, the winter is past, the rain is over and gone. The flowers appear on the earth; the time of singing has come, and the voice of the turtledove is heard in our land (Song of Solomon 2:11–12).

The dove is described in Scripture as a symbol of the Holy Spirit, and I believe, after my personal study of Scripture over the last sixty-two-plus years, that the Lord will return to His own in the spring when *"the voice of the turtledove is heard in our land."*

- *"cut them in two, down the middle, and placed each piece opposite the other"*: God is setting the stage for a "covenant-cutting" ceremony. The sacred nature of this bond was attested to by the shedding of lifeblood.

- *"when the vultures came down on the carcasses, Abram drove them away"*: The birds of prey symbolize the nations of the world that would attempt to assimilate the seed of Abraham into foreign cultures and religions from generation to generation. In extreme cases, some nations would attempt to utterly exterminate Abraham's seed. By driving the predators away, Abram was protecting the spiritual tie between the Almighty and the future of Israel.

- *"a deep sleep fell upon Abram; and behold, horror and great darkness fell upon him"*: Abram's mind needed to be free to grasp the radical revelation he was about to receive. God isolated Abram's thoughts, bringing him into a "wholly yielded state."[16] This "deep sleep" was the same sleep with which God sedated Adam in the Garden of Eden to create Eve. In this case, the "deep sleep" prophetically reveals the birth of a nation (Israel) that would ultimately bring forth God's Only Begotten Son.

  Pink asserts that God further showed Abram he would not inherit the land during his natural life; instead, he must go to the grave and in due time inherit it together with the Promised Seed. In his awaking from this sleep, Abram received a "veiled promise of resurrection from the dead."[17] Bottom line: The way to Abram's inheritance was through death and resurrection—a type and shadow of our own redemption through the death and resurrection of Christ.

This deep sleep also revealed the tribulations that lay ahead for Abram's descendants. God showed Abram the darkness and bitterness of the future Hebrew exiles through the four-fold expressions of *"horror," "darkness," "great,"* and *"fell."* This manifestation, which overtook Abram's spirit, referred to the four ancient kingdoms listed in the book of Daniel (chapters 2 and 7).

The *"horror"* depicts Babylon; *"darkness"* represents Media-Persia; *"great"* refers to Greece; and *"fell"* symbolizes Rome. God forewarned Abram that if Israel sinned, the people would be exiled from their land and kept in subjugation by these kingdoms.

The Lord then confirmed to Abram that possession of the Promised Land would still come, but only after the Egyptian exile of his people.[18]

- *"your descendants will be strangers in a land…and will serve them, and they will afflict them four hundred years. And also the nation whom they serve I will judge; afterward they shall come out with great possessions.…Now as for you, you shall go to your fathers in peace.…But in the fourth generation they shall return here"*: These verses contain a sevenfold prophecy, all of which would be literally fulfilled. It foretells the time of Abram's descendants in the land of Egypt, their bondage, their redemption, and their return to Canaan.

1. You will be strangers in another country (Egypt) (Psalms 105:11–15).
2. You will be slaves in Egypt (Exodus 1:8–14).
3. You will be oppressed four hundred years (Exodus 12:40–42).
4. God will judge Egypt (Acts 7:6–8).

5. Israel will come out with many possessions (Exodus 3:21–22; 12:35–36).
6. Abram will not live through this period of slavery (Genesis 25:7–8).
7. In the fourth generation (four hundred years), Israel will return to the land (Exodus 6:26).

The Bible provides all the proof necessary to show how each of these prophecies was fulfilled, as illustrated by the above scriptures and many more, such as the following:

Exodus 6:16–26 gives the genealogy of Levi, the third son of Jacob, representing the first generation of those who entered Egypt. The second generation was Levi's son Kohath. The third generation was Amram, the son of Kohath, and the fourth generation was Aaron and Moses, who were described as *"the same Aaron and Moses to whom the LORD said, 'Bring out the children of Israel from the land of Egypt according to their armies'"* (Exodus 6:26).

- *"Now as for you, you shall go to your fathers in peace; you shall be buried at a good old age"*: The Lord was telling Abram that he would be spared all of the trials and tribulations that his people would endure.

- *"But in the fourth generation they shall return here, for the iniquity of the Amorites is not yet complete"*: The Amorites represented all the Canaanite nations. God showed Abram that the slavery of the Hebrews in Egypt, their exodus, and their conquest of the Promised Land were part of His long-term plan.

  It would take four hundred years for the sins of the Amorites to reach such magnitude until God saw fit to expel them from the land. Joshua's subsequent invasion of the Amorite nations was not an act of aggression on Joshua's part, but a fulfillment of God's promise. Genesis 15: *"And the LORD drove out from before us all the people, including the Amorites who dwelt in the land"* (Joshua 24:18).

- *"there appeared a smoking oven and a burning torch that passed between those pieces"*: The burning torch symbolized the glory of the Lord. Only God passed between the pieces, indicating that it was *His covenant* and He would assume full responsibility for its administration—Abram's only requirement was to believe.[19]

  Think of it—the great I AM was making a covenant with *Himself,* based on His own integrity!

  The fulfillment of the covenant had nothing to do with the faithfulness of Abraham or the Jewish people. Replacement theologians present the concept that this covenant was broken because of Israel's failure to keep it; therefore, the Church has replaced Israel in the economy of God.

  Nothing could be further from the truth.

  God never lies—this irrevocable covenant depends solely on the Almighty fulfilling His part. Nothing man can do or say will ever change this eternal promise between God, Abraham, and the land—the ratification of Abraham's covenant is as "sure as the ongoing life of the Lord."[20]

- *"On the same day the LORD made a covenant with Abram...I have given this land . . .":* Here the Lord confirmed the boundaries of the Promised Land grant.[21]

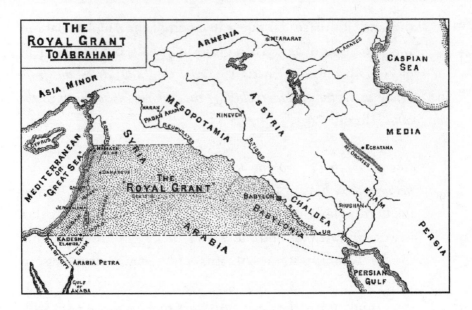

THE ISHMAEL BLESSING—
WHO OWNS THE LAND?

The most pressing geopolitical crisis of our time is the Arab-Israeli dispute over who owns the Promised Land of Israel. The chasm between the Jews and Arabs began after Abram, at the urging of doubting Sarai, took Hagar as his concubine. Hagar conceived Ishmael, and soon after Hagar and Sarai began to despise each other (Genesis 16:5–6).

Abram's regretful decision to follow Sarai's lead created enmity between the two women. This animosity is the root cause of the hostility that exists between Abraham's descendants (Arabs and Jews) to this day.

Some Arabs believe that because they too are the seed of Abraham, the Promised Land belongs to them. It is true that the Arab nations have Abraham as their father through Ishmael, and it is also true that Abraham loved his firstborn and wanted him to be included in the covenant, pleading to God, *"Oh, that Ishmael might live before You!"* (Genesis 17:18).

How did God respond to Abraham's request? His answer was instant and resolute: *"No, Sarah your wife shall bear you a son, and you shall call his name Isaac; I will establish My covenant with him for an everlasting covenant, and with his descendants after him"* (Genesis 17:19).

Paul reiterated God's position in Galatians 4:

Now we, brethren, as Isaac was, are children of promise. But, as he who was born according to the flesh then persecuted him who was born according to the Spirit, even so it is now. Nevertheless what does the Scripture say? "Cast out the bondwoman and her son, for the son of the bondwoman shall not be heir with the son of the freewoman." So then, brethren, we are not children of the bondwoman but of the free (vv. 28–31).

The Lord honored Abraham's request to bless Ishmael, for the Bible records:

And as for Ishmael, I have heard thee: Behold, I have blessed him, and will make him fruitful…twelve princes shall he beget, and I will make him a great nation. But my covenant will I establish with Isaac, which Sarah shall bear unto thee at this set time in the next year" (Genesis 17:20–21).

Fast-forward to the twentieth century, when the twelve princes of Ishmael became part of the OPEC nations, which is one of the wealthiest oil conglomerates on planet Earth. They are truly blessed of God because of Abraham.

The world's most heated geopolitical issue can be explained in two simple sentences: *One father had two sons. One inherited the real estate, and the other inherited the oil.* When you go to Israel, you are blessing Isaac; when you fuel your car, you are blessing Ishmael.

THE ULTIMATE SACRIFICE

During the most dramatic scene of Abram's vision, the Almighty's divine presence, represented by a *"burning torch,"* passed between the cut halves of the sacrificial animals. It was at this time that God chose to bind Himself to a unilateral obligation. This one divine act constituted the ratification of the everlasting covenant He made with Abram.

> *And it came to pass, when the sun went down and it was dark, that behold, there appeared a smoking oven and a burning torch that passed between those pieces. On the same day the Lord made a covenant with Abram* (Genesis 15:17–18).

Abram was not required to perform this ritual for he had no obligation under the terms of the covenant. The *"smoking oven and a burning torch"* symbolized *one* single blazing fire—the Shekinah glory of God. This same *"cloud and thick darkness"* would appear *"as the smoke of a furnace"* at the revelation of the Torah (God's Word) to Moses in Exodus 19, and the *"torch"* was the *"fire"* that manifested on Mount Sinai (Deuteronomy 5:4).

The Great I Am, Creator of heaven and earth, was the promising party within the covenant, and His oath was unconditional. This divine deed reflects one of the most beautiful truths in Scripture: God is the great Promise Keeper.

THE SIGN OF THE COVENANT

After years of silence, Abram was reminded that he must come to the end of himself before God sealed His covenant with him. By addressing Himself as *"I am the Almighty God"* or *"El Shaddai,"* God was reaffirming the covenant's fulfillment (Genesis 17:1).

This is the first time the term *El Shaddai* is used to refer to God in Scripture. He was and is sufficient in Himself to fulfill all that He promised. God would multiply Abram abundantly. He was and is the Life Giver who would restore reproductive ability to Abram and Sarai, for they were as good as dead.

The next step in the fulfillment of Abram's divine destiny was the changing of his name. God gave Abram a new name—he would no longer be known as Abram or patriarch; now he would be addressed as Abraham, the father of a multitude of nations (v. 5).

Think of it: Every time Abraham spoke his own name or heard it spoken, he would be reminded of God's eternal promise.

When Abraham was ninety-nine years old the Lord established the *sign* of the covenant through the act of circumcision. This physical symbol of Abraham's inclusion in God's irrevocable promise was such a significant milestone in the history of the Jewish people that the Torah precisely records it as occurring 2,047 years after creation.[22]

Abraham's circumcision was a required preparatory procedure before the miraculous conception of Isaac, the "son of promise," could occur. It was at this time that God reaffirmed His covenant to Abraham,

> *I will make you exceedingly fruitful; and I will make nations of you, and kings shall come from you. And I will establish My covenant between Me and you and your descendants after you*

*in their generations, for an everlasting covenant, to be God to you and your descendants after you. Also **I give to you** and your descendants after you the land in which you are a stranger, all the land of Canaan, as an everlasting possession; and **I will** be their God. . . .*

*Then God said: "No, Sarah your wife shall bear you a son, and you shall call his name Isaac; **I will** establish My covenant with him for an everlasting covenant, and with his descendants after him....But My covenant **I will** establish with Isaac, whom Sarah shall bear to you at this set time next year"* (Genesis 17:6–8, 19, 21).

God is the great I AM. When He says *I will*, He is establishing His intent and will perform what He has spoken.

Remember this truth: God's promises are prophetically accomplished facts from the moment He speaks them into existence and are fully realized at His selected time. God's words are so sure in their fulfillment that when He declares in Genesis 17:5, *"I have made you a father of many nations"* and then again, in verse 7: *"to you and your descendants"*—it is as good as done!

Abraham's son Isaac, whom God clearly blessed, inherited the covenant in Genesis 26. It was then given to Jacob and his descendants in Genesis 32. Eventually, these descendants collectively became the *"children of Israel"* (Exodus 6:26) or the Jewish people, and the Promised Land is the land of Israel.

Please understand that the Abrahamic covenant is not just another relic of antiquity; it is the taproot to the Old Testament and the fulfillment of the New Testament—it is alive and well. Dwight Pentecost described God's covenant with Abraham and his descendants as the pillar on which the Holy Scripture stands:

> The eternal aspects of this covenant [Abrahamic], which
> guarantee Israel a permanent national existence, perpetual
> title to the land of promise, and the certainty of material and
> spiritual blessings through Christ, and guarantee Gentile
> nations a share in these blessings, determine the whole escha-
> tological program of the Word of God.[23]

Abraham is the *"father of all those who believe"* (Romans 4:11), and this fact is the foundation of the Judeo-Christian bond. The land of Israel, with its God-given boundaries, belongs exclusively to His Promised Seed. The Abrahamic covenant made by Almighty God with the Jewish people is not only eternal; it cannot be altered or amended by governments or mankind. And because of this certainty, Israel lives today, tomorrow, and forever, for as King David declared:

> *And who is like Your people, like Israel, the one nation on the earth whom God went to redeem for Himself as a people, to make for Himself a name—and to do for Yourself great and awesome deeds for Your land—before Your people whom You redeemed for Yourself from Egypt, the nations, and their gods? For You have made Your people Israel Your very own people forever; and You, LORD, have become their God* (2 Samuel 7:23–24).

The greatest legacy of the Abrahamic covenant is that it is the cornerstone of Israel's eternal relationship to God—all other Bible promises are based on this truth.

CHAPTER 11

DANIEL'S VISION— THE FOUR KINGDOMS

...and Daniel had understanding in all visions and dreams.
—Daniel 1:17

From the beginning of time until we enter the dimension called eternity, where time shall be no more, Israel and the Jewish people have been and will continue to be God's prophetic timepiece. When major events take place that determine the destiny of mankind, God uses His Covenant nation to alert the world.

Many brilliant minds have devoted their life's work to the study of ancient biblical prophecies, the works of Christian and Jewish scholars, and even the prognostications of secular sources to better understand the timeline of the End of Days. One such scientific genius was Sir Isaac Newton (1643–1727).

Newton is credited with astrophysical, mathematical, and scientific findings that include the invention of calculus, the construction of the first reflecting telescope, and of course the discovery of the laws of motion and gravity. However, few know that Newton was also a prominent Christian theologian who spent significant time studying Bible prophecy.

Newton applied his unique scientific approach to the study of Scripture, the Hebrew language, and the teachings of the Talmud, which is a compilation of Jewish oral law and stories. To Newton, science and faith were part of the same domain. He theorized that the Scriptures provided a "code" to the natural world. Newton believed that the study of God's Word was a type of science that, if properly interpreted, could predict what was to come.

One of the Hebrew texts Newton studied was the book of Daniel. He concluded that among the biblical prophets, Daniel was most distinct in order of time and should be used as the key to learning more about the End of Days.[1]

Josephus said that Daniel "not only predicted the future, like the other prophets, but specified when the events would happen."[2]

In order to better comprehend Daniel's writings, it is important to know a little of what happened to the Jewish people up to his time in history and how these events specifically affected Daniel's life. Therefore, the following is an abridged overview of 1,555 years in Israel's history.[3]

ABRAHAM TO DANIEL

Some 290 years after God made the covenant with Abraham, the Jews entered into 430 years of Egyptian bondage.[4] Their captivity ended with their well-known Exodus of 1440 BCE, when the Lord provided deliverance through His miraculous parting of the Red Sea. After a forty-year trek in the wilderness (Numbers 14:33; Exodus 16:35) under Moses's leadership, the mantle was handed to Joshua. This warrior led the Israelites into a highly celebrated period in Jewish history, beginning with their crossing of the Jordan into the Promised Land (Genesis 15:16; Joshua 3:1).

After Joshua came the golden age of Israel, which reached the pinnacle of its glory under the rule of King David (2 Samuel 5:3–3) and King Solomon (1 Kings 1:38–39). However, dissension reigned after the death of Solomon, dividing the nation of Israel into two parts: the Northern and the Southern Kingdoms (1 Kings 12:16, 19). The discord between the two kingdoms led to their turbulent and bloodstained decline, resulting in the eventual fall of Jerusalem in 586 BCE (2 Kings 24:10–16).

The northern ten tribes (Kingdom of Israel) chose national idolatry over obedience to God's Word. Consequently, they were the first to be captured by the Assyrians in 722 BCE. Then, in the course of time, the remaining two southern tribes (Kingdom of Judah) also embraced pagan worship and were conquered by the Babylonians in 586 BCE. Following the overthrow, King Nebuchadnezzar deported the Jewish captives into Babylon (2 Kings 25:9–19; 2 Chronicles 36:18–19; Jeremiah 52:12–25; Daniel 1:1–21). These tragic events marked the end of Israel's first commonwealth.

Still, amid the carnage and decline of the Jewish nation, the seeds of hope remained alive for Israel's rebirth. Although the Assyrians completely absorbed the Northern Kingdom into their vast empire, the Babylonians chose not to colonize the conquered Southern Kingdom of Judah. Nebuchadnezzar permitted the Jewish remnant to stay in their land, maintain their identity, and continue to worship the One True God. Only the Creator of the Universe could have orchestrated these unique circumstances, which preserved the roots of Judaism.

This chapter in history, which recorded Israel as a nation—beginning with God's covenant promise with Abraham to the glorious reign of King David—had ended. What followed was a time of chaos and anguish for the Jewish people in Babylon, referred to in Israel's history as the Exile.

THE EXILE

Thus Daniel continued [in Babylon] until the first year of King Cyrus (Daniel 1:21).

The Assyrians were strategic warfare experts and were viciously aggressive in controlling their captured territories. They would forcibly remove the educated and influential upper class of the conquered nation and relocate them to other parts of their massive empire. By doing so, they ensured that the people in the seized lands remained pacified.

Subsequently, the Assyrians settled their own citizens in the conquered territory. This strategy displaced the captured remnant, triggering a domino effect as they lost their land and their distinctive culture. Through this well-executed tactic of forced relocation and assimilation, the conquered people lost their God-given identity.

This integration policy forced the tribes of the Northern Kingdom to scatter in small numbers throughout the massive Assyrian Empire. These peoples are referred to as the "Ten Lost Tribes of Israel" because they systematically disappeared from the pages of history. They silently and submissively assimilated into various ethnic communities throughout the Middle East, resulting in the abandonment of their Jewish identities, including Hebrew names, culture, and faith.

Unlike the Assyrians, when the Babylonians conquered the Kingdom of Judah, they relocated over ten thousand Israelites to *one* city: Babylon. Here the Jewish people were allowed to live in their own separate community, providing them the opportunity to retain their identity and their religion, which was based on their belief in the God of Abraham, Isaac, and Jacob.[5]

After the siege of Jerusalem, Nebuchadnezzar confiscated many priceless Temple implements, but he also took a far more valuable treasure: Judah's finest and brightest youth. These young men were taught by their fathers to be loyal to the Lord and observant to His laws. This biblically mandated instruction would prove to be crucial for surviving their time of testing in Babylonian captivity (Proverbs 3:3).

Nebuchadnezzar had no interest in destroying the Kingdom of Judah, though he did demand allegiance and subservience. He made great efforts in providing a Babylonian-based education in culture and religion for his elite captives. Nebuchadnezzar's calculated goal was to reprogram these young and bright Jewish minds through a three-year indoctrination within the "king's college."

Later, he planned to resettle these newly trained Hebrew leaders into the conquered territories as official representatives of the Babylonian government. Through this deliberate approach, it would be nearly impossible for the Kingdom of Judah to survive their future generation's assimilation into a pagan society.

Nebuchadnezzar's premeditated plan of integration, along with his oppression of the Jewish remnant, should have rationally led to Israel's extinction. However, we must remember that Israel was God's nation by way of His irrevocable covenant with Abraham, and nothing—including displacement, integration and oppression—would erase what God had established by His blood covenant.

Within the despair of the Exile, the Great Architect of the Ages was not only creating a path to survival for His chosen people; He was also laying the foundation for the imminent restoration of the nation of Israel. To accomplish this divine plan, God anointed a young man for royal ministry within King Nebuchadnezzar's college. His name was Daniel, a Jewish captive from Jerusalem, who would eventually become the "prince of the prophets."

THE BRIDGE TO ETERNITY

Daniel modestly described himself as a Jewish prisoner of war who was a servant in Babylonian captivity. However, he was so much more: he was an advisor to kings, the interpreter of dreams, a model of faith and courage, and a prophet of Israel's future conquest and redemption. Most importantly, the accounts of Daniel's visionary insight would become one of the vital keys to understanding the End of Days for all generations.

Daniel, a contemporary of Jeremiah and Ezekiel, was credited with writing the book titled with his name, which in Hebrew means "God is my judge" (Daniel 8:1; 9:2, 20; 10:2). Jesus referred to Daniel's insights in His Olivet Discourse, which is recorded in Matthew 24, and in His teaching on the signs of the times and the end of the age in Luke 21.

The events and prophecies presented within Daniel's writings were meant to encourage and comfort the Jewish people in exile through hope in the God of Israel. Jewish scholars teach that the "divine hand" was preparing the way for the exiles when He placed Daniel in the academy of the king's court. His writings, along with Christ's Olivet Discourse and the book of Revelation, would prove to be the anchors of the bridge to eternity for future generations.

A MATTER OF FAITH

The book of Daniel is divided into two parts. Part I is composed of chapters 1 through 6, which record Daniel's life and service in Babylon. Here, six vivid stories are presented in the third person and tell of Daniel's time of testing and God's miraculous intervention. These accounts reflect the faithfulness of God and attest to the righteous character of Daniel and his three friends: Hananiah, Mishael, and Azariah.

Part II includes chapters 7 through 12 and chronicles four visions or revelations given to Daniel by God or His angelic messenger. These narratives are set in first person and depict the Great Statue, the Four Beasts, the Seventy Weeks, and Daniel's Final Vision. Their message speaks of Israel's future, most of which has been fulfilled, and the End of Days, which has yet to be fully reached.

All that Daniel detailed in his writings was a testimony to the supernatural power of Israel's God. Everything that happened to Daniel and his friends while in exile was intended to separate them from God. Yet, because of the Word embedded in their hearts, they remained loyal to and became more dependent upon the Almighty. Their faith-based allegiance became a beacon of inspirational light for generations to come.

Shortly after the four entered the king's college, their names were changed, a normal practice for Babylonian captives. The young men were given Hebrew names at birth, which were derived from the names of God, while their new Babylonian names epitomized pagan gods.

For example, Daniel's name was changed to Belteshazzar, meaning "prince of the king." The Babylonians may have changed their names, but they could not change their commitment to Jehovah God. This test and others like it only galvanized the faith of these young men in the One True God of Israel.

Additionally, part of the daily regimen for those in the king's care included eating only the finest foods, but there was a problem—these items were first offered to idols as was the custom.[6] By consuming these delicacies, one would give allegiance to the gods of Babylon and not the God of Abraham.

Daniel and his friends refused the pagan offerings and persuaded the eunuch assigned to them to provide a simple diet of water and vegetables. They did not enter into a short-term fast but chose to abstain from eating meat for the duration of their captivity. God honored their allegiance and, inexplicable to their captors, the young men appeared healthier than those who ate the rich royal foods offered to pagan gods.

Daniel and his companions never measured God by the size of their problem; they had faith that the Lord would provide for their good in any situation. And for their faith, God rewarded Daniel and his friends: to Shadrach, Meshach, and Abed-Nego, God gave wisdom and knowledge; and to Daniel, He gave the gift of prophecy (Daniel 1:17).

Ask yourself these questions: Why were Daniel and his friends so adamant about remaining loyal to the God of Israel while in Babylon? Why were they willing to stand before a powerful king in a foreign land and boldly hold to their convictions at the risk of death?

The answer is simple: their fathers had faithfully taught them that there was only One True God. This creed has been the sacred foundation of the Jewish people since the Great I Am spoke these words to Moses: *"Hear, O Israel: The LORD our God, the LORD is one!"* (Deuteronomy 6:4).

God chose Abraham to be the father and founder of Israel for one reason:

For I have known him, in order that he may command his children and his household after him, that they keep the way of the LORD, to do righteousness and justice (Genesis 18:19).

Daniel and his friends recognized that the false gods of Nebuchadnezzar had the government's backing but not the approval of the Almighty.

By the same logic,

- Why have our college and university campuses ceased to teach the Biblical principles of righteousness and instead become cesspools of deception, rebellion, secular humanism, and radical socialism?
- Why does anarchy reign in the streets of our cities? Why are there daily reports of heart-wrenching acts of violence, murderous mayhem, assassinations of policemen, anarchy burning down our cities, and anti-Semitism throughout America and the nations of the world?
- Why are idol worship and satanism rampant throughout the global media outlets?
- Why is this generation full of lovers of pleasure and not lovers of God Almighty? Why has righteousness been rejected and rebellion been glorified?

The answer to these questions is also simple: We no longer teach our children the ways of the Lord, nor do we seek His guidance. We have rejected the light of truth and embraced darkness. When you reject the love of God, all that is left is the hatred. Most fathers today do not impart the truth of God's Word to their families, nor do they speak the power of the blessing over them. Without the blessing of God Almighty, our loved ones are left exposed and naked before the Prince of Darkness. In fact, many of today's fathers are absent from their homes—either physically, spiritually, or both.

Derek Prince describes the effect of this cultural downward spiral of parental and authoritarian neglect:

Men have failed in their basic responsibility and women have taken over the male role. The inevitable outcome, whether in a family, nation or civilization, can be summed up in one word: *confusion*.[7]

Fathers and mothers of this generation must return to the moral and spiritual instruction of their children, encouraged by these words from the Bible: *"Train up a child in the way he should go, and when he is old he will not depart from it"* (Proverbs 22:6).

Instead of teaching the Word of God to our children, we have taught them to worship the gods of our hedonistic society: fantasy superheroes, law-breaking professional athletes, foul-mouthed actors, mind-numbing simulated games, and singing "idols." Without moral boundaries, our children have fallen prey to a godless, overindulgent alternate reality.

Many parents do not teach their children to make good choices or allow them to suffer the consequence of bad ones. Today's generation is simply not held accountable and consequently do not respect delegated authority. The United States is only able to function successfully if we all have respect for the law of God and civil authority. Likewise, the rule of law is only legitimate if it is enforced justly and the rights of all Americans are protected. These are mutually exclusive; one cannot exist without the other.

We have also failed to pass on the work ethic that previous generations passed to us. As a result, today's youth are looking for entitlements and handouts instead of taking pride in earning an honest living.

Remember this truth: You deserve nothing until you work for it. Our country's future does not depend on what the federal government does for our children, but it *does* depend on what we do, as parents, to teach our children the ways of God. While many of today's university students are demanding "safe spaces" to shelter their hurt feelings brought on by their own confusion, Christians United for Israel (CUFI) is training brave, self-assured young college campus advocates throughout America to stand up for their faith and for the nation of Israel.[8]

These students are taught the importance of obeying the biblical mandate to support Israel and the Jewish people through programs such as the CUFI on Campus Bonhoeffer Fellowship. These same young men and women courageously stand on the front lines against the rising tide of anti-Semitism on their campuses—they are the young Daniels of this generation. They have discovered what the Lord requires of all of us:

> *He has shown you, O man, what is good; and what does the LORD require of you but to do justly, to love mercy, and to walk humbly with your God* (Micah 6:8).

Daniel defied the king's commands to stop praying to the God of Abraham and he faced certain death in the lions' den as a result of his choice (Daniel 6:16). Shadrach, Meshach, and Abed-Nego were willing to walk into the fiery furnace instead of bowing to the golden image commissioned by Nebuchadnezzar (Daniel 3:21). *Why?*

Because they believed that no matter the circumstance, their God was able to deliver them. Since childhood, they had been trained in His mandates, which shaped their outlook with an unequivocal faith that allowed them to prevail during times of trial.

> *My son, keep my words, and treasure my commands within you. Keep my commands and live, and my law as the apple of your eye. Bind them on your fingers; write them on the tablet of your heart* (Proverbs 7:1–3).

Most of America's youth cannot withstand any form of testing. Instead, they have conformed to the current trends of this idolatrous society, losing their God-given identities as men and women, as citizens, and as righteous believers. Just as Daniel and the rest of Israel's elite youth were sent into Babylon's indoctrination program, so have the young minds of our generation been brainwashed with revisionist history and liberal progressive propaganda wrapped in a package labeled "higher education." There is one stark difference: Daniel and his friends passed the test (Daniel 1:3–5, 19–20); the majority of our youth will not.

What shall we do?

We must launch a righteous revolution within our homes that begins with the father coming back into the God-given role of family leadership. We must disciple young mothers to stand in support of their husbands as together they lead their families in the ways of the Lord. We must live by the following truth as we raise our children: *"The fear of the LORD is the beginning of wisdom, and the knowledge of the Holy One is understanding"* (Proverbs 9:10).

We must decide to instill the Ten Commandments into the hearts, minds, and souls of our children. It is the only way they will succeed in their time of testing. It is the only way the America we know will survive the troubles of this world. Be assured that it is not a matter of *if* trials will come; it is only a matter of *when*!

Remember this truth: Righteous power stems from righteous choices.

Daniel decided to stand with the Lord and not be tempted by the greatest metropolis of his time, and God rewarded him with supernatural power. Daniel passed the test, and when it was time for him to graduate from the king's college, he was stronger in body and faith and had *"understanding in all visions and dreams"* (Daniel 1:17). In short, Daniel became God's appointed messenger to his generation and for the future generations of the world.

The Lord of Hosts rewarded the steadfast faith of this young sage by trusting him with supernatural revelations of the world tomorrow.

Daniel would serve as prime minister during Nebuchadnezzar's forty-four year reign, and he would continue to serve as a highly respected leader under the rest of the Babylonian monarchs and subsequent rulers of the Medo-Persian Empire. Daniel continued his royal service *"until the first year of King Cyrus"* (Daniel 1:21).

Even though Daniel was entrusted to lead the whole Medo-Persian Empire, I believe that one of Daniel's greatest missions was to show King Cyrus the two-hundred-year-old prophecies of Isaiah concerning the rebuilding of the temple and those of Jeremiah's foretelling the end of Babylonian captivity.

> *[The LORD] says of Cyrus, "He is My shepherd, and he shall perform all My pleasure, saying to Jerusalem, 'You shall be built,' and to the temple, 'Your foundation shall be laid'"* (Isaiah 44:28).

> *For thus says the LORD: After seventy years are completed at Babylon, I will visit you and perform My good word toward you, and cause you to return to this place* (Jeremiah 29:10).

Take a moment and imagine Daniel negotiating the liberation of his exiled brethren. It must have been an overwhelming joy for Daniel to chart their path to redemption—a path that he himself would not walk.

THE OFFICE OF PROPHET AND SAGE

The word "prophet," or *navi* in Hebrew, is derived from the term *niv sefatayim*, meaning "fruit of the lips," emphasizing the prophet's role as a speaker.[9] While the gift of prophecy includes the capacity to see forthcoming events as revealed by God, a prophet exhibits far more qualities. The Bible portrays prophets as role models of righteousness; they are well learned and, most importantly, have a close relationship to God.

The Almighty appoints a prophet to speak on His behalf for the purpose of delivering His precise message or select teaching. It is the *Shekinah* or divine spirit of the Lord that rests upon a prophet or prophetess to accomplish the God-given task set before them.

The *Tanakh* or Hebrew Bible is composed of three sections: the Law *(Torah)*, the Prophets (*Nevi'im*), and the Writings (*Ketuvim*). The book of Daniel is not included as part of the Prophets but rather in the Writings. It is believed that Daniel had visions that were divinely inspired, and therefore he is considered a sage in Judaism.[10]

Jewish scholars teach that there are two types of visions: prophetic and divine inspiration. A prophet studies the future and points to the opportunities for righteousness on life's journey. A sage looks into the past and shows how man can make way for God's healing presence and loving power in the choices he makes and the paths he follows. The prophet fortifies us with the gift of hope. The sage strengthens us with the gift of meaning.[11] Daniel did both.

He was led by divine inspiration and received power to take action, to speak wisdom, and to exhort. The book of Daniel includes visions and forthcoming revelations, which were not meant for the people of his time but were intended for future generations.[12] Daniel's writings, however, brought encouragement to his fellow captives and established positive examples of how to live the abundant life of a believer among unbelievers.

THE KING'S DREAM

Nebuchadnezzar favored Daniel and his three friends, keeping them within his palace until their appointed time. Four years after Daniel was taken captive, the king had a tormenting dream:

Now in the second year of Nebuchadnezzar's reign, Nebuchadnezzar had dreams; and his spirit was so troubled that his sleep left him (Daniel 2:1).

The king was furious that none of his soothsayers could reveal or interpret his dream and, consequently, condemned them all to death—a sentence that would also include Daniel and his three friends.

Daniel learned of his imminent execution and requested more time to interpret the king's dream. He gathered his friends and went before God to ask for the meaning of the king's mysterious nightmare. The Almighty honored their request, and as a result of their prayer, the *"secret was revealed to Daniel in a night vision"* (v. 19).

It is thought-provoking to note that the Lord sent a tormenting dream to a pagan king so that Daniel's supernatural powers could be revealed, establishing him as the voice of God in a godless society. There is no equal to the sovereign power and purpose of the Almighty.

I believe the second chapter of Daniel presents a more exhaustive interpretation of the things to come than any other chapter in the Bible. God's supernatural revelation of the king's dream gave a geopolitical panorama from Daniel's day to eternity.

Nebuchadnezzar's dream defines the theme of Daniel's book, which is "the superseding of the 'times of the Gentiles' as rulers of the earth [specifically Israel] by a kingdom which is to be set up in the earth by the God of Heaven, which shall be everlasting and universal."[13]

THE REVELATION

I can see it now: The king sits on his throne, frozen with fear, sweat beads of suspense dripping from his face as he anticipates Daniel's next words. And there stands God's messenger, divinely inspired, confident in demeanor, strong in his faith, and bold in his courage as he enlightens this distraught ruler of Babylon's great empire.

Daniel presents God's divine interpretation: The reign of Nebuchadnezzar's empire will be followed by four world empires, all of which will be destroyed by a supernatural power, *"the stone cut out of a mountain without hands"* (v. 45).[14] After the destruction of these empires, God will establish a fifth kingdom that will endure forever.

Daniel describes the king's dream with exactness—a statue of a man composed of four metals (2:24–45). These metals symbolize the four Gentile empires that would sequentially rule over Israel, plus a fifth that would be established much later:

1. The head of gold represented the Babylonian Empire, which ruled 612–539 BCE.
2. The crossed arms of silver symbolized the Medo-Persian Empire, which would succeed Babylon in 539–332 BCE.
3. The belly and thighs of brass represented the Greeks, which followed the Medo-Persian rule in 332–63 BCE.
4. The legs of iron depicted the Roman Empire, which ruled in 63 BCE–476 CE.
5. The feet and toes of iron and clay foreshadow the revived Roman Empire of the End of Days—the New World Order that now stands at the doorway of history.

Next, Daniel gives clear details of the final portion of the king's dream:

Inasmuch as you saw that the stone was cut out of the mountain without hands, and that it broke in pieces the iron, the bronze, the clay, the silver, and the gold—the great God has

made known to the king what will come to pass after this. The
dream is certain, and its interpretation is sure (Daniel 2:45).

The stone Daniel describes represents the Kingdom of God.
This Kingdom will suddenly appear, overrule, and destroy all earthly
powers, no matter their strength. The Lord promised to strip
the Gentiles of their dominion over Israel which they had since
Nebuchadnezzar conquered Zedekiah and destroyed Jerusalem in
586 BCE (2 Kings 25:4–9).

Can you imagine what the king felt when Daniel stood before
him and clearly described every detail of his tormenting nightmare?
Nebuchadnezzar recognized that this young Hebrew had the accurate understanding of the vivid image that haunted him. The king
also acknowledged that Daniel's God was the *"God of gods,"* and as
a reward for his service, Daniel and his three friends were promoted
"over the affairs of the province of Babylon" (Daniel 2:46–49).

THE TIMES OF THE GENTILES

Daniel plainly described Gentile empires in his writings, and as I
mentioned earlier, Jesus also referred to this period in His teachings.
In Luke 21, the Rabbi from Nazareth was speaking to His followers
about the signs of the times and the End of the Age:

> *"They will fall by the edge of the sword and will be taken as*
> *prisoners to all the nations. Jerusalem will be trampled on by the*
> *Gentiles until the times of the Gentiles are fulfilled"* (v. 24 NIV).

What was Jesus referencing?
The *"times of the Gentiles"* is the period of history when Gentile
nations dominated the world—specifically Israel. Jesus declared
that Jerusalem would be seized, its people dispersed, and then suffer

subjugation under the rule of numerous Gentile nations. Gentile control would begin to end with Israel's rebirth in 1948. This prophecy was fulfilled when Jerusalem was reunified with the Covenant nation of Israel as an outcome of the Six-Day War of 1967.

After the *"time of the Gentiles"* ends, the Messianic kingdom will arise and encompass the whole earth—and of His kingdom there will be no end (Isaiah 9:7; Daniel 2:44; 7:14; Luke 1:33).

VISION OF THE FOUR BEASTS

The last six chapters of the book of Daniel (Part II) include visions and dreams, and the prophecies applicable to them. These visions and dreams occurred in the same time period of the first six chapters of the book (Part I). Parallel imagery can be found in both the books of Ezekiel (17:3) and Revelation (13:12).[15]

Daniel wrote down the relevant facts of his vision, which occurred fifty years after his exile and fourteen years before Babylon's fall (Daniel 7:1–8). This vision mirrors Nebuchadnezzar's dream, but with the use of animals. An important fact to note is that each of the nations represented in the great image of chapter 2 and the four beasts of chapter 7 were in force in Daniel's day and are still players on the world stage today.

In the first year of Belshazzar king of Babylon, Daniel had a dream and visions of his head while on his bed. Then he wrote down the dream, telling the main facts. Daniel spoke, saying, "I saw in my vision by night, and behold, the four winds of heaven were stirring up the Great Sea" (Daniel 7:1–2).

Each of the beasts pictured in Daniel's vision represent four world powers and correspond with the kingdoms of Nebuchadnezzar's image. The first beast is the lion (king of the animals) with eagle's wings (king of the birds), both rightly represent the Babylonian Empire.

The second image is of a bear, symbolizing the Medes (ancient citizens of northwest Iran) and the Persians (modern-day Iran). The bear is raised on one side, indicating that the Persians had greater power than the Medes. The ribs in its mouth signify the three kingdoms that the Medo-Persians "devoured"—Babylon (part of modern-day Iraq), Lydia (part of modern-day Turkey), and Egypt.

The third beast is a swift leopard with four wings and four heads, representing Greece. The four wings symbolize the speed with which Alexander the Great conquered the entire known world. After Alexander's death, his kingdom was divided among his four generals, who led Macedonia (modern-day north central Greece), Egypt, Syria, and Thrace (parts of modern-day Turkey, Greece, and Bulgaria).[16]

The fourth and final image is not named because it is incomparable to any other animal or human. This beast is described as *"dreadful and terrible, exceedingly strong"* (Daniel 7:7). It has teeth of iron and ten horns. Iron is the same metal that represented the Roman Empire in Nebuchadnezzar's image (Daniel 2:40), and the horns represent a federation of nations within the revived Roman Empire. Both the images in Daniel chapters 2 and 7 represent a future kingdom possessing great power led by an evil ruler. This kingdom will be reinvented in the form of a New World Order, possibly evolving out of the European Union (Daniel 7:7).

Then Daniel sees God, the "Ancient of Days," majestically seated on His throne. And from this throne He will judge the kingdoms of this world (Daniel 7:9–10). Daniel witnesses *"the Son of Man, coming in the clouds of heaven"* (v. 13). This is Jesus Christ, our Blessed Redeemer, who will have all dominion over the earth. He will rule the final empire that will last through eternity (vv. 13–14).

DANIEL'S CALENDAR

Fast-forward—Daniel is now about eighty years old and has been in captivity for about sixty years, according to several biblical timelines associated with the Babylonian and Medo-Persian Empires. Daniel was a faithful student of the Holy Scriptures and was longing for the time when Jehovah would rebuild Jerusalem and its temple as He promised.[17] Daniel specifically reflected on Jeremiah's prophecy regarding the seventy years before Israel's redemption and their return to the Holy City of Jerusalem:

> *This whole land will be a desolation and a horror, and these nations will serve the king of Babylon seventy years* (Jeremiah 25:11 NASB).

> *For thus says the LORD: After seventy years are completed at Babylon, I will visit you and perform My good word toward you, and cause you to return to this place* (Jeremiah 29:10).

Daniel believed that the time of Jeremiah's prophecy was ending, and so would Israel's Babylonian captivity. Yet there was no visible change in sight to confirm this promise. Daniel once again chose the safe haven of prayer in which to seek his answer. God the Father wants all His children to seek Him in prayer—to find refuge in prayer, to search for guidance and wisdom in prayer, and to hear His voice in prayer.

Remember this truth: God's promises are often conditional to the actions of His people, and He has ordained prayer as one measure in which to communicate and accomplish His divine purpose.

I have always taught my congregation the importance of precise and detailed prayer. First, we must always pray according to God's Word, and second, we should pray with an exact and sincere regard for our need. This way when the provision comes, we have no doubt that it was God who answered our prayer. The Almighty is all-knowing, all-powerful, and ever-present, and He will give us the desires of our heart; however, He wants us to take the first step of faith through prayer.

Daniel presented an exemplary prayer that began with praise to God, repentance, and finally his specific petition for the restoration of his beloved Jerusalem (Daniel 9:4–19). Prayer and praise are the gateway to God the Father, and repentance is the key to answered prayer. Repentance has no doctrine or denomination—it is a gift for all mankind. Daniel did not assume to be faultless by way of a puffed-up attitude; instead, he willingly shared the guilt of his people.

Centuries later, it was God who had His only Son, the spotless Lamb, identify with our guilt in the Great Exchange at the cross:

For He made Him who knew no sin to be sin for us, that we might become the righteousness of God in Him (2 Corinthians 5:21).

The present-day church, which has been afforded so many blessings, must never forget this miraculous exchange and avoid any form of self-righteousness, for it demonstrates the same prideful attitude that caused the fall of Lucifer. The Evil One, knowing his time is short, will only increase his chaotic schemes against the body of Christ, and because of this intense warfare, arrogance can play no part in the believer's sincere relationship with God.

Remember this truth: The gateway to true intercession is the cry, "Lord Jesus, forgive me, for I have failed!" After all, who among us has not sinned against God at some time in our lives?[18]

AN ENCOUNTER OF
THE ANGELIC KIND

Daniel cried out to God and asked Him to fulfill the prophecy He had given Jeremiah. And it was in the midst of Daniel's heartfelt supplication that he received one of the most significant prophetic revelations of all time:

> *Yes, while I was speaking in prayer, the man Gabriel, whom I had seen in the vision at the beginning, being caused to fly swiftly, reached me about the time of the evening offering [set time of Prayer]. And he informed me, and talked with me, and said, "O Daniel, I have now come forth to give you skill to understand"* (Daniel 9:21–22).

Daniel had a deep desire to know the truth about the future of the Jewish people in Babylonian captivity. Remember, it is not the *truth* that sets us free, but rather the *knowledge* and *understanding* of the truth which produces liberty. Truth exists whether we are aware of it or not. The truth can stand inches from us, but it provides no benefit without our knowledge and acceptance of it.

Daniel longed to discover the mystery of God's message to Jeremiah. He asked the Lord for the ability to understand the "seventy years" in the writings of Jeremiah and he received much more. The angel Gabriel gave Daniel a glimpse of Israel's redemption from the bondage of Babylon to their ultimate restoration under the Messiah.[19]

THE SEVENTY WEEKS

The Angel revealed the precise meaning of Jeremiah's seventy-year prophecy to Daniel as instructed by God Himself.

Seventy weeks are determined for your people and for your holy city, to finish the transgression, to make an end of sins, to make reconciliation for iniquity, to bring in everlasting righteousness, to seal up vision and prophecy, and to anoint the Most Holy.

Know therefore and understand, that from the going forth of the command to restore and build Jerusalem until Messiah the Prince, there shall be seven weeks and sixty-two weeks; the street shall be built again, and the wall, even in troublesome times.

And after the sixty-two weeks Messiah shall be cut off, but not for Himself; and the people of the prince who is to come shall destroy the city and the sanctuary. The end of it shall be with a flood, and till the end of the war desolations are determined. Then he shall confirm a covenant with many for one week; but in the middle of the week he shall bring an end to sacrifice and offering. And on the wing of abominations shall be one who makes desolate, even until the consummation, which is determined, is poured out on the desolate (Daniel 9:24–27).

The term *"seventy weeks"* has confounded many a Bible student, but it can best be understood with the phrase "seventy weeks of years." The interpretation of the word *week* is not a week of seven days but a *week* of seven years; therefore, the expression *"seventy weeks"* is referring to a time period of 490 years.

This unique computation is also observed in Leviticus 25:8, which refers to the Year of Jubilee (a time of restoration) and a seven-year (sabbatical cycles) rest for the land of Israel:

"And you shall count seven sabbaths of years for yourself, seven times seven years; and the time of the seven sabbaths of years shall be to you forty-nine years."

Daniel miscalculated Jeremiah's timetable, believing his people's captivity would *literally* last seventy years. He believed that only two years of the conventional seventy-year time period remained. Daniel could not understand how the remaining three world empires (Medo-Persian, Greek, and Roman) were to come and go within such a short time before the Jews could be restored to their "national existence."

Gabriel disclosed to Daniel that the seventy years was in truth a "type" of a longer time span. Everything God promised, as well as what the Jews longed for concerning Israel's future, was summed up with Gabriel's revelation of the "seventy weeks" as recorded in Daniel 9:24–27. Saint Peter refers to the same when he said, *"the times of restoration of all things, which God has spoken by the mouth of all His holy prophets since the world began"* (Acts 3:21).[20]

Bible scholar Clarence Larkin, who died in 1924, long before the rebirth of the nation of Israel, believed the following:

> The vision of the seventy weeks is not only an interpretation of "Prophetic Chronology" but it is the "Key" that unlocks the "Scriptures of Truth." It also discloses another important fact that the "Seventy Weeks" only cover the period when the Jews are dwelling in their own land, and does not cover the present period of their dispersion [the condition of the Jews at the time of Larkin] but takes up their history again when they return to their own land [the ingathering], thus covering the time from the going forth of the decree to "restore and rebuild Jerusalem" until the second coming of Christ.[21]

Rev. Larkin would not witness the prophesied rebirth of Israel in 1948 (Isaiah 66:8); however, the ingathering of the Jews from their diaspora had begun in his lifetime. The Jewish people began the return to their Promised Land in the late 1800s at the encouragement of Theodor Herzl's call to establish a Jewish state. The prophet Isaiah foretold of this ingathering:

> *Fear not, for I am with you; I will bring your descendants from the east, and gather you from the west; I will say to the north, "Give them up!" And to the south, "Do not keep them back!" Bring My sons from afar, and My daughters from the ends of the earth* (Isaiah 43:5–6).

After the initial ingathering, the British government endorsed the establishment of a Jewish home in Palestine. This decision was made public in a letter from the British foreign secretary, Lord Arthur James Balfour, to Lord Walter Rothschild. The contents of this letter became known as the Balfour Declaration.

> *Foreign Office*
> *November 2nd, 1917*
>
> *Dear Lord Rothschild,*
>
> *I have much pleasure in conveying to you, on behalf of His Majesty's Government, the following declaration of sympathy with Jewish Zionist aspirations which has been submitted to, and approved by, the Cabinet:*
>
> *"His Majesty's Government view with favour the establishment in Palestine of a national home for the Jewish people, and will use their best endeavours to facilitate the achievement of this object, it being clearly understood that nothing shall be done which may prejudice the civil and religious rights of existing non-Jewish communities in Palestine, or the rights and political status enjoyed by Jews in any other country."*

> *I should be grateful if you would bring this declaration to*
> *the knowledge of the Zionist Federation.*
>
> *Yours sincerely, Arthur James Balfour*[22]

However, the seventy-week countdown of Daniel 9 began long before the Balfour Declaration.

GOD'S PROPHETIC CLOCK

The angel Gabriel revealed to Daniel that Israel's refining judgments would come to an end and, at a specific time, the Messiah's everlasting righteousness would begin. Simply put: the computation of seventy weeks establishes the times governing Israel's destiny from its Babylonian captivity to its rebirth as a nation until the coming of Messiah.

The duration of the complete seventy-weeks is divided into three periods for a total of 490 years:

1. The seven weeks (49 years)
2. The sixty-two weeks (434 years)
3. The one week (7 years)

As stated previously, these periods specifically deal with the Jewish people and Jerusalem—both part of God's prophetic clock.

The first period of the "weeks of years" begins with seven sevens, or forty-nine years. This period, dated from the decree of King Artaxerxes (444 BCE), allowed for the Jewish people to return to Israel from Babylon with the expressed commission of rebuilding Jerusalem (Nehemiah 2:1–8). The prophetic return culminated in the celebration of the Feast of Tabernacles (395 BCE).

The following sixty-two sevens (434 years) ends with the triumphal entry of Christ into Jerusalem (32 CE).

✗⅄ The one remaining "week" or seven years has yet to be fulfilled and will constitute the seven years of the Tribulation. It will be a time when the Antichrist makes a peace treaty with Israel, which will be violated after three and a half years, resulting in the righteous Jews fleeing to the city of Petra in Jordan. There they will be protected by the hand of God for three and a half years until the Messiah comes to lead them home.

God's purposes for the seventy weeks are stated in Daniel 9:24:[23]

1. To cancel man's first disobedience thereby annihilating death and restoring eternal life.
2. To abolish all sins against God through the redemption of Christ.
3. To make reconciliation for iniquity through Christ's Great Exchange at the cross.
4. To bring in everlasting righteousness and divine holiness.
5. To perfect all the ancient prophecies relating to the Messiah.
6. To anoint the Most Holy—the coming Messiah.

God the Father was once again leading His chosen people to their divine destiny. However, could He also have been making provisions for us—the Gentiles—within the seventy weeks?

THE GENTILE EXPRESS

It is important to restate that the seventy weeks are not consecutive—there is a distinct gap of time between the sixty-ninth and seventieth weeks. Daniel 9:26 refers to two prophetic milestones; the death of Christ (33 CE) and the destruction of the temple (70 CE)—then God's prophetic clock stops.

Why did the clock stop ticking, and when will it begin again?

Remember, the seventy weeks relate solely to God's dealings

Artaxerxes's Decree
for Nehemiah
445 BCE

445 BCE—Artaxerxes's Decree to restore and rebuild Jerusalem—Nehemiah 2:1-8

The Presentation of
Messiah as Prince
32 CE

The Covenant
of Antichrist
with Israel

4 BCE—The birth of our Lord

32 CE—The Crucifixion of Christ

The Return
of Messiah to
Establish the
Kingdom of
God

Sixty-Nine Weeks or 483 Years (Dan. 9:25)		Gap of Time (Dan. 9:26)	The Seventieth Week (Dan. 9:27)
49 Years to Complete Rebuilding of Jerusalem	434 Years (62 Weeks)	Messiah Cut Off — Jerusalem and Sanctuary Destroyed (70 CE)	Desolation by Antichrist (Dan. 9:24)

with the Jewish people—the church of Jesus Christ is nowhere mentioned. The New Testament church occupies that gap from the day of Pentecost until the Rapture of the church as foretold by St. Paul in 1 Corinthians 15:52.

What marked the beginning of the Church age, when will it end, and when will the seventieth week begin?

The Church was birthed at Pentecost, and its age will last until Christ raptures His bride into the third heaven—it is the Dispensation of Grace.[24] Bible scholar Myer Pearlman quotes Louis C. Talbot's writing, which presents a perfect word picture of the time space we are referring to:

> Some years ago, I was on a train…and for a while we ran on schedule, to the very minute. Then my train was sidetracked for two and a half hours. Finally, I asked the conductor why we were sidetracked all that while. He answered: "We are waiting for the express to go through." After a while, I heard the shrill whistle and saw the fast train whizz by. Then my own train was put back on the mainline, and on we went, according to schedule.
>
> I thought of God's train for Israel. For sixty-nine sevens of years His people ran according to schedule. Then their train was switched to a sidetrack, as it were, in order that the heavenly express might go through. From Pentecost to the Rapture, the gospel train of this age is on the main line.
>
> One of these days, the journey will be over, and we shall be ushered into the presence of the Lord. Then the Jewish train will be put back on the main track.[25]

Think of the Jewish nation as being placed on the side-track by God Himself, awaiting the arrival and fulfillment of the "Gentile Express" (see Romans 11:25). Replacement Theology or Supersessionism teaches that the "church" has replaced Israel and the Jewish people. This false doctrine advocates that the first covenant (Old Testament) was supplanted by the new covenant (New Testament).

The scourge of anti-Semitism severely lashed Jewish backs

through Pharaoh's slavery, Haman's gallows, Spain's inquisitions, and Hitler's Final Solution. As generations of God's Chosen still struggle to recover from these evils, it is tragic that they must now confront the rising tide of global anti-Semitism and, even more heartbreaking, the continued false teachings within some Christian churches.

There is *one* Bible, beginning with Genesis 1:1 and ending with the "amen" of Revelation 22:21.

All Scripture is given by inspiration of God, and is profitable for doctrine, for reproof, for correction, for instruction in righteousness, that the man of God may be complete, thoroughly equipped for every good work (2 Timothy 3:16–17).

Remember this truth: The Old Testament is God's will *concealed,* and the New Testament is God's will *revealed*—every word is equally anointed, relevant, and eternally true.

The temporary sidetracking of the Jewish nation has made space for the fast-tracking of the Gentile nation. This pause on the path to the ultimate redemption we all long for is God's grace in action and in no way violates His promise to the Jewish people.

*If his sons forsake My law and do not walk in My judgments, if they violate My statutes and do not keep My commandments, then I will punish their transgression with the rod and their iniquity with stripes. But **I will not break** off My lovingkindness from him, nor deal falsely in My faithfulness. My covenant **I will not violate**, nor will I alter the utterance of My lips. OnceI have sworn by My holiness; **I will not lie** to David. His descendants shall endure forever and his throne as the sun before Me. **It shall be established** forever like the moon, and the witness in the sky is faithful (Psalm 89:30–37 NASB).*

We, who were grafted into the blessings of Abraham, owe a great debt of gratitude to the Jewish people. Saint Paul wrote about this debt in the book of Romans:

> For if the Gentiles have been partakers of their [Jewish people] spiritual things, their [Gentiles'] duty is also to minister to them [Jewish people] in material things (15:27).

The Old Testament is the very solid foundation of our Christian faith. As I stated earlier, Judaism does not need Christianity to explain its existence—Christianity, however, cannot explain its existence without Judaism.

THE PORTRAIT OF THE SON OF SATAN

Sometime in the immediate future, the bride of Jesus Christ will be taken from the earth in the *"twinkling of an eye"* (1 Corinthians 15:52). Believers refer to this prophetic event as the Rapture of the Church (1 Thessalonians 4:16–17). However, I can assure you that those who are left behind will most likely call this phenomenon the "Great Disappearance."

This sudden departure of the Church will instantly take hundreds of millions of believers from the earth and subsequently out of the workplace. An immediate global economic crisis will result as a consequence of this sudden vacuum. Believers will not only be out of the workforce; we will not be paying taxes, attending universities, or buying goods and services.

Why is this significant? Remember that a European economic crisis launched Adolf Hitler to absolute control over Germany and eventually most of Europe.

Scripture declares that there will be one final, supremely evil, and enormously powerful ruler who will dominate the human race.

This charismatic despot is called the Antichrist—a person who has not yet been revealed to mankind.

Daniel painted a vivid picture of the Antichrist in the last six chapters of his book. This ruthless dictator will come from the revived Roman Empire (Daniel 7:20). Satan will empower this willful ruler whose goal is to bring destruction to the world (Daniel 7:23). Referred to as the "little horn," this vile, self-exalting despot will do as he pleases and reign in utter deception Daniel 7:8; 8:25; 11:45).

Isaiah called him the *"king of Babylon"* and *"Lucifer"* (Isaiah 14:4, 12). Saint Paul recognized him as *"the lawless one"* (2 Thessalonians 2:8), and John the Revelator identified him as the rider on the white horse (Revelation 6:2) and the *"beast rising up out of the sea"* (13:1–2).

Larkin describes the Antichrist as a "superman" that will appear as a great humanitarian posing as a charismatic friend to the nations of the world—especially the Jewish people. When in reality, this incarnate of evil will be the embodiment of all kinds of wickedness and blasphemy. He will persuade the masses that he has come to usher in the "golden age," as termed by the prophets, and the world will eagerly receive him as their messiah.[26]

THE ILLUSTRIOUS

The first thirty-five verses of Daniel's eleventh chapter spans approximately two hundred years. Daniel provides a description of the Persian and Grecian Empires; the skirmishes of the kings of Syria and Egypt; and presents an exposition of the Syrian king, Antiochus Epiphanes—the great persecutor of the Jewish people.

Antiochus, *"The Illustrious,"* reigned over an established federation of nations and instituted a one-world religion. He banned Judaism, desecrated the Temple with pig sacrifices, burned scrolls of the Torah, and subsequently demanded that all the Jews worship him.

This was one of the foremost attempts by the Gentile world to rob the Jewish people of their faith in Jehovah God, but it would not be the last. While some Jews bowed their knee to this Evil Prince, thousands of the devout suffered and died for their belief in the One True God of Israel. Jesus referred to these past and future rulers in Matthew 24:15–16 as He spoke to His twelve disciples on the Mount of Olives.

> *"Therefore when you see the 'abomination of desolation,' [by Antiochus Epiphanes and the Antichrist] spoken of by Daniel the prophet, standing in the holy place"[Temple] ... "then let those who are in Judea [in the future] flee to the mountains [Petra in Jordan]."*

The final verses in this chapter fast-forward to the End of Days and deal with the rise of the Antichrist, the Tribulation, Israel's deliverance, and the resurrection of the dead.[27]

THE FINAL WARNING

Remember that the Jewish people are people of destiny. They are called to lead the nations back to God. This divine calling is reason enough for Satan to target them for destruction in the book of Revelation—but he will fail. God will soon demonstrate His awesome power against the nations that attack the "apple of God's eye."

Daniel's dream declares that after the time of trouble the wicked and the righteous will be raised from the dead. Those who are found *"written in the book"* will receive *"everlasting life"* and those who are not will spend eternity in *"shame and everlasting contempt"* (12:1–2). This is the first and only time the term *everlasting life* is used in the Old Testament—and it refers to the Jewish people—*not* the Church.

The book of Daniel ends with God's mandate to *"shut up the words, and seal the book until the time of the end"* (12:4). Why? Perhaps the book is *closed* so that believers can lead righteous lives characterized by obedience, commitment, and faith, as Daniel did. And *sealed* so we do not dwell on the unknown but rather trust in the God of our redemption for He promises to never fail nor forsake us.

No matter the interpretation, no one can afford to ignore the life-transforming truths God has chosen to reveal to His people—all of them significant and eternal. Myer Pearlman condenses the message of the book of Daniel with one profound statement:

Throughout the chances and changes of this fleeing life, throughout political change and international upheavals— we can walk with the Eternal who never changes. And though we may not live to witness the final triumph in our own days, we can take leave of this life with the assurance that one day, God shall remake this troubled world after His own heart.[28]

CHAPTER 12

EZEKIEL'S VISION—
THE FINAL GAME OF
THRONES BEGINS

---

*Now it came to pass in the thirtieth year, in the fourth month,
on the fifth day of the month, as I was among the captives by
the River Chebar, that the heavens were opened and I saw
visions of God. —Ezekiel 1:1*

As a nation, we have become more polarized than ever. Seemingly gone are the days of "agreeing to disagree." Instead, we have adopted a "cancel culture"; where once reasonable opinions were allowed, and in some instances encouraged, they are now singled out and condemned once they don't agree with the radical liberal agenda. Now, a difference of opinion, unmet with a groveling apology or bended knee, can lead to one's expulsion from civil society. People and businesses are boycotted and, in some cases, literally shut down. Just consider biased media outlets and those that are politicizing the

COVID-19 crises to benefit their political agendas. Know this—the longer the pandemic drags on closer to the 2020 elections, the better the campaign chances for the socialist democrats.

This is not to discount the devasting threat or effect of this pandemic—but simply to challenge our response to it. It appears COVID-19 was hijacked from the start through inflated and draconian projections of infection and deaths, creating havoc, fear, and hopelessness in the hearts of the American people. Pandemics are not new.

Some may remember the Hong Kong flu pandemic of September 1968. The estimated number of deaths was 1 million worldwide and approximately 100,000 in the US. Most deaths were among people sixty-five years and older. That virus (H3N2) continues to circulate worldwide as the seasonal influenza A.*

In response to the Hong Kong pandemic, nations ran business as usual without isolations, restrictions, or the shutdown of their economic engines. The world kept turning and life was relatively normal; why was the response to COVID-19 so radically different?

Could it be that the global community is now conditioned to accept all they hear as absolute truth—no matter the source?

As a whole, untainted journalism in America has died. Truth is ignored in the blinding lust for sensational headlines. No matter if innocent people are destroyed, if impeccable reputations are ruined, if promising careers are crushed or worldwide pandemonium breaks out, causing businesses to fail, family farms to shut down, and supply and demand to halt—print the story!

Mark R. Levin, author and news commentator, has written,

I often wonder what Thomas Jefferson, George Washington, James Madison, John Adams, George Mason, Benjamin

* https://www.cdc.gov/flu/pandemic-resources/1968-pandemic.html.

Franklin and the other Founders would think about today's America....Surely, they would object.

What will the future hold for our children and grand-children? What will be left of our constitutional system? Will the Bill of Rights have the force of law?...How many will remember or care to learn about our founding princi-ples, as concisely and brilliantly set forth in the Declaration of Independence?...What of civil society...? Will it have frayed beyond repair? Will we have been conquered from within, as Thomas Jefferson, Joseph Story, and Abraham Lincoln feared might be our fate? Will we have avoided the doom of Athens and Rome? If we are honest with ourselves we must agree that the outcome is unclear.[1]

A GEOPOLITICAL SNAPSHOT

For years there has been an aligning of Gentile nations in prepara-tion for the tribulation period. The Kingdom of the West will be led by the Antichrist and comprised of a ten-king federation—the final form of the revived Roman Empire. Russia and her allies will make up the Northern Kingdom; the Eastern Kingdom will include China and its confederacy; and the Southern Kingdom will con-sist of radical Islamic nations whose common denominator is their absolute hatred of Israel.

The actions of these four neo-axis powers are plainly referred to in Scripture and represent one of the major themes of prophecy. All of these major players are now rapidly moving into place. Most have nuclear weapons and are focused on Israel and the Middle East.

On the world front, we turn to North Korea, defended by China, courted by South Korea, and led by Kim Jong-un. In February 2019, President Trump and Kim Jong-Un met at a historic summit in Vietnam. The United States displayed a willingness to extend a hand to North Korea, if the regime would adopt the so-called "Libya model" to end its weapons of massive destruction programs.

Under this approach, the regime would engage in the full "dismantling [of] their nuclear infrastructure," including their chemical and biological warfare programs, ballistic missiles, launchers.* The North Koreans rejected the proposal outright and abruptly ended the meeting.

Despite his willingness to meet with America, Kim Jong-Un has not changed his agenda. He is just pulling a page out of the tactical propaganda journals used by Hitler, Yasser Arafat, and now President Hassan Rouhani of Iran—and that is: tell the world what they want to hear and continue planning for its destruction.

Concerning Iran: Make no mistake, regardless of President Trump's reinstatement of economically suffocating sanctions, Iran remains a terror state whose citizens are programmed to swarm the streets shouting, "Death to America" and "Death to Israel."

In fact, Iran's supreme leader, the Ayatollah Ali Khamenei, continues to threaten Israel and its allies. In a tweet rampage dated late May 2020, the Ayatollah once again compared Israel to a "cancerous tumor" and the deadly coronavirus. He called for the nation [Israel] to be "uprooted and destroyed." Furthermore, Khamenei warned against the west who he believes has "stemmed the Iranian regime's nuclear ambitions and stated mission to destroy Israel."†

Iran is entrenched in the teachings of the Ayatollah Ruhollah Khomeini, the founder of the Islamic Republic and "Khomeinism," who declared, "We shall export our revolution to the whole world.

---

* https://www.cnbc.com/2019/03/30/with-a-piece-of-paper-trump-called-on-kim-to
-hand-over-nuclear-weapons.html.
† https://apnews.com/a033042303545d9ef783a95222d51b83.

Until the cry 'there is no god but God [Allah]' resounds over the whole world, there will be struggle." As Prime Minister Benyamin Netanyahu so aptly concluded, "The Nazis believed in a master race. Militant Islamists believe in a master faith."

Iran's aspiration is to export their Islamic Revolution throughout the Middle East and the world, via their backing of proxy terrorist organizations. The war with radical Islam that intensified after 9/11 has only just begun. America and the West cannot let their guard down, because nations like Iran will not relent until the world is under its extreme Islamic rule.

In Europe, on one end of the spectrum, you have the British government, who recognized that Iran has engaged in the "systematic non-compliance" of the JCPOA.* Accordingly, under the leadership of conservative Prime Minister Boris Johnson, Britain has expressed a desire to see Europe's Iran nuclear agreement replaced with the "Trump Deal."†

On the other end, the French and the European Commission have consistently sought to resuscitate the flawed Iran nuclear agreement. French President Emmanuel Macron went so far as to unilaterally invite Iran's foreign minister to a 2019 meeting of the G7.‡ The other signatories to the Iran Deal, Germany, China and Russia, presently remain party to the agreement—but with varying levels of interest in maintaining it.

As I stated, since withdrawing from the Iran nuclear accord, the US has steadily increased sanctions against key Iranian industries, entities, and individuals associated with the regime's leadership nuclear weapons programs, and terrorist support. In addition, America has vigorously responded to Iran's use of proxy terrorist organizations which seek to destroy our nation and its allies.

---

* https://www.bbc.com/news/uk-politics-51104386.
† https://www.bbc.com/news/uk-politics-51104386.
‡ https://www.cnn.com/2019/08/25/politics/g7-iran-zarif-france-intl/index.html.

In January of 2020, the US conducted an airstrike killing Maj. Gen. Qasem Soleimani, the head of Iran's brutal Islamic Revolutionary Guard Corps Quds Force.* Soleimani oversaw Iran's effort to back terrorist groups like Hezbollah and other Shiite extremists. He was the architect of the strategy behind Iran's anti-Western war of terror. As President Trump noted after the successful attack, Soleimani is "directly and indirectly responsible for the deaths of millions of people."[†]

For Russia and China, addressing the dispute over Iran's nuclear weapons ambitions is not about curtailing that ambition, but rather manipulating the situation to their own countries' geopolitical benefit.

Fundamentally, Chinese foreign policy reflects their engagement in a "zero-sum" geopolitical game with the West, where one state can only make gains if others lose. In the Middle East, this plays out in China's efforts to engage the region economically. In fact, the Chinese have become "the biggest trade partner and external investor for many countries in the region."[‡] This economic power is translating into security influence over the Middle East. A prime example was the Chinese government being "instrumental in persuading Tehran to sign the Iran nuclear deal."[§]

The rivalry between the US and China functions in all arenas, including military expansion, space exploration, economic growth, technological advancements, strategic and security alliances, and within political and cultural models. International advisors have even gone as far as recommending that the US accept China's rise to power, allowing them a greater say in the shaping of global rules.[¶]

---

* https://www.bbc.com/news/world-middle-east-50979463.
† Ibid.
‡ https://www.ecfr.eu/publications/summary/china_great_game_middle_east.
§ Ibid.
¶ https://nationalinterest.org/feature/growing-us-china-conflict-why-and-now-what-61227.

In late May of 2020, General Jack Keane asserted that Chinese president Xi had "weaponized the spread of the coronavirus around the world to destroy Western democracies' economies and stifle its competition."[*]

China has vowed not to seek international domination, despite the fact that President Xi declared he intends to "fully dominate the Sino-Pacific region."[†] Few are aware of China's ambitious Belt and Road Initiative (BRI), which covers much of the world. This project currently links China with more than 138 countries across Asia, Africa, Europe, and Oceania through trade and infrastructure projects, such as shipping lanes, railroads, and airports.

To accomplish its goal of stronger international ties, China is lending vast amounts of money to participating nations, totaling 18 trillion dollars. This endeavor sounds progressively innovative, yet America views this initiative as a direct challenge to its own supremacy.[‡]

Supporters believe BRI is an opportunity for China to strengthen connections by investing in emerging markets. On the other hand, critics contend, "It is a way for China to use money to leverage political gains and increase its global power." By generating these loans, China is engaging in "debt-trap diplomacy," which is the strategy of "extracting political concessions out of a country that owes it money."[§]

The Belt and Road Initiative is made up of two parts: the "belt," which recreates the old Silk Road land route, and the "road," which is a route through various oceans. It is interesting to note that the

---

[*]   Charles Creitz, Fox News. "General Jack Keane: China 'weaponized' corona virus to 'destroy' Western democracies' economies."

[†]   Ibid.

[‡]   https://www.businessinsider.com/what-is-belt-and-road-china-infrastructure -project-2018-1.

[§]   Ibid.

Silk Road was an ancient land route across Europe and Asia that connected traders and travelers from regions like China, Persia, and the Roman Empire,* nations representing some of the major players in the Final Game of Thrones.

America and China, the world's two largest economies and military powers, are headed for a major conflict—primarily because of the US-China economic trade wars, the coronavirus catastrophe, and the clash concerning Hong Kong's endangered capitalistic autonomy. Such a confrontation would cripple the already fragile global order, similar to what took place after the First World War— "the war to end all wars"—when international order disappeared altogether.[†]

Russia, under the cunning leadership of former KGB officer Vladimir Putin, is methodically rebuilding the international power and prestige once associated with the former USSR. Central to Putin's efforts is the need to remain in total control of the region. To that end, Putin advanced constitutional changes in Russia enabling him to continue to seek re-election, guaranteeing that he could retain power through 2036.[‡] Putin wants Russia to be a superpower again, and to America and Israel's detriment, a key component of his efforts revolves around the Middle East.

But why is Russia interested in Israel?

Putin is interested in Israel's warm water ports and natural gas resources. Russia signed a forty-nine-year agreement with Syria in January 2017. Under the terms of the agreement, Russia is able to, at no cost, expand their presence and have sovereign control of their existing naval facility at the Syrian port of Tartus.

---

*   Ibid.

†   https://asiasociety.org/policy-institute/avoidable-war-alternative-future-us-china-relations.

‡   https://www.rferl.org/a/russia-putin-signs-off-constitutional-changes-extend-power/30487735.html.

The treaty states that Russia can keep eleven warships, including nuclear vessels, at Tartus with full privileges and "full immunity from civil and administrative jurisdiction of Syria."[2] By the end of 2017, Russia announced it was "forming a permanent grouping" at the Tartus naval facility as well as at its Hmeymim air base.[3] Recently, Russia announced it would invest 500 million dollars in their Syrian-based posts.*

Security analyst Daniel Nisman states, "The Russians have had varying levels of activity and personnel in Syria since the cold war."[4] Meanwhile, Russia and Syria have been cooperating militarily, as well as sharing intelligence, for decades. You can be sure that the Russians do not intend to leave the region any time soon—quite the contrary. In due time, Russia will lead Iran and the Islamic nations in an invasion of Israel.

Russia was a key player throughout the Syrian civil war, going so far as to protect Syria's brutal regime from UN Security Council action. They also engaged with militarily forces fighting in opposition to Syrian dictator Bashar al-Assad.†

Putin's involvement in the region is not limited to simply protecting his interests in Syria. Know that the web of alliances in the Middle East is tangled, where perceived ideological foes often cooperate. As an example, Russia has a newly formed dictatorship, whereas Iran is a tyrannical theocracy. But because of Moscow's focus on Syria, an ally of Iran and thus the Iranian proxy-terrorist army Hezbollah, Russia has what it views as a legitimate relationship with Hezbollah, the most potent terrorist group in the Middle East.

---

* https://www.businessinsider.com/base-in-syria-helps-russia-expand-presence-in -mediterranean-2019-9.

† https://www.theguardian.com/world/2016/sep/25/russia-accused-war-crimes-syria-un -security-council-aleppo.

But don't think that Russia is the only global power that has a strong presence in the Middle East. China will start running the port of Haifa in 2021. The US, which is opposed to the move, currently docks its 6th Fleet at the same port. Israel is very much interested in learning from the Chinese the advanced technology of its deep seaport in Shanghai which is almost completely automated. However, there is a genuine worry that the "Chinese would weave in some back-door or old-fashioned spying into the Haifa Port mix."*

Has anyone noticed that this commotion is taking place in Israel's backyard the epicenter of the forthcoming Gog-Magog wars?

In February 2018, a weaponized, unmanned drone originating from a base in Homs, Syria, was shot down by the IDF before it could reach its intended target in Israel. In May of that year, I stood at the Israeli-Syrian border the day after the Quds Force launched twenty missiles toward Judea and Samaria, just thirty short miles from Damascus.

An IDF representative traveling with us stated that four rockets were intercepted and destroyed by the Israeli Iron Dome aerial defense system, while sixteen others fell short of their targets. In response to the assault, the IDF said Israeli fighter jets struck seventy military targets belonging to Iran.

The action, called "Operation House of Cards," nearly wiped out Iran's entire infrastructure in Syria. This, I might add, occurred with Putin's full knowledge and support.[5] Bear in mind, the key for Russia is to play multiple sides against each other. Moscow's projection of power thrives in the chaos of conflict. Israel may try to "draw the red lines" restricting the impact of Iran and Hezbollah in Syria—but it is Putin who is in control.[6]

---

* https://www.jpost.com/israel-news/china-wins-on-haifa-port-but-fights-with-us-for
-the-future-analysis-610510 https://en.globes.co.il/en/article-pompeo-presses
-israel-to-distance-from-china-1001328517.

A Hezbollah commander revealed in late 2016 that the relationship between Hezbollah fighters and Russian ground troops is "not a new development. He said Hezbollah and the 'cream of the Russian army,' specifically special forces and anti-tank missile (ATM) teams, had been fighting together in Aleppo for their mutual benefit. [The commander continued,] 'If you play with a good football team, you will learn something from them.'"[7]

In fact, Russia's special forces soldiers, the infamous Spetsnaz, have been seen alongside Hezbollah troops.[*] And when a Russian SU-24 attack aircraft was shot down by Turkey, there were reports that Hezbollah terrorists acted as the search-and-rescue team hunting for the plane's pilots.[†]

Hezbollah's secretary general, Sheikh Hassan Nasrallah, declared, "What has been prepared for Israel differs from the battle we are fighting [in Syria] against the armed groups." What does he mean?

Hezbollah is not going to just fight Israel in large formations, through conventional airstrikes, or with Russian tanks. It will also penetrate Israel's borders with small-unit configurations and specially trained cadres to conduct numerous and simultaneous ambushes and raids.[8] This is why Israel so fiercely defends and protects all of its borders.

Furthermore, as detailed earlier, Hezbollah has 150,000 thousand Iranian rockets ready to launch against Israel at a moment's notice. An online article found in Dahiya, a Lebanese pro-Hezbollah website, reported that the Syrian president Bashar al-Assad has ordered his army to build and camouflage missile silos to allow Hezbollah to increase its missile arsenal to five hundred thousand units in Syria alone.[9]

---

[*] https://freebeacon.com/national-security/u-s-spots-russian-commandos-in-syria/.
[†] Ibid.

WHY SO MANY ROCKETS?

The well-known "Iron Dome," a mobile all-weather air defense system, currently protects Israel. The moment a rocket is launched toward Israel, the Iron Dome locks in on the incoming missile, computes its route, and immediately establishes whether it will hit a populated area.

If so, a defensive missile is instantly fired, intercepting the incoming warhead, thereby blowing it up. According to an article in *Aviation Week*, Hezbollah launched 4,594 rockets in a fifty-day period from the Gaza Strip, and the Iron Dome destroyed all but seventy missiles, yielding a 90 percent success rate.[10]

However, the Iron Dome has an Achilles' heel. When we are talking about saving human lives, 90 percent is not good enough. The Dome can only process a limited number of incoming projectiles per minute, which is why Hezbollah has stockpiled over 150,000 rockets in Lebanon.

When the next war starts, Hezbollah will flood Israel's airspace with rockets and attempt to compromise the capability of the Iron Dome system. Their goal is to overwhelm the Dome at the same time they infiltrate Israel's borders with multiple incursions. If this happens, the results could be catastrophic.

This destructive strategy has already begun. At the end of May 2018, over 114 mortars and rockets were fired into Israel from Gaza in a twenty-four-hour period. This missile attack was the largest assault on Israeli civilians since the 2014 Gaza war, forcing over one million Israelis into bomb shelters. After hearing the piercing Red Alert sirens, warning of an incoming projectile, families had less than thirty seconds to react.

The Iranian-backed terrorist groups Hamas and Palestinian Islamic Jihad issued a joint statement claiming "credit" for the attack on Israel. During the eight weeks of the Hamas-led riots along the Gaza-Israel border that I mentioned in a previous chapter, Hamas openly bragged that they would "tear down their fence just like we will tear out their [the Israeli's] hearts from their chests."[11]

RE-ENTER RUSSIA

In February of 2019, Vladimir Putin received Prime Minister Benjamin Netanyahu at the Kremlin to discuss the volatile situation in Syria and Iran's threating role in the Middle East. Putin confirmed that "getting the Iranians and all foreign fighters out of Syria is also [as with Israel] one of Russia's stated goals."[*] However, later that year, as a result of Russia's continued calculating control in the area, a trilateral meeting between the US, Israel, and Russia was called.

During the June meeting, held in Jerusalem, Russian Security Council Secretary Nikolai Patrushev urged Israel and the United States to show "restraint" toward the Islamic Republic,[†] stating, "The attempts to present Iran as the main threat to the region and equate it to international terrorist groups are *not acceptable.*"[‡]

This is typical KGB doublespeak. In one interchange Russia claims it will minimize Iran's invasive role in the Middle East, and in the next, they demand that the US and Israel show restraint toward Tehran.

Zvi Bar'el, PhD, a highly credentialed Middle East affairs analyst, succinctly summarizes Russian's impact this way: "Jordan, Saudi Arabia, Egypt, Turkey and Israel all understand that the only great power capable of working a miracle in Syria is Russia. Thus each of them is now seeking guarantees from Moscow that its interests will

---

* https://www.haaretz.com/israel-news/russia-wants-to-get-iran-out-of-syria-netanyahu-says-after-putin-meet-1.6978647.
† https://www.ynetnews.com/articles/0,7340,L-5536046,00.html.
‡ Ibid.

be protected."[12] Henry Wooster, Deputy Assistant Secretary of State for the Near East, explains it this way: "The Kremlin uses…military power, proxies and disinformation…to expand its influence across the [Mediterranean]."*

It is obvious a massive war will suddenly arise in the Middle East, and Israel will be the target. There will be no time to win the global media war, which historically sides against Israel. There will be no time to fight the fake news that distorts the truth. For their survival, Israel must either use the "first strike option," as Moshe Dayan did at the start of the Six-Day War, or wait to respond, which will be costly in Jewish blood.

Israeli intelligence officials have reported that weapons are hidden in mosques, schoolyards, and civilian houses. It is a known fact that Hamas's leadership war room is in a bunker beneath Gaza's largest hospital.[13] As in previous wars, Hezbollah and Hamas will hide behind terrified women and children as they launch rockets from their homes into Israel.

If Israel *does not* respond swiftly and fiercely, they will suffer massive loss of life. Yet if they *do* respond aggressively, the global "blame Israel first" liberal media will condemn the Israelis for bombing houses from which the rockets are being launched toward Israel.

The geopolitical players are in place, and this coming war will be the birth pangs of the Gog and Magog Wars, as foretold by God to the prophet Ezekiel.

EZEKIEL'S CALL

Ezekiel, whose name means "may God strengthen" in Hebrew, was a prophet of priestly descent and a contemporary of Jeremiah and

---

* https://www.washingtonpost.com/opinions/global-opinions/america-on-the-wane
  -russias-scavenger-diplomacy-is-succeeding-in-the-middle-east/2020/05/07/a4bbec6c
  -9097-11ea-9e23-6914ee410a5f_story.html.

Daniel. He was sent into Babylonian exile, along with ten thousand other captives, in 597 BCE—eleven years before the destruction of Jerusalem (Ezekiel 1:3; 2 Kings 24:14–16; Jeremiah 29:1).

Ezekiel was confronted by a divine vision of God's glory, which he vividly described as a great cloud coming out of the north. He saw a wheeled platform engulfed in a raging fire, carried by four living creatures, on which was enthroned the Lord's fiery majesty (1:1–28).

Thus began Ezekiel's commission as a watchman, who would warn Israel of the devastating consequences of their wicked ways (3:17). Jewish teachings state that Moses revealed what *could have been* and Ezekiel revealed *what was* (Exodus 6:2–8). Israel *could have been* the parchment upon which God's Word was written (Proverbs 3:1–4); *could have been* a living, breathing Torah scroll; *could have been* an eternal example that true wisdom and understanding were the product of God's Word fulfilled (Proverb 7:4).

Israel *could have been*, had they only heeded God's voice (Deuteronomy 28:1–14). Instead, they took their own path and lived in exile until the Almighty's providential ingathering. Ezekiel witnessed the presence of the Lord depart from the Holy City and the Holy Temple (1 Kings 8:10; Ezekiel 10:18). Without God's Shekinah, Jerusalem lost its splendor, and the temple, although still beautiful, was empty of His glory.[14]

The Jewish people believed that the temple of God was insurance for their survival and their "sacrifices an antidote to the spiritual poison afflicting them." Not so. The temple and its service reflected the people—if the nation was empty of a moral code, then the temple was a mere shell; if their deeds were evil, then their sacrifices were an abomination to God.[15]

The God of Abraham, Isaac, and Jacob had lifted His protection, and the Jewish people were now defenseless against Nebuchadnezzar's invasion and subsequent deportation to Babylon (2 Kings

24). The Lord commissioned Ezekiel to be the prophet to the exiles. His message was that one day, God Almighty would gather the Jewish people from the four corners of the earth and restore them to the land of Israel (Ezekiel 28:25). Once reunited with their covenant promise, they would never be removed again (Joel 3:16–21).

Ezekiel mourned the decline and destruction of Jerusalem. His vision encompassed the heavens, and his words revealed the rebirth of the Jewish nation. And it was Ezekiel whom Jehovah God chose to give His revelation of the final battles that would usher in earth's last empire.

THE FIVE W'S OF
THE GOG AND MAGOG WARS

There are five questions I ask my executive assistant to answer regarding every incoming phone call or speaking invitation: who, what, when, where, and why? This way, the groundwork has been established for a clear and complete understanding of the pending conversation or engagement.

Remember this truth: A clear understanding prevents a complete misunderstanding. With this concept in mind, let us ask the same five questions pertaining to the Gog and Magog Wars.

Jewish and Christian students of the last days state that there is a king, whose name is Gog, who will rule over the nations of Magog (Ezekiel 38).

The lands of Magog, established by the second son of Japheth and grandson to Noah, will include the former Soviet Empire. These nations, who share the Islamic faith, currently number nearly 75 million people. Gog, their supreme leader, will cause them to rise up against Israel.

Ezekiel speaks of future events concerning Gog:

1. Gog's plan to bring his mighty military armies against Israel (Ezekiel 38:10).
2. Jehovah's wrath overcomes Gog and Magog inside His Covenant Land (Ezekiel 38:18–22; Joel 2:20; Zechariah 14).
3. Israel's seven-month cleansing of the devastating aftermath (Ezekiel 39:12).

Some Jewish theologians believe that Gog and Magog are a series of wars that includes the war in the "middle of the week," or three and a half years after the Antichrist negotiates a peace treaty with Israel (Daniel 9:27). The battle of Armageddon, the mother of all wars, happens seven years after the signing of the peace treaty. Once again, the hand of God will come against the invading armies who attack Israel (Psalm 121:4).

1. Who Is Involved in This War?

Russia

*"Son of man, set your face against Gog, of the land of Magog, the prince of **Rosh**, Meshech, and Tubal, and prophesy against him* (Ezekiel 38:2).

Bible scholars widely believe that Rosh is Russia and recognize Meshach and Tubal (Noah's grandsons) as the Russian cities of Moscow and Tobolsk.[16]

Magog, Tubal, and Meshach can be traced back to Genesis 10:1–2 as the sons of Japheth:

*Now this is the genealogy of the sons of Noah: Shem, Ham, and Japheth. And sons were born to them after the flood. The sons of Japheth were Gomer, **Magog**, Madai, Javan, **Tubal**, **Meshech**, and Tiras.*

Certain anthropologists believe that Noah and Japheth migrated "to the north beyond the Caspian and Black Seas after the great flood, instead of going south, as did Shem (the Shemites) and Ham (the Hamites). Noah and Japheth then settled in the area of Rosh, which is modern-day Russia."[17]

The prophet Ezekiel was commanded by God Almighty to deliver a message against a man (Gog) and his kingdom (Magog).

> *Now the word of the Lord came to me, saying, "Son of man, set your face against Gog, of the land of Magog, the prince of Rosh, Meshech, and Tubal, and prophesy against him, and say, 'Thus says the Lord God: "Behold, I am against you, O Gog, the prince of Rosh, Meshech, and Tubal. I will turn you around, put hooks into your jaws, and lead you out, with all your army, horses, and horsemen…"'"* (Ezekiel 38:1–4a).

Persia

The prophet Ezekiel stated that the following nations will join the King of the North, in a massive military invasion of Israel:

> *Persia, Ethiopia, and Libya are with them, all of them with shield and helmet* (Ezekiel 38:5).

Persia is modern-day Iran and has been on the world stage since the sixth century BCE. The Persians are brilliant, cunning, and artful masters of long-term planning. The Persian Empire was described in Daniel's vision (7:5) as one of the four global empires, which ruled over Israel and will come against them in the Gog and Magog Wars.

Persia's name changed in 1935 at the prompting of Nazi associates of the Persian ambassador to Germany. Under the leadership of Mohammad Reza Shah, a name that better identified Persia and Germany's close alliance was created. That name was Iran, which mirrored the word *Aryan*.[18]

In 1979, the radical Muslim Shiite Ayatollah Khomeini took power, and Iran once again changed its name, this time to the Islamic Republic of Iran.[19] Iran's republic is an extremist, death-worshipping, religious theocracy that funds Middle East terror organizations and threatens to use nuclear force against America and Israel at every opportunity.

Ethiopia and Libya

J. Dwight Pentecost taught that Ethiopia (modern-day Sudan) and Libya represent two separate Arab states. Why? When Moses fled Egypt after killing an Egyptian slave master (Exodus 2:15), he did not go south into African Ethiopia but into the Ethiopia of the Arabian Peninsula (Midian). Therefore, when Ezekiel spoke of Ethiopia and Libya (a region west of the Nile), he was speaking of the Arab states around Israel.[20] Ethiopia was founded by Cush, Ham's eldest son, and Libya was established by Put, Ham's third son.

Germany and Turkey

In Ezekiel 38:6, we read about

> *Gomer and all its troops; the house of Togarmah from the far north and all its troops.*

Gomer was the first son of Japheth and grandson to Noah (Genesis 10:2). Josephus noted that the Gomerites were identified with the Galatians, who inhabited what today is central Turkey.[21] His extensive listing of the nations included the sons of Gomer. Gomer's eldest son, Ashkenaz, founded the Ashkenazians (Germany), who were identified by the Greeks as Rheginians.[22]

David Jeremiah, in his book *The Book of Signs*, cited John Phillips regarding Germany past, present, and future:

> A united and greater Germany (Gomer and all its bands) had come within a hair of winning World War II…It had taken all the combined might of the British Empire, the Soviet Union and the United States to fight Germany to a standstill. What if a united and anti-Semitic Germany were to seek its future fortunes while allied to an anti-Semitic Russia?[*]

The "house of Togarmah" was established by Gomer's third son, Noah's great-grandson through Japheth. This is modern-day Turkey and is located north of Israel.

The above nations will join Russia in a massive land invasion of Israel called the Gog and Magog Wars.

2. What Will Ignite the Gog and Magog Wars?

Following the Rapture of the church, the world will be in a state of chaos, both economically and socially. The Antichrist will rise to power and organize the collapsed European Union into the ten-nation revived Roman Empire. Israel will make a seven-year peace treaty with the Antichrist with assurance that the treaty will give it complete protection from Russia and Iran. However, Israel will be sadly disappointed.

In three and a half years, this treaty will be broken by the Antichrist. At this time, the Jewish people will equate the Beast to Amalek, the first recorded anti-Semite (Exodus 17:8). Israel will

---

[*] John Phillips, *Exploring the Future: A Comprehensive Guide to Bible Prophecy.* (Nashville, Tennessee: Thomas Nelson, 1983), 327.

be attacked in a land invasion led by Russia and followed by Iran, Libya, Turkey, and Arab Islamic nations. It will be a massive incursion, for Ezekiel prophesied concerning Russia and its proxies in 38:6, saying, *"Many people are with you* [Gog]. *"*

In recent years, Iran, Hezbollah, Syria, and Hamas have repeatedly attacked Israel directly or through proxies. Europe's leadership is in disarray—the United Kingdom has officially left the European Union, and Germany is swamped with radical Islamic immigrants who are bringing utter chaos to the already fractured region. Angela Merkel, chancellor of Germany, said, "The world is coming apart at the seams."[23]

France is also unstable. Vicious Islamic terrorists are spilling French blood, using speeding trucks to kill and maim men, women, and children as they celebrate Bastille Day,[24] stabbing and killing two young innocent women at the Marseille-Saint-Charles train station,[25] and gunning down concertgoers and café patrons, taking 130 lives and injuring 352 more.[26]

The Jews of France are fleeing to the nations of the world due to growing anti-Semitism in Europe, spurred by assaults such as the deadly Jewish market attack in Paris.[27] Anti-Semitic hate crime in France spiked by 74 percent in 2018 and rose another 27 percent in 2019.[*]

Meanwhile, anti-Semitism in Germany has grown so common that the country's commissioner, Felix Klein, issued a shocking caution against wearing a *kippah* (Jewish head covering) in public.[†] Moreover, the United Kingdom's Labour Party, led by anti-Semite Jeremy Corbyn, is currently under investigation by the UK Equality

---

[*] Simone Rodan-Benzaquen, "Europe's Lessons for the Struggle Against Anti-Semitism" (March 2, 2020), *The Atlantic*, https://www.theatlantic.com/ideas/archive/2020/03/what-europe-can-teach-america-about-fighting-anti-semitism/607162/, accessed April 3, 2020.

[†] Ibid.

and Human Rights Commission (as of December 2019) for "insti-
tutional anti-Semitism"* due to allegations of anti-Semitism against
the party.†

Diana and I had the privilege of visiting Omaha Beach in
Normandy, France. This site and others like it were bloody battle-
fields during World War II. I walked the beaches where American
soldiers were cut in half by machine gun fire. Others were blown
to bits by the German guns positioned in the cliffs overlooking the
sandy killing fields. History records that the waters of the sea were
turned red with the blood of Allied soldiers fighting for the world's
freedom. We must never forget their supreme sacrifice.

Tears ran down our faces as we walked through the pristine military cemeteries, cradling the graves of tens of thousands of America's
precious sons who paid the ultimate sacrifice on the altar of freedom. I looked at row after row of the final resting places of the
fallen. I noticed the ages on their grave markers; most were eighteen
to twenty years of age, their hopes and dreams forever abandoned
that ours might be fulfilled.

I engaged our French tour guide in personal and detailed conversation. When he understood my knowledge of the geopolitical crisis in Europe, he made the following statement concerning France:
"History is about to repeat itself. When Hitler came to power, the
door of opportunity to leave France was opened only briefly. I'm
leaving France soon before the flag of radical Islam flies over Paris."

3. When Will the Gog-Magog War Happen?

*After many days you will be visited. In the latter years you [Gog]
will come into the land of those brought back from the sword and*

---

* Ibid.
† "Investigation into the Labour Party" (December 11, 2019), Equality and Human Rights
Commission, https://www.equalityhumanrights.com/en/inquiries-and-investigations
/investigation-labour-party, accessed April 3, 2020.

gathered from many people on the mountains of Israel, which had long been desolate; they [the Jewish people] were brought out of the nations, and now all of them dwell safely.... Then you [Russia] will come from your place out of the far north, you and many people with you, all of them riding on horses, a great company and a mighty army. You will come up against My people Israel like a cloud, to cover the land. It will be in the latter days that I will bring you against My land, so that the nations may know Me [the Lord God of Israel], when I am hallowed in you, O Gog, before their eyes (Ezekiel 38:8, 15–16).

These verses provide the answer to the question, especially verse 15: *"Then you [Russia] will come from your place out of the far north."* On September 15, 2015, Russia moved its military forces *"out of the far north"* into the Middle East, specifically Syria.

The *New York Times* headline read, "Russian Moves in Syria Widen Role in Middle East." From backing terrorists, when it is beneficial for them, to direct military engagement with Turkey, Russia's presence in the Middle East has dramatically expanded. In addition, the Russians have sought to strengthen their influence into northern Africa as well.

Most disconcerting has been Russia's deepening relationship with Egypt.* With close ties to Syria in Israel's north and increasing ties with Egypt to Israel's south, it's quite clear Russia's diplomatic and military moves in the Middle East have positioned them in a place of vital strategic relevance when it pertains to influencing the safety and security of Israel.

Iran and Syria have had a crucial alliance ever since the start of the Iran-Iraq War in 1980. I believe Russia and Iran are currently

---

* https://www.mei.edu/publications/sochi-summit-highlights-growing-russia-egypt-ties.

plotting the genesis of the Gog and Magog Wars that Ezekiel clearly stated shall take place *"in the latter years"* (38:8).

In the Latter Years

The Gog-Magog wars will take place "in the latter years" after Israel is reborn as a nation (Ezekiel 38:8).

> *"For I will take you from among the nations, gather you out of all countries, and bring you into your own land"* (Ezekiel 36:24).

The Balfour Declaration of November 2, 1917, which acknowledged Britain's support for a Jewish homeland, opened the door for Ezekiel's prophecy to become reality:

"In the latter years" is when God supernaturally breathed upon the valley of dry bones, making Israel's physical rebirth possible.

> *Thus says the Lord GOD to these bones: "Surely I will cause breath to come into you, and you shall live"* (Ezekiel 37:5).

The word *breath* in Hebrew is *ruach*, meaning "spirit." When God created Adam, he was not complete until God breathed His Spirit into him. It was only then that Adam became a living soul. There is no doubt that Ezekiel's prophecy referred to God breathing life back into His chosen nation: *"These bones are the whole house of Israel"* (v. 11).

"In the latter years..." the miracle of miracles happened on May 14, 1948, when Prime Minister David Ben-Gurion bounded up the steps of the Tel Aviv Museum of Art to read the Declaration of Independence for the State of Israel over the radio as the world listened in absolute amazement. And it was President Harry Truman

who recognized the Jewish state eleven minutes after Ben-Gurion announced Israel's rebirth.

I was eight years of age, sitting at our kitchen table in Channelview, Texas, listening to the radio with my father as this historic announcement was made. My father, a pastor and Bible scholar, seldom wept, but as we listened to the broadcast, tears ran down his face. I knew this event was earthshaking, although I did not know why.

I remember his words to this day: "Son, this is the most important fulfillment of prophecy in the twentieth century. It proves the words of the prophets and the promises of the Bible are absolutely true. The State of Israel has been reborn. Messiah is coming!"

The Jewish people have been liberated from their Gentile graves. They have returned home. They are prospering and thriving in every dimension of life.

Israel lives! Shout it from the housetops! Israel lives! Israel lives!

The Jubilee Prophecies

Israel's restoration to the Promised Land was prophesied by Rabbi Judah ben Samuel, who lived in Regensburg, Germany, during the twelfth and thirteenth centuries (1140–1217). Rabbi ben Samuel stated that God measures time in modules of fifty years, called "Jubilees." The Bible refers to the Jubilee in Leviticus 25:10–11:

*And you shall consecrate the fiftieth year, and proclaim liberty throughout all the land to all its inhabitants. It shall be a **Jubilee** for you; and each of you shall return to his possession, and each of you shall return to his family. The fiftieth year shall be a Jubilee to you; in it you shall neither sow nor reap what grows of its own accord, nor gather the grapes of your untended vine.*

A Jubilee was a time when God Almighty poured out His blessings on Israel and the Jewish people. Specifically, a Jubilee year in ancient Israel meant that all debts were forgiven, indentured servants were liberated, all lands were given back to the original owner, and a time when the land was allowed to rest.

Rabbi ben Samuel's prophecy was as follows:

> When the Ottomans [Turks]…conquer Jerusalem they will rule over Jerusalem for eight jubilees. Afterwards Jerusalem will become no-man's land for one jubilee, and then in the ninth jubilee it will once again come back into the possession of the Jewish nation—which would signify the beginning of the Messianic end time.[28]

Let's do the math. The first Jubilee Prophecy predicted that the Turks would rule over Jerusalem for eight Jubilees or four hundred years. The Turks gained control of Jerusalem in 1517 and held power for exactly four hundred years until British forces led by General Allenby took control of Jerusalem on Hanukkah, December 17, 1917. Please note: the Turks took possession of Jerusalem three hundred years after Rabbi ben Samuel's death, making the Rabbi's prophecy astonishingly accurate.

Rabbi ben Samuel continues: "Afterwards Jerusalem will become no-man's land for one jubilee."

Under the British Mandate of 1917, Jerusalem was an international city and declared a "no-man's-land." Fifty years later, or one Jubilee, on June 17, 1967, the Israeli army reclaimed the city of Jerusalem during the Six-Day War. Jerusalem was under Jewish control for the first time since the city was destroyed in 70 CE by General Titus and the Roman Legion. Another part of ben Samuel's prophecy was fulfilled.

The final part of his prophecy stated that one Jubilee following Jerusalem's reunification would begin the year of the "Messianic end time."

When you add fifty years to 1967, you have the year 2017. This was the year that Jerusalem celebrated a Jubilee year—fifty years since it was reunited with the State of Israel. It was also a time when God Almighty poured out His blessings on Israel and the Jewish people with a momentous announcement.

On December 6, 2017, President Donald J. Trump recognized Jerusalem as the eternal and undivided capital of the State of Israel by deciding to move the US embassy from Tel Aviv to the Holy City. On May 14, 2018, seventy years to the day that Israel was reborn as a nation, Diana and I were privileged to be in Jerusalem to witness biblical history in the making. I was honored to be asked by the US ambassador to Israel, David Friedman, to give the closing benediction:

> Our most gracious heavenly Father, God of Abraham, Isaac, and Jacob, the God who calls the stars by name and measures space with the span of His hand—King of the universe.
>
> We gather here today to thank You for the joy of living to see this glorious and historic day. We thank You for the State of Israel, the lone torch of freedom in the Middle East, who lives and prospers because of Your everlasting love for the Jewish people.
>
> It was You, O Lord, who gathered the exiles from the nations and brought them home again. It was You who made statehood possible.
>
> It was You that gave a miraculous victory in 1967 when Jerusalem reopened to worshippers of all faiths.

✓ Jerusalem is the city of God. Jerusalem is the heartbeat of Israel.

✓ Jerusalem is where Abraham placed his son on the altar on the Temple Mount and became the father of many nations.

✓ Jerusalem is where Jeremiah and Isaiah penned the principles of righteousness that became the moral foundations of Western civilization.

✓ Jerusalem is where Messiah will come and establish a kingdom that will never end.

We thank You, O Lord, for President Donald Trump's courage in acknowledging to the world a truth established three thousand years ago, that Jerusalem is and always shall be the eternal capital of the Jewish people.

And because of that courage of our president, we gather here today to consecrate the ground upon which the United States embassy will stand, reminding the dictators of the world that America and Israel are forever united.

We thank You for our ambassador, David Friedman, and pray Your anointing upon him as he opens the doors to the US embassy to receive the nations of the world.

✓ Let the word go forth from Jerusalem today...Israel lives! Shout it from the housetops that Israel lives!

✓ Let every Islamic terrorist hear this message—Israel lives!

✓ Let it be heard in the halls of the United Nations—Israel lives!

✓ Let it echo down the marble halls of the presidential palace in Iran—Israel lives!

✓ Let it be known to all men that Israel lives because, "He that keepeth Israel [shall] neither slumber nor sleep" [Psalm 121:4 KJV].

As King David prayed three thousand years ago, we pray for the peace of Jerusalem and for all its inhabitants.

Let the name of the Lord be glorified today for the Defender of Israel today, tomorrow, and forever is here!

Can we all shout Hallelujah? Amen!

> Prayer of Dedication for the US embassy
> Jerusalem, Israel May 14, 2018

Sadly, *"in the latter years"* is also the time when scientists produced nuclear weapons that have the power to turn the earth into a spinning graveyard in space. Einstein said of this time: "I know not with what weapons World War III will be fought, but World War IV will be fought with sticks and stones."

The Bible very clearly indicates there will be a nuclear war in the future for control over the city of Jerusalem, which was precisely described by the prophet in Zechariah 14:12:

> *And this shall be the plague with which the LORD will strike all the people who fought against Jerusalem: their flesh shall dissolve while they stand on their feet, their eyes shall dissolve in their sockets, and their tongues shall dissolve in their mouths.*

Zechariah's word picture depicts what happens to the human body when exposed to the heat of a nuclear blast. Temperatures of such an explosion can reach those of the interior of the sun, or about one hundred million degrees Celsius.[29] With this devastating amount of blazing heat, it requires little imagination to visualize the prophet's words. The cities of Hiroshima and Nagasaki, Japan, experienced the horrific destruction of the first atomic bomb, but its aftermath pales in comparison to the incalculable lethal power of the coming nuclear bomb.

4. Where Will the Gog and Magog Wars Take Place?

Israel is surrounded by her enemies on three fronts—north, east, and south—and the Mediterranean Sea on the west. Therefore, the Gog and Magog Wars will arise on every side of Israel. There is no escape by land or sea.

> *After many days you will be called to arms. In future years you will invade a land that has recovered from war, whose people were gathered from many nations to the mountains of Israel, which had long been desolate. They had been brought out from the nations, and now all of them live in safety* (Ezekiel 38:8).

> *The mountains shall be thrown down, the steep places shall fall, and every wall shall fall to the ground. "I will call for a sword against Gog throughout all My mountains," says the Lord GOD* (Ezekiel 38:20–21).

The reference to the "mountains" of Israel refer to those that surround the city of Jerusalem. Before Jerusalem was reunited with the State of Israel it was controlled by Jordan. It was not until after the Six-Day War that the State of Israel included mountains by means of Jerusalem.*

5. Why Is Russia Coveting Israel?

Theologians have debated this question for many years. Some say

---

* Mark Hitchcock, *The End: A Complete Overview of Bible Prophecy and the End of Days* (Carol Stream, Il.: Tyndale House, 2012), 310.

Russia is trying to gain more territory. But why? Look how vast Russia is geographically. Who needs a postage stamp–sized nation like Israel when you have such a mammoth landmass?

As I stated earlier, the Russians are clearly interested in Israel's natural gas resources. The *Wall Street Journal* stated that the recent offshore gas and oil discoveries in Israel are sufficient to meet Israel's gas needs for one hundred years.[30] Moscow is concerned that this massive discovery will threaten their manipulative supply of natural gas to Europe, which will negatively affect Russia's entire economy. This, however, is not the only reason for invasion: Russia also covets Israel's warm water ports.

I asked a former Israeli intelligence officer about Russia's interest in Israel. The officer used a standing global map to show me where Russia has its naval bases. He said, "Russia's navy is frozen in place for several months each year. For Russia to achieve military dominance in the Middle East and Europe it must find a warm-water port to the oceans of the world."

I further inquired, "So how does Israel figure into global warm-water ports?" The officer spun the globe to Israel's coastline, which borders the Mediterranean Sea at the Port of Haifa, and answered, "Israel is one of the few nations in the Middle East that has warm-water access to the oceans of the world year-round. Russia must have this kind of entry to those oceans for military dominance."

The Mediterranean Sea leads to the north and south Atlantic oceans. Going south from Haifa, the warm water takes you to the Red Sea, which leads to the Indian Ocean to the North Pacific and the oceans of the world. In one sentence, the officer captured why the nation of Israel is invaluable from a military perspective.

Israel's natural gas resources and warm-water ports may be the goal of Israel's enemies, but oil is the hook in their jaw set by God

Almighty (Ezekiel 38:4). Russia must have both the natural resources and strategic port access to reclaim its position as a global superpower. No matter their purpose, the King of the universe will drag Russia and its anti-Semitic coalition to their graves instead.

Unwalled Villages

Ezekiel 38:9–11 describes the great military invasion against Israel orchestrated by Gog's evil plans:

> You will ascend, coming like a storm, covering the land like a cloud, you and all your troops and many peoples with you. "Thus says the Lord God: 'On that day it shall come to pass that thoughts will arise in your mind, and you will make an evil plan.' You[Gog] will say, "I will go up against a land of unwalled villages; I will go to a peaceful people, who dwell safely, all of them dwelling without walls, and having neither bars nor gates."

Why is Israel referred to as "a land of unwalled villages"? Walls, then and now, are protection against invasion. At this time, concrete walls surround much of Israel to safeguard them from enemy sniper fire. But the Jewish people, who have been under ceaseless attack since the rebirth of their nation, will trust in the peace treaty they sign with the Antichrist. They will let their guard down and dismantle the walls believing they can finally live without fear of destruction. The Jews will pay a great price for relying on men instead of trusting the God of Abraham.

Ezekiel 38:13 reads, "Have you come to take plunder? Have you gathered your army to take booty, to carry away silver and gold, to take away livestock and goods [oil and technology], to take a plunder?"

I can see it now—diplomats attempting to negotiate away Russia's aggression, all the while ignoring the impending danger against Israel. I can assure you, Russia will thumb its nose and ignore all inept world governments who challenge its plan. They will invade God's Covenant nation with the help of a radical Islamic Confederation.

God's Response

Israel's enemies have formed a confederacy and for centuries have boasted that they would *"cut them [Israel] off from being a nation, that the name of Israel may be remembered no more"* (Psalm 83:4). This will happen—but not to Israel. God will make sure of that! King David prophesied this exact situation in the second chapter of Psalms:

Why do the nations rage, and the people plot a vain thing? The kings of the earth set themselves, and the rulers take counsel together, against the LORD and against His Anointed, saying, "Let us break Their bonds in pieces and cast away Their cords from us."

He who sits in the heavens shall laugh; the Lord shall hold them in derision. Then He shall speak to them in His wrath, and distress them in His deep displeasure: "Yet I have set My King on My holy hill of Zion."

"I will declare the decree: The LORD has said to Me, 'You are My Son, today I have begotten You. Ask of Me, and I will give You the nations for Your inheritance, and the ends of the earth for Your possession. You shall break them with a rod of iron; You shall dash them to pieces like a potter's vessel.'"

Now therefore, be wise, O kings; be instructed, you judges of the earth. Serve the LORD with fear, and rejoice with trembling. Kiss the Son, lest He be angry, and you perish in the way, when His wrath is kindled but a little. Blessed are all those who put their trust in Him.

Jehovah, the King of the universe, the Defender of Israel, watches over His people night and day as He sits on His Holy Throne. When the Russian-Islamic armada storms His Land, He will shout, for the Lord of hosts has been waiting for this moment since Amalek fought against the Israelites (Exodus 17:8–16).

Ezekiel declared in his prophecy: God's righteous fury will pour out judgment and vengeance on all nations that have historically persecuted and slaughtered the Jewish people:

> *It will be **in the latter days** that I will bring you against My land, so that the nations may know Me, when I am hallowed in you, O Gog, before their eyes* (Ezekiel 38:16).

> *"And it will come to pass at the same time, when Gog comes against the land of Israel," says the Lord GOD, "that My fury will show in My face. For in My jealousy and in the fire of My wrath I have spoken"* (Ezekiel 38:18–19).

God's Fury Released

The face of God is generally portrayed as one of absolute peace, tranquility, and love without limit, and these are surely among His many attributes. However, Ezekiel described God's face as enraged, nostrils flared, eyes blazing, incensed with the invasion of *"the apple of His eye"* by enemy nations and kings (Zechariah 2:8).

It is as if God is saying, "You weren't satisfied with the massacre of My people throughout the empires, while in exile, during the Inquisition, and in the Holocaust. Now you have come to the only place on earth I have created for Abraham's seed to live in safety and security to slaughter them! I think not!"

Jewish theologian Rabbi Solomon ben Isaac, more commonly referred to as "Rashi," also saw the Gog and Magog Wars as a time of reckoning for all the evils that the nations have perpetrated against Israel over the centuries. The armies of Magog are coming, and God Almighty is waiting for them with His day of retribution.

The nations of the world will watch the Russian-Islamic alliance lead a vast military invasion into the Holy Land, and it will appear that Israel is finished. However, this agnostic generation has completely forgotten the "God Factor."

The children of Israel have experienced this Divine intervention time and time again. When Moses led his people out of Egypt and through the desert, they were overcome by fear as six hundred of Pharaoh's fastest chariots pursued them all the way to the banks of the Red Sea. The people cried out to Moses, saying, *"Because there were no graves in Egypt, have you taken us away to die in the wilderness?"* (Exodus 14:11).

What was God's response? He caused the Red Sea to part and His children walked *"into the midst...on the dry ground."* Then God told Moses, *"Stretch out your hand over the sea, that the waters may come back upon the Egyptians, on their chariots, and on their horsemen."* The result: *"Not so much as one remained"* (Exodus 14:19–22, 26, 28).

God has miraculously redeemed His people before through Joshua, Deborah, Jehoshaphat, Hezekiah, and Esther, to name a few—and He will do it again. While the nations of the world anxiously watch, as the Jewish people appear to be standing on the brink of annihilation, Almighty God is measuring every step of the invading armies as they march toward Israel. When their pagan feet touch its sacred soil, God's fury will be released once more:

For in my jealousy and in the fire of My wrath I have spoken: "Surely in that day there shall be a great earthquake in the land of Israel, so that the fish of the sea, the birds of the heavens, the beasts of the field, all creeping things that creep on the earth, and all men who are on the face of the earth shall shake at My presence" (Ezekiel 38:19–20).

God is going to use the mountains around Israel to crush and bury its invaders. The Lord has used earthquakes throughout the history of man to communicate with those who refuse to obey His sovereign will. When God purposed to renew the human race to righteousness through Noah, He used an earthquake to open the *"fountains of the great deep."* This huge disturbance unbridled the global flood (Genesis 7:11).

Korah, Dathan, and Abiram rebelled against Moses and Aaron. God caused the earth to split open and swallow them, their households, and all they owned in judgement of their disobedience (Numbers 16: 23–34).

God shook the earth at Calvary to testify to the Roman Empire that Jesus of Nazareth was indeed the King of the Jews (Matthew 27:51). An earthquake released Jesus from the tomb on the third day (Matthew 28:2) and an earthquake released Paul and Silas from the prison in Philippi (Acts 16:26) to testify to all that they were men sent from God.

The earthquake of Ezekiel 38 will be the round-up of anti-Semitic nations, which will bring a supernatural disaster of colossal scale and result in:

1. The destruction of the invading armies of Gog-Magog (38:18–23).
2. The revelation of God's greatness and holiness being demonstrated among the nations (38:23).
3. Israel's national atonement (39:25–29).

Then the Creator of the universe will declare,

*So I will show my greatness and my holiness and make myself
known in the eyes of many nations. Then they will know that I
am the Lord* (Ezekiel 38:23 ESV).

*"I will gather them to their own land, not leaving any behind.
I will no longer hide my face from them, for I will pour out
my Spirit on the people of Israel, declares the Sovereign Lord"*
(Ezekiel 39:29 NIV).

Friendly Fire

God follows up His "welcome to Israel" earthquake with the tactic
of friendly fire—when a military force mistakenly fires upon its own
troops. The earthquake will fill the air with a thick black cloud of
dust and dirt, and then *"every man's sword will be against his brother"*
(Ezekiel 38:21).

Screams of terror coming from those falling into mass graves
will confuse and disorient the enemy's armies, causing them to turn
their weapons on each other. Blood will flow, and legions will die
because the very weapons intended for the slaughter of the Jewish
people will now be used to execute God's judgment against their
enemies.

This is also not the first time God has used friendly fire to crush
the enemies of Israel. Gideon was commanded by the Lord to have
three hundred men blow trumpets and charge the enemies of Israel
with pitchers filled with torches. Then *"The LORD set every man's
sword against his companion throughout the whole camp"* (Judges
7:22). The Midianites killed each other!

When invading armies come to call on the chosen people, God

will once again open His combat manual and initiat
Chaos."

There are questions about the "latter days" that we do not i.
the answers to, but the following is what we do know, based on
God's infallible Word:

- Immediately following the rapture of the church, the seven-year tribulation begins with the Antichrist making a seven-year treaty with Israel that will resolve the Israel Arab dispute. (Daniel 9:27; Ezekiel 38:8, 11)
- The Third Temple will be built in Jerusalem. (Daniel 9:27; Revelation 11:1)
- The Antichrist will form a global government with one currency, one religion, and ten leaders he will appoint to rule the world under his absolute dictatorship. (Daniel 2:40–44; 7:7)
- After three and a half years, the 144,000 Jewish messengers will begin their ministry.
- The Gog-Magog wars will begin with Russia leading Iran and other Islamic nations in an invasion of Israel. God will crush this invading army killing five out of six of the invaders.
- The Antichrist will set up his image to be worshipped as God by the nations of the world.
- He will be shot in the head and recover miraculously... emulating the death and resurrection of Jesus Christ. (Daniel 11:45)
- The Antichrist will turn on the Jewish people, who will flee to Petra, where God will protect and provide for them until Messiah comes. (Matthew 24:16–20)

- Elijah and Enoch will begin their miracle ministry in Israel for three and a half years. (Revelation 11:2–3)
- The False Prophet will introduce the mark of the Beast; those who do not receive it will be decapitated. (Revelation 13:16–18)
- Toward the end of the Tribulation, the seven bowls of Judgment are poured out over the earth in rapid succession. (Revelation 16)
- The Battle of Armageddon begins. (Revelation 16:16)
- Elijah and Enoch are killed in Jerusalem by the Antichrist and lie dead in the streets for three and a half days, after which they are resurrected. This is witnessed by a global audience, which is terrified at the sight. (Revelation 11:7–12)
- Jesus Christ returns to earth at the Mount of Olives with His Triumphant Church, where He slaughters the armies that have invaded Israel.
- There is a banquet for buzzards who are called by God to eat the flesh of the invaders.
- Satan and the Antichrist are cast into hell. (Revelation 20:1–9)
- The Final Kingdom begins for 1,000 years of perfect peace where the lion will lie down with the lamb and will study war no more. (Revelation 20:4–6)
- Satan is released from hell for a short time to deceive the nations. He will attack Jerusalem, where he will be destroyed with the Beast and the False Prophet by God Almighty. (Revelation 20:7–10)
- The Great White Throne Judgment for the wicked dead. (Revelation 20:11–15)
- The earth is burned with fire and recreated to be like the Garden of Eden. (Revelation 21:1)

- And time shall be no more...Eternity, world without end, begins. (Revelation 21:9–22:5)

There are only two kingdoms on earth and in eternity: the Kingdom of Light and the Kingdom of Darkness. From the beginning of Genesis until the End of Days, the Kingdom of Light prevails.

Each one of us will belong to one kingdom or the other—which will you choose?

SECTION FOUR

THE FINAL GAME OF THRONES

CHAPTER 13

SATAN'S THRONE

I will ascend into heaven, I will exalt my throne above the stars of God; I will also sit on the mount of the congregation on the farthest sides of the north; I will ascend above the heights of the clouds, I will be like the Most High. (Isaiah 14:13–14)

History most definitely repeats itself. The twentieth century saw the harbinger of the coming Antichrist: his name was Adolf Hitler. He is recorded in history as flooding the earth with a river of innocent blood, as did other megalomaniac monsters, such as Haman, Herod, Nero, Stalin, Mussolini, Tojo, Saddam Hussein, Assad, and Khamenei of Iran.

HITLER LIVES

The mere mention of Hitler's name triggers horrifying accounts of World War II, culminating in the systematic slaughter of 6 million Jewish people. Since his cowardly suicide in 1945, more than 120,000 publications about his psychotic life have been written, and even now the ghost of Hitler walks across the nations of the globe.

Steven Spielberg's intense and heart-wrenching movie *Schindler's List* brilliantly captured a glimpse of the Holocaust and the living hell it produced. I believe God Almighty put this artistic genius on the earth to create this graphic depiction of the unspeakable horrors committed against the Jewish people. The world must never forget the satanic evil of the Final Solution, the Nazis' code name for the murder of two-thirds of Europe's Jewish population. *Schindler's List* should be required viewing for every student in America's public schools to diminish the poisonous stream of anti-Semitism that still flows rampant throughout the world.

Although Hitler has been dead for over seventy-five years, you can still watch nightly documentaries that feature his hypnotic speeches to throngs of spellbound Germans as they recited their perverted prayer of adoration: "Adolf Hitler, you are our great leader. We praise thee! Heil Hitler!"[1] The Third Reich was their religion, and Hitler was their god.

There are countless biopics on Hitler's weapons of war, works of art, connection to the occult, obsession with racial purity, the Third Reich (his personal empire), and of course his gruesome attempt to annihilate the Jewish people. Why are we still so obsessed with this diabolical madman?

The headline in a March 2018 *New York Times* world news article screamed, "Indian Children's Book Lists Hitler as a Leader 'Who Will Inspire You.'" The publisher "came under fire…for including Hitler in a children's book about world leaders who have 'devoted their lives for the betterment of their country and people.'"

"'This description would bring tears of joy to the Nazis and their racist neo-Nazi heirs,' [responded] Rabbi Abraham Cooper, associate dean of the Simon Wiesenthal Center, an international Jewish human rights organization.…On the book's cover, a stony-faced

Hitler is featured alongside...Mahatma Gandhi, Nelson Mandela and India's prime minister, Narendra Modi."[2]

Make no mistake: the tactic of the radical extremists is to place a monster like Hitler in the company of respectful leaders to confuse impressionable young minds concerning this human devil, his methodical extermination of six million Jews, and the bloody war he launched that killed more than 40 million people in Europe.

We say, "Never again"; but the floodtide of anti-Semitism *is* surging once more.

Remember this truth: There is soon to appear on the earth an unequivocally depraved evil genius far worse than Adolf Hitler. The Bible calls him the Antichrist—the Beast and the chief son of Satan. His evil empire will engulf and enslave the world, and his deeds will make Adolf Hitler look like a choirboy. But before he reveals his true nature, the Antichrist will appear like a charismatic leader who brings peace to the nations.

Destruction Through False Peace

The offer of peace is not a new tactic for world dominance. Hitler manipulated the peace process as a weapon of war just as the Antichrist will do in the near future:

> And through his policy also he [the Antichrist] shall cause craft [deceit] to prosper in his hand; and he shall magnify himself in his heart, and by [false] peace shall destroy many [Great Tribulation]: he shall also stand up against the Prince of princes [Christ]; but he shall be broken without hand (Daniel 8:25 KJV).

> "He shall confirm a covenant with many for one week [seven years]" (9:27).

False Peace in Our Time

On September 30, 1938, the Munich Pact was signed between Great Britain's prime minister, Neville Chamberlain; French premier Édouard Daladier; Italy's leader, Benito Mussolini; and Germany's chancellor, Adolf Hitler. This pact allowed Hitler to enter Czechoslovakia unhindered, bolstering his goal of German expansion.[3]

Prime Minister Chamberlain was willing to sacrifice the people of Czechoslovakia to avoid another world war—it was his "land for peace" agreement. Chamberlain flew home to London victoriously waving the signed peace treaty, proclaiming, "This means peace in our time." However, it was Hitler's ploy, intended to seduce the British into complacency—while taking Europe "one piece of land at a time." Hitler even duped the German people into believing peace was at hand:

> Circumstances have forced me [Hitler] to almost only speak of peace for decades. It was only through the continued emphasis on the German desire for peace and peaceful intentions that it was possible to give the German people the arms that were always a requirement for the next step.[4]

The "peace treaty" was actually a blatant act of deception devised by a demonized dictator whose lust to control Europe knew no limits. Hitler continued his ruse for fraudulent peace via the 1939 Hitler-Stalin Pact, which allowed him to invade Poland while the Russians looked the other way. Before the signing of the non-aggression pact, President Franklin D. Roosevelt warned Stalin that, "It was as certain as that the night followed the day that as soon as Hitler had conquered France he would turn on Russia and it would be the Soviets' turn next."[5]

In response to Hitler's invasion of Poland, France and Britain declared war on Germany on September 1939. Hitler had a massive head start in the war effort due to the territory and resources he had seized in Eastern Europe. Then on June 22, 1941, Hitler broke his treaty with Stalin and launched one of the largest surprise attacks since Germanic warriors struck down three entire Roman Legions in 9 CE.* Russia paid an enormous price for accepting Hitler's so-called peace process. By the end of World War II, twenty million Russian soldiers and civilians had lost their lives.

The man who saved England, and arguably Western civilization, from this evil incarnate was Sir Winston Churchill. He saw through Hitler's charade and with a voice of a lion, he roared at those who thought negotiating with Hitler was a plausible tactic to maintain peace. Churchill thundered, "You cannot reason with a tiger when your head is in his mouth."[6]

When most in the British Parliament wanted to collaborate with Adolf Hitler, Winston Churchill issued instead a call to arms in his first speech after being appointed prime minister of Great Britain. While the armies of the Third Reich were treading across Europe in an unrelenting quest to conquer as much of it as possible, Churchill instinctively recognized that appeasement was not the answer to Hitler's aggression.

The survival of Great Britain was uncertain at best, yet Churchill managed to unite his people when he bellowed before Britain's legislative body, "You ask, what is our aim? I can answer in one word. It is victory, victory at all costs, victory in spite of all terror, victory, however long and hard the road may be; for without victory, there is no survival."[7]

We too are walking toward a similar skyline, where one will appear out of Europe, a bewitching, multilingual political superstar

---

* https://militaryhistorynow.com/2016/12/07/didnt-see-it-coming-nine-of-military
-historys-most-amazing-surprise-attacks/.

who will lead a ten-nation coalition. This false messiah will enter into a seven-year peace treaty with the State of Israel and his motive will be like that of Hitler—to conquer the nations of the world and set up his personal empire.

Peace, One Piece at a Time

The leaders of the world have been attempting to broker peace in the Middle East long before Israel was reborn as a nation. Every major politician in the West wants the Middle East Peace Treaty notch on their belt. Some negotiators have become so obsessed with reaching a deal that they have not considered the cost.

The core dilemma is that all the concessions for peace in the Middle East to this point in history have been made by Israel. While the Arab nations say they want peace, in reality, like Hitler, they only want it *one piece of land at a time* and will not be content until they control all of Israel to include Jerusalem.

The question arises, What kind of peace treaty will the Antichrist negotiate that will cause the geopolitically savvy leaders of Israel to sign? How will the Antichrist deceive them?

Why not offer a seven-year peace treaty that will promise the Jewish people total control of Israel, to include the Temple Mount? Why not include the authorization of the building of the Third Temple? What about offering Israel complete jurisdiction over all the holy sites? I can assure you that this cunning man of deception will offer the moon! It will not matter what the Antichrist offers or what Israel accepts, because the Great Deceiver does not intend to keep the pact anyway—peace was never his objective.

Doubtless, once the treaty is signed, the Antichrist will receive the Nobel Peace Prize after he is deluged with global praise from the United Nations and the liberal world media. Even some of the Jewish people will believe that this "man of peace" is the Messiah.

However, this lawless ruler has two main objectives: present himself as God and destroy the nation of Israel.

This promise of seven years of peace is, in reality, part of the Antichrist's calculated tactic—it will become his vehicle for war. The treaty and the ten-nation federation that the Antichrist will lead are mentioned by Daniel and John the Revelator (Daniel 9:27; 2:40–44; Revelation 11:1; 17:12). They foretell of the Antichrist's breach of this ill-fated accord exactly forty-two months after it is made and his ensuing military attack on Israel.

Spellbinding Deception

One of the most celebrated film clips of the Third Reich is of Adolf Hitler standing on a massive platform surrounded by the German high command, his voice booming like claps of thunder, as thousands of Nazi soldiers scream, "Heil Hitler." Historians may give Hitler high marks as a public speaker, but his oratory skill does not explain the mesmerizing effect he had on the masses.

Men and women wept uncontrollably and hysterically shouted praise while they assembled by the hundreds of thousands to hear him rant. It was as if they were spellbound as they listened to the pseudo-savior of Germany.

In my book *The Three Heavens*, I detail Hitler's involvement with the occult and his close association with Dietrich Eckart, who was a committed occultist. It was Eckart who "trained Hitler in self-confidence, projection, persuasive oratory, body language and ranting discord." However, it was not "by his own power" that Hitler deceived millions, nor will it be by the Antichrist's personal power that he captivates the masses.[8] "*His [the Antichrist's] power shall be mighty, but not by his own power*" (Daniel 8:24); he will have Satan's demonic anointing and ability to deceive, bringing nations to submission with his oratory:

> *And he [the Antichrist] was given a mouth speaking great things*
> *and blasphemies, and he was given authority [by Satan] to con-*
> *tinue for forty-two months* (Revelation 13:5).

THE FORESHADOWERS

There have been many foreshadowers of the Antichrist who have slithered through the pages of history: Nimrod, Pharaoh, Nebuchadnezzar, the Roman Caesars, and Antiochus Epiphanes, to name but a few. These vile men had many things in common with the Antichrist:

- They rebelled against God and His authority.
- They persecuted and murdered the chosen people at will.
- They erected images of themselves for self-seeking adulation.

Adolf Hitler fits perfectly in this list of wickedness—he too can be described as a forerunner of the Antichrist. After his ascension to power in 1933, Hitler required German schoolchildren to recite a prayer that equated him with Christ. Hitler, like Satan and the Antichrist, craved praise and worship.

Historian Joseph J. Carr records, "Nazism was no mere political movement of racist gangsters and misfits, as is commonly believed, but rather, it was an occultic religion in which Adolf Hitler was the Messiah, Heinrich Himmler the High Priest and the blood-drenched men of the SS Death's Head Formation the clergy."[9]

Nazism was an evil New World Order where Hitler saw himself as god and the Third Reich his kingdom. His National Socialist Party was more than a political movement—it was a formal faith with rituals, rites, doctrine, scripture, and a messiah. However, Hitler's reign of destruction, dispensed by his evil hordes, will pale in comparison to the demonic triune that will compete in the Final Game of Thrones.

DEMONIC TRIUNE

One of Satan's desires is to emulate God. A prime example of this obsession is his defilement of the Holy Trinity. God's Trinity consists of the Father; Jesus Christ, the Son; and the Holy Spirit. Their sacred union is defined by righteousness, truth, and life.

The Holy Trinity refers to the one God who exists in three coequal and coeternal Persons—nothing and no one can emulate this divine union. The "unholy triune" is completely opposite and consists of Satan, the Antichrist, and the False Prophet. These evil entities depict pure wickedness, deception, and death.

Satan

Satan's fixation to be *"like the Most High"* (Isaiah 14:14), began in the midst of heaven. The following are a few key facts concerning this obsession:

- God created an indescribably beautiful angel named Lucifer. He was the most glorious of all the angels, a wise overseer of the Garden of God and he was chosen as the worship leader for paradise (Third Heaven).
- Lucifer displayed such splendor and radiance that he was called *"son of the morning"* (Isaiah 14:12). *Lucifer* is the English translation of the Hebrew name *helel*, which means "to shine" or "to bear light." He reflected the magnificent majesty of God's radiance. Isaiah vividly depicted Lucifer:

> *Thus says the Lord God: "You were the seal of perfection, full of wisdom and perfect in beauty. You were in Eden, the garden of God; every precious stone was your covering.... The workmanship of your timbrels and pipes was prepared for you on the day you were created. You were the anointed*

cherub who covers; I established you; you were on the holy mountain of God; you walked back and forth in the midst of fiery stones" (28:12–14).

- Lucifer's wings "covered" the place where God's glory was manifested in His heavenly temple, just as the cherubim in the tabernacle of Moses covered the mercy seat and the place where the visible glory of God appeared (Exodus 37:9). *So what went wrong?*

    By his own confession, Lucifer made a declaration of defiance:

*You have said in your heart: "**I will** ascend into heaven, **I will** exalt my throne above the stars of God: **I will** also sit on the mount of the congregation....**I will** ascend above the heights of the clouds, **I will** be like the Most High"* (Isaiah 14:13–14).

I mentioned earlier the "I will" of God concerning His promises to Abraham, and in his insurrection, Lucifer too declared his *"I will."* Because of his pride, Lucifer became dissatisfied with his position, exalted though it was. He lusted for God's throne and was consumed by his desire to be worshipped, an ambition that will be momentarily satisfied when he gives power to the man of sin—the Antichrist (2 Thessalonians 2:3; Revelation 13:4).

As penalty for Lucifer's rebellion, God banished him from the Third Heaven. The beautiful Lucifer was no more. In that instant, the chief cherub was no longer the "bearer of light"—he would forever be called Satan—the prince of darkness.

Once banished, the rebel of all rebels established his throne in the Second Heaven. The Lord referred to Satan's seat of power in the letter to the church of Pergamos (Revelation 2:12–17). And if there is a throne, there is an empire. Through this evil empire, Satan and his fallen angels rule over all the kingdoms of the world, for the Word of God declares that *"the whole world lies under the sway of the wicked one"* (1 John 5:19).

The Scriptures reveal many of the names given to Satan based on his evil nature:

- The accuser (Job 1:6; Zechariah 3:1–2; Revelation 12:10)
- The tempter (Matthew 4:3)
- The ruler of demons (Matthew 12:24)
- The strong man (Mark 3:27)
- Beelzebub (Luke 11:15)
- A murderer (John 8:44)
- The father of lies (John 8:44)
- The ruler of this world (John 14:30)
- The prince of the air (Ephesians 2:2)
- The power of death (Hebrews 2:14)
- Adversary the devil (1 Peter 5:8)
- A roaring lion (1 Peter 5:8)
- The wicked one (1 John 5:19)
- The angel of the bottomless pit (Revelation 9:11)
- The great dragon (Revelation 12:9)
- The serpent of old (Revelation 12:9)

Satan has directed his savage anger toward God's faithful remnant. Since the time of his fall until now, the wicked one has attempted to foil God's plan of redemption by destroying His chosen line from which our Messiah comes.

There was Cain, who *"was of the wicked one"* (1 John 3:12). There was the evolution of universal disobedience that caused God to redeem mankind through Noah (1 Peter 3:19–20), whose lineage included Abraham, Isaac, and Jacob—the fathers of God's chosen people.

The good news is that the serpent will fail to thwart the Father's plan. This ages-long conflict between good and evil will reach its climax when:

> *The devil, who deceived them, was cast into the lake of fire and brimstone where the beast and the false prophet are. And they will be tormented day and night forever and ever* (Revelation 20:10).

The Antichrist

The second entity of the demonic triune is the Antichrist. The Scriptures are replete with descriptions that capture his vile nature:

- The little horn, with *"eyes like the eyes of a man"* (Daniel 8:9).
- A prince who is to come, who *"shall destroy the city and the sanctuary"* (Daniel 9:26).
- The one who makes desolate *"on the wing of abominations"* (Daniel 9:27).
- A foolish shepherd *"who will not care for those who are cut off"* (Zechariah 11:15–17).
- The son of perdition: *"the man of sin"* (2 Thessalonians 2:3–10).
- The lawless one, *"according to the working of Satan"* (2 Thessalonians 2:8–9).
- The rider on the white horse who *"went out conquering and to conquer"* (Revelation 6:2).
- The beast out of the sea, *"and on his heads a blasphemous name"* (Revelation 13:1–2).

The Bible describes one possessing great oratory skills who will rise in power filling a global leadership vacuum. Sound familiar?

Who would have ever believed that a man as insignificant as Adolf Hitler could rise to global power from such absolute obscurity in such a short period? Carr writes, "Physically, Hitler was colorless and unimpressive enough to make one wonder how he could inspire the 'ideal' Nordic beast of his SS formations, much less an entire nation."[10]

He stood only five foot nine, and he had dark hair and a pasty, pale complexion—a far cry from the blond-haired, blue-eyed Nordics that were being exalted as the super race. If it were not for his crazed grayish-blue eyes that seemed to be ablaze, he would have been lost in an average crowd. He was not even physically fit enough to meet the admission qualifications for his own SS.

Hitler, and Antiochus IV Epiphanes before him, was a type and shadow of the Antichrist to come.

The Antichrist will appear in the "latter days," after the Rapture of the church (Daniel 8:23; 2 Thessalonians 2:3). He will arise from the revived Roman Empire (Daniel 9:26) and lead the last form of Gentile world government (Revelation 13:1). His empire will be the most extensive in history, encompassing the entire globe (Revelation 13:8). The Antichrist's rule will be the most demonic the world has ever experienced (Daniel 11:36; 2 Thessalonians 2:3; 9-19).

> Then I stood on the sand of the sea. And I saw a beast [Antichrist] rising up out of the sea [the world], having seven heads and ten horns, and on his horns ten crowns [leaders of ten nations], and on his heads a blasphemous name (Revelation 13:1).

At an appointed time, the Beast of Revelation 13 will have three of the ten European leaders killed (Daniel 7:8,24). He will place the fallen kings' crowns on his head and will increase his power as the dynamic and visionary leader of the revised G7. This savior-like figure will astound the masses with his innate skill to solve the world's insurmountable problems (Daniel 7:8; 20; 8:23).

The Antichrist will rise to power through his seemingly brilliant Middle East peace treaty with Israel and her enemies, which he will break (Daniel 9:27). However, as the Antichrist consolidates his satanic supremacy, his true nature will be revealed.

He will emerge as a demonically empowered individual who hates God and is determined to annihilate those who believe in Him—both Jews and Christians. For this reason, he is identified as the Antichrist (1 John 2:18), for he will stand against God, the Father of Abraham, Isaac, and Jacob, and His anointed one, Jesus Christ (Daniel 11:36–37; 2 Thessalonians 2:4; Revelation 13:5).

Many Jewish people will accept the Antichrist as a great political leader and diplomat and will place their trust in him (2 Thessalonians 2:11). But the moment he reveals himself halfway through the Tribulation by blaspheming God, the righteous Jews will revolt (Ezekiel 28:2; Daniel 7:25). They will reject him as the Messiah, at which point this willful king (Daniel 11:36) will respond savagely by attempting to annihilate them—the spirit of Haman and Hitler will live again (Daniel 7:21; 25).

I believe that just as the Maccabees revolted against the abominations of Antiochus Epiphanes, a righteous Jewish revolution will rise up against the Antichrist, ending with him suffering a mortal wound to the head:

And I saw one of his heads as it were wounded to death; and his deadly wound was healed: and all the world wondered after the beast (Revelation 13:3 kjv).

This incident will lead to one of Satan's greatest deceits—the Antichrist will shockingly survive and present himself anew to the world as an indestructable god. After defeating a coalition that comes against him, the Antichrist will establish his military head-quarters between the Mediterranean Sea and Mount Zion (Daniel 11:42–45).

The Antichrist will align himself with the corrupt world religion (the Great Harlot) that will attempt to control him, but he will ultimately destroy it (Revelation 17:3; 17:16–17). He will set up his image in the Third Temple in Jerusalem and demand that the world worship him and those who refuse will be executed. (Daniel 7:25; 9:27; 11:36; Revelation 13:5; 15).

God will judge the Antichrist in the battle for Jerusalem at Christ's second coming (Daniel 7:22; 2 Thessalonians 2:8). After his defeat, the Beast, along with the False Prophet who performed signs and wonders to deceive those who took the mark of the Beast, will be cast into the lake of fire (Ezekiel 28:8–10; Revelation 19:19–20).

Saint Paul called the Antichrist the son of perdition and described him as *"the mystery of lawlessness"*:

> *Let no one deceive you by any means; for that Day will not come unless the falling away comes first, and the man of sin is revealed, the son of perdition [Antichrist], who opposes and exalts himself above all that is called God or that is worshiped, so that he sits as God in the temple of God, showing himself that he is God. . . .*
>
> *For the mystery of lawlessness [the spirit of Antichrist] is already at work; only He [the Holy Spirit] who now restrains will do so until He is taken out of the way [the Rapture]. And then the lawless one will be revealed, whom the Lord will consume with the breath of His mouth [Revelation 19:15] and*

destroy with the brightness of His coming. The coming of the lawless one is according to the working of Satan, with all power, signs, and lying wonders, and with all unrighteous deception among those who perish, because they did not receive the love of truth, that they might be saved (2 Thessalonians 2:3–4, 7–10).

What exactly does the term *mystery of lawlessness* mean? The Antichrist is the illegitimate claimant to the throne of Christ. Satan, being the ultimate impersonator, is determined to desecrate what God has made holy. Jesus Christ is described as the *"mystery of godliness,"* which is God manifested in the flesh (1 Timothy 3:16).

Our all-knowing Father in heaven foretold Satan's future when He rebuked the serpent in the Garden of Eden: *"And I will put enmity between you [Satan] and the woman, and between your seed [Antichrist] and her Seed [Jesus Christ]"* (Genesis 3:15). Therefore, the term *mystery of lawlessness* or *the lawless one* means "wickedness incarnate." The Antichrist is called the "man of lawlessness" or "man of sin" because it is his nature. His very life is characterized by blasphemous sin against God.[11]

But until that day when Jesus Christ returns, it is Satan's offspring, the Antichrist, who will bring a reign of terror upon the earth that it has never seen before.

Nature of the Beast

Bible scholar A. W. Pink says of the coming Antichrist, "Across the varied scenes depicted by prophecy there falls the shadow of a figure at once commanding and ominous. Under many different names like the aliases of a criminal, his character and movements are set before us."[12]

The following are a few of the characteristics that define the nature of the Antichrist who is called the Beast by John the Revelator (Revelation 3:1).

- A warmonger, a man of bloodshed and deceit (Psalm 5:6).
- A *"deceitful and unjust man"* (Psalm 43:1).
- A worker of deceit (Psalm 52:2).
- His words are *"smoother than butter"* (Psalm 55:21).
- Boastful (Daniel 7:8).
- Strong-willed; demands his own way and arrogantly speaks against the Almighty (Daniel 7:25).
- Mighty, *"but not by his own power"* (Daniel 8:24).
- Has no *"desire of women"* (Daniel 11:37).
- Possessed by Satan, just as Judas was (Luke 22:3).
- Has Satan's power and authority (2 Thessalonians 2:9; Revelation 13:2).
- Speaks arrogant words and blasphemies (Revelation 13:5).

The immoral and depraved nature that the Antichrist displays is best summed up in the distinct references assigned to him in Scripture:

- The insolent king (Daniel 8:23)
- The vile person (Daniel 11:21)
- The willful king (Daniel 11:36)
- The worthless shepherd (Zechariah 11:17)
- The abomination (Matthew 24:15)
- The man of sin (2 Thessalonians 2:3)
- The son of perdition (2 Thessalonians 2:3)

Christ versus Antichrist

The Antichrist is the antithesis of Jesus Christ. Pink expands on this truth: "The word *Antichrist* has a double significance. Its primary meaning is one who is *opposed* to Christ; but its secondary meaning is one who is *instead* of Christ. He will attempt to become another Christ, a pretender to the name of Christ. The Antichrist will set himself up as the true Christ, but he will be the Devil's counterfeit."[13] It is not hard to fathom how even the elect will be deceived (Matthew 24:24).

Scripture provides several references illustrating how the Antichrist is a counterfeit of Jesus Christ:

CHRIST	THE ANTICHRIST
Christ was despised and afflicted (Isaiah 53:3).	The Antichrist will be admired and lauded (Revelation 13:3–4).
Jesus makes an everlasting peace covenant with Israel (Ezekiel 37:26).	The Antichrist makes a seven-year peace treaty with Israel, which he breaks (Daniel 9:27).
Jesus Christ was resurrected from the dead (Matthew 28:6).	The Antichrist will miraculously recover from a fatal wound to the head (Revelation 13:3, 14).
Christ came to save (Luke 19:10).	The Antichrist will come to destroy (Daniel 8:24).
Christ came from heaven (John 6:38).	The Antichrist will come from the bottomless pit (Revelation 11:7).
Christ came in His Father's name (John 5:43).	The Antichrist will come in his own name (John 5:43).
Christ came to do His Father's will (John 6:38).	The Antichrist will come to do his own will (Daniel 11:36).

CHRIST	THE ANTICHRIST
Christ is the Good Shepherd (John 10).	The Antichrist will be the evil shepherd (Zechariah 11:16, 17).
Christ is the truth (John 14:6).	The Antichrist will be *the lie* (2 Thessalonians 2:11).
Jesus Christ is part of the Holy Trinity (Father, Son, and Holy Spirit) (Matthew 28:19).	The Antichrist is part of a demonic triune (Satan, the Antichrist, and the False Prophet) (Revelation 13).
Christ is the mystery of godliness, God manifested in the flesh (1 Timothy 3:16).	The Antichrist will be the "mystery of lawlessness," Satan manifested in the flesh (2 Thessalonians 2:7–9).
The Lord's name is exalted in all the earth (Psalm 148:13).	The Antichrist will exalt himself above all (2 Thessalonians 2:4).
Jesus mandates men to only worship God (Matthew 4:10).	The Antichrist seduces men to worship Satan (Revelation 13:4).
Christ seals His servants' foreheads with God's name (Revelation 7:3; 14:1).	The Antichrist forces his followers to be branded with his counter mark (666) on their foreheads or right hands (Revelation 13:16–18).
Christ is Lord of lords and King of kings (Revelation 17:14).	The Antichrist will be given authority by Satan over the ten kings (2 Thessalonians 2:9; Revelation 17:12–13).
Jesus Christ will descend from heaven, riding a white horse (Revelation 19:11).	The Antichrist rides on the white horse of the Apocalypse (Revelation 6:2).
Jesus Christ is crowned with many crowns (Revelation 19:12).	The Antichrist has ten horns with ten crowns (Revelation 13:1).

CHRIST	THE ANTICHRIST
God will establish Christ's throne (2 Samuel 7:12–14; Psalm 132:11).	The Antichrist will sit on Satan's throne (Revelation 13:2).
Christ will reign over His Eternal Kingdom (Revelation 11:15).	The Antichrist will have a temporary kingdom (Revelation 17:17).

The False Prophet

The third entity of the demonic triune is the "second beast," or the False Prophet (Revelation 16:13;19:20; 20:10). Satan charges him with the malevolent mission of leading the masses in the worship of the Antichrist. He is the antithesis of the Holy Spirit.

> *Then I saw another beast [False Prophet] coming up out of the earth, and he had two horns like a lamb and spoke like a dragon. And he exercises all the authority of the first beast [Antichrist] in his presence, and causes the earth and those who dwell in it to worship the first beast....He [False Prophet] performs great signs, so that he even makes fire come down from heaven on the earth in the sight of men. And he deceives those who dwell on the earth by those signs which he was granted to do in the sight of the beast* (Revelation 13:11–14).

Based on the Scriptures, this false prophet will be a globally renowned religious figure who will help the Antichrist control the world for seven years during the Tribulation. He will call fire from heaven and cause a statue of the Antichrist to speak, convincing the nations of the world that Satan's messiah is the living god (Revelation 13:11–15).

Just as the Third Reich's propaganda machine vaulted Hitler to power, the False Prophet will catapult the Antichrist to the throne of his evil empire.

Satan is now a step closer to satisfying one of his eternal pursuits—the utter destruction of God's chosen people. He hates God and therefore hates the Jewish people. What God establishes, the Great Adversary opposes. Satan may have his battle plans drawn, but the God of Israel has decided on the battle site—the Valley of Megiddo. This is the setting for the bloodiest military battle humanity will ever witness—Armageddon.

It is the place where those who come to destroy the Jewish people are themselves destroyed by the hand of God. *"Behold, He that keepeth Israel neither slumber nor sleep"* (Psalm 121:4 KJV).

CHAPTER 14

THE APOCALYPSE

Write the things which you have seen, and the things which are, and the things which will take place after this. (Revelation 1:19)

Who can judge time in terms of eternity—Only God Himself. In the first portion of this book, I presented a short synopsis of over 1,550 years of biblical history from the time of Abraham to Daniel. Now let us take a brief journey from here to eternity—from the End of Days to time without end.

Abraham, Jeremiah, Ezekiel, Daniel, Joel, Amos, and Zechariah were shown visions of the future, including the End of Days. However, one man stands out as having "unveiled" the impending events leading to the Final Game of Thrones—his name was John the Revelator.

The last of John's five manuscripts included in the Bible is the book of Revelation. It is often referred to as the "Apocalypse," or the "unveiling." Revelation deals with eschatology, or "a study of the last days" pertaining to the imminent conclusion of the world as we know it. More importantly, the prophecies surrounding the end of the age are the fulfillment of the purposes of God and an encouragement to prepare believers for the coming of the Lord.

God the Father reveals the final book of the Bible to His Son, Jesus Christ. Christ makes its message known to *"His angel"* (Revelation 1:1), who then unveils it to the apostle John on the Island of Patmos. Fundamentally, God is the Author and John is His scribe.

The Lord emphasized the importance of knowing the *things to come* in this passage: *"Blessed is he who reads and those who hear the words of this prophecy, and keep those things which are written in it; for the time is near"* (Revelation 1:3).

God's perfect will and revelation of truth are found throughout His Word—it is the protoplasm of life. God's Word is an exercise in righteousness; it is medicine for the sick, peace for a troubled heart, direction for the wayward soul, and encouragement to the hopeless— it is everything His children will ever need to lead an abundant life. It is no wonder that the Enemy of God—the Great Deceiver—has devised a campaign to mock and diminish this sacred Book.

We supposedly live in a time of enlightenment—the Information Age[1]—but exactly whose information are we receiving? In a recent *Gentlemen's Quarterly* (*GQ*) magazine article titled "21 Books You Don't Have to Read," the Holy Bible was listed as number twelve. Novelist Jesse Ball writes:

The Holy Bible is rated very highly by all the people who supposedly live by it but who in actuality have not read it. Those who *have* read it know there are some good parts, but overall it is certainly not the finest thing that man has ever produced.[2]

God's truth always transcends that of man, and His Word declares:

All Scripture is given by inspiration of God, and is profitable for doctrine, for reproof, for correction, for instruction in righteousness, that the man of God may be complete, thoroughly equipped for every good work (2 Timothy 3:16–17).

The Word of God is greater than all other books as the blazing sun is greater than a single candle on a child's birthday cake, as the oceans of the earth are greater than a dripping faucet, or as Mount Everest is greater than a grain of sand. The Bible is not a good book—it is *The Book* by which all other books are judged.

The history of the world has proven repeatedly that mankind has been at odds with the Creator since the days of Adam. Yet what few realize is that the Architect of the Ages is not swayed by our failings—instead, He has fashioned a plan of ultimate redemption through the glorious and triumphant return of His Son, which is the core event in the book of Revelation.

THE THINGS YOU HAVE SEEN

Man has anticipated the end of time for centuries, yet never before have so many prophetic events been fulfilled leading to the Rapture of the Church, the appearance of the Antichrist, and the second coming of Christ. As John unfolds the revelation of the End of Days, we can begin to connect the dots of what is soon to come.

The first section of the book of Revelation deals with what John witnesses as a follower of Jesus. He attempts to portray the Lord and His profound majesty by describing Him as the One, *"who is and who was and who is to come…the Alpha and the Omega, the Beginning and the End"* (Revelation 1:4, 8).

Because of the righteous deeds John personally saw Christ do, he declared His Master to be the Conqueror of death, the Ruler of the nations, and the resurrected Savior of the world (Revelation 1:5; John 4:42).

This "beloved disciple" dropped his nets by the shores of Galilee as a teenager and followed the Rabbi from Nazareth. John later played a vital role in the expansion of the early church. His writings are intended to give the reader an understanding of Christ through His words and works. And in turn, those who believe in Him will *"have [eternal] life in His name"* (John 20:31).

Jesus called John and his older brother, James, the *"Sons of Thunder"* (Mark 3:17), most likely because of their fervent passion and steadfast loyalty for the things of God (Mark 9:38; Luke 9:54). The two brothers, along with Peter, where chosen by Christ to be in His inner circle (Matthew 17:1). The Scripture refers to John as the disciple *"whom Jesus loved,"* so much so, that the Lord asked him to watch over His mother Mary, after His death (John 13:23; 19:27).

John saw firsthand Jesus turn water into wine (John 4:46), he witnessed the healing of the lame man at the pool of Bethesda (John 5:9), and he was there when Jesus miraculously fed the multitudes by the Sea of Galilee (John 6:13). John was the only disciple to witness Christ's crucifixion (John 19:30), and he visited with the Lord following His supernatural resurrection (John 21:14). John received the power of the Holy Spirit in Jerusalem along with Christ's mother and the other believers who gathered in the Upper Room when the New Testament church was born within the wind and fire of Pentecost (Acts 2:4).

After Christ's ascension, Herod continued to persecute the church through imprisonment and execution, causing believers to scatter outside of Jerusalem (Acts 12:1–17). John found temporary refuge in Ephesus but was eventually captured by the Roman emperor Domitian and exiled to the island of Patmos (Revelation 1:9). It was here that the angel of the Lord gave to John the book of Revelation.

There are major similarities between the Book of Revelation and the description given by Jesus of the signs of the end of the age in the Book of Matthew.

- War (Matthew 24:6–7; Revelation 6:3–4)
- Famine (Matthew 24:7; Revelation 6:5–6)
- Death (Matthew 24:7–9; Revelation 6:7–8)
- Martyrdom (Matthew 24:9–10, 16–22; Revelation 6:9–11)
- Signs in the heavens (Matthew 24:29; Revelation 6:12–14)
- Divine judgment (Matthew 24:32–25:26; Revelation 6:15–17).*

THE THINGS THAT ARE

As John begins his account, he describes the Holy Trinity—God the Father, sitting on His throne; Jesus, one like the Son of Man; and (the Seven Spirits, which embody the presence of the Holy Spirit) (Revelation 1:4). He also sees seven lampstands and seven stars, which symbolize the seven churches of Asia Minor and their pastors (Revelation 1:12, 16).[3]

The second portion of John's book deals with the letters Christ addresses to these churches. Think of it as Christ the Author and John the "Postman of Patmos."[4] The churches were located in Ephesus, Smyrna, Pergamos, Thyatira, Sardis, Philadelphia, and Laodicea. Every church is defined by its traits, all but one are commended, some are reproved, and all are given a promise.

---

* J. Dwight Pentecost, *Things to Come*, pp. 280–82.

The promises given to the seven churches are also afforded to every believer in Christ (Revelation 2–3). These promises include:

- Access to the Tree of Life (2:7; 22:14)
- The victor's crown (2:10; 3:11)
- A new name (2:17)
- Power to rule over nations (2:26)
- An everlasting place in the Book of Life (3:5)
- Deliverance from the Great Tribulation (3:10)
- Sharing in the throne of Christ (3:21)

Earlier we discussed the Dispensation of Grace—it is the age in which we currently live. This sixth age of God's amazing mercy will be followed by the Day of the Lord (Seventh Age), which will bring judgment, wrath, and ultimate victory.

THE THINGS THAT WILL TAKE PLACE

The third and final section of the book of Revelation begins with Christ pulling back the veil of eternity to His faithful disciple. It is here that John sees the throne room of God (Revelation 4).

You have heard me say that man cannot fully describe the glory and grandeur that awaits every believer in heaven. I am certain that even John, who actually caught a glimpse of this splendor, still paints a pale portrait of the beauty that surrounds the heavenly throne of the Almighty (1 Corinthians 2:9; Revelation 4:1–11).

Twenty-Four Elders

John first sees twenty-four elders seated on individual thrones around the throne of God. These men represent the twelve Old Testament Patriarchs (sons of Jacob) and the New Testament apostles. The white robes they are wearing reflect their righteousness (Revelation 3:18), and the crown of life on their heads depicts their victory over death (Revelation 2:10). These elders are in heaven now and are worshiping Him who sits on the throne, singing the song of Moses and the song of the Lamb (Revelation 4:9–10; 15:3; Deuteronomy 32:1–43).

The Rapture of the Church

The next most important event that will occur for the faithful believers in Christ Jesus is the Rapture of the church. Let us engage in our "five-W" exercise that we used earlier to summarize this highly anticipated event.

What is the Rapture? It is a date certain, known only to God, when *"in a twinkling of an eye,"* the church of Jesus Christ will be taken from this earth and united with our Lord and Savior in heaven (1 Corinthians 15:52).

Who will participate? All believers in Christ, living and dead, will meet the Lord Jesus in the air. The dead in Christ will rise first, and the living will be *"caught up together with them,"* and be with the Lord forever (1 Thessalonians 4:17).

When will it happen? The timing of the Rapture is highly debated; however, I will answer this question based on the following Scriptures. John's Revelation account largely addresses a time when God will pour out His divine wrath on those who rejected the Gospel. Furthermore, Christ promised to deliver believers from the "hour of trial" that is soon to come (Revelation 3:10; 1 Thessalonians 5:9).

Finis Dake says the "church will continue to hinder lawlessness until the Rapture. And then the Antichrist will be revealed."[5] Our Lord is a Promise Keeper who does not lie; therefore, I believe the Rapture of the church will take place before the start of the seven-year

Tribulation—a time of unparalleled turmoil and suffering on earth (Revelation 4:1).

Where will the Rapture take place? This phenomenon will be a worldwide occurrence. All who are in Christ Jesus will be taken up with Him *in the clouds* and will ascend into the Third Heaven (1 Thessalonians 4:16–17).

Why will the Rapture happen? To release the End of the Age. At this moment in time, the bride of Christ is keeping the wrath of God from being executed on the ungodly. Once the righteous in Christ are gone, those left behind will encounter the full power of lawlessness, which is presently being *restrained* by the Holy Spirit. Saint Paul taught that *"the mystery of lawlessness"* will be *unconstrained* by the Holy Spirit when He ascends to heaven with the believers (2 Thessalonians 2:7).

At that very moment the church is taken up, empty cars will careen down the highway, their drivers and occupants suddenly absent. Homes of believers will be vacated without notice, with dishes on the dining table, food bubbling on the stove, and water running in the sink. Instantly people will be frantically looking for their loved ones on all social media platforms, and the headlines will read,

THE GREAT DISAPPEARANCE— MILLIONS MISSING!

In the following months, churches will be overflowing with despondent people who have realized, all too late, that God's Word is true. The world will spiral out of control and will enter a time simply known as the Tribulation. The Scriptures repeatedly warn of the Rapture and the time of trouble that follows. Even Jesus taught on this season several times, during His prophecy seminar (Matthew 24:1–36), in the parable of the ten virgins (Matthew 25:1–13), right before His ascension into heaven (Acts 1:7), and at the Mount of Olives with His disciples:

> *But of that day and hour no one knows, not even the angels in heaven, nor the Son, but only the Father. Take heed, watch and pray; for you do not know when the time is. It is like a man going to a far country, who left his house and gave authority to his servants, and to each his work, and commanded the door keeper to watch. Watch therefore, for you do not know when the master of the house is coming—in the evening, at midnight, at the crowing of the rooster, or in the morning—lest, coming suddenly, he find you sleeping. And what I say to you, I say to all: Watch!* (Mark 13:32–37)

The Judgment Seat of Christ

Every one of us will face a day of judgment—either the Judgment Seat of Christ (the judgment of the righteous) or the Great White Throne Judgment (the judgment of the unrighteous). According to Scripture, *"it is appointed for men to die once, but after this the judgment"* (Hebrews 9:27).

After the Rapture of the church, the righteous will appear before the Judgment Seat of Christ. God Almighty will judge us for the lives that we lived. This judgment does not qualify us for heaven—we are already there. It will determine the kind of reward we will receive for the life we led.

> *For we must all appear before the judgment seat of Christ, so that each one may be recompensed for his deeds in the body, according*

to what he has done, whether good or bad (2 Corinthians 5:10 NASB).

Jesus Christ will judge us based on our personal words and deeds. It is here that *"the fire will test each one's work, of what sort it is"* (1 Corinthians 3:11–15). As believers, we will be judged and rewarded in part on how faithfully we served Christ (1 Corinthians 9:4–27; 2 Timothy 2:5), how well we obeyed God's mandates (Deuteronomy 28:1–14; 1 Peter 4:17), whether we participated in the Great Commission (Matthew 28:18–20), and how we personally triumphed over sin (Romans 6:1–4).

Scripture describes five crowns that believers will receive: the victor's crown (1 Corinthians 9:25–27), the crown of life (Revelation 2:10), the crown of glory (1 Peter 5:2–4), the crown of righteousness (2 Timothy 4:8), and the crown of rejoicing, also called the soul winners' crown (1 Thessalonians 2:19–20).[6]

Think of it—we will all stand before God Almighty and answer for every word, thought, and deed. I ask, are you ready to give an account to God for your life?

Marriage Supper of the Lamb

Once the bride—the blood-bought church—is adorned in her wedding robe and crowns, Jesus Christ, the Bridegroom, will welcome the wedding guests to the marriage supper. In Revelation 19:9, John is told to write, *"Blessed are those who are called to the marriage supper of the Lamb!"* Here, we will gather with the Old and New Testament saints.

It will be a truly magnificent occasion, beyond the power of words to describe. Imagine the guests passing through the gates of splendor and onto the streets of heaven lined with mansions of glory. They will then enter the banquet hall of the King of kings and sit at the table of the marriage supper of the Lamb—the Messiah, the Son of David, the Son of Abraham—Jesus Christ, our Redeemer. Hallelujah to the Lamb!

The Scroll

Roman law required a last will and testament to be sealed seven times as demonstrated in the wills left by Emperors Augustus and Vespasian for their successors.* These seals were used to prevent an unauthorized reading of a document.

The apostle John saw God sitting on His throne holding a scroll in His right hand. Let's study three important words of this vision— *God, right hand,* and *throne.* The fact that God held the scroll symbolizes its sovereignty and divine origin. His right hand denotes might and authority (Exodus 15:6; Psalm 20:6; 44:3; 110:1; Lamentations 2:3–4; etc.), and the throne itself refers to coming judgment (see Proverbs 20:8; Matthew 27:19; Acts 25:6).

The fact that the scroll had writing on both sides indicates a completed work. The scroll is stamped with seven seals, which serve as symbols of the hidden plan of God which will be revealed at the breaking of each seal. John sees the Lamb of God, the only One worthy to open the scroll, take it from His Father's hand while those surrounding the throne bow down and sing a new song (Revelation 5:8–10).

The lamb is scripturally significant in Judaism—it was a symbol of redemption. Animal sacrifices in general are found throughout the Old Testament. They were an integral part of worship for the Tabernacle in the wilderness and, later, in the Holy Temple of Jerusalem.

The blood of the sacrificial lamb represented an atonement for sin (Leviticus 4:35). If sin was present then cleansing and redemption

---

* Ethelbert Stauffer, *Christ and the Caesars*, pp. 182–83.

was necessary, *"And according to the law almost all things are puri-fied with blood, and without shedding of blood there is no remission"* (Hebrews 9:22).

The blood of the Passover lamb was offered as a sacrifice for Israel's redemption from Pharaoh's bondage (Exodus 12:12–13). This liberation was a type and shadow of God's redemptive plan for all humanity from the spiritual bondage of sin through the sacrifice of His Son on the cross (John 1:35–36; 11:25–26; 1 Peter 1:19).

John mentions the Lamb repeatedly within his writings and refers to Him as the Lion of the Tribe of Judah (Revelation 5:5; see Genesis 49:8–10) and the Root of David (Revelation 22:16; see Isaiah 11:1–10; Romans 15:12), signifying His identity as the messianic King (John 4:25–26). He also describes the Lamb as having seven horns, symbolizing the Lord's strength and power, and seven eyes, representing His perfect wisdom and understanding (Revelation 5:6). The Lamb in Revelation is represented as One sovereign in His own authority, omnipotent in power, and worthy as the Redeemer who died.*

Seven in the Bible represents completeness and perfection. Scripture is filled with events and images associated with the number seven. Aside from the length of creation, the first verse of Genesis consists of seven Hebrew words; the Sabbath is on the seventh day, and many Jewish feasts are seven days long.

The land of Israel was mandated to rest every seventh year, the menorah in the Temple has seven branches, and the walls of Jericho fell after the Israelites encircled it for seven days.[7] Christ used the imagery of sevens throughout the book of Revelation.

The scroll has seven seals. Each time a seal is opened, a new part of the scroll is revealed, until the final seal is broken. John referred to

---

* John F. Walvoord, *The Revelation of Jesus Christ*, Section 5, The Lamb and the Seven Sealed Books.

four successive judgments in multiples of seven represented by seven seals, seven thunders, seven trumpets, and seven bowls. However, twenty-one apocalyptic symbols—the seven seals, seven trumpets, and seven bowls—sequentially represent the chain of events surrounding the church. They embody her trials, her persecution, her final triumph, and eternal prosperity.

These judgments are part of the Great Tribulation. It is a time when God pours out His righteous wrath on those who have rejected His Son and tormented His chosen. This period is marked by God's fury, Israel's longing for the coming Messiah, and the preparation of Christ's return. Repeatedly, John uses the phrase *God's wrath* to describe this turbulent time.

Silence and the Seventh Seal

The Lord, through the prophets, promised that judgment would come, and now it is here. Fittingly, there is half an hour of absolute silence in heaven as the Lord opens the seventh seal, pulls back the curtain of time, and reveals the judgments He will execute upon the nations of the world.

Imagine a quiet so intense that not even your own breath is heard. Suddenly, after thirty minutes, the prayers of the saints who have been crying out for vengeance break the deafening silence. And then "*...there were noises, thunderings, lightnings, and an earthquake*"—all happening at once, ushering in a synchronized clamor of cataclysmic proportions (Revelation 8:5). The thunders and lightnings are the prologue to the earthquake, when the earth literally convulses as the time of the Gentiles comes to an end.

The seventh seal is the last seal, marking the prophetic judgments of God. With the sounding of the seven trumpets, (Revelation 8:6), seven angels are given seven vials or bowls containing God's wrath (15:7; 16:1). This is His verdict on those who have rejected His Son, tormented the saints (church) and the elect ((Jewish people), and received the mark of the Antichrist.

The Trumpets

The first four trumpets announce earthly disasters that will cause massive destruction upon the earth (Revelation 8:7–13). The fifth trumpet describes a "star" falling from heaven—this is Satan. He is given the key to the bottomless pit, which he opens, and out springs a smoke so dense that even the sun is darkened by its intensity (Revelation 9:1–2).

Coming from this blinding smoke is a horde of demons resembling huge, scorpion-like creatures. Satan will lead these instruments of misery as they afflict all of humanity. Even the rich and powerful, whose bodies are covered with agonizing sores, cry out for death as a means to relieve their suffering (Revelation 9:3–6).

Whereas the fifth trumpet brought torture and torment, the sixth produces death. At a very precise time, the sound of the sixth trumpet will release four angels, whose assignment is to kill one-third of mankind in one day (Revelation 9:13-15). The severity of human suffering during the Great Tribulation is beyond the mind of man to fathom.

Remember this truth: The only thing that equals the love of God is the wrath of God. The Almighty will direct His righteous anger on those who refuse to repent *of the works of their hands, that they should not worship demons, and idols of gold, silver, brass, stone, and wood,…their murders or their sorceries or their sexual immoralities or their thefts*" (Revelation 9:20–21).

This time of travail is a precursor to Christ's millennial reign.

The Two Witnesses

Once the Antichrist comes to absolute power, his evil reign will not be hindered. However, not everyone will fall under his demonic spell. Among the many who refuse to submit to the Antichrist's subjugation will be two invincible witnesses sent by God to torment him. John does not identify who they are; however, many Bible scholars believe they are Elijah and Enoch, the only two people who were taken to heaven from this earth without experiencing death.

It is as if God were preparing them for a great assignment. The prophet Malachi clearly identified Elijah as one of them, and Enoch is the only other man who was translated without dying (Genesis 5:24; 2 Kings 2:11; Malachi 4:5; Hebrews 11:5).

These two witnesses will be filled with the Holy Spirit and will testify of God's glory (Zechariah 4:6). They will prophesy within the city of Jerusalem and perform great miracles. God will supernaturally protect them by giving them the power to kill their enemies with the fire that comes from their mouths. For three and a half years, no harm will prevail against these two witnesses until their mission is complete.

When their divine assignment is accomplished, the Antichrist will kill Elijah and Enoch. He will leave their bodies exposed on the streets of Jerusalem without proper burial, to be seen by the entire world on global television and "shared" by millions through social media. The people of the earth will celebrate their murder for three and a half days, until God raises them from the dead and they ascend to heaven. The awesome power of God will strike fear in the hearts of every person on earth after their resurrection. Within an hour, a great earthquake will take place, destroying a tenth of the city, killing seven thousand people (Revelation 11:1–13).

The 144,000—the Sealed of Israel

John describes four angels originating from the four corners of the earth, holding the four winds. They represent God's total control over all He has created. They are commanded not to sound their trumpets until the fifth angel marks the foreheads of the righteous with the seal of the living God, protecting them from death at the hand of the Antichrist (Revelation 7:1–3; 14:1).

This seal is the *"Father's name"* (Revelation 14:1) placed on their foreheads, visible to all—just as the mark of the Beast (666) will be seen on the foreheads or right hands of those who bow to the Antichrist (Revelation 13:8; 14:9).

Saint Paul refers to these souls as the *"remnant according to the election of grace"* (Romans 11:5). They number 144,000—composed of 12,000 Jewish evangelists from each of the twelve tribes of Israel. Reverend Clarence Larkin makes a very important point concering the chosen tribes of Israel. The tribes of Dan and Ephraim are not included in the 144,000; whereas the tribes of Joseph and Levi are (Revelation 7:7, 8).

Why? Because the Lord promised that any *"man or woman or family or tribe"* who introduced idolatry into Israel would be set apart from the other tribes and blotted out from under heaven (Deuteronomy 29:18–21). Both Dan and Ephraim worshipped the golden calves (1 Kings 12:25– 30). The God of Abraham, Isaac, and Jacob does not forget a promise and fulfills His Word when He chooses this select group.[8]

The Tribulation and the Great Tribulation

Following the Rapture of the Church, there will be a revival of the Roman Empire (federation of European states), generating great evil in the world (Revelation 17:3–13). At the Lord's chosen time, the

Antichrist (Daniel 7:8; 2 Thessalonians 2:3; Revelation 11:7; 13:1; 19:20) will walk onto the world stage and enter into a seven-year Middle East peace treaty with Israel, signaling the beginning of the Tribulation (Daniel 9:27).

The Tribulation is a future, seven-year period of unspeakable horror that can be best described as "hell on earth." It will be marked by a destruction of the present world order—political, social, and religious. All will be reduced to chaos by the breaking down of all moral authority and social stability.

It is a time when God will unleash His wrath on all those who have rejected Him and the Gospel of the Kingdom. The Tribulation is also described as the Day of the Lord (Isaiah 2:12; 13:6–9; Joel 2; 1 Thessalonians 5:2; Zephaniah 1:14; Acts 2:20) and as a day of trouble, wrath, and distress (Deuteronomy 4:30; Ezekiel 7:19; Zephaniah 1:15; Romans 2:5).

The Antichrist will betray Israel in the *"middle of the week,"* exactly three and a half years after signing his peace treaty with them (Daniel 9:27). This demarcation is when the Antichrist will be revealed as the son of Satan. The "lawless one" will ban Jewish sacrifices in the temple and exalt himself as the head of a New World Religion (Revelation 13:11–15).

These incidences signify the beginning of the Great Tribulation, when Satan, the Antichrist, and the False Prophet (the demonic trinity) will rule the earth. Please note that the Tribulation represents the full seven-year period, while the Great Tribulation specifically marks the second half.

Christ expressly distinguishes the horrific impact of the Great Tribulation from any other time of trials: *"For then there will be great tribulation, such as has not been since the beginning of the world until this time, no, nor ever shall be"* (Matthew 24:21).

The Great Tribulation Saints

John then sees a countless number of people from all nationalities before the throne of God. They represent those who have been martyred during the Great Tribulation (Revelation 7:9, 14), who were killed after declining the mark of the Beast (Antichrist) and refused to worship his image in the temple of Jerusalem.

These believers have remained loyal to God through great suffering. Because of their faithfulness, God will *"wipe every tear from their eyes"* and give them eternal life (Revelation 7:14–17).

The Four Horsemen of the Apocalypse

John the Revelator is told to *"come and see"* (Revelation 6:1) as the Lamb opens the first four seals, which reveal four riders on four horses.

The first rider sits on a white horse, wears a crown, and represents the world ruler of the false peace movement. He is the Antichrist. The second rider holds a great sword and straddles a red horse; he symbolizes worldwide warfare and bloodshed. The next rider carries a pair of scales and rides a black horse. He embodies severe scarcity, poverty, and lack. The fourth rider sits on a pale horse; he represents death, which will strike one-third of the earth's population through famine, pestilence, and the attack of wild beasts, which are all represented by the previous three seals.

The fifth seal reveals an altar upon which the martyrs cry out for God's righteous judgment upon the enemies of His people. They will be beheaded by the Antichrist for their witness and refusal to take the mark of the Beast.

The sixth seal represents earth-shattering natural disasters, which will herald the second coming of the Lord. They include great earthquakes, the darkening of the sun, the moon becoming as blood, the stars falling from the sky, and mountains and islands that will be moved from their natural position.

Some of these phenomena are described in other books of the Bible:

For the stars of heaven and their constellations will not give their light; the sun will be darkened in its going forth, and the moon will not cause its light to shine (Isaiah 13:10).

The sun shall be turned into darkness, and the moon into blood, before the coming of the great and awesome day of the LORD (Joel 2:31).

But the day of the Lord will come as a thief in the night, in which the heavens will pass away with a great noise, and the elements will melt with fervent heat; both the earth and the works that are in it will be burned up (2 Peter 3:10).

The Battle of Armageddon

In review, at the beginning of the seven years of tribulation, Satan's messiah will make a treaty with Israel that will ensure their national security and allow them to rebuild their temple (Daniel 9:27; Ezekiel 38:8, 11). At the halfway mark, the armies of Gog and Magog will invade the land of Israel.

God Almighty will destroy these invading armies, killing five out of six combatants, demonstrating to the world that He is the mighty Shield of Israel—the One True God of Abraham, Isaac, and Jacob (Ezekiel 38–39; Daniel 9:27; 11:40–41; Ezekiel 39:2; Psalms 18:2).

After the Antichrist breaks his treaty with the Jewish people, he will take over Jerusalem and establish the throne of his evil empire in the Third Temple. With the help of the False Prophet, the Antichrist will erect his image in the temple and demand that the world worship him as God. This is the *"abomination of desolation"* that Jesus mentions in Matthew 24:15. The Jewish people, recognizing the Antichrist for who he is, will flee Judea and be sheltered by the hand of God in Petra for the last half of the Tribulation (Matthew 24:16). Just as God Almighty provided for the children of Israel for forty years, so will He provide for the Jewish remnant for three and a half years.

There are two major wars fought during the seven years of the Tribulation. The first is the Gog and Magog Wars of Ezekiel 38–39, and the last is the Battle of Armageddon, which happens at the end of the Tribulation in the Valley of Megiddo.

The armies of the king of the West (the Antichrist), representing a vast military armada, and the kings of the East (China and its allies), with an army of two hundred million, will march down the dry riverbed of the Euphrates to reach Israel on the battlefield of the Valley of Jezreel. Here they will face off in the mother of all wars for world domination (Revelation 9:16).

When the kings of the West and East battle for global supremacy, the war ends not with an invasion from the north, south, east, or west, but with an invasion from heaven.

Jesus Christ, the rabbi from Nazareth, will return to earth riding on a magnificent white horse, ushering in the final triumph over the enemies of Israel. The army riding with Him, the church of Jesus Christ and the Old Testament saints, will be mounted on white horses and clothed in pure white linen.

This massive army, traveling faster than the speed of light through space and time, will fly over Petra, where the hand of God has protected the Jewish people from the Antichrist. They will see the city of Jerusalem. They will look on Mount Calvary where our Redeemer died for the sins of the world. They will see the Mount of Olives, where Christ will rule the earth with a rod of iron as He establishes the Final Kingdom that shall never pass away.

It is here that Jesus Christ slaughters the combatants of Armageddon until the blood flows to the bridle of a horse (Revelation 14:20). Once again, the Defender of Israel fulfills the promise that He who keeps Israel neither slumbers nor sleeps (Psalms 121:4).

The Second Coming of Christ

John records the amazing revelation of the Second Coming with the words, *"Now I saw heaven opened . . ."* (Revelation 19:11). When translated in the Greek, this phrase literally means that when Christ returns to earth, this gateway to and from heaven will open, and will remain open, for all eternity. It reminds us of Jacob's ladder, with the angels ascending into heaven and descending to earth at will (Genesis 28:12).

How long will it take to go from heaven to earth and back again in our supernatural bodies? According to the length of Daniel's prayer, it will only be a matter of seconds:

> *Now while I was speaking, praying, and confessing my sin and the sin of my people Israel, and presenting my supplication before the LORD my God for the holy mountain of my God, yes, while I was speaking in prayer, the man Gabriel, whom I had seen in the vision at the beginning, being caused to fly swiftly, reached me.... "At the beginning of your supplications the command went out, and I have come to tell you, for you are greatly beloved"* (Daniel 9:20–23).

The Scriptures are replete in offering the purposes of Christ's return to earth. He will come to:

- Fulfill His promise (Zechariah 14:4; Matthew 25:31; Acts 1:9–11).
- Gather and restore His people (Isaiah 43:5–6; Jeremiah 30:10; 33:6–9; Ezekiel 36:24–38; 37:1–28).
- Judge the nations for their wickedness (Matthew 25:31–46; Revelation 19:2).
- Resurrect the dead who refused the mark of the Beast (Daniel 12:1–4; Revelation 20:4–6).
- Reign as the King of kings (Revelation 19:6).

Righteous Judge, Victorious Warrior, and Lord of Lords

The apostle John, who was an eyewitness to Christ's ascension, records His triumphant return:

> Now I saw heaven open, and behold, a white horse. And He who sat on him was called Faithful and True, and in righteousness He judges and makes war. His eyes were like a flame of fire, and on His head were many crowns, He had a name written that no one knew except Himself. He was clothed with a robe dipped in blood, and His name is called The Word of God. And the armies in heaven, clothed in fine linen, white and clean, followed Him on white horses. Now out of His mouth goes a sharp sword, that with it He should strike the nations. And He Himself will rule them with a rod of iron. He Himself treads the winepress of the fierceness and wrath of Almighty God. And He has on His robe and on His thigh a name written: KING OF KINGS AND LORD OF LORDS (Revelation 19:11–16).

428 | THE FINAL GAME OF THRONES

Christ's position on a white horse signifies His conquest in battle (Revelation 6:2; see also Psalm 45:4). He is first the Conqueror over death, hell, and the grave. Second, He is the Conqueror of Satan and his evil empire and all the enemies of Israel.

Jesus appears in this scriptural setting as ultimate Judge, Warrior, and Lord of lords. His judgment is indicated by His *"eyes...like a flame of fire,"* and He is bearing many crowns, declaring His absolute power and Kingship (Revelation 19:12).

A Robe Dipped in Blood

Having been in the ministry for sixty-two plus years, I have heard Revelation 19:13—*"He was clothed with a robe dipped in blood"*— explained in many ways. However, I believe the prophet Isaiah's account. First, Isaiah posed the question:

> *Who is this who comes from Edom, with dyed garments from Bozrah, this One who is glorious in His apparel, traveling in the greatness of His strength?* (Isaiah 63:1a)

Then the answer was given:

> *"I who speak in righteousness, mighty to save." Why is Your apparel red, and Your garments like one who treads in the winepress? "I have trodden the winepress alone, and from the peoples no one was with Me. For I have trodden them in My anger, and trampled them in My fury; their blood is sprinkled upon My garments, and I have stained all My robes. For the day of vengeance is in My heart, and the year of My redeemed has come"* (Isaiah 63:1b–4).

When we think of Jesus, we do not consider Him as vengeful. His death on the cross was not an act of retribution but one of absolution and love. He forgave the thief who died next to Him, (Luke 23:43) and even on behalf of those guilty of His crucifixion, He pleaded, *"Father, forgive them for they know not what they do" (Luke 23:34).* Jesus Christ forgave the Romans who entered into a Calvary conspiracy to kill him. He even forgave the handful of Pharisees in Pilate's courtyard who hated Him (Matthew 21:31).

However, the Lord's righteous anger against Israel's enemies will not be contained. What Isaiah is describing is the greatest destruction that earth will ever see. Millions will be destroyed at Armageddon. The One who treads the winepress with His garments splattered and soaked in crimson blood is the description of God's day of vengeance upon the adversaries of Israel.

The Winepress
John the Revelator describes God's winepress:

> *And another angel came out from the altar, who had power over fire, and he cried with a loud voice to him who had the sharp sickle saying, "Thrust in your sharp sickle and gather the clusters of the vine of the earth, for her grapes are fully ripe." So the angel thrust his sickle into the earth and gathered the vine of the earth, and threw it into the great winepress of the wrath of God. And the winepress was trampled outside the city [Jerusalem], and blood came out of the winepress, up to the horses' bridles, for one thousand six hundred furlongs"* (Revelation 14:18–20).

John sees the armies of the Antichrist surrounding the city of Jerusalem. They are the *"clusters of the vine,"* which are *"fully ripe."*

What they don't realize is that God is waiting for them. Every commander and every soldier in that army is about to experience the winepress of God in His version of *The Grapes of Wrath*.

The prophet Zechariah declared,

"Behold, the day of the LORD cometh [Day of Judgment]... [when] I will gather all nations against Jerusalem to battle... and fight against those nations" (14:1–3 KJV).

King David spoke of God's protection over His people:

"As the mountains surround Jerusalem, so the LORD surrounds His people [the Jewish people] from this time forth and forever" (Psalms 125:2).

Moses prophesied that the hand of God will annihilate the invading armies of Israel:

"For He will avenge the blood of His servants, and render vengeance to His adversaries; He will provide atonement for His land and His people" (Deuteronomy 32:43).

The Gog and Magog Wars and the Battle of Armageddon will be God's retribution on those who have sought to destroy the Jewish people. It is important for Christians to comprehend the depths of God's love for the Jews, who have suffered so much for their steadfast faith in Him. God called Israel *"My son, My firstborn"* (Exodus 4:22).

The Jews are His chosen; they are a Covenant people; they are a cherished people. God chose the nation of Israel to provide the source of divine truth. Through Israel, the Almighty gave mankind

His sacred Word, the Patriarchs, the prophets, and our Redeemer, Jesus Christ. Because Satan hates what God establishes, the spirit of anti-Semitism has prevailed through the ages in an effort to destroy this scarlet thread of redemption.

God made mankind this promise concerning the Jewish people: *"I will bless those who bless you, and I will curse him who curses you"* (Genesis 12:3).

God will call the buzzards of the earth to consume the bloated corpses of the armies that come against His people. Their lifeless bodies will stretch across the great span of Armageddon's battlefield. This is a testimonial of God's ultimate fury on the nations of the world who persecuted the nation of Israel (Ezekiel 39:17–20; Revelation 19:17).

The bodies of kings, captains, commoners, and horses will become a banquet for the birds of prey, fulfilling the prophecy of Jesus:

> *"For wherever the carcass is, there will the eagles be gathered together"* (Matthew 24:27–28).

Why is God doing this? He answers this question in Ezekiel 39:22, 29:

> *"So the house of Israel shall know that I am the LORD their God from that day forward....And I will not hide My face from them anymore; for I shall have poured out My Spirit on the house of Israel,"* says the Lord GOD.

The Authority of God's Word

Christ, mounted on His white horse, circles over the battlefield of Armageddon with the heavenly host, He opens *"His mouth [and out] goes a sharp sword, that with it He should strike the nations"* (Revelation 19:15).

The Spoken Word of God based on the will of God is an awesome force. The Bible says that Jesus *"will consume with the breath of His mouth and destroy with the brightness of His coming"* (2 Thessalonians 2:8).

In the beginning it was the authority of God's Word that created the heavens and the earth. It was the authority of Jesus' Spoken Word that healed the sick, raised the dead, and caused demons to tremble. And for the grand finale, it will be the awesome power of God's Spoken Word that will utterly destroy the armies of the Antichrist and of the kings of the East.

The Seventy-Five Day Interval

According to the prophet Daniel, there is a literal seventy-five day interval between the second coming of Christ and the official inauguration of the Kingdom of God. Daniel explained this gap in time:

And from the time that the daily sacrifice is taken away, and the abomination of desolation is set up, there shall be one thousand two hundred and ninety days. Blessed is he who waits, and comes to the **one thousand three hundred and thirty-five days** (Daniel 12:11–12).

Revelation 11:3 states, *"And I will give power to my two witnesses, and they will prophesy* **one thousand two hundred and sixty days,** *clothed in sackcloth."*

The difference between 1,335 days and 1,260 days makes up the seventy-five-day interval between the end of the Tribulation and Christ's return to the Mount of Olives, which means the official beginning of the Millennial Age. So what will happen in those seventy-five days?

There is no exact timeline; however, somewhere during this seventy-five-day period it is clear that the Lord is getting Israel's house in order.

- He will remove the abomination of desolation from the temple.
- He will cast the Antichrist and the False Prophet alive into the lake of fire (Revelation 19:20).
- He will bind Satan and cast him into the bottomless pit (Revelation 20:2–3).
- He will execute the judgment of the Gentiles (Matthew 25:31–46).
- The Old Testament saints (righteous Jews) will be resurrected (Isaiah 26:19; Daniel 12:2).
- The Tribulation saints will be resurrected (Romans 14:10; 2 Corinthians 5:10; Revelation 20:4).
- The Marriage Feast of the Lamb will take place (Revelation 19:9).

Earth's Last Empire

Bible scholar John Phillips beautifully describes that next step in the Final Game of Thrones:

> The remnant of the Jews and the redeemed of the Jews and the redeemed from among the Gentiles will go into the millennial kingdom, the nucleus of the New Kingdom. The millennial kingdom will be worth waiting for.[9]

CHAPTER 15

THE MILLENNIAL REIGN

Blessed and holy is he who has part in the first resurrection. Over such the second death has no power, but they shall be priests of God and of Christ and shall reign with Him a thousand years (Revelation 20:6).

During the seven years of the Tribulation, a global evangelism campaign will take place. This time of testimony begins with the 144,000 Jewish evangelists of Revelation 7, who are protected from the Antichrist with the seal of God's Name on their foreheads. How will these 144,000, chosen from the twelve tribes of Israel, come to the knowledge of Christ? By supernatural revelation.

They will have an encounter with the Lord similar to that of the Apostle Paul on the road to Damascus. Christ arrested the brilliant yet antagonistic Pharisee with His presence, blinding him, and then sent him to Ananias for healing before being commissioned to preach the Gospel (Acts 9:1–20). Thereafter, Paul established the

New Testament church and shook the Roman Empire with the power of the good news of Jesus Christ. In short, the Lord of Hosts will reveal Himself to the 144,000.

God will also release three angels, giving them the assignment of *"flying in the midst of heaven, having the everlasting gospel to preach to those who dwell on the earth—to every nation, tribe, tongue and people"* (Revelation 14:6–9).

Add to this avalanche of evangelism the two witnesses, Elijah and Enoch, who, without experiencing death, were taken up to heaven thousands of years earlier. The last promise God made to the Jewish people in the final chapter of the last book of the Old Testament was the promise of Elijah's return: *"Behold, I will send you Elijah the prophet before the coming of the great and dreadful day of the LORD"* (Malachi 4:5).

Planet Earth has never seen such an awesome demonstration of God's power from previous evangelists. Countless numbers of people will accept Jesus as Messiah after hearing their testimonies while remembering the sudden disappearance of millions of people caused by the Rapture of the church.

THE JUDGMENT OF THE NATIONS

The Judgment of Nations (all Gentile nations) will immediately follow the return of Christ to earth and occur before the start of His millennial reign. This is when Jesus Christ will execute His final verdict:

> *"Behold, the days are coming," says the LORD, "that I will raise to David a branch of righteousness; a King [Jesus Christ] shall reign and prosper, and execute judgment and righteousness in the earth"* (Jeremiah 23:5).

What is the basis for this judgment? Jesus Christ is calling the people of all nations to give an account of how they treated the Jewish people, as recorded in Matthew 25:31–46. Those who blessed the Jewish people will hear, *"Come, you blessed of My Father, inherit the kingdom prepared for you from the foundation of the world"* (v. 34).

Where is the Jewish connection? Listen to the words of Jesus in verse 40:

> *And the King [Jesus] will answer and say to them, "Assuredly, I say to you, inasmuch as you did it to one of the least of these My brethren [Jewish people], you did it to Me."*

Before the cross, Jesus never called the Gentiles "My brethren." It was not until His death that His precious blood signed the adoption papers on the parchment of His flesh and made the outcast Gentiles His very own (Ephesians 2:12).

What happens to those who witnessed the suffering of the Jewish people throughout the ages and did nothing? The Rabbi from Nazareth provides the answer: *"And these [who did nothing to help the suffering Jews] will go away into everlasting punishment"* (Matthew 25:46).

Remember what God told Abraham the first time He spoke to him thousands of years ago: *"I will bless those who bless you, and I will curse him who curses you"* (Genesis 12:3). This mandate is still recorded in the books of heaven by pens of iron with points of diamond. Allow me to ask you a very important question: What are you doing to bless the house of Israel?

Israel and the Jewish people are at the epicenter of prophecy from the moment God made His Covenant with Abraham, and they will remain so throughout eternity. All other nations and celebrated cities will fall by the wayside, but Israel and Jerusalem will live forever. Jerusalem is the shoreline of eternity; it is the city of God.

The late theologian John Walvoord clearly summarized the purpose and effect of the Judgment of the Nations:

> The sheep [righteous] who have manifested their faith in Christ under trying circumstances by befriending a Jew are now rewarded by being ushered into the millennial kingdom with its blessings of Christ's righteous rule and beneficent care over all who trust in Him. By contrast, the goats [unrighteous] who followed the course of this world and undoubtedly participated in the persecution of the Jewish people as well as neglecting their acts of kindness now come under the divine judgment which they justly deserve, and are cast into everlasting fire.[1]

SATAN BOUND
FOR A THOUSAND YEARS

Before the glorious millennial reign of perfect peace, Satan is bound in chains and cast into *"the bottomless pit"* for a thousand years.

> *Then I saw an angel coming down from heaven, having the key to the bottomless pit and a great chain in his hand. He laid hold of the dragon, that serpent of old, who is the Devil and Satan, and bound him for a thousand years; and he cast him into the bottomless pit, and shut him up, and set a seal on him, so that he should deceive the nations no more till the thousand years were finished. But after these things he must be released for a little while* (Revelation 20:1–3).

It will only take one angel, at God's direction, to imprison Satan—think about it...*just one angel!* Why should that encourage you? Because the Bible clearly states that every believer has at least *two angels* as their security escort at all times.

> *For He [God Almighty] shall give His angels [more than one] charge over you, to keep you [defend] in all your ways. In their hands they shall bear you up, lest you dash your foot against a stone. You shall tread upon the lion and the cobra, the young lion and the serpent you shall trample underfoot* (Psalm 91:11–13).

God Almighty gives His angels charge over you! They are created to protect you, defend you, and minister to you. We serve an awesome heavenly Father! When the serpent comes to torment you with doubt, strife, disease, and hardship, imagine him chained in the bottomless pit so deep that he cannot see the Light that imprisoned him for one thousand years.

THE JEWISH ELECT

As soon as Jesus Christ sets His foot on the Mount of Olives, He is going to gather His chosen ones from all over the earth. *"And He will send His angels with a great sound of a trumpet, and they will gather together His elect from the four winds, from one end of heaven to the other"* (Matthew 24:31).

Who are *"His elect"*? They are the Torah-believing Jews of the world.

The Jewish people do not recognize Jesus as Messiah because, according to the teachings of Paul in Romans, chapters 9 through 11, they have been judicially blinded by the hand of God to the identity of Jesus as Messiah. God intentionally blinded them in order for the Gentiles (non-Jews) to have their day of salvation (Romans 11:25).

Those who teach that the Church has replaced the Jewish people in God's eternal plan are promoting a false doctrine. Listen to Paul: *"I say then, has God cast away His people [Jewish people]? Certainly not! For I also am an Israelite, of the seed of Abraham, of the tribe of Benjamin"* (Romans 11:1).

Paul's logic is clear. He classifies himself as completely Jewish with a threefold certification. He continues his argument, stating that if God is still using him, then He will not cast aside the rest of the Jewish people.

As a side note, when Jesus returns to earth, He will be introduced as the Lion of Judah. *Judah* is the root word from which we get the word *Jew*. Jesus was born a Jew from the tribe of Judah. He ministered as a rabbi from Nazareth. When Jesus comes to earth a second time, He remains a Jew and He will identify Himself with His Jewish brethren. The Jewish people have not been replaced by anyone, and they will be front and center in the millennial reign. Saint Paul succinctly presented the evidence:

What then? Israel has not obtained what it seeks; but the elect [like Paul] have obtained it, and the rest [Jewish people] were hardened (blinded). Just as it is written: "God has given them a spirit of stupor, Eyes that they should not see, And ears that they should not hear, To this very day."...For I do not desire, brethren, that you should be ignorant of this mystery [judicial blindness of the Jews concerning Christ's true identity], lest you be wise in your own opinion, that hardening in part [of the Messiah] has happened to Israel until the fullness of the Gentiles has come in (Romans 11:7–8, 25).

The blindness of Israel is a judicial act by the hand of God. The phrase *"has happened to"* occurs in the active voice as an act that ensued from outside the Jewish people's own effort or control. Their blindness or "inability to see" is restricted only to the aspects of the death, burial, and resurrection of Jesus Christ. Again, the purpose of this judicial blinding is so that salvation could come to the Gentiles.

Romans 11:28 reads, *"Concerning the gospel they are enemies for your sake, but concerning the election [the Jewish people] they are beloved [of God Almighty] for the sake of the fathers."* The "enemies" refer to the Pharisees, appointed by Rome, who were persecuting Christians in Paul's day, and the "fathers" are Abraham, Isaac and Jacob.

Paul warns Gentile Christians who brag of their relationship with God the Father outside of their Jewish roots: *"Do not boast against the branches [Jewish people]. But if you [Gentiles] do boast, remember that you do not support the root [Abraham, Isaac, and Jacob], but the root supports you"* (Romans 11:18).

I have stated repeatedly and state it again—Judaism does not need Christianity to explain its existence, but Christianity cannot explain its existence without Judaism. It will be the "elect," the righteous observant Jewish person of Matthew 24:31, who will recognize Jesus as Messiah when He returns (Zechariah 12:10–14).

MESSIAH'S REIGN

The *Millennium* literally refers to the era of one thousand years when Christ begins His kingship on earth shortly after His victory at Armageddon. During this time, Satan will be locked in the abyss, and there is no earthly theocratic kingdom aside from Christ's—it will be a golden age like no other in history.

Why will this era arise? The millennial reign exists solely on Christ and the fulfillment of His Word:

How can the curse be repealed; how can death be overcome; how can all the fearful evils pertaining to man and nature be removed; how can the unspeakably great blessings be obtained: all of which are to be realized in this Kingdom under Messiah's reign.[2]

The prophets Isaiah, Jeremiah, and Ezekiel recorded the words of the Lord concerning His triumphant return and His joyous reign!

Now it shall come to pass in the latter days that the mountain of the LORD's house shall be established on the top of the mountains, and shall be exalted above the hills; and all nations shall flow to it. . . .He shall judge between the nations, and rebuke many people; they shall beat their swords into plowshares, and their spears into pruning hooks; nation shall not lift up sword against nation, neither shall they learn war anymore (Isaiah 2:2, 4).

"Behold, the days are coming," says the LORD, "that I will perform that good thing which I have promised to the house of Israel and to the house of Judah: 'In those days and at that time I will cause to grow up to David a Branch of righteousness; He shall execute judgment and righteousness in the earth. In those days Judah will be saved, and Jerusalem will dwell safely. And this is the name by which she will be called: THE LORD OUR RIGHTEOUSNESS'" (Jeremiah 33:14–16).

Then they shall dwell in the land that I have given to Jacob My servant, where your fathers dwelt; and they shall dwell there, they, their children, and their children's children, forever; and My servant David shall be their prince forever. Moreover I will make a covenant of peace with them, and it shall be an ever-lasting covenant with them; I will establish them and multiply them, and I will set My sanctuary in their midst forevermore. My tabernacle also shall be with them; indeed I will be their God, and they shall be My people. The nations also will know that I, the LORD, sanctify Israel, when My sanctuary is in their midst forevermore (Ezekiel 37:25–28).

THE GOVERNMENT OF
THE MILLENNIAL KINGDOM

The millennial kingdom will be a theocracy, as it was in the days before the reign of King Saul, when Israel was under the direct government rule of God Himself (1 Samuel 9:16–17; 10:1). In the millennium, Christ is King of kings over the entire earth (Psalm 72:8).

The prophet Isaiah declared, *"For unto us a Child is born, unto us a Son is given; and the government will be upon His shoulder. And His name will be called Wonderful, Counselor, Mighty God, Everlasting Father, Prince of Peace"* (9:6).

The promise of an Eternal Kingdom was spoken to Mary by the angel Gabriel:

Then the angel said to her, "Do not be afraid, Mary, for you have found favor with God. And behold, you will conceive in your womb and bring forth a Son, and shall call His name JESUS. He will be great, and will be called the Son of the Highest; and the Lord God will give Him the throne of His father David. And He will reign over the house of Jacob forever, and of His kingdom there will be no end" (Luke 1:30–33).

Christ alone will rule with the Word of God and a rod of iron:

Now out of His mouth goes a sharp sword, that with it He should strike the nations. And He Himself will rule them with a rod of iron. He Himself treads the winepress of the fierceness and wrath of Almighty God (Revelation 19:15).

THE SIZE OF
THE ROYAL LAND GRANT

The Lord God of Israel holds the original title deed of the Promised Land, and He transferred the ownership to Abraham, Isaac, and Jacob and their descendants forever. Then God recorded the transfer of ownership in the Holy Scriptures to be witnessed by the world.

God made two promises to Abraham concerning the nation of Israel:

1. The promise of becoming a great nation (Genesis 12:1–3; 13:16; 15:5; 17:7; 22:17–18).
2. The promise that the land of Israel was an everlasting inheritance (Genesis 12:7; 13:14–17; 15:18–21).

The Royal Land Grant given by God to Abraham and his descendants extended from the *"river of Egypt [Nile] to the great river, the River Euphrates"* (Genesis 15:18), from Hamath, northeast of Damascus, to Kadesh on the south[3] (Ezekiel 48:1–29). The land promise includes all the land Israel now owns, Judea and Samaria (West Bank), Gaza, parts of Egypt, Syria, Lebanon, and Iraq (Genesis 15:18–21). The Covenant Land promised to the Jewish people is literal and unconditional and will be fulfilled in the millennial reign.

The Palestinian claim to Israel is without merit. Those who call themselves Palestinians today are actually descendants of Arabs who lived in the land referred to as Palestine. But where did the name *Palestine* originate? It is derived from the Egyptian/Hebrew word *peleshet*, or "wanderers."[4]

The Egyptians used this term in a derogatory reference against the Hebrew children who came to live in their country during the great famine of Joseph's time. The Egyptians feared Abraham's people as they grew into a great multitude, so they enslaved and persecuted them (Exodus 1:7–11). Once again, the demonic spirit of anti-Semitism reared its ugly head, but the God of Abraham, Isaac, and Jacob used Moses to lead them out of Egyptian bondage and back into the Promised Land.

Later, a quasi-form of the word *Palestine* appeared in the fifth century BCE when the Greek historian Herodotus called the area *Palaistin*.[5] In the second century CE, the Romans quashed the revolt of Shimon Bar Kokhba and as a result created a new Roman province from the merger of Roman Syria and Roman Judaea. In an attempt to sever any Jewish ties with the land of Israel, the Romans, under Emperor Hadrian, renamed the area *Palaestina*.[6]

Centuries later under the Ottoman Empire, the territory south of Syria was *unofficially* designated as Palestine until 1914. After World War I, during the British Mandate (1920–1948), the same territory was *officially* labeled by the British as Palestine and included present-day Israel and present-day Jordan. Incidentally, the international press only labeled *Jews* as Palestinians and not Arabs before Israel's independence in 1948.[7]

Prior to 1948, the British government established the Royal Commission of Inquiry (1936) under the leadership of Lord Robert Peel to investigate the causes of unrest among Arabs and Jews. The findings of the Peel Commission also substantiate the Jewish claim to the Covenant Land of Israel:

The Jewish nation was presented as the only nation linked to the land by a historical presence and religious connections. The Commission argued that it was only in the land of Palestine that the Jewish people could achieve political freedom. The Report notes that the Jewish people are indigenous to the Land of Israel/Palestine because of their historical presence in the land. For example, the Commission described in detail the flourishing and influential Jewish community in Safed in the Sixteenth Century.[8]

The Palestinian refugee debate began shortly after the Arab-Israeli war of 1948, when five Arab armies invaded Israel just hours after President Truman recognized it as a state. At the direction of their Arab leaders, over 750,000 Palestinian Arabs fled their homes to avoid the war. Israel's adversaries gave them assurance of returning once their armies defeated the new Jewish state.

Instead, the Lord God of Israel intervened on behalf of His people and miraculously delivered them from their enemies. The Palestinian claim to any part of the land of Israel is nothing more than political propaganda, which is what the Jewish people have had to contend with for centuries. The concept that the Palestinians ever owned the land of Israel is one of the great frauds of history.

The covenant God made with King David gave him a royal dynasty that would continuously rule over an eternal kingdom.

And your house and your kingdom shall be established forever before you. Your throne shall be established forever (2 Samuel 7:16).

When Jesus Christ, the Son of David, sits on His throne on the Temple Mount in Jerusalem during the millennial reign…this covenant will be fulfilled. Our God is *the Great Promise Keeper!*

JERUSALEM:
THE HOLY CITY OF THE FUTURE

Jerusalem is so much more than the eternal capital of the State of Israel. The Scriptures are filled with descriptions and stories that reflect why it holds such a special place in God's heart and why millions from around the world seek refuge behind its gates:

- Jerusalem is where Abraham placed his son Isaac on the altar on Mount Moriah (Temple Mount) (Genesis 22:2, 9).
- Jerusalem is where King David conquered the city from the Jebusites (1 Chronicles 11:4).
- Jerusalem is where God has placed His Name (2 Chronicles 6:6).
- Jerusalem is where the angel of the Lord destroyed Sennacherib and his army of 185,000 when they threatened to destroy the Holy City (2 Kings 19:35).
- Jerusalem is the City of God (Psalms 48:1–2, 8).
- Jerusalem is the city from which living waters will flow (Zechariah 14:8).
- Jerusalem is where Jesus was crucified for the sins of the world (Luke 23:33; 24).
- Jerusalem is where Christ rose from the dead (Matthew 28:6).
- Jerusalem will be the seat of government for the world, from the millennial reign into eternity (Revelation 20:4).

THE COMING TEMPLE

The Third Temple will be rebuilt per the specifications found in Ezekiel chapters 40 through 44. Then, after the return of Messiah at the start of the Millennium, the Aaronic priesthood is reestablished and the sons of Zadok will officiate and offer sacrifices once more.

"But the priests, the Levites, the sons of Zadok, who kept charge of My sanctuary when the children of Israel went astray from Me, they shall come near Me to minister to Me; and they shall stand before Me to offer to Me the fat and the blood," says the Lord GOD. "They shall enter My sanctuary, and they shall come near My table to minister to Me, and they shall keep My charge" (Ezekiel 44:15–16).

THE MILLENNIAL BLESSINGS AND FEASTS

Scripture describes this thousand-year period as one like no other since the Garden of Eden. It will be a time when the land of Israel will be fully restored (Joel 3:18), man and nature will live together in peace (Isaiah 11:6–9), and humanity will once again live long, healthy lives (Zechariah 8:4; Ezekiel 47:12). It will be a time of blessings for all.

Moreover, great blessings will be afforded to the Jewish people during the millennial reign. After centuries of abuse, ridicule, and hatred, they will be celebrated and sought after. God's love and favor for His Chosen will finally be recognized by all the nations on earth:

Yes, many peoples and strong nations shall come to seek the LORD of hosts in Jerusalem, and to pray before the Lord....In

those days ten men from every language of the nations shall grasp
the sleeve of a Jewish man, saying, "Let us go with you, for we
have heard that God is with you" (Zechariah 8:22–23).

The teachings of the God of Abraham, Isaac, and Jacob will be a
major theme during this time of peace:

"'…to the house of the God of Jacob [the Jewish people]; He
will teach us His ways, and we shall walk in His paths.' For out
of Zion the law shall go forth, and the word of the LORD *from*
Jerusalem" (Micah 4:2).

Gentile believers will *"grasp the sleeve"* of the Jewish people and
ask about the foundations of the *true faith*. What is the true faith?

It is what Christianity was meant to be devoid of Babylonian
paganism, which is still very much a part of modern-day Christianity.
True faith is the pure precepts of Judaism, as revealed to Moses by
God on Mount Sinai, enriched by God's grace and unmerited favor
through the death and resurrection of Jesus Christ, His only begotten Son.

What is meant by the phrase "grasp the sleeve"? The word *sleeve*
refers to the Hebrew word *tallith*, or "prayer shawl." What is a prayer
shawl? It is a fringed garment worn by Jews to specifically fulfill biblical precepts. The prayer shawl is an outward symbol of an observant Jew's devotion to the God of Abraham, Isaac, and Jacob.

Jesus wore a prayer shawl the entirety of His adult life—while
He taught His followers, healed the sick, gave sight to the blind,
and raised Lazarus from the dead. Jesus was buried with His prayer
shawl. After His resurrection, it was found neatly folded in the
place where His body had been laid (John 20:7). Christ will return

wearing a prayer shawl, as He is the fulfillment of the law (Numbers 15:38–40; Matthew 5:17).

The Feast of Passover (Exodus 12:1–14) and the Feast of Tabernacles (Zechariah 14:16) will be observed during the millennial reign. The majority of Gentile believers are ignorant of the importance of the feasts and will seek out their Jewish brethren for instruction and interpretation of these *appointed times*.

The word *feast* in Hebrew means "a set or appointed time." The feasts are like a dress rehearsal of things to come. The combined seven feasts, divinely instituted shortly after the Israelites were delivered from Egypt's bondage, will be a spiritual blueprint of what lies ahead for Israel, Jerusalem, and the rest of the world—they paint a portrait of God's prophetic plan.

Remember this truth: Everything God will do, He has already done. Gentile believers will need a teacher, and the Jewish people will be delighted to share the Jewish roots of Christianity as found in God's Word.

SATAN LOOSED

As the curtain of time on the glorious millennial reign of Jesus Christ draws to a close, the angel who put Satan in the *"bottomless pit"* (Revelation 20:1–3) will turn him loose to deceive the nations of the world.

> *Now when the thousand years have expired, Satan will be released from his prison and will go out to deceive the nations which are in the four corners of the earth* (Revelation 20:7–8).

After one thousand years without stress, worry, or wars, why would God allow this monster to be released upon the earth once again? There can only be one answer. Despite all God has the ability to do, He will never force someone to believe in Him. All mankind is given free will. The Word reminds us that it is required of every person to *"choose for yourselves this day whom you will serve"* (Joshua 24:15).

God releases Satan from the bottomless pit so that those who have not had the opportunity to exercise their free will of choosing between good or evil will do so. The millions who have been born during this time still have the same sinful Adamic nature as all who were born before, as the late J. Vernon McGee perfectly described:

> The human heart alone remains unchanged under these circumstances and many will turn their backs on God and will go after Satan....This rebellion following the Millennium reveals how terrible the heart of man is....We just cannot bring our old nature into subjection to God.[9]

When Satan is loosed from his prison, people from all nations of the earth will believe his lies and follow him back to the gates of hell. It seems impossible to fathom that after a thousand years of glorious peaceful living, many will choose to turn their backs on God Almighty and heed Satan instead, but it will happen. So great is the sinful nature of man that even in the clear triumph of the Gospel, Satan leads many into blatant rebellion.

Who can understand what drives men to sin? For those who are living in earthly bodies, even as we are now, the law of sin is like the law of gravity. No matter how much we want to rise above it, it draws us down. Romans 8:7 says, *"The carnal mind is enmity against God; for it is not subject to the law of God, nor indeed can be."* It is only through the power of Christ that we can ascend above iniquity.

Since sin will still have a foothold in mankind, it must be eradicated. It is at the end of the thousand-year reign of Christ when the final conflict between God and Satan will take place. Unfortunately, just as men failed in previous ages, mankind will fail during this period as well. Though most will obey Christ, many will rebel against Him, under Satan's leadership.

Remember that the millennial reign of Christ will be a time similar to the Garden of Eden. And just as Adam and Eve, who were placed in a perfect environment created by God Almighty, chose to sin, so will mankind choose the same during Christ's reign. Even under ideal circumstances—an abundant earth, no sickness, and no war—the human heart will prove that it remains unchanged unless regenerated by the power of Christ. Sadly, many will reject the God who has sustained them and follow the evil one.[10]

Notice that the book of Revelation mentions Gog and Magog in the verses describing the final conflict, but this is not part of the same Gog and Magog Wars described in Ezekiel 38–39. J. Vernon McGee believed that "the rebellion of the godless forces from the north will have made such an impression on mankind that after one thousand years, the last rebellion of man bears the same label—Gog and Magog." Just as we have called two conflicts World War I and World War II, the people of that time could call this last battle Gog and Magog II.[11]

When the glorious millennial reign has ended, Satan will gather the largest army ever assembled to war against Jesus Christ and the Jewish nation. These rebellious armies will advance against Jerusalem, where Jesus rules and reigns from the Temple Mount.

Now when the thousand years have expired, Satan will be released from his prison and will go out to deceive the nations which are in the four corners of the earth, Gog and Magog, to gather them together to battle, whose number is as the sand of the sea. They went up on the breadth of the earth and surrounded the camp of the saints and the beloved city (Revelation 20:7–9).

There they will learn that rebellion against God always ends in destruction. To purge creation of the evil effects of sin finally and forever, the Almighty will destroy the earth with great heat and fire. This final conflict will end swiftly and victoriously, because the Great I AM is ready to destroy Satan and his hordes forevermore! Saint Peter described this complete obliteration of the earth: *"The heavens will pass away with a great noise, and the elements will melt with fervent heat; both the earth and the works that are in it will be burned up"* (2 Peter 3:10).

God Almighty will consume all the people who fought against Jerusalem. However, what about Satan?

And fire came down from God out of heaven and devoured [annihilated] them. The devil [Satan], who deceived them, was cast into the lake of fire and brimstone where the beast [Antichrist] and the false prophet are. And they will be tormented day and night forever and ever (Revelation 20:9–10).

The statement *"…tormented day and night forever and ever"* clearly establishes the fact that there is no end to eternity. At this time, the Antichrist and the False Prophet are still in the lake of fire, in constant anguish. This eternal inferno was prepared specifically for Satan and his fallen angels (Matthew 25:41), not to consume them, but to punish them forever.

The Enemy—the one who has tempted, tested, and tormented

Jews and Christians through the ages—will be permanently bound. But today he still roams the earth, seeking to rob, kill, and destroy.

At the end of the Millennium, those who chose to side with Satan will be destroyed. God will bring an end to rebellion, and all who participated, alive or dead, will face judgment and be confined to eternal hell and torment. The Almighty will then create a new heaven and a new earth that will last for all eternity.[12]

THE GREAT WHITE THRONE JUDGMENT

The final rebellion of Satan prepares the way for the Great White Throne Judgment. The theme of this judgment is the eternal destiny of those who were not part of the Rapture. Those appearing before this judgment are coming to be officially sentenced to everlasting punishment.

Clarence Larkin describes those who will participate:

The Church is not in this judgment, nor is Israel, for both have been already judged.…This [judgment] is after the Millennium when Christ shall sit on the Great White Throne.…In this judgment, "Death" and "Hell" are personified. By "Death," we are to understand the "Grave," which holds the "body" until the resurrection. By Hell the compartment of the underworld or Hades where the souls of the wicked dead remain until the resurrection of the wicked. That both Death and Hell are cast into the lake of fire signifies that Death and Sin will not be found on the New Earth.[13]

There are two resurrections—the resurrection of the just and that of the unjust:

"I have hope in God, which they themselves also accept, that there will be a resurrection of the dead, both of the just and the unjust" (Acts 24:15).

In John 5:27–29, Jesus Christ says that the Father

has given Him [Christ] authority to execute judgment also, because He is the Son of Man. Do not marvel at this; for the hour is coming in which all who are in the graves will hear His voice and come forth—those who have done good, to the resurrection of life, and those who have done evil, to the resurrection of condemnation.

The resurrection of the just takes place in three phases. The first phase was at Calvary when men came out of their graves and were seen in the city of Jerusalem. The second phase will be the Rapture of the church, when the dead in Christ shall rise first. The third phase will occur at the end of the Tribulation, when martyred saints are taken into heaven (Daniel 12:2; Revelation 20:4). All men, both righteous and unrighteous, will experience a resurrection day.

After the resurrection of the unjust, John describes the throne where their sentencing takes place:

Then I saw a great white throne and Him who sat on it, from whose face the earth and the heaven fled away. And there was found no place for them. And I saw the dead, small and great, standing before God, and books were opened. And another book was opened, which is the Book of Life. And the dead were judged according to their works, by the things which were written in the books. The sea gave up the dead who were in it, and Death and Hades delivered up the dead who were in them. And they were judged, each one according to his works. Then Death and Hades were cast into the lake of fire. This is the second death (Revelation 20:11–14).

Notice that God has two sets of books, for the Apostle John says, *"books were opened."* There is the Book of Life, which contains the name of every person who accepted Jesus Christ while they were on the earth. When the wicked dead approach the Great White Throne Judgment, God will first look for their names in the Book of Life, and obviously, they will not be found.

Then He will open the "books" that are His written records of every word, thought, and deed of the wicked.[14] John describes what happens next: *"And anyone not found written in the Book of Life was cast into the lake of fire"* (Revelation 20:15).

Either your name is in the Book of Life or it is not. You can receive Christ in this life, or you can choose to follow Him in the Tribulation at the cost of having your head cut off by the Antichrist. It is *your* choice.

If you choose to do neither, you will be made to account for every word, thought, and deed of your life as you stand at the Great White Throne Judgment. Following this judgment, you will be formally sentenced to spend eternity in the lake of fire.

It is *your* choice. I want to be perfectly clear—this is not a future fable I am describing—this is fact. Every one of us is going to spend eternity somewhere: either with God, the Son, and the Holy Spirit in the New Jerusalem, or in the lake of fire with Satan, the Antichrist, and the False Prophet. But until this time comes, the Great Deceiver is still seeking whom he will devour.

Imagine Satan in the lake of fire, cursing the glory of God and mocking those he has fooled to follow him. His only reward is the damned souls that will share in the torment of his eternal home. His only regret will be he did not win the Final Game of Thrones.

SATAN'S FINAL SONG

Long ago, I planned in my embodied pride,
That today I would reign as king.
But where is my kingdom, where is my crown?
Is the bitter song I sing.

What bliss have I won through my evil designs?
What pleasure in my soul-wrecking plan?
I hoped to conquer both Heaven and Earth,
But have won nothing more than man.

Where are my princes, my legions of imps,
And the millions of souls I have won?
My chains and my torment are greater by far,
Because of the evil I've done.

Come on, all you dupes, you millions of men,
Who heeded my wishes like fools;
Take your share of the vexing chains,
Under Him who in Triumph rules.

You have lived and died for my wretched cause,
Your souls are eternally marred;
You shall see no more than glimpses of the Light of Heaven,
from which you are barred.

Then cast your despair, my friends, to the winds,
As the echo of silence replies,
You will feel henceforth the deeper degrees,
Of the Hell within which we lie.

—Author Unknown[15]

I pray you will choose the path to redemption that will lead you to the Eternal Throne of the Living God and not be one of the many who will follow Satan into eternal damnation.

As the millennial reign comes to an end, God will create His new heaven and His new earth:

But the heavens and the earth which now exist are kept in store by the same word, reserved for fire until the day of judgment and perdition [destruction] of ungodly men....But the day of the Lord [judgment] will come as a thief in the night, in which the heavens will pass away with a great noise, and the elements will melt with fervent heat; both the earth and the works that are in it will be burned up (2 Peter 3:7, 10).

Once this purification by fire has been completed, the New Jerusalem will descend from the Third Heaven, and God the Father will set up His Eternal Throne and establish the Final Kingdom.

CHAPTER 16

THE FINAL THRONE

And there shall be no more curse, but the throne of God and
of the Lamb shall be in it, and His servants shall serve Him.
(Revelation 22:3)

We live in an information age, yet I believe we are one of the most uninformed generations in the history of humanity when it comes to the knowledge of the truth. We listen to "fake news," we refuse to read books, and we allow historical revisionists to hijack the foundational truths of our nation's birth.

Reality TV has made voyeurism a family pastime. We watch You-Tube tirades and consider Facebook the Holy Grail, yet we don't know how to communicate with our loved ones across the dinner table.

Scientists can split the atom, create deadly chemical and biological weapons, and build nuclear missiles of war in an effort to secure world power. We know how to use complicated electronic gadgetry, children can fly a plane via virtual video games, we can go to the moon and back, and radical terrorists can create deadly bombs with internet blueprints.

Yet all this high-tech information is a recipe for disaster if we refuse to recognize the veracity of God's Word: *"The entirety of Your word is truth, and every one of Your righteous judgments endures forever"* (Psalms 119:160).

If you do not believe Genesis 1:1, then you will not believe the balance of God's Word. However, if you *do* believe God's Word, then you can look at the past, the present, and into the future with absolute confidence and certainty.

THE AGES OF AGES

Prophecy scholar Clarence Larkin refers to the "Creative Ages" of Genesis as the "Alpha Ages" and the "End of the Ages" of Revelation as the "Omega Ages." When time as we know it ceases, the "Eternal Ages," or the "Ages of the Ages," will begin.

This is what the apostle Paul called the *"ages to come"* in his letter to the Ephesians (2:7). John, in the book of Revelation, said that Satan, the Beast, and the False Prophet shall be tormented day and night forever and ever (Revelation 20:10), or through the "Ages of the Ages." During this same period, the servants of God shall reign in the new earth (Revelation 22:5).

God only knows what the "Ages of Ages" will reveal; however, believers will experience the glorious things He has planned.[1] The "Ages of Ages" will usher in the Final Throne.

THE NEW EARTH

God's purging fire will destroy man's rebellious social order for the last time. This divine cleansing will mark the end of sin's contamination of the world. The Apostle John opens his book by pulling back the veil of eternity through Christ's revelation, and he closes it by describing a *"new heaven and a new earth"*: *"I saw a new heaven and a new earth, for the first heaven and the first earth had passed away. Also there was no more sea"* (Revelation 21:1).

The seas that were created in Genesis 1:2 will be put back into heaven and in the center of the earth, where they originated. The earth will be "renewed to its original state as before the fall of Lucifer and before the first rebellion of the earth against God." The world's new water source will come from rivers, lakes, and small seas.[2]

His dominion shall be "from sea to sea, and from the River to the ends of the earth" (Zechariah 9:10).

And in that day it shall be that living waters shall flow from Jerusalem, half of them toward the eastern sea [Dead Sea] and half of them toward the western sea [Mediterranean]; in both summer and winter it shall occur (Zechariah 14:8).

And he showed me a pure river of water of life, clear as crystal, proceeding from the throne of God and of the Lamb (Revelation 22:1).

The new earth will have everything you will ever need. However, there are things you will not find there:

- No tears: *"And God will wipe away every tear from their eyes"* (Revelation 21:4).
- No death: *"there shall be no more death"* (21:4).
- No mourning: *"nor sorrow, nor crying"* (21:4).
- No pain: *"no more pain, for the former things have passed away"* (21:4).
- No curse: *"there shall be no more curse,"* forever conquered through the cross of Christ (22:3).

- No night: *"for the Lord God gives them light"* (22:5).
- No sin: *"anything that defiles, or causes an abomination or a lie"* (21:27).

God has also eradicated all evil: *"But the cowardly, unbelieving, abominable, murderers, sexually immoral, sorcerers, idolaters, and all liars shall have their part in the lake which burns with fire and brimstone, which is the second death"* (Revelation 21:8).

THE NEW JERUSALEM

The pinnacle of God's eternal plan for mankind is a new heaven and a new earth. The old has passed away. Sin and decay are no more. God promises *"he who overcomes,"* an inheritance in an eternal paradise with Christ Jesus (Revelation 21:7).

We will live forever in the Final Kingdom, worshipping God Almighty as He sits on His Eternal Throne in the new city of Jerusalem. The New Jerusalem will be a city of celestial origin. It is the city Jesus told His followers He is preparing for them in heaven (John 14:2).

For me, this is one of the most exciting descriptions in the book of Revelation. I can imagine it in the theater of my mind—the heavens opening, and this perfect, foursquare city in all its glory descending onto the new earth. It will be established in the center of the Promised Land. What a remarkable sight!

The New Jerusalem will have many unique traits, for John the Revelator takes the time to describe its appearance, its foundations, the buildings, its location, its measurements, its materials, and its rulers. One of the most important truths about this beautiful city is that God the Father, Jesus Christ the Son, and the Holy Spirit will dwell there (Revelation 21:22; 22:17).

Seven Characteristics of the New Jerusalem

1. It will be known by many names, among them are:
   - The Holy City (Isaiah 52:1; Revelation 21:2).
   - The tabernacle of God (Psalm 46:4; Revelation 21:3).
   - The city of the living God (Hebrews 12:22).
   - My Father's house (John 14:2).
2. God is the Architect, the Builder, and the Owner (Revelation 21).
3. The glory of God and the light of the Lamb will illuminate it (v. 23).
4. It will be made of gold and precious stones (vv. 18–21).
5. It will have walls and foundations (vv. 12–14).
6. It will have twelve gates of solid pearl and twelve streets made of pure, transparent glass-like gold (v. 21).
7. There will be no temple there, *"for the Lord God Almighty and the Lamb are its temple"* (v. 22).

New Tree of Life

The original Tree of Life was in the midst of the Garden of Eden (Genesis 2:9). The new earth will have a new Tree of Life, whose leaves will be for the healing of the nations, preserving the lives of all who live in the Final Kingdom.

It will bear twelve variety of fruits—one for every month: *"In the middle of its street, and on either side of the river, was the tree of life, which bore twelve fruits, each tree yielding its fruit every month. The leaves of the tree were for the healing of the nations"* (Revelation 22:2).

Who Will Inhabit the New Earth?

According to John the Revelator, the inhabitants of the new earth will be angels (Revelation 21:12), the redeemed of Israel (v. 12), the Church of Jesus Christ (v. 14), and the *"nations of those who are saved"* (v. 24).

However, the most important inhabitants are the members of the Holy Trinity—God Himself, His Son, and the Holy Spirit: *"And I heard a loud voice from heaven saying, 'Behold, the tabernacle of God is with men, and He will dwell with them, and they shall be His people. God Himself will be with them and be their God'"* (Revelation 21:3).

Finis Dake says of the Trinity and the new earth, "The Father, the Son and the Holy Spirit will reign together throughout all eternity, as before the rebellion, which made it necessary for them to take separate parts in the creation and redemption of all things."[3]

The heavenly city embraces the glory of God, it contains His Final Throne, and those who dwell there shall see the face of God (Ezekiel 43:7; Revelation 21:23; 22:4). The Great I AM will dwell among His people forever, which is the final realization of the eternal plan of God for man and the earth.

Who Will Be King?

Several empires and kings have walked across the stage of history. They have conquered men and nations and taken their seat on gilded thrones. Through the centuries, thrones have been fought over and toppled, ascended to and sat upon, and the majority have passed away.

A throne symbolizes power and authority over kingdoms and empires. Subjects throughout the world have bowed, knelt, and prostrated themselves before them. To be considered an empire, an expanse of land must be led politically by a monarch, an emperor, or an oligarchy. Aside from this leadership model, the only thing these empires and rulers have in common is that they have all disappeared.

However, there is One who was, and is, and is to come. He will take His rightful place on the Final Throne in His Eternal Kingdom. There is only one throne and one King—the Almighty God, Creator of heaven and earth. The Final Throne is where God manifests His power, and great glory, and declares His absolute sovereignty. *"Your throne, O God, is forever and ever; a scepter of righteousness is the scepter of Your kingdom"* (Psalms 45:6).

God Almighty, the Great I AM, the Alpha and Omega, who sits upon His throne and is:

- Majestic: *"We have such a High Priest, who is seated at the right hand of the throne of the Majesty in the heavens"* (Hebrews 8:1).
- Perfect justice: *"Righteousness and justice are the foundations of His throne"* (Psalm 97:2).
- Holy: *"God reigns over the nations; God sits on His holy throne"* (Psalm 47:8).
- Worthy of praise: *"But You are holy, enthroned in the praises of Israel"* (Psalm 22:3).
- Pure: *"And in their mouth was found no deceit, for they are without fault before the throne of God"* (Revelation 14:5).
- Grace: *"Let us therefore come boldly to the throne of grace, that we may obtain mercy and find grace to help in time of need"* (Hebrews 4:16).

My dear friend Derek Prince described one of the most splendid scenes that will surround the Throne of the Living God. It is the praise of His people:

What a beautiful revelation that is—when we realize that the throne God sits upon is the praises of His people. God is Holy. God is a King. He's the King of kings and Lord of lords. We do not make Him a King by praising Him, but we offer Him the throne, which is His due.

You see, Jesus said: "When two or three are gathered together in My name, there am I in the midst." His presence in our midst is guaranteed. It depends upon His faithfulness, not our response. But when He comes in our midst—as the King of kings and the Lord of lords—it's very right and appropriate that we respond to Him as a King.

As a King, He merits a throne; nothing else becomes Him. And it is our privilege to offer Him the throne. When we praise Him, when we exalt Him, when we sing praises and glorify His Name and extol His majesty, then we are acknowledging His Kingship and we are responding in a way that is appropriate. We are offering Him a throne to sit upon—the throne of our praises.[4]

One day all creation will bow to the majesty of God's throne (Philippians 2:9–11). The regal beings surrounding the throne will lay their crowns before God and say, *"You are worthy, O Lord, to receive glory and honor and power"* (Revelation 4:11).

The Bible presents a perfect and complete circle. Everything that God created in the Garden of Eden, after several thousand years of blood, tears, and suffering, has returned to be an exact replica of paradise—what God intended all along. We will live in a realm where there will be no more death, nor sorrow, nor suffering. There will be no pain, for the former things have all passed away. *Will you be there?*

One of the greatest preachers and soul winners of all time was a prince of the Gospel named Charles Haddon Spurgeon. Over a century ago, he presented a sermon at Metropolitan Tabernacle on the throne of God. The following is the call to salvation he offered the hearer. I could think of no better way to end this book than to afford you, the reader, the same opportunity.

> We do not suppose that a man is shooting at a target if he does not look that way; nor can we imagine that a man's ambition is fixed on heaven if he has no heavenward thoughts or aspirations. The pilgrim turns his steps towards the place he is desirous to reach....Till the day breaks and the shadows flee away, let us wait for the Bridegroom's appearing, and the home-bringing of the bride.
>
> As virgins that look forward to the marriage day let us keep our lamps trimmed, and see to it that there is oil in our vessels, lest when the cry is heard, "The Bridegroom cometh" any of us should need to nurse the dimly-burning spark, or despairingly cry, "Our lamps are gone out." Let us all be ready that we may go in through the gates into the city.
>
> Some of you, alas! are not able to feel the joy which this subject excites in our breasts. You cannot take delight in the throne of God and of the Lamb. God grant you may. Come, now, to the throne of grace with open confession and secret contrition.
>
> It is the throne of God, who knows the nature of your sin; it is the throne of the Lamb, who bore the penalty of sin, and can put it away. Come to the throne of the Lamb that was slain. I entreat you to come now. So shall you find peace and reconciliation, and you shall be made meet to enter into the joy of your Lord.[57]

If you are presently experiencing a time of tears, a time of suffering and sorrow, there is hope for your troubled heart. Remember: We are moving ever closer toward the perfection that God has created for the righteous. The King of kings is preparing for the appointed time when He will set up earth's Last Empire—on the new earth, in the New Jerusalem, reigning forevermore on His Final Throne.

"Surely I am coming quickly." Amen. Even so, come, Lord Jesus! (Revelation 22:20)

THE ETERNAL THRONE

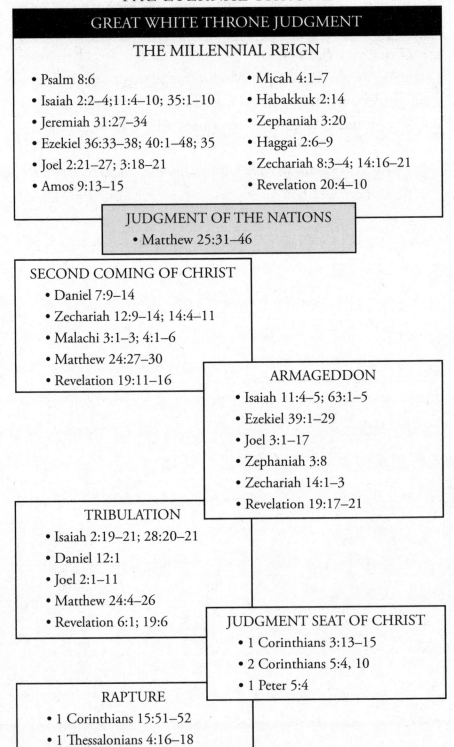

GREAT WHITE THRONE JUDGMENT

THE MILLENNIAL REIGN

- Psalm 8:6
- Isaiah 2:2–4;11:4–10; 35:1–10
- Jeremiah 31:27–34
- Ezekiel 36:33–38; 40:1–48; 35
- Joel 2:21–27; 3:18–21
- Amos 9:13–15

- Micah 4:1–7
- Habakkuk 2:14
- Zephaniah 3:20
- Haggai 2:6–9
- Zechariah 8:3–4; 14:16–21
- Revelation 20:4–10

JUDGMENT OF THE NATIONS
- Matthew 25:31–46

SECOND COMING OF CHRIST
- Daniel 7:9–14
- Zechariah 12:9–14; 14:4–11
- Malachi 3:1–3; 4:1–6
- Matthew 24:27–30
- Revelation 19:11–16

ARMAGEDDON
- Isaiah 11:4–5; 63:1–5
- Ezekiel 39:1–29
- Joel 3:1–17
- Zephaniah 3:8
- Zechariah 14:1–3
- Revelation 19:17–21

TRIBULATION
- Isaiah 2:19–21; 28:20–21
- Daniel 12:1
- Joel 2:1–11
- Matthew 24:4–26
- Revelation 6:1; 19:6

JUDGMENT SEAT OF CHRIST
- 1 Corinthians 3:13–15
- 2 Corinthians 5:4, 10
- 1 Peter 5:4

RAPTURE
- 1 Corinthians 15:51–52
- 1 Thessalonians 4:16–18

EARTH'S
LAST EMPIRE

NOTES

SECTION ONE: ALL ROADS LEAD TO JERUSALEM

My Jerusalem

1   Yehuda Amichai, "Jerusalem, 1967," in *The Poetry of Yehuda Amichai*, ed. Robert Alter (New York: Farrar, Straus and Giroux, 2015), 88.

Chapter 1

1   Simon Sebag Montefiore, *Jerusalem: The Biography* (New York: Alfred A. Knopf, 2011), xix.

2   Rabbi Jill Jacobs, in an article for the website My Jewish Learning, explains, "While we speak often of 'the Midrash,' there is no single book with this title, but only a series of compilations composed and edited over the course of more than a millennium. These works are generally categorized as either *halachic* (legal) or *aggadic* (narrative)....One of the works that best exemplifies this intermingling of legal and narrative material is Midrash Tanhuma, a collection of stories, discussions of specific laws, and rabbinic homilies, all connected with the five books of the Torah and named for Rabbi Tanhuma, the first character to appear in the collection." Adapted from Jill Jacobs, "Midrash Tanhuma," My Jewish Learning, accessed June 16, 2018, https://www.myjewishlearning .com/article/midrash-tanhuma/.

3   Midrash Tanhuma, Kedoshim 10.

4   Teddy Kollek, *Jerusalem: Policy Papers 22* (Washington, DC: Washington Institute for Near East Policy, 1990), 19–20.

5   Eric H. Cline, *Jerusalem Besieged: From Ancient Canaan to Modern Israel* (Ann Arbor: University of Michigan Press, 2004), 311.

6   Israel Ministry of Foreign Affairs, "Jerusalem 3000: When Did King David Conquer Jerusalem?" MFA Archive, June 2, 1993, http://www.israel.org/MFA/MFA-Archive /1993/Pages/JERUSALEM%203000-%20When%20did%20King%20David %20conquer%20Jerusa.aspx.

7   William G. Dever, *Who Were the Early Israelites and Where Did They Come From?* (Grand Rapids, MI: Eerdmans, 2003).

8   Israel Ministry of Foreign Affairs, "Israel's War of Independence (1947–1949)," About Israel: History, accessed June 16, 2018, http://mfa.gov.il/MFA/AboutIsrael/History /Pages/Israels%20War%20of%20Independence%20-%201947%20-%201949.aspx.

9   JIMENA, "Jewish Refugees from Arab Countries: Country Profiles," Jews Indigenous to the Middle East and North Africa, http://www.jimena.org/jimena-country-by-country/.

10 Meir Loewenberg, "What Happened on the Original Yom Yerushalayim in 1967?" Behind the News in Jerusalem, http://israelbehindthenews.com/happened-original -yom-yerushalayim-1967/14682/.

11 Jewish Virtual Library, "The Six-Day War: Background and Overview/The Stunning Victory," accessed June 16, 2018, http://www.jewishvirtuallibrary.org/background-and -overview-six-day-war. (Jewish Virtual Library hereafter cited as JVL.)

12 Howard M. Sachar, *A History of Israel: From the Rise of Zionism to Our Time* (New York: Knopf, 2007), 676; CAMERA (Committee for Accuracy in Middle East Reporting in America), "Immediate Aftermath: The 3 No's of Khartoum," The Six-Day War, accessed June 18, 2018, http://www.sixdaywar.org/content/khartoum.asp.

13 UN General Assembly, Resolution 3379 (30), Elimination of All Forms of Racial Discrimination, November 10, 1975, 83–84, https://documents-dds-ny.un.org/doc /RESOLUTION/GEN/NR0/000/92/IMG/NR000092.pdf?OpenElement.

14 CNN Library, "Camp David Accords Fast Facts," CNN, last updated September 3, 2017, https://www.cnn.com/2013/08/23/world/meast/camp-david-accords-fast-facts /index.html.

15 William E. Farrell, "Sadat Assassinated at Army Parade as Men amid Ranks Fire into Stands: At Least 8 Killed," *New York Times*, October 7, 1981, https://archive.nytimes .com/www.nytimes.com/learning/general/onthisday/big/1006.html.

16 Peter Bergen, "The Cleric Who Altered the Course of Modern History," CNN, February 19, 2017, https://www.cnn.com/2017/02/19/opinions/9-11-spiritual-guide-dies-bergen/.

17 JVL, "Israel's Wars and Operations: Operation Opera—Raid on Iraqi Nuclear Reactor/ Diplomacy Fails," accessed June 18, 2018, http://www.jewishvirtuallibrary.org /operation-opera-raid-on-iraqi-nuclear-reactor.

18 Dario Leone, "Operation Opera: How 8 Israeli F-16s Destroyed an Iraqi Nuclear Plant 33 Years Ago Today," *Aviationist* (blog), June 7, 2014, https://theaviationist.com/2014 /06/07/operation-opera-explained/.

19 JVL, "First Lebanon War: Background and Overview/Burgeoning Violence," accessed June 18, 2018, http://www.jewishvirtuallibrary.org/background-and-overview-of-first -lebanon-war.

20 Henry Kissinger, "From Lebanon to the West Bank to the Gulf," *Washington Post*, June 16, 1982, accessed June 28, 2018, https://www.washingtonpost.com/archive/politics /1982/06/16/from-lebanon-to-the-west-bank-to-the-gulf/76008a90-a029-4bc3-88b9 -ece961df8a22/?utm_term=.7b8b414229c4.

21 JVL, "First Lebanon War: Israeli Civilian Casualties on the Lebanese Border," accessed June 18, 2018, http://www.jewishvirtuallibrary.org/israeli-civilian-casualties-on-the -lebanese-border-1985-1999.

22 Michael Omer-Man, "This Week in History: Operation Moses Begins, *Jerusalem Post*, November 19, 2010, www.jpost.com/Features/In-Thespotlight/This-week-in-History -Operation-Moses-begins.

23 Michael Slackman, "Some Palestinian Jordanians Lose Citizenship," *New York Times*, March 13, 2010, https://www.nytimes.com/2010/03/14/world/middleeast/14jordan .html; Hussein bin Talal, "Address to the Nation," English translation of speech delivered in Amman, Jordan, July 31, 1988, http://www.kinghussein.gov.jo/speeches_letters.html.

24 JVL, "Terrorism against Israel: Comprehensive Listing of Fatalities," accessed June 18, 2018, http://www.jewishvirtuallibrary.org/comprehensive-listing-of-terrorism-victims-in-israel.

25 Rich Valkanet, "Bible Timeline," Bible Hub, accessed June 18, 2018, Biblehub.com/timeline/.

26 Brian Whitaker, "The Mitchell Report: End the Violence Now, So That Peace Talks Can Start Again," *Guardian*, May 21, 2001, https://www.theguardian.com/world/2001/may/22/israel1.

27 Dona J. Stewart, *The Middle East Today: Political, Geographical and Cultural Perspectives* (New York: Routledge, 2009), 165.

28 Sharon Otterman, "Middle East: The Road Map to Peace," Council on Foreign Relations, February 7, 2005, www.cfr.org/backgrounder/middle-east-road-map-peace.

29 Israel Ministry of Foreign Affairs, "Declaration of the Establishment of the State of Israel," May 14, 1948, www.mfa.gov.il/mfa/foreignpolicy/peace/guide/pages/declaration%20of%20establishment%20of%20state%20of%20israel.aspx.

30 Daniel Ayalon, "In Gaza, a Test Case for Peace," *Washington Post* Opinions, July 20, 2005, http://www.washingtonpost.com/wp-dyn/content/article/2005/07/19/AR2005071901552.html.

31 Human Rights Watch, "Why They Died: Civilian Casualties in Lebanon during the 2006 War," *Human Rights Watch* 19, no. 5(E) (September 2007), www.hrw.org/reports/2007/lebanon0907/lebanon0907webwcover.pdf.

32 Aaron Klein, "Israeli Strike in Syria Eliminates Reviled Perpetrator of Attack 'So Sickening' Details 'Give Pause to Israel's Enemies,'" Breitbart, December 20, 2015, http://www.breitbart.com/jerusalem/2015/12/20/israeli-strike-in-syria-eliminates-reviled-perpetrator-of-attack-so-sickening-details-give-pause-to-israels-enemies/.

33 Dudi Cohen, "Iran Honors Murderer Samir Kuntar," Ynetnews, January 30, 2009, https://www.ynetnews.com/articles/0,7340,L-3664187,00.html.

34 Ali Hashem, "How Will Nasrallah Retaliate for Death of Hezbollah Leader in Syria?" Lebanese-Canadian Coordinating Council, December 24, 2015 (news release from Al-Monitor, December 23, 2015), http://eliasbejjaninews.com/archives/34153/ali-hashem-how-will-nasrallah-retaliate-for-death-of-hezbollah-leader-in-syria/.

35 JVL, "Operation Cast Lead: IDF Soldiers Killed," accessed June 19, 2018, http://www.jewishvirtuallibrary.org/idf-soldiers-killed-during-operation-cast-lead.

36 COGAT, "Hamas Terror Tunnels—Built with Gazans' Stolen Money," Coordination of Government Activities in the Territories, May 18, 2017, http://www.cogat.mod.gov.il/en/Our_Activities/Pages/Hamas-Terror-Tunnels-18.5.17.aspx.

37 "Israeli Humanitarian Operations: Aid to the Gaza Strip (June 2010-Present)," Jewish Virtual Library, https://www.jewishvirtuallibrary.org/israeli-humanitarian-aid-to-the-gaza-strip.

38 "Cement Intended for Gaza Reconstruction Ends Up on Black Market," *Algemeiner*, December 3, 2014, https://www.algemeiner.com/2014/12/03/cement-intended-for-gaza-reconstruction-ends-up-on-black-market/.

39 JVL, "Israel's Wars and Operations: Operation Protective Edge/Statistics," accessed June 19, 2018, http://www.jewishvirtuallibrary.org/operation-protective-edge.

40 Yaniv Kubovich and Noa Shpigel, "Israel Shoots Down Syrian Drone Infiltrating 10 Kilometers into Israeli Airspace," *Haaretz*, July 11, 2018, https://www.haaretz.com /israel-news/israel-shoots-down-drone-infiltrating-from-syria-1.6267047.

41 Michael Bachner and TOI Staff, "Hamas Said to Offer Israel Long-Term Ceasefire in Gaza," *Times of Israel*, May 7, 2018, www.timesofisrael.com/hamas-said-to-offer -israel-long-term-ceasefire-in-gaza-report/.

42 Reuters, "Israeli Fire Kills Palestinian During Protest at Gaza Border," *New York Post*, April 5, 2018, www.nypost.com/2018/04/05/israeli-fire-kills-palestinian-during -protest-at-gaza-border/.

43 Tamara Pileggi and TOI Staff, "PA Warned Paris That Gaza Border Clashes Financed by Iran—Report," *Times of Israel*, June 5, 2018, https://www.timesofisrael.com/pa-warned -paris-that-gaza-border-clashes-financed-by-iran-report/.

Chapter 2

1 Edward Flannery, *The Anguish of the Jews: Twenty-Three Centuries of Anti-Semitism* (Mahwah, NJ: Paulist, 1985), 295.

2 Dagobert D. Runes, *The War Against the Jew*, epigraph (New York: Philosophical Library, 1968), xxv.

3 "31 Countries Adopt New Definition of Anti-Semitism that Includes Anti-Zionism," *Tower*, June 3, 2016, http://www.thetower.org/3462-31-countries-adopt-new-definition -of-anti-semitism-that-includes-anti-zionism/.

4 Martin Lockshin, "Haman's Antisemitism: What Did He Not Like about the Jews?" TheTorah.com, March 8, 2017, https://thetorah.com/hamans-antisemitism-what -did-he-not-like-about-the-jews/.

5 Elon Gilad, "The Revolt of the Maccabees: The True Story behind Hanukkah," *Haaretz*, December 10, 2014, https://www.haaretz.com/jewish/.premium-maccabean-revolt -the-true-story-1.5343197.

6 Flannery, *Anguish of the Jews*, 13.

7 Ibid., 8.

8 Josephus, *The Jewish War*, trans. G. A. Williamson (Harmondsworth: Penguin, 1959).

9 Jewish Virtual Library (www.jewishvirtuallibrary.org) and Rabbi Eisen. Eisen serves as senior rabbinical lecturer at the Orthodox Union (OU) Jerusalem World Center, where he has taught for thirty years. His lecture series include completed studies of Ethics of the Fathers, The Kuzari and Guide of the Perplexed series in early Biblical commentaries, Talmudic Aggadah, and classic Jewish thought and philosophy. For over twenty years, he also taught Talmud and Midrash, with a special focus on Jewish thought philosophy at Yeshivat Hakotel's Foreign Students and Israeli Hesder programs. Rabbi Eisen has also been a Torah lecturer in the Israel Defense Forces (IDF) Rabbinate Torah Lecture Corps (reserves), and has also volunteered as a board member of Operation Dignity, a relief organization on behalf of the former residents of Gush Katif, after their expulsions.

More recently he has been involved in "building bridges" with the Christian community through lectures and informal meetings in Israel, North America, and Europe, as well as via the Internet (especially through Yeshivath Sharashim).

10 Bruce L. Shelley, "325 The First Council of Nicea," *Christian History* 28 (1990), www .christianitytoday.com/history/issues/issue.../325-first-council-of-nicea.html.

11 From the Letter of the Emperor to all those not present at the Council, found in Philip Schaff and Henry Wallace, *Nicene and Post-Nicene Fathers*, second series, vol. 1 (New York: Cosimo, 2007), 524.

12 Erin Doom, "Dating Easter: A Concise History of the Division," Eighth Day Institute, May 4, 2015, https://www.eighthdayinstitute.org/dating_easter_a_concise_history _of_the_division.

13 Ignatius of Antioch, Epistle to the Magnesians, chap. 8–10.

14 Justin Martyr, "Dialogue with Trypho" chaps. 16, 21, in *Saint Justin Martyr: The First Apology, The Second Apology, Dialogue with Trypho, Exhortation to the Greeks, Discourse to the Greeks, The Monarchy or The Rule of God*, trans. Thomas B. Falls, The Fathers of the Church, vol. 6 (Washington, DC: Catholic University of America Press, 2008), 172, 178.

15 Attributed to John Chrysostom, quoted by Rabbi Ken Spiro, "History Crash Course #46: Blood Libel," Aish.com, September 29, 2001, http://www.aish.com/jl/h/cc /48951151.html.

16 Charlotte Elisheva Fonrobert, "Jewish Christians, Judaizers, and Christian Anti-Judaism," chap. 10 in *Late Ancient Christianity, A People's History of Christianity*, vol. 2 (Minneapolis, MN: Fortress Press, 2005).

17 John Chrysostom, *Against the Jews* 1:5, in "Early Church Fathers—Additional Texts," ed. Roger Pearse, Tertullian.org, http://www.tertullian.org/fathers/chrysostom _adversus_judaeos_01_homily1.htm.

18 Augustine, *Confessions* 12.14

19 *Oxford Dictionary of Byzantium*, ed. Alexander P. Kazhdan (New York: Oxford University Press, 1991), s.v. "Codex Theodosianus."

20 History, "Pope Urban II Orders the First Crusades," www.history.co.uk/this-day-in -history/27-november/pope-urban-ii-orders-the-first-crusades.

21 S. Grayzel, *The Church and the Jews in the 13th Century*, 1966.

22 Madeleine Schwartz, "The Origins of Blood Libel," *The Nation*, January 28, 2016, www.thenation.com/article/the-origins-of-blood-libel/.

23 Itamar Marcus, "Islam's War Against the Jews: Quotes from the Palestinian Authority," Aish.com, July 21, 2001, http://www.aish.com/jw/me/48883732.html.

24 Martin Luther, *On the Jews and Their Lies* (1543), quoted in "Anti-Semitism: Martin Luther—'The Jews and Their Lies,'" Jewish Virtual Library, accessed June 22, 2018, https://www.jewishvirtuallibrary.org/martin-luther-quot-the-jews-and-their-lies-quot.

25 Jeanne Favret-Saada, "A Fuzzy Distinction: Anti-Judaism and Anti-Semitism (An excerpt from Le Judaisme et ses Juifs)," *HAU: Journal of Ethnographic Theory* 4, no. 3 (Winter 2014), https://www.journals.uchicago.edu/doi/full/10.14318/hau4.3.021.

26 John Calvin, quoted in *The Calvin Handbook*, ed. Herman J. Selderhuis, trans. Henry J. Baron (Grand Rapids, MI: Eerdmans, 2009), 146.

27 John Calvin, quoted in "Anti-Semitism of the 'Church Fathers,'" Yashanet, accessed June 25, 2018, http://www.yashanet.com/library/fathers.htm.

28 Barbara Newman, *The Passion of the Jews of Prague: The Pogrom of 1389 and the Lessons of a Medieval Parody Church History 81:1* (March 2012), 1–26.

29 "Jewish Ghetto, Venice: History of the Jewish Ghetto," Sacred Destinations, accessed June 23, 2018, http://www.sacred-destinations.com/italy/venice-ghetto.

30 Anna Foa, *The Jews of Europe after the Black Death* (Berkeley: University of California Press, 2000), 146.

31 "Jewish Massacre Denounced: East Side Mass Meeting Plans to Help Victims of Russians in Kishinev," *New York Times*, April 28, 1903, 6.

32 John Doyle Klier, *Russians, Jews, and the Pogroms of 1881–1882* (New York: Cambridge University Press, 2011), 58.

33 Wilhelm Marr, *The Victory of Judaism over Germanism: Viewed from a Nonreligious Point of View*, 8th ed., trans. Gerhard Rohringer (Bern: Rudolph Costenoble, 1879), accessed June 23, 2018, http://www.kevinmacdonald.net/marr-text-english.pdf.

34 United States Holocaust Memorial Museum (hereafter cited as USHMM), *Holocaust Encyclopedia*, s.v. "Protocols of the Elders of Zion," accessed June 23, 2018, www.ushmm.org/wlc/en/article.php?ModuleId=10007058.

35 Ibid.

36 "Audio: Hitler and the Jews," History, BBC, accessed June 23, 2018, http://www.bbc.co.uk/history/worldwars/genocide/hitler_audio.shtml.

37 USHMM, *Holocaust Encyclopedia*, s.v. "Anti-Jewish Legislation in Prewar Germany," accessed June 23, 2018, https://www.ushmm.org/wlc/en/article.php?ModuleId=10005681.

38 Jeremy Noakes and Geoffrey Pridham, eds., *Documents on Nazism 1919–1945* (NY: Viking, 1975), 463–67; *Encyclopaedia Judaica*, vol. 15: Nat–Per, eds. Fred Skolnik and Michael Berenbaum, s.v. "Nuremberg Laws" (Farmington Hills, MI: MacmillanReference, 2007), https://ketab3.files.wordpress.com/2014/11/encyclopaedia-judaica

39 USHMM, *Holocaust Encyclopedia*, s.v. "Antisemitic Legislation 1933–1939," accessed June 23, 2018, https://www.ushmm.org/wlc/en/article.php?ModuleId=10007901.

40 USHMM, *Holocaust Encyclopedia*, s.v. "Kristallnacht," accessed June 23, 2018, https://www.ushmm.org/wlc/en/article.php?ModuleId=10005201#seealso.

41 "Extract from the Speech by Hitler, January 30, 1939," SHOAH Resource Center, Yad Vashem, accessed June 23, 2018, http://www.yadvashem.org/odot_pdf/Microsoft%20Word%20-%201988.pdf.

42 David B Green, "This Day in Jewish History // 1939: Hitler Makes First Call for Jews' 'Annihilation,'" *Haaretz*, January 30, 2014, https://www.haaretz.com/jewish/premium-1939-hitler-makes-first-call-for-jews-annihilation-1.5316931.

43 "Reading 20: The Voyage of the St. Louis," from Margot Stern Strom, *Holocaust and Human Behavior*, chap. 7 (Brookline, MA: Facing History and Ourselves National Foundation, 1994), a teaching resource on Facing History and Ourselves (website), accessed June 23, 2018, https://www.facinghistory.org/holocaust-and-human-behavior/chapter-7/voyage-st-louis. See also "Reading 15: World Responses to Kristallnacht," https://www.facinghistory.org/holoaust-and-human-behavior/chapter-7/world-responses-kristallnacht.

44 "U.S. Policy During the Holocaust: The Tragedy of *S.S. St. Louis*," Jewish Virtual Library, accessed June 23, 2018, https://www.jewishvirtuallibrary.org/the-tragedy-of-s-s-st-louis.

45 USHMM, *Holocaust Encyclopedia*, s.v. "Voyage of the St. Louis," accessed June 23, 2018, https://www.ushmm.org/wlc/en/article.php?ModuleId=10005267.

46 Aish.com staff, "German Expansion and War," Holocaust Studies, Aish.com, December 31, 1969, http://www.aish.com/ho/o/48955271.html.

47 "Why Did the League of Nations Fail to Keep the Peace in the 1930s?" Modern World History \ International Relations 1900–1939, Marked by Teachers, accessed June 23, 2018, http://www.markedbyteachers.com/gcse/history/why-did-the-league-of-nations-fail-to-keep-peace-in-the-1930-s.html.

48 Christopher Klein, "History Stories: The Secret Hitler-Stalin Pact," August 22, 2014, History, www.history.com/news/the-secret-hitler-stalin-pact-75-years-ago.

49 "Timeline of Events: After 1945," USHMM, accessed June 23, 2018, https://www.ushmm.org/learn/timeline-of-events/after-1945.

50 "Timeline of Events: After 1945," USHMM, accessed June 23, 2018, https://www.ushmm.org/learn/timeline-of-events/after-1945.

51 Michael Berenbaum, "Wannsee Conference," *Encyclopaedia Britannica*, accessed June 23, 2018, www.britannica.com/event/Wannsee-Conference.

52 "Section 1: Nazi Camps," in Tony Joel and Mathew Turner, "Week 7: The 'Auschwitz Experience' and Other Settings of Mass Death and Devastation," Contemporary Histories at Deakin, accessed June 25, 2018, https://blogs.deakin.edu.au/holocauststudents/wpcontent/uploads/sites/48/2014/03/WEEK-7 FINAL.pdf.

53 Some suggested resources are: Franklin H. Littell, *The Crucifixion of the Jews* (New York: Harper & Row, 1975); Edward Flannery, *The Anguish of the Jews: Twenty-Three Centuries of Anti-Semitism* (Mahwah, NJ: Paulist, 1985); Dagobert D. Runes, *The War Against the Jew* (New York: Philosophical Library, 1968).

54 Raul Hilberg, "The Destruction of the European Jews: Precedents," chap. 1 in *Holocaust: Origins, Implementation, Aftermath,* ed. Omer Bartov (New York: Routledge, 2000), 25.

55 Laura Bult, "Nobel Peace Prize Winner Elie Wiesel's Best Quotes on Survival, Activism and Humanity," *New York Daily News*, July 2, 2016, http://www.nydailynews.com/news/world/elie-wiesel-quotes-survival-spirituality-humanity-article-1.2697132.

56 From an interview with Carol Rittner and Sandra Myers, *The Courage to Care: Rescuers of Jews During the Holocaust* (New York: New York University Press, 1986), 2.

Chapter 3

1 Kenneth Marcus, "The Horror of Holocaust Denial," Louis D. Brandeis Center, June 3, 2014, http://brandeiscenter.com/the-horror-of-holocaust-denial/.

2 Adapted from "Holocaust Denial: Denial Forms," Auschwitz-Birkenau: Former German Nazi Concentration and Extermination Camp, accessed June 25, 2018, http://auschwitz.org/en/history/holocaust-denial/denial-forms.

3 United States Holocaust Memorial Museum (hereafter cited as USHMM), *Holocaust Encyclopedia*, s.v. "Introduction to the Holocaust," https://www.ushmm.org/wlc/en/article.php?ModuleId=10005143.

4 "Extract from the speech by Hitler, January 30, 1939," SHOAH Resource Center, Yad Vashem, accessed June 23, 2018, http://www.yadvashem.org/odot_pdf/Microsoft%20Word%20-%201988.pdf.

5 Katie, "December 12th 1941: Adolf Hitler Announces Extermination of the Jews," This Day in History, *Today in History* (blog), December 13, 2011, http://todayinhistory.tumblr.com/post/14168048136/december-12th-1941-adolf-hitler-announces.

6 Julius Streicher, from an article in *Der Stuermer*, November 4, 1943, quoted in "Nuremberg Trial Defendants: Julius Streicher," Jewish Virtual Library, accessed June 25, 2018, https://www.jewishvirtuallibrary.org/nuremberg-trial-defendants-julius-streicher.

7 Eric Lichtblau, "The Holocaust Just Got More Shocking," Sunday Review, *New York Times*, March 1, 2013, https://www.nytimes.com/2013/03/03/sunday-review/the-holocaust-just-got-more-shocking.html.

8 USHMM, *Holocaust Encyclopedia*, s.v. "Jewish Population of Europe in 1933: Population Data by Country," https://www.ushmm.org/wlc/en/article.php?ModuleId=10005161.

9 "Gas Chambers and Crematoria: The Nazi Murder Machine Operated at Peak Efficiency," Aish.com, December 31, 1969, http://www.aish.com/ho/o/Einsatzgruppen-The-Killing.html.

10 Ibid.

11 The History Place, "Biographies of Nazi Leaders: Adolf Eichmann," accessed June 25, 2018, www.historyplace.com/worldwar2/biographies/eichmann-biography.htm.

12 Ibid.

13 Louis Bülow, "Rudolf Hoess, Death Dealer of Auschwitz," Auschwitz.dk, accessed June 25, 2018, http://www.auschwitz.dk/hoess.htm.

14 Ibid.

15 Ibid.

16 Ibid.

17 "A Description of the Mass Murder of Jews in the Gas Chambers of Auschwitz," excerpted from Autobiografia Rudolfa Hössa, komendanta obozu oświęcimskiego, Warsaw, 1989, 202–3, http://en.auschwitz.org/lekcja/12_miejsce_pamieci/kurs/s405/fragmenty.pdf.

18 Ibid., s.v. "Jewish Population of Europe in 1945," https://www.ushmm.org/wlc/en/article.php?ModuleId=10005687.

19 Mark Weber, "Wilhelm Höttl and the Elusive 'Six Million,'" *Journal of Historical Review* 20, no. 5/6 (September/December 2001): 25.

20 Raul Hilberg, *The Destruction of the European Jews*, 3rd ed. (New Haven, CT: Yale University Press, 2003). First published 1961 by Quadrangle Books (Chicago).

21 Lucy S. Dawidowicz, *The War against the Jews* (New York: Holt, Rinehart and Winston,1975).

22 Wolfgang Benz, *Dimension des Völkermords: Die Zahl der jüdischen Opfer des Nationalsozialismus* (Munich: Dtv,1996).

23 Adolf Eichmann, "Eichmann's Own Story, Part 2: 'To Sum It All Up, I Regret Nothing,'" *Life*, December 5, 1960, 161, https://books.google.com/books?id=900EAAAAMBAJ &pg=PA46&source=gbs_toc_r&cad=2#v=onepage&q=I%20regret%20nothing&f=false.

24 History Place, Adolf Eichmann.

25 Ibid.

26 Kate Connolly, "'Accountant of Auschwitz' Goes on Trial in Germany," *Guardian*, April 21, 2015, US edition, https://www.theguardian.com/world/2015/apr/20/former-auschwitz-death-camp-guard-oskar-groning-on-trial-germany; see also Matthias Geyer, "An SS Officer Remembers: The Bookkeeper from Auschwitz, Part 2: Counting the Money of the Dead," trans. Christopher Sultan, *Spiegel* Online International, May 9, 2005, http://www.spiegel.de/international/spiegel/an-ss-officer-remembers-the -bookkeeper-from-auschwitz-a-355188-2.html.

27 Associated Press, "'Accountant of Auschwitz' Oskar Groening Loses Prison Appeal," CBS News, December 29, 2017, https://www.cbsnews.com/news/nazi-accountant-of -auschwitz-oskar-groening-loses-prison-appeal/.

28 Ed Wight, "Hall of Shame," *The Sun*, January 31, 2017, www.thesun.co.uk/news /2750293/nazi-ss-guards-auschwitz-concentration-camp/.

29 Laurence Rees, *Auschwitz: The Nazis & the "Final Solution"* (London: BBC Books, 2005).

30 USHMM, *Holocaust Encyclopedia*, s.v. "Ohrdruf," accessed June 25, 2018, https://www .ushmm.org/wlc/en/article.php?ModuleId=10006131.

31 "U.S. Policy During WWII: U.S. Army & the Holocaust," JVL, accessed June 25, 2018, https://www.jewishvirtuallibrary.org/u-s-army-and-the-holocaust.

32 *Holocaust Encyclopedia*, s.v. "Ohrdruf."

33 Nicholas Lemann, "The Murrow Doctrine: Why the Life and Times of the Broadcast Pioneer Still Matter," *New Yorker*, January 23, 2006, https://www.newyorker. /magazine/2006/01/23/the-murrow-doctrine.

34 "Extract from the Nuremberg Trial," Buchenwald (Germany), JewishGen (website),https://www.jewishgen.org/ForgottenCamps/Camps/BuchenwaldEng.htm.

35 Holocaust Education & Archive Research Team, "Buchenwald Concentration Camp," Holocaust Research Project, accessed June 25, 2018, http://www .holocaustresearchproject.org/othercamps/buchenwald.html.

36 "Ed Murrow Reports from Buchenwald—April 15, 1945," Media Resource Center Moffitt Library, UC Berkeley, accessed June 26, 2018, http://www.lib.berkeley.edu /MRC/murrowbuchenwaldtranscript.html.

37 Erwin Lutzer, quoted in Pastor Rudy, "Will It Happen Again?" *Cape May County Herald*, September 19, 2014, http://www.capemaycountyherald.com/opinion/columns/article _f189573a-7d3a-5e91-a3da-88690fde657b.html.

38 Judi Heit, "Adelaide Hautval," *Heroines of the Resistance* (blog), September 17, 2015, http://resistanceheroines.blogspot.com/2015/09/adelaide-hautval-1906-1988.html.

39 Yad Vashem, "Dr. Adelaide Hautval," The Stories of Six Righteous among the Nations in Auschwitz: Flickers of Light, accessed June 26, 2018, http://www.yadvashem.org/yv/en /exhibitions/righteous-auschwitz/hautval.asp.

40 Ibid.

41 Roddie's Code: Be the Hero, "The Story of Master Sergeant Roddie Edmonds," accessed June 26, 2018, http://www.roddieedmonds.com/bio/.

42 Jewish Telegraphic Agency, "American Soldier Named Righteous among the Nations for First Time," December 2, 2015, https://www.jta.org/2015/12/02/news-opinion /united-states/american-soldier-named-righteous-among-the-nations-for-first-time.

43 Ibid.

44 Judaism 101, Sh'ma.

45 Peter Longerich, *Holocaust: The Nazi Persecution and Murder of the Jews* (New York: Oxford University Press, 2010).

46 Gerhard SP and Spiegel, "How Denmark Saved Its Jews from the Nazis," ABC News, November 3, 2013, https://abcnews.go.com/International/denmark-saved-jews-nazis /story?id=20750027.

47 Michael Ignatieff, "Denmark and the Holocaust: One Country Saved Its Jews. Were They Just Better People?" Aish, May 24, 2014, http://www.aish.com/ho/i/Denmark--the -Holocaust.html.

48 Rabbi Israel Ba'al Shem Tov, quoted in David Silberklang, "More Than a Memorial: The Evolution of Yad Vashem," *Yad Vashem Quarterly Magazine*, Special Commemorative Edition (Fall 2003), 7.

Chapter 4

1 Theodor Herzl, *The Jewish State* (Der Judenstaat), trans. Sylvie D'Avigdor (American Zionist Emergency Council, 1946), quoted in Jewish Virtual Library (hereafter cited as JVL), "Texts Concerning Zionism: *The Jewish State*," https://www.jewishvirtuallibrary. org/quot-the-jewish-state-quot-theodor-herzl; Britannica Educational Publishing, *Judaism: History, Belief, and Practice*, ed. Matt Stefon (New York: Rosen Education Service, 2011), 346.

2 David Brog, "The Jews Come Home," chap. 3 in *Reclaiming Israel's History: Roots, Rights, and the Struggle for Peace* (Washington, DC: Regnery, 2017), 61–82.

3 "The Mandate for Palestine," Israel Ministry of Foreign Affairs, http://www.mfa.gov.il /mfa/foreignpolicy/peace/guide/pages/the%20mandate%20for%20palestine.aspx.

4 "The Weizmann-Feisal Agreement," Israel Ministry of Foreign Affairs, http://www .mfa.gov.il/mfa/foreignpolicy/peace/mfadocuments/pages/the%20weizmann-feisal %20agreement%203-jan-1919.aspx.

5   Jacqueline Shields, "Pre-State Israel: Arab Riots of the 1920s," JVL, https://www
    .jewishvirtuallibrary.org/arab-riots-of-the-1920-s.

6   Richard Bass, *Israel-Palestine for Critical Thinkers* (self-pub., 2015), 56.

7   Ibid., 60.

8   Jacqueline Shields, "Pre-State Israel: Arab Riots of the 1920s," JVL, https://www
    .jewishvirtuallibrary.org/arab-riots-of-the-1920-s.

9   Ibid.

10 Ibid.

11 "The Holocaust: The Mufti and the führer," JVL, https://www.jewishvirtuallibrary.org
    /the-mufti-and-the-f-uuml-hrer.

12 "Israeli War of Independence: Background & Overview," JVL, https://www
    .jewishvirtuallibrary.org/background-and-overview-israel-war-of-independence.

13 Ibid.

14 David Patterson, "The Muslim Brotherhood and the Evolution of Jihadist Antisemitism,"
    January 17, 2018, Flashpoint 50, Institute for the Study of Global Antisemitism and
    Policy, https://isgap.org/flashpoint/the-muslim-brotherhood-and-the-evolution-of
    -jihadist-antisemitism/.

15 Ibid.

16 "The Muslim Brotherhood" (white paper), The Investigative Project on Terrorism, http://
    www.investigativeproject.org/documents/misc/135.pdf.

17 Ibid.

18 See "Timeline of Ancient Israel" at TimeMaps, https://www.timemaps.com/civilizations
    /ancient-israel/.

19 "Palestine Liberation Organization: The Original Palestine National Charter (1964),"
    JVL, https://www.jewishvirtuallibrary.org/the-original-palestine-national-charter
    -1964.

20 Ibid.

21 "Israel's Wars & Operations: Operation Isotope (May 1972)," JVL, https://www
    .jewishvirtuallibrary.org/operation-isotope.

22 "Munich Olympic Massacre: Background & Overview (September 1972)," JVL, https://
    www.jewishvirtuallibrary.org/background-and-overview-munich-olympic-massacer.

23 "Israel's Wars & Operations: The Entebbe Rescue Operation (July 1976)," JVL, https://
    www.jewishvirtuallibrary.org/the-entebbe-rescue-operation.

24 "First Lebanon War: Background & Overview (1982–1985)," JVL, https://www
    .jewishvirtuallibrary.org/background-and-overview-of-first-lebanon-war.

25 David Daoud, "On the Roots and Branches of Shi'a Anti-Semitism," *Tower*,
    September 2015, http://www.thetower.org/article/on-the-roots-and-branches
    -of-shia-anti-semitism/.

26 Ibid.

27 "Hamas: Background & Overview," JVL, https://www.jewishvirtuallibrary.org
    /background-and-overview-of-hamas.

28 Ian Mount, "The U.S. Sent Another $1.3 Billion to Iran after Hostages Were Released," Fortune, September 7, 2016, http://fortune.com/2016/09/07/us-iran-billion -hostages-arms-deal/.

29 Ibid., 96.

30 "Hezbollah: Overview," Counter Extremism Project, https://www.counterextremism .com/threat/hezbollah#overview.

31 Ibid.

32 Ibid.

33 Jerusalem, February 9, 2018 Rockets, Missiles and More; Predicting the Third Lebanon War.

34 Aaron Bandler, "Ayatollah Khamenei Tweets That Israel Is a 'Cancerous Tumor.' Israel Claps Back," *Jewish Journal*, June 4, 2018, http://jewishjournal.com/news/israel/234736 /ayatollah-khamenei-tweets-israel-cancerous-tumor-israel-claps-back/.

35 "Iran Prepares to Boost Uranium Enrichment Capacity," TRT World, June 6, 2018, https://www.trtworld.com/mea/iran-prepares-to-boost-uranium-enrichment -capacity-18001.

36 Patterson, "Muslim Brotherhood."

37 "ISIS: Overview," Counter Extremism Project, https://www.counterextremism.com /threat/isis#overview.

38 Hamas: Background & Overview," JVL, https://www.jewishvirtuallibrary.org /background-and-overview-of-hamas.

39 Richard Bass, *Israel for Critical Thinkers* (CUFI Edition, 2006), pgs 87–91. Copyright © Richard Bass, info@forcriticalthinkers.com.

40 Ibid., 96.

41 "Hamas War Tactics: Attacks from Civilian Centers," JVL, https://www .jewishvirtuallibrary.org/jsource/images/hamastactics.pdf.

42 Dan Williams and Nidal al-Mughrabi, "Gazans Send Fire-Starting Kites into Israel; Minister Threatens Lethal Response," Reuters, June 5, 2018, https://www.reuters.com /article/us-israel-palestinians-kites/gazans-send-fire-starting-kites-into-israel-minister -threatens-lethal-response-idUSKCN1J127C. The Times of Israel 10 July 2019 Judah Ari Gross.

43 Judah Ari Gross, "Despite Concerns, Senior IDF Technology Officer Says Anti-Kite Drones a Success," *Times of Israel*, June 8, 2018, https://www.timesofisrael.com /disputing-news-report-colonel-declares-idfs-anti-kite-drones-a-success/.

44 "Tenuous Cease-Fire Reached in Gaza after IDF Pounds Hamas Posts," Israel Hayom, July 15, 2018, http://www.israelhayom.com/2018/07/15/tenuous-cease-fire-reached -in-gaza-after-idf-pounds-hamas-posts/.

45 "PM: Anyone Who Attacks Israel Will Meet Forceful Counterattack," Israel Hayom, July 15, 2018, http://www.israelhayom.com/2018/07/15/pm-anyone-who-attacks -israel-will-meet-forceful-counterattack/.

46 Lahav Harkov, "Palestinians Increase Payments to Terrorists to $403 Million," *Jerusalem*

Post, March 6, 2018, https://www.jpost.com/Arab-Israeli-Conflict/Palestinians-increase
-payments-to-terrorists-to-403-million-544343.

47 Raphael Ahren, "'Pandemic' of Anti-Semitism Taking Shape Worldwide, Even Threatens
America, Warns Top US Jewish Leader," *Times of Israel*, February 27, 2017, https://www
.timesofisrael.com/pandemic-of-anti-semitism-taking-shape-worldwide-even-threatens
-america-warns-top-us-jewish-leader/, emphasis added.

48 Ahren, "'Pandemic' of Anti-Semitism Taking Shape Worldwide."

49 Reprise to "Sixteen Going on Seventeen" by Oscar Hammerstein in the theatrical (not
film) version of *The Sound of Music*, http://www.thepeaches.com/music/composers
/hammerstein/SixteenGoingOnSeventeen.htm.

50 Commentary on "Watchman," BibleGateway, https://www.biblegateway.com/resources
/encyclopedia-of-the-bible/Watchman.

51 Commentary on Isaiah 62:6, "Who shall never be silent by day or by night," The Israel
Bible, https://theisraelbible.com/bible/isaiah/chapter-62.

52 Yehuda Bauer, quoted in "Voice of the Jewish News: Thou Shalt Not Be a Bystander,"
Jewish News Online, January 28, 2016, http://jewishnews.timesofisrael.com/voice-of-the
-jewish-news-thou-shalt-not-be-a-bystander/.

SECTION TWO: THE EMPIRES

Chapter 5

1 Peter Davidson, *Atlas of Empires: The World's Great Powers from Ancient Times to Today*
(East Petersburg, PA: CompanionHouse Books, 2018), from the introduction.

2 "Ancient Rome," UShistory.org, Independence Hall Association, accessed June 12, 2018,
http://www.ushistory.org/civ/6.asp.

3 "The Fall of the Roman Empire," Ushistory.org, Independence Hall Association, accessed
June 12, 2018, http://www.ushistory.org/civ/6f.asp.

4 Michael Frassetto et al., "Roman Catholicism," *Encyclopedia Britannica*, last updated May
17, 2018, https://www.britannica.com/topic/Roman-Catholicism.

5 "Holy Roman Empire," *Almanach de Saxe Gotha*, accessed June 11, 2018, http://www
.almanachdegotha.org/id131.html.

6 Ibid.

7 Stephen L. Baehr, "From History to National Myth: Translatio Imperii in Eighteenth-
Century Russia," *Russian Review* 37, no. 1 (1978): 1, http://www.jstor.org/stable/128360.

8 Dariusz Kasprzak, "The Theological Principles Underlying Augustine's 'City of God,'"
Theological Research 1 (2013): 104, http://dx.doi.org/10.15633/thr.153.

9 Spyridon Flogaitis, *The Evolution of Law and the State in Europe: Seven Lessons* (Portland,
OR: Hart, 2014), 10.

10 "Holy Roman Empire," *Saxe Gotha*.

11 Ibid.

12 "The Origins of Anti-Semitism," Alpha History, accessed June 14, 2018, http://
alphahistory.com/holocaust/origins-of-anti-semitism/.

13 "Medieval anti-Semitism," Alpha History, accessed June 14, 2018, http://alphahistory
.com/holocaust/medieval-anti-semitism/.

14 David B. Green, "Holy Roman Emperor Orders All Jewish books—Except the Bible—
Be Destroyed," *Haaretz*, August 19, 2013, https://www.haaretz.com/jewish
/this-day-an-emperor-rounds-up-books-1.5322641.

15 Katy Gibbons, "Five of the Most Violent Moments of the Reformation," The
Conversation, January 20, 2017, http://theconversation.com/five-of-the-most-violent
-moments-of-the-reformation-71535.

16 David B. Green, "1670: The Holy Roman Emperor Banishes the Jews from Austria,"
Haaretz, March 1, 2015, https://www.haaretz.com/jewish/.premium-1670
-austrian-jews-banned-1.5330064.

17 David B. Green, "1802: Jews Ask Holy Roman Empire to Upgrade Them to
Citizens,"*Haaretz*, November 15, 2013, https://www.haaretz.com/jewish/.premium
-1802-jews-seek-german-rights-1.5290758.

18 "Holy Roman Empire," *Saxe Gotha*.

19 "Napoleon Bonaparte," Jewish Virtual Library, accessed June 14, 2018, http://www
.jewishvirtuallibrary.org/napoleon-bonaparte.

20 Gemma Betros, "The French Revolution and the Catholic Church," *History Review*, no.
68 (December 2010), https://www.historytoday.com/gemma-betros/french-revolution
-and-catholic-church.

21 Michael Adkins, "North German Confederation (1866–1871): History," Dead Country
Stamps and Banknotes, accessed June 14, 2018, http://www.dcstamps.com/north
-german-confederation-1866-1871/.

22 David Kaiser, "Treaty of Versailles," *The Reader's Companion to Military History*, ed.
Robert Cowley and Geoffrey Parker (New York: Houghton Mifflin, 1996), 488–89
(hereafter cited as *Reader's Comp.*; citations refer to the 2001 paperback ed.); Gideon
Rose, "Reparations," *Reader's Comp.*, 385–86.

23 "Encyclopedia Judaica: Emancipation: Germany," Jewish Virtual Library, American-
Israeli Cooperative Enterprise (AICE), http://www.jewishvirtuallibrary.org/emancipation.

24 Elizabeth Vlossak, "Alsace-Lorraine: Alsace-Lorraine between France and Germany,
1871–1914," International Encyclopedia of the First World War, last updated October
21, 2016, https://encyclopedia.1914-1918-online.net/article/ abylo-lorraine.

25 "Understanding the Kulturkampf," History, Unan Sanctam Catholicam, accessed
June 14, 2018, http://www.unamsanctamcatholicam.com/history/79-history/394
-kulturkampf.html.

26 "The Attack on the Social Democrats," German Empire: The Making of the Empire,
Encyclopedia Britannica, accessed June 14, 2018, https://www.britannica.com/place
/German-Empire#ref339177 (hereafter cited as German Empire, *Britannica*).

27 "Foreign and Colonial Policy," German Empire, *Britannica*.

28 "The Fall of Bismarck," German Empire, *Britannica*.

29 BBC, "Wilhelm II (1859–1941)," *History: Historic Figures*, accessed June 14, 2018,
http://www.bbc.co.uk/history/historic_figures/wilhelm_kaiser_ii.shtml.

30 United States Holocaust Memorial Museum, "The Weimar Republic," *Holocaust Encyclopedia*, accessed June 14, 2018, https://encyclopedia.ushmm.org/content/en /article/the-weimar-republic.

31 Michael H. Kater, "Everyday Anti-Semitism in Prewar Nazi Germany: The Popular Bases," *Yad Vashem Studies* 16 (1984): 129–59, https://www.yadvashem.org/odot_pdf /Microsoft%20Word%20-%203261.pdf.

Chapter 6

1 Michael Novak, *On Two Wings: Humble Faith and Common Sense at the American Founding* (San Francisco: Encounter Books, 2002), 5–13.

2 Novak, *On Two Wings*, 34–39.

3 See James Madison's argument in *Federalist* No. 47, in Alexander Hamilton, James Madison, and John Jay, *The Federalist Papers*, ed. Clinton Rossiter (New York: Mentor Books, 1961), 269.

4 Alexis de Tocqueville, *Democracy in America*, trans. George Lawrence, ed. J. P. Mayer (New York: Harper & Row, 1969), 292.

5 For a discussion of the structural features of the three branches of government, see Jeffrey K. Tulis, *The Rhetorical Presidency* (Princeton, NJ: Princeton University Press, 1987), 41–45.

6 *The Federalist Papers* is the best place to start to understand the Framers' vision for the American presidency. Hamilton's quote can be found in No. 75.

7 *Federalist*, No. 70.

8 This discussion is based heavily on the work of Stephen Skowronek, who first articulated this understanding of American history as a series of partisan regime cycles. See Stephen Skowronek, *The Politics Presidents Make: Leadership from John Adams to George Bush* (Cambridge, MA: Belknap Press, 1993); and Stephen Skowronek, *Presidential Leadership in Political Time: Reprise and Reappraisal* (Lawrence, KS: University Press of Kansas, 2008).

9 On the early American party system, see Richard Hofstadter, *The Idea of a Party System: The Rise of Legitimate Opposition in the United States, 1780–1840* (Berkeley: University of California Press, 1969).

10 For a detailed account of early American party politics, see Richard P. McCormick, *The Presidential Game: The Origins of American Presidential Politics* (New York: Oxford University Press, 1982).

11 For a thorough look at Jacksonian politics, see Gerard N. Magliocca, *Andrew Jackson and the Constitution: The Rise and Fall of Generational Regimes* (Lawrence, KS: University Press of Kansas, 2007).

12 John C. Calhoun, "On the Oregon Bill," speech delivered in the Senate of the United States, June 27, 1848.

13 Abraham Lincoln referenced this quote by Indiana senator John Pettit in his "Speech at Peoria, Illinois," October 16, 1854.

14 Lincoln, "Speech at Peoria."

15 "Republican Party Platform of 1856," June 18, 1856, The American Presidency Project: Political Party Platforms, http://www.presidency.ucsb.edu/ws/index.php?pid=29619.

16 Scott v. Sandford, 60 U.S. (19 How.) 393 (1856).

17 Alexander H. Stephens, "Corner-Stone Speech," Savannah, GA, March 21, 1861.

18 The most complete exploration of Theodore Roosevelt's political philosophy is Jean M. Yarbrough, *Theodore Roosevelt and the American Political Tradition* (Lawrence, KS: University Press of Kansas, 2012).

19 For a thorough account of Wilson's place in Progressive politics, see Ronald J. Pestritto, *Woodrow Wilson and the Roots of Modern Liberalism* (Lanham, MD: Rowman & Littlefield, 2005).

20 Calvin Coolidge, "The Inspiration of the Declaration" (speech), July 5, 1926.

21 On the Great Depression, see Amity Shlaes, *The Forgotten Man: A New History of the Great Depression* (New York: Harper Perennial, 2008). On Roosevelt's transformation of the executive branch, see Sidney M. Milkis, *The President and the Parties: The Transformation of the American Party System Since the New Deal* (New York: Oxford University Press, 1993).

Chapter 7

1 "Remarks of President Donald J. Trump—As Prepared for Delivery: Inaugural Address," Washington, DC, January 20, 2017, https://www.whitehouse.gov/briefings-statements /the-inaugural-address/.

2 Goldwater's own political philosophy is most succinctly expressed in Barry Goldwater, *The Conscience of a Conservative* (Shepherdsville, KY: Victor, 1960).

3 A succinct discussion of these differences can be found in Paul Gottfried and Thomas Fleming, *The Conservative Movement* (Boston: Twayne, 1988). The most comprehensive history of the post-war conservative movement is George H. Nash, *The Conservative Intellectual Movement in America Since 1945* (Wilmington, DE: ISI Books, 2006).

4 For a comprehensive account of the period leading up to Reagan's victory, see Steven F. Hayward, *The Age of Reagan: The Fall of the Old Liberal Order, 1964–1980* (New York: Forum, 2001).

5 On the idea of a culture war and cultural realignment, see James Davison Hunter, *Culture Wars: The Struggle to Define America* (New York: Basic Books, 1991).

6 Scott v. Sandford, 60 U.S. (19 How.) 393 (1856); Roe v. Wade, 410 U.S. 113 (1973).

7 "Ronald Reagan, 'Evil Empire Speech' (8 March 1983)," Voices of Democracy, http:// voicesofdemocracy.umd.edu/ abylo-evil-empire-speech-text/.

8 On Reagan's presidency, see Andrew E. Busch, *Ronald Reagan and the Politics of Freedom* (Lanham, MD: Rowman & Littlefield, 2001). See also Steven F. Hayward, *The Age of Reagan: The Conservative Counterrevolution, 1980–1989* (New York: Crown Forum, 2009).

9 See transcript of "Saddleback Civil Forum on the Presidency," in which Pastor Rick Warren interviewed then Senator Barack Obama during the 2008 presidential race (August 16, 2008), http://transcripts.cnn.com/TRANSCRIPTS/0808/16/se.02.html.

10 David Remnick, "Going the Distance: On and Off the Road with Barack Obama," *New Yorker*, January 27, 2014, https://www.newyorker.com/magazine/2014/01/27 /going-the-distance-david-remnick.

11 On the polarization in American politics and its source in the 1960s, see James E. Campbell, *Polarized: Making Sense of a Divided America* (Princeton, NJ: Princeton University Press, 2016).

12 Shannon, Pettypiece, "Trump Signs $1.5 Trillion Tax Cut in First Major Legislative Win," Bloomberg, December 22, 2017, https://www.bloomberg.com/news/ articles /2017-12-22/trump-signs-1-5-trillion-tax-cut-in-first-major-legislative-win.

13 Council of Economic Advisors, "U.S. Unemployment Rate Falls to 50-Year Low" (October 4, 2019), https://www.whitehouse.gov/articles/u-s-unemployment-rate -falls-50-year-low/.

14 "Conscience Protection Act: What It Is and Why It's Needed," Speaker Paul Ryan's Press Office (July 12, 2016), https://www.speaker.gov/general/conscience-protection-act -what-it-and-why-it-s-needed.

15 "Mairead McArdle, "U.S. Pulls Out of 'Biased' UN Human Rights Council," *National Review,* June 19, 2018, https://www.nationalreview.com/news/ united-states-pulls-out-of-united-nations-human-rights- council/.

16 Yair Lapid, "The U.N. and Antisemitism: 10-Year Report Card," The Jerusalem Post, July 12, 2018, https://www.jpost.com/Opinion/The-UN-and-antisemitism-10-year -report-card-562377.

Chapter 8

1 For more detail on this subject, see John Hagee, *Three Heavens: Angels, Demons and What Lies Ahead* (Nashville: Worthy, 2015).

2 Flavius Josephus, "Concerning the Tower of Babylon, and the Confusion of Tongues," bk. 1, chap. 4, in *The Antiquities of the Jews, in The Genuine Works of Flavius Josephus*, William Whiston, ed. (Halifax: William Milner, 1849), 30.

3 Shaul Wolf, "The Life and Times of Nimrod, the Biblical Hunter," Chabad.org, https:// www. chabad.org/library/article_cdo/aid/3162874/jewish/The-Life-and-Times-of-Nimrod -the-Biblical-Hunter.htm.

4 Source of quote unknown, though widely attributed to Alexander Hislop, *The Two Babylons*, 2nd American edition (Neptune, NJ: Loizeaux Brothers, 1959), 5, 24.

5 "Historical Pictures of Christianity: Babylonian Priests Migrate," http://historical .benabraham.com/html/abylonian_priests_migrate.html.

6 Socrates Scholasticus, *Ecclesiastical History*, bk. 5, chap. 22.

7 Christian Tomuschat, ed., *The United Nations at Age Fifty: A Legal Perspective* (The Hague: Martinus Nijhoff, 1995), 77.

8 Attributed to Dietrich Bonhoeffer. For more on his life, see Eberhard Bethge and Victoria Barnet, ed., *Dietrich Bonhoeffer: A Biography* (Minneapolis: Fortress Press, 2000).

9 Ibid.

10 United Nations, "European Union Indispensable Partner of United Nations, Ready to Build

Cooperative New World Order, Its Top Diplomat Tells Security Council," Meetings coverage: Security Council 7935th meeting, May 9, 2017, https://www.un.org/press/en/2017/sc12814 .doc.htm.

11 MSN, "Who's Stockpiling?," slides 27–31.

12 MSN, "Who's Stockpiling Gold?" (slideshow), slides 26 (China) and 25 (Russia), https:// www.msn.com/en-us/money/markets/this-is-who-owns-most-of-the-worlds-gold/ss -BBGmtjN?fullscreen=true#image=22.

13 Freedom-channel, "New World Currency."

14 "Russian President Dmitry Medvedev Pulls New World Currency from His Pocket," *Telegraph*, July 10, 2009, https://www.telegraph.co.uk/finance/currency/5796892 /Russian-President-Dmitry-Medvedev-pulls-new-world-currency-from-his-pocket.html.

15 Freedom-channel, "A New World Order and a New World Currency in 2018?," Steemit, https://steemit.com/money/@freedom-channel/a-new-world-order-and-a-newworld -currency-in-2018.

SECTION THREE: FROM AMALEK TO ARMAGEDDON

Chapter 9

1 Adapted from Riley Winters, "The Ancient Roots of Doomsday Prophecies and End of the World Beliefs," Ancient Origins, January 15, 2015, https://www.ancient-origins.net /history/ancient-roots-doomsday-prophecies-and-end-world-beliefs-002571.

2 "Ancient Jewish History: The Assyrians (1170-612 BCE)," Jewish Virtual Library, https:// www.jewishvirtuallibrary.org/the-assyrians.

3 Mark Strauss, "Ten Notable Apocalypses That (Obviously) Didn't Happen, *Smithsonian*, November 12, 2009, https://www.smithsonianmag.com/history/ten-notable -apocalypses-that-obviously-didnt-happen-9126331/.

4 John Roach, "End of World in 2012? Maya 'Doomsday' Calendar Explained," *National Geographic*, December 20, 2011, https://news.nationalgeographic.com/news /2011/12/111220-end-of-world-2012-maya-calendar-explained-ancient-science/.

5 Jack Schofield, "The Millennium Bug: Special Report," Money We Spent, *Guardian*, US edition, January 4, 2000, https://www.theguardian.com/technology/2000/jan/05/y2k .guardiananalysispage.

6 Adapted from Martin Ralph DeHaan, *Signs of the Times* (Grand Rapids, MI: Zondervan, 1951), 168–69.

7 J. Dwight Pentecost, *Prophecy for Today: God's Purpose and Plan for Our Future*, rev. ed. (Grand Rapids, MI: Discovery House, 1989), 16.

8 Derek Prince, *Foundational Truths for Christian Living: Everything You Need to Know to Live a Balanced, Spirit-Filled Life* (Lake Mary, FL: Charisma House, 2006), 22–23.

9 "353 Prophecies Fulfilled in Jesus Christ," According to the Scriptures, http://www .accordingtothescriptures.org/prophecy/353prophecies.html.

10 Brian H. Edwards, *Nothing but the Truth: The Inspiration, Authority and History of the Bible Explained* (Darlington, UK: Evangelical Press, 2006), 116–43.

Chapter 10

1   Adapted from Hersh Goldwurm, *Daniel: A New Translation with a Commentary Anthologized from Talmudic, Midrashic, and Rabbinic Sources*, Artscroll Tanach Series (Brooklyn: Artscroll Mesorah, 1979), xxiv.

2   Ibid.

3   Arthur W. Pink, *Gleanings in Genesis* (Chicago: Moody Press, 1922), 142.

4   Richard Cavendish, "Spanish Bankruptcy," *History Today*, November 11, 2007, https://www.historytoday.com/richard-cavendish/spanish-bankruptcy.

5   Soeren Kern, "The Islamization of Germany in 2016: 'Germany Is No Longer Safe," January 2, 2017, Gatestone Institute International Policy Council, https://www.gatestoneinstitute.org/9700/germany-islamization.

6   James S. Robbins, "The Iran Nuclear Deal Was the Worst Deal Ever. No Wonder Donald Trump Nixed It," *USA Today*, May 8, 2018, https://www.usatoday.com/story/opinion/2018/05/08/iran-nuclear-deal-worst-donald-trump-column/589828002/.

7   Pink, *Gleanings in Genesis*, 162–63.

8   Ibid., 166.

9   Meir Zlotowitz, *Bereishis/Genesis*, Artscroll Tanach Series (Brooklyn: ArtScroll Mesorah, 1986), 504.

10 Derek Prince, "God's Covenant with Abraham," https://www.derekprince.org/Articles/1000085415/DPM_USA/Archive_of_UK/Keys/Relationships/Relationship_with_God/Gods_Covenant_with.aspx.

11 J. Dwight Pentecost, *Things to Come: A Study in Biblical Eschatology* (Grand Rapids, MI: Zondervan, 1958), 69.

12 Adapted from Ibid., 68.

13 *Bereishis*, ArtScroll Tanach Series, vol. 1(a), (Brooklyn, NY: Mesorah Publications, Ltd., 1969), 519–20, note 1.

14 Pink, *Gleanings in Genesis*, 169.

15 "Birdwatching from a Christian Perspective: Birds of the Bible," *Lee's Birdwatching Adventures Plus* (blog), https://leesbird.com/bb/.

16 Finis J. Dake, *Dake's Annotated Reference Bible–KJV* (Lawrenceville, GA: Dake, 2014), 20.

17 Pink, *Gleanings in Genesis*, 170.

18 Zlotowitz, *Bereishis/Genesis*, 524.

19 *The Nelson Study Bible: NKJV* (Nashville, TN: Thomas Nelson, 1997), 27.

20 Ibid., 29.

21 Clarence Larkin, "Royal Grant to Abraham" (chart), in "The Jews: Dispensational Truth," chap. 9, Blue Letter Bible, https://www.blueletterbible.org/study/larkin/dt/09.cfm#c41.

22 *The Chumash*, ArtScroll Stone Edition (Brooklyn, NY: Mesorah Publications, Ltd., 1998), 72, note 17.

23 Pentecost, *Things to Come*, 71.

Chapter 11

1 Aron Heller, "Sir Isaac's Jewish Writings Enter the 21st Century," *Times of Israel*, February 19, 2012, https://www.timesofisrael.com/sir-isaacs-jewish-writings-enter-the-21st-century/.

2 Flavius Josephus, *Antiquities of the Jews* (Book X, Chapter 11, section 7), Internet Sacred Text Archive, http://sacred-texts.com/jud/josephus/ant-10.htm.

3 "General Timeline Abraham to Nehemiah," accessed July 3, 2018, http://livingstonesclass.org/Archive/Daniel%20Introduction.pdf.

4 "What Is the Basic Timeline of the Old Testament?" Compelling Truth, accessed July 3, 2018, https://www.compellingtruth.org/Old-Testament-timeline.html.

5 "The Jewish Temples: The Babylonian Exile (597–538 BCE)," Jewish Virtual Library, https://www.jewishvirtuallibrary.org/the-babylonian-exile.

6 Tom Bradford, Old Testament Studies (Lesson 4, Daniel 1, cont.), Torah Class, http://www.torahclass.com/old-testament-studies-tc/1816-old-testament-studies-daniel/1385-lesson-4-daniel-ch-1-cont.

7 Derek Prince, *Husbands and Fathers: Rediscover the Creator's Purpose for Men* (Grand Rapids, MI: Chosen Books, 2000), 28.

8 See "What We Do," CUFI on Campus, https://www.cufioncampus.org/about.

9 Tracey R. Rich, "Prophets and Prophecy," Judaism 101, accessed July 20, 2018, http://www.jewfaq.org/prophet.htm.

10 Yehuda Shurpin, "Why Isn't the Book of Daniel Part of the Prophets?: The Difference between Prophecy and Divine Inspiration," Chabad, https://www.chabad.org/library/article_cdo/aid/1735365/jewish/Why-Isnt-the-Book-of-Daniel-Part-of-the-Prophets.htm.

11 Lewis Eron, "Prophets and Sages," Reconstructing Judaism, https://www.reconstructingjudaism.org/dvar-torah/prophets-and-sages.

12 *The William Davidson Talmud*, Megillah 14a, Sefaria, https://www.sefaria.org/Megillah.14a?lang=bi.

13 W. C. Stevens, *The Book of Daniel* (Camp Hill, PA: Christian Publications, 1915), 41.

14 Clarence Larkin, *The Book of Daniel* (Glenside, PA: Rev. Clarence Larkin Estate, 1990; first published 1919), 50.

15 *The Woman's Study Bible: NKJV*, 2nd ed. (Nashville, TN: Thomas Nelson, 2006), 1089.

16 *NKJV Study Bible*, 2nd ed. (Nashville, TN: Thomas Nelson, 2007), 1349.

17 Adapted from Myer Pearlman, *Daniel Speaks Today* (Springfield, MO: Gospel Publishing House, 1943), 81.

18 Ibid., 82–83.

19 John F. Walvoord, *Daniel: The Key to Prophetic Revelation* (Chicago: Moody Press, 1971), 214–16.

20 Adapted from Pearlman, *Daniel Speaks*, 85.

21 Larkin, *The Book of Daniel*, 176.

22 Jennifer Rosenberg, "The History of the Balfour Declaration," ThoughtCo, updated June 11, 2018, https://www.thoughtco.com/balfour-declaration-1778163.

23 Joseph Benson, *Commentary of the Old and New Testament* (New York: Carlton and Porter, 1857).

24 John Hagee, *The Three Heavens* (Nashville, TN: Worthy, 2015).

25 Pearlman, *Daniel Speaks*, 87–88.

26 Clarence Larkin, *The Greatest Book on 'Dispensational Truth' in the World*, chap. 19 (self-pub., 1920).

27 Pearlman, *Daniel Speaks*, 99.

28 Ibid., 118.

Chapter 12

1 Mark R. Levin, *Rediscovering Americanism: And the Tyranny of Progressivism* (New York: Threshold Editions, 2017), 1, 238.

2 Tass, "Moscow Cements Deal with Damascus to Keep 49-Year Presence at Syrian Naval and Air Bases," January 20, 2017, http://tass.com/defense/926348; "New Russia-Syria Accord Allows up to 11 Warships in Tartus Port Simultaneously," Deutsche Welle. January 20, 2017, https://www.dw.com/en/new-russia-syria-accord-allows-up-to-11-warships-in -tartus-port-simultaneously/a-37212976.

3 "Moscow Moves to Make Military Presence in Syria Permanent," *Times of Israel*, December 27, 2017, https://www.timesofisrael.com/moscow-moves-to-make-military -presence-in-syria-permanent/.

4 Inna Lazareva, "Russian Spy Base in Syria Used to Monitor Rebels and Israel Seized," *Telegraph*, October 8, 2014, https://www.telegraph.co.uk/news/worldnews/europe/russia/11148857 /Russian-spy-base-in-Syria-used-to-monitor-rebels-and-Israel-seized.html.

5 Matthew RJ Brodsky, "Russia Is Reaping the Benefits of Israel's Actions in Syria," *National Interest*, May 20, 2018, http://nationalinterest.org/feature/russia-reaping-the-benefits -israels-actions-syria-25897.

6 Anshel Pfeffer, "Israel Struggles to Draw New Red Lines in Russia's Syria Playground," Analysis, *Haaretz*, February 11, 2018, https://www.haaretz.com/middle-east-news/syria /premium-israel-struggles-to-draw-new-red-lines-in-russia-s-syria- playground-1.5806718.

7 IHS Jane's, "Hizbullah's Expanded Role in Syria Threatens Israel," an analysis report from HIS Jane's Military and Security Assessments Intelligence Centre, 2017, http://www .janes.com/images/assets/885/68885/Hizbullahs_expanded_role_in_Syria_threatens _Israel.pdf.

8 Ibid.

9 MEMRI, "Pro-Hizbullah Lebanese Website: Hizbullah Has 70,000 Iranian Missiles across Syria Ready to Launch into Israel; in a Year It Will Have 500,000," Special Dispatch No. 7328, February 12, 2018, https://www.memri.org/reports/pro-hizbullah-lebanese -website-hizbullah-has-70000-iranian-missiles-across-syria-ready.

10 Alon Ben David, "Iron Dome Blunts 90% of Enemy Rockets," *Aviation Week*, September 1, 2014, http://aviationweek.com/defense/iron-dome-blunts-90-enemy-rockets.

11 CUFI Talking Points, "More Rockets Fired into Israel over the Past 24 Hours Than During Past 3 Years," Christians United for Israel, https://www.cufi.org/cufi-talking-points-more -rockets-fired-into-israel-over-the-past-24-hours-than-during-past-3-years/.

12 Zvi Bar'el, "Russia Seeks Hamas-Fatah Reconciliation in Order to Save Assad, Weaken Iran,"

Haaretz, September 13, 2017, https://www.haaretz.com/middle-east-news/ palestinians/ .premium-russias-next-potential-victory-hamas-fatah-reconciliation -1.5450299.

13 Steve Erlanger, "A Gaza War Full of Traps and Trickery," *New York Times*, January 10, 2009, https://www.nytimes.com/2009/01/11/world/middleeast/11hamas.html.

14 Adapted from Moshe Eisemann, *Yechezkel/Ezekiel*, Artscroll Tanach Series (Brooklyn: ArtScroll Mesorah, 1989), xx.

15 "Ezekiel 38," *Scofield Reference Notes*, 1917 ed., Bible Study Tools (website), https://www .biblestudytools.com/commentaries/scofield-reference-notes/ezekiel/ezekiel-38.html.

16 Ibid. xv.

17 J. Dwight Pentecost, *Prophecy for Today: An Exposition of Major Themes in Prophecy* (Grand Rapids, MI: Zondervan, 1961), 107–8.

18 Ehsan Yarshater, "Communication," *Iranian Studies* 22, no. 1 (1989): 62–65, https:// www .jstor.org/stable/4310640?seq=1#page_scan_tab_contents.

19 "History of Iran: Islamic Revolution of 1979," Iran Chamber Society, http://www .iranchamber.com/history/islamic_revolution/islamic_revolution.php.

20 Pentecost, *Prophecy for Today*, 108.

21 Josephus, *Antiquities* 1.6.1.

22 Bodie Hodge, "Josephus and Genesis Chapter Ten: A Wonderful Stepping-Stone," Answers in Genesis, November 18, 2009, https://answersingenesis.org/genesis/josephus -and-genesis-chapter-ten/.

23 Nick Miller, "Angela Merkel Proposes Partial Burqa Ban ahead of German Election," *Sydney Morning Herald*, December 7, 2016, https://www.smh.com.au/world/angela -merkel-proposes-partial-burqa-ban-ahead-of-german-election-20161207-gt5gth.html.

24 Associated Press, "Nice Truck Attack Claims 86th Victim," *Star Tribune* (Minneapolis, MN), August 19, 2016, https://web.archive.org/web/20160821175505/http:/www.startribune .com/nice-truck-attack-claims-86th-victim/390715371/.

25 Angelique Chrisafis, "Man Shot Dead by French Army after Killing Two People at Marseille Train Station," *Guardian*, October 1, 2017, https://www.theguardian.com /world/2017/oct/01/french-police-operation-under-way-at-marseille-train-station.

26 Eleanor Steafel, "Paris Terror Attack: Everything We Know on Saturday Afternoon," *Telegraph*, November 21, 2015, https://www.telegraph.co.uk/news/worldnews/europe/france /11995246/Paris-shooting-What-we-know-so-far.html.

27 Griff Witte, "In a Kosher Grocery Store in Paris, Terror Takes a Deadly Toll," *Washington Post*, January 9, 2015, https://www.washingtonpost.com/world/europe/paris-kosher -market-seized-in-second-hostage-drama-in-nervous-france/2015/01/09/f171b97e-97ff -11e4-8005-1924ede3e54a_story.html?utm_term=.45094e12a036.

28 "12th-Century Rabbi Predicted Israel's Future," World Net Daily, November 11, 2012, http://www.wnd.com/2012/11/12th-century-rabbi-predicted-israels-future/.

29 "Thermal Radiation," Effects of Nuclear Weapons, Atomic Archive, http://www .atomicarchive.com/Effects/effects7.shtml.

30 Charles Levinson and Guy Chazan, "Big Gas Find Sparks a Frenzy in Israel," *Wall Street Journal,* updated December 30, 2010, https://www.wsj.com/articles /SB10001424052970204204004576049842786766586.

SECTION FOUR: THE FINAL GAME OF THRONES

Chapter 13

1 Joseph J. Carr, *The Twisted Cross* (Shreveport, LA: Huntington House, 1985), 39.

2 Kai Schultz, "Indian Children's Book Lists Hitler as Leader 'Who Will Inspire You,'" *New York Times,* March 18, 2018, https://www.nytimes.com/2018/03/17/world/asia/india-hitler -childrens-book.html.

3 Daryl Worthington, "The Munich Pact," New Historian, September 30, 2014, http:// www.newhistorian.com/munich-pact/1340/.

4 Ian Kershaw, "The Führer Myth: How Hitler Won Over the German People," Spiegel Online, January 30, 2008, http://www.spiegel.de/international/germany/the-fuehrer-myth-how -hitler-won-over-the-german-people-a-531909-3.html.

5 Christopher Klein, "The Secret Hitler-Stalin Pact," History Stories, History, August 22, 2014, https://www.history.com/news/the-secret-hitler-stalin-pact-75-years-ago.

6 A line from the movie *Darkest Hour,* as reported by Navnee Likhi in "One Man Who Took a Stand," *Tribune* (Chandigarh, India), December 10, 2017, http://www .tribuneindia.com/news/spectrum/entertainment/one-man-who-took-a-stand /510703.html.

7 Winston Churchill, "Blood, Toil, Tears and Sweat, 1940," National Churchill Museum, accessed July 17, 2018, https://www.nationalchurchillmuseum.org/blood-toil-tears-and -sweat.html.

8 John Hagee, *The Three Heavens* (Franklin, TN: Worthy, 2015), 164.

9 Carr, *Twisted Cross*, 13.

10 Ibid.

11 John F. Walvrood, Chapter 8 The Revelation of the Man of Sin http://walvoord.com /article/177.

12 Arthur W. Pink, *The Antichrist* (Grand Rapids: Kregel, 1923; 1988), 9.

13 Ibid., 62.

Chapter 14

1 Manuel Castells, *The Information Age: Economy, Society and Culture*, 3 vols. (Cambridge, MA: Wiley-Blackwell, 1999).

2 "21 Books You Don't Have to Read," *GQ*, April 19, 2018, https://www.gq.com/story /21-books-you-dont-have-to-read.

3 Finis J. Dake, *Dake's Annotated Reference Bible–KJV* (Lawrenceville, GA: Dake, 2014), 501.

4 G. A. Hadjiantoniou, *The Postman of Patmos: The Letters to the Seven Churches of Revelation* (Grand Rapids, MI: Zondervan, 1961).

5 Dake, *Annotated Reference Bible*, 405.

6   Clarence Larkin, *Dispensational Truth, or God's Plan and Purpose in the Ages* (1920; repr., Brattleboro, VT: Echo Point, 2015), 110; Hagee, *Three Heavens*, 270–75.

7   Adapted from Geoffrey Dennis, "Judaism and Numbers," My Jewish Learning, accessed July 18, 2018, https://www.myjewishlearning.com/article/judaism-numbers/.

8   Clarence Larkin, *The Book of Revelation* (Glenside, PA: Rev. Clarence Larkin Estate, 2004), 66.

9   John Phillips, *Exploring the Book of Daniel: An Expository Commentary* (Grand Rapids, MI: Kregel, 2004), 222–23.

Chapter 15

1   John F. Walvoord, *The Nations in Prophecy* (Grand Rapids, MI: Zondervan, 1967), http://walvoord.com/book/export/html/318.

2   Geo. N. H. Peters, *The Theocratic Kingdom of Our Lord Jesus: The Christ, as Covenanted in the Old Testament, and Presented in the New Testament* (New York: Funk & Wagnalls, 1884), 3:220.

3   See map, Clarence Larkin, "Royal Grant to Abraham" (chart), in *The Jews: Dispensational Truth*, chap. 9, Blue Letter Bible, https://www.blueletterbible.org/study/larkin/dt/09.cfm#c41.

4   David Abulafia, *The Great Sea: A Human History of the Mediterranean* (New York: Oxford University Press, 2011), 55.

5   Anson F. Rainey, "Herodotus' Description of the East Mediterranean Coast," *Bulletin of the American Schools of Oriental Research*, no. 321 (February 2001), 57–63, https://www.jstor.org/stable/1357657.

6   Louis H. Feldman, "Some Observations on the Name of Palestine," *Hebrew Union College Annual* 61 (1990): 19, https://www.jstor.org/stable/23508170.

7   Noah Rayman, "Mandatory Palestine: What It Was and Why It Matters," *Time*, September 29, 2014, http://time.com/3445003/mandatory-palestine/; "Israel: Origins of the Name 'Palestine,'" Jewish Virtual Library, https://www.jewishvirtuallibrary.org/origin-of-quot-palestine-quot; "British Palestine Mandate: History and Overview (1922–1948)," Jewish Virtual Library, https://www.jewishvirtuallibrary.org/history-and-overview-of-the-british-palestine-mandate.

8   Shaul Bartal, "The Peel Commission Report of 1937 and the Origins of the Partition Concept," *Jewish Political Studies Review* 28, no. 1/2 (Spring 2017): 54, https://www.jstor.org/stable/44510475. See also: William R. W. Peel, et al., "Zionism," in chap. 1, "The Historical Background," *Palestine Royal Commission Report*, 11–15, https:// biblio-archive.unog.ch/Dateien/CouncilMSD/C-495-M-336-1937-VI_EN.pdf; General Council (Va'ad Leumi) of the Jewish Community of Palestine, *Three Historical Memoranda, submitted to the United Nations Special Committee on Palestine*, 5707/1947 (Jerusalem: Hasman Press, 1947), 56–60; Bernard Lewis, "Studies in the Ottoman Archives—I," *Bulletin of the School of Oriental and African Studies, University of London* 16, no. 3 (1954): 469–501, https://www.jstor.org/stable/608618.

9   J. Vernon McGee, *Thru the Bible: 1 Corinthians–Revelation*, vol. 5 (Nashville, TN: Thomas Nelson, 1983), 1058.

10 John Hagee, *The Battle for Jerusalem* (Nashville, TN: Thomas Nelson, 2001), 244–47.

11 J. Vernon McGee, *Revelation Chapters 14–22: The Prophecy* (Nashville, TN: Thomas Nelson, 1991), 152.

12 Hagee, *Battle for Jerusalem*, 244–47.

13 Clarence Larkin, The Book of Revelation, Rev. Clarence Larkin Estate, Glenside, Pennsylvania, 1919, p 193.

14 John Hagee, ed., "Top 20 Questions: 15. What is the Great White Throne Judgment?," *NKJV Prophecy Study Bible* (Nashville, TN: Thomas Nelson, 1997), 1597.

15 Adapted from Finis Jennings Dake, *God's Plan for Man* (1949; Lawrenceville, GA; Dake Bible Sales, 1981), 1009.

Chapter 16

1   Adapted from Clarence Larkin, *The Book of Revelation* (Glenside, PA: Rev. Clarence Larkin Estate, 2004), 209.

2   Finis Jennings Dake, *God's Plan for Man* (1949; Lawrenceville, GA: Dake Bible Sales, 1981), 987.

3   Ibid.

4   Derek Prince, "A Throne for the King," devotional on Facebook, May 19, 2018, https:// www.facebook.com/dpmlegacy/posts/10156535190977975.

5   Charles Haddon Spurgeon, "The Throne of God and of the Lamb," sermon no. 1576, delivered at Metropolitan Tabernacle, Newington (1881), *Metropolitan Tabernacle Pulpit: Volume 27: Sermons Preached and Revised in 1881* (repr., Pasadena, TX: Pilgrim Publications, 1975); available for viewing online at The Spurgeon Center for Biblical Preaching at Midwestern Seminary, https://www.spurgeon.org/resource-library/sermons/the-throne-of -god-and-of-the-lamb#flipbook/.

ABOUT THE AUTHOR

JOHN HAGEE is the founder and senior pastor of Cornerstone Church in San Antonio, Texas, a non-denominational evangelical church with more than 22,000 active members. He is the author of forty books including several *New York Times* bestsellers. Pastor Hagee is known for his support of Israel and his teachings on prophecy with such books as *The Beginning of the End, Jerusalem Countdown, In Defense of Israel, Four Blood Moons,* and *The Three Heavens.* John Hagee is the founder and chairman of Christians United for Israel (CUFI) with over 4.3 million members. His television and radio outreach spans America and the nations of the world.